Remembering
the
Maine

REMEMBERING ★ T ★ H ★ E ★ MAINE

Peggy and Harold Samuels

SMITHSONIAN INSTITUTION PRESS
Washington and London

Designer: Janice Wheeler
Editor: Diane Amussen

Library of Congress Cataloging-in-Publication Data

Samuels, Peggy.
    Remembering the Maine / Peggy and Harold Samuels.
       p.   cm.
    Includes bibliographical references (p.   ) and index.
    ISBN 1-56098-474-0 (acid-free paper)
     1. Maine (Battleship)   2. Spanish-American War, 1898—Causes.
  I. Samuels, Harold. II. Title.
  E721.6.S19 1995
  973.8'95—dc20   94-34649
                                                    CIP

British Library Cataloguing-in-Publication Data is available

Manufactured in the United States of America

02 01 99 98 97 96 95   5 4 3 2 1

∞ The paper used in this publication meets the minimum requirements of the
American National Standard for permanence of Paper for Printed Library Materials
Z39.48–1984

Table of Contents

★ ★ ★ ★ ★ ★ ★ ★

Acknowledgments

★ ★ ★ ★ ★ ★ ★ ★ ★

Mark L. Hayes, Historian, Early History Branch, Department of the Navy, read the manuscript before publication and offered invaluable suggestions and comments in detail. Michael J. Crawford, Head, Early History Branch, lent his aid, as did Harold D. Langley, Curator of Naval History, National Museum of American History.

REFERENCES TO SOURCES

Sources are listed in the Bibliography (pp. 339–52) and, for a particular item, in the Notes section (pp. 311–38) and identified there by page number and a phrase from the text.

Resolving a Naval Mystery

★ ★ ★ ★ ★ ★ ★ ★

A century ago, the Congress of the United States authorized the construction of a wholly new type of warship. For the first time, an armored battleship was to be built to an American design, entirely of domestic materials, in an American navy yard. The vessel was the battleship *Maine*. Her commissioning in 1895 was a proud moment for a country coming of age.

Early in 1898 President William McKinley ordered the *Maine* to make an uninvited entry into the port of Havana in the hostile Spanish colony of Cuba. The ship's unstated mission was to intimidate the Spanish authorities in the tense months preceding the Spanish-American War. Soon after the *Maine* was shut down on February 15 for what seemed to be a routine night at her mooring in Havana harbor, she exploded. Hundreds of sailors were drowned, burned to death, or mutilated in the wreck that became a submerged tomb. The cause of the disaster was not apparent, although the ship's captain reported that the *Maine* was blown up, not that it blew up.

In less than a week the Navy Department formed a court of inquiry composed of outstanding and unimpeachable senior officers. After twenty-three days of intensive investigation through divers and naval experts called as witnesses, the court found that the source of the calamity was a submarine mine that had burst under the bottom of the ship, igniting gunpowder in the forward magazines. No guilty party was named. Three weeks later the United States Senate charged the Spanish government with responsibility for the catastrophe. The stage was set for war.

Almost unnoticed in the United States, a Spanish court of inquiry made a feeble rebuttal to the Navy Department's report in an attempt to force international arbitration. Then, too late to prevent the war, European naval authorities analyzed the published testimony in the Navy's report and proved that the court had made an unbelievably gross error. The explosion was not located where the report had placed it. In addition, the European experts demonstrated to their satisfaction that the explosion was really an accident. The *Maine* had been designed with a coal bunker adjacent to the reserve gunpowder and shell magazine. The coal in the bunker had ignited spontaneously, the Europeans said, detonating the gunpowder. There had not been a mine explosion at all. The fault lay in inexperienced ship design and negligent shipboard routine, not in Spanish treachery.

The European refutations had no more impact in the United States than the Spanish report. The war had begun. Admiral George Dewey had already given Commander Charles Gridley permission to fire "when he was ready" in Manila Bay. The United States defeated Spain handily on the sea and on the land.

A decade later doubts about whether the Spaniards had actually detonated a mine under the *Maine* were still very much alive. In addition to continuing questions in Europe, the basic attitude toward the war had changed in the United States from pride in the country's military triumph to qualms about what was increasingly seen as an unnecessary and immoral war.

To settle these doubts, a second naval court was convened. This time the members were of an even higher level of expertise. In part as a response to veterans' organizations that were pressing Congress for the recovery of the bones of the scores of sailors whose corpses remained in the wreck, a cofferdam was constructed around the *Maine* and the water was pumped out. The new court was able to see the bottom of the ship. Like the first court of inquiry, the new one found that the cause of the explosion had been a mine underneath the *Maine*. The difference was that the location of the explosion conformed to the European findings. There had not been, the court reported, spontaneous combustion of the coal.

At that point the intact segment of the *Maine* was refloated, towed from Havana harbor, and given a ceremonial burial in the depths of the open ocean. The history of the celebrated ship was ended, but the mystery persists.

Not surprisingly, the European experts remained unconvinced. Even in the United States, the matter of culpability for the explosion of the *Maine* was considered by some to be unresolved. The answer was given one way, then another, over the years. The Spanish government blew up the *Maine*, or ultra-Spanish military fanatics did, or the Cuban insurgents, or minions of publisher William Randolph Hearst, or the disaster was an accident. Or perhaps the devastation had been so complete that no one could ever tell from the testimony and the photographs of the dewatered wreckage whether the *Maine* blew up accidentally or was blown up by a mine. The questions that endured were, first, what actually did happen to the *Maine* that overcast February evening? and second, who if anyone was responsible?

At the time of the Vietnam War, espousing the accident theory was an easy way to assault the record of the naval branch of the U.S. military establishment. In 1974, Admiral Hyman Rickover, the father of the nuclear navy, read an article that debunked the findings of the two American investigative boards. The maverick admiral had made a career of battling the naval establishment and was sympathetic to the author's point of view.

Rickover enlisted a pair of naval scientists to apply modern techniques to re-examine the phenomena of the disaster. He then decided that the *Maine* explosion really had been accidental, and that there had been no mine under the *Maine*. The 267 American deaths had been caused by spontaneous combustion, not by the Spaniards. Rickover said the Spanish War had been fought for false reasons. The Navy Department did not dispute the charge that at best its two courts had been in error, and at worst, were part of a cover-up to protect the *Maine*'s designers and officers.

Today, however, a look at the Rickover findings indicates the possibility of error. His deductions were based on a mistake concerning the size of the mine, thus invalidating his conclusions. His proof was circumstantial, and would for example be insufficient for a criminal conviction in a U.S. court. Consequently, the mystery of the *Maine*'s destruction continues after almost a hundred years. Competent and honest men have reached different conclusions about what happened.

Internationally, the explosion of the *Maine* was a turning point in the relations of the United States with the European powers. Previously, the nation had been regarded abroad as brash and overconfident, gaining rapidly in strength and wealth but still immature. By virtue of the bravura performance of its military in the Spanish War, however, the country pushed its way to a high rank among the nations of the world.

The sinking of the *Maine* in Havana harbor contributed to the outbreak of the Spanish War and thus to the rise of American imperialism. The history of the turn of the last century, and of much that has taken place since then, was affected by what happened after the battleship exploded. Yet it is only now, almost a century later, that decisive clues to the cause of the explosion have been discovered.

Rebellion in Cuba

★ ★ ★ ★ ★ ★ ★ ★

THE BUTCHER'S DISCIPLES

During the late nineteenth century the United States viewed Spain and the Spanish temperament with suspicion and dislike. Spaniards were thought to be treacherous and lazy, and brutality was seen as their dominant trait.

This unflattering portrait seemed justified in American eyes by Spain's administration of its nearby colony, Cuba. The Spaniards' most significant contribution to Cuba had been 400 years of cruelty to the Cuban people. That was Spain's pattern. In the course of the first hundred years of Spanish rule over the lush tropical island, the Indians who had greeted the Spanish explorers were methodically exterminated. To replace the Indians with a hardier work force, Blacks were captured in Africa, enslaved, and shipped to the Caribbean.

Through physical coercion and religious fanaticism Spain became a great colonial power with a wide-ranging empire. This produced a deep hatred of the Spanish regime in Cuba. By the 1870s revolt had become chronic there. The dissatisfaction included upper classes who had come to identify them-selves as Cuban rather than Spanish.

Early in 1895 the United States Congress enacted a protectionist subsidy for American producers of sugar and world sugar prices dropped. The Cu-ban economy was seriously depressed. Another insurrection against Spain began in February, and was still growing a year later when the moderate General Martinez Campos failed to put down the rebellion and was recalled to Spain.

His successor was General Valeriano Weyler y Nicolau who quickly employed harsh methods to end the rebellion. The *New York Journal* called him "the most cruel and bloodthirsty general in the world," and with reason. Popularly known in the United States and in Cuba as "the butcher," Weyler was the villain in the story of the *Maine*.

Weyler's arrival in Havana on February 10, 1896, was welcomed with enthusiasm by the ultra-Spanish members of the Conservative faction in Cuba. They made him the focus of a Loyalist cult, expecting him to live up to his reputation by ridding the island of the elusive multiracial rebels. The general's notoriety in Cuba came from his previous service on the island in the 1870s. He was still hated for the atrocities he had ordered then. He was also in disrepute abroad because of the barbarities he had inflicted on the Moors in Africa.

Born in 1839, Weyler was short, a Napoleon whose appearance was distinguished by black eyes, black hair, black beard, and a very dark complexion—and he wore black clothing to match. Newspaper correspondents who interviewed Weyler described him as thin, physically weak, and almost shriveled. He was highly intelligent, having graduated at the head of his staff college class, but coarse and unsoldierly in bearing.

The description of Weyler in these accounts is of a flawed, talented, and contradictory figure—unpleasant in appearance but irresistibly magnetic to his hotheaded officers, a master of diplomacy as well as of violence, and ambitious for immortality regardless of means. Crafty, unscrupulous, and fearless, he displayed an unshakable perseverance. In the final analysis, he was unlovable and unloving, but exalted in his faith in his own capacities.

In the field, Weyler found that although his army numbered one soldier for every ten Cubans, including women and children, the rebel guerrillas were operating successfully in every part of Cuba. He sent his infantry to fight the rebels but could not make them stand for a pitched battle. Beyond the murder of civilians thought to be siding with the insurgents, nothing was accomplished. Instead of pursuing with cavalry, Weyler dissipated his strength by constructing a defensive line of small forts across the island. Without doing more, he announced to his superiors that the populous western provinces were pacified. They were not.

Having failed to defeat the rebels militarily, Weyler tried to crush the insurrection by instituting a program that would be followed in most guerrilla wars during the twentieth century—the repression of noncombatants to deprive the rebels of their base of support. Hundreds of thousands of Cuban peasants were compelled to leave their self-sufficient farms in rural districts and forced into deadly concentration camps on the outskirts of the garrison towns where there was neither food nor sanitary facilities. Homes and farm buildings were burned behind them.

Weyler believed he would starve the insurgents into submission by depriving them of their means of subsistence in the countryside. Instead, while two hundred thousand uprooted Cuban peasants died unfed and wasted by disease, the insurgents were inspired to greater resistance against Weyler's huge army. The war became more savage as the rebels in turn executed Cubans who cooperated with the Spaniards. They destroyed factories and plantations to eliminate any source of income for Spain. Brutality to civilians by both sides was out of hand. By nineteenth-century standards, the disastrous consequences for the helpless had rarely been surpassed.

As the rebellion and butchery continued, indignation in the United States led to an official investigation by incoming President McKinley in March 1897. There was a growing perception in Spain that the atrocities under Weyler might provoke armed intervention from Cuba's neighbor to the north. Officials in Madrid were uneasy, but the determined Weyler remained blindly dedicated to ending the insurrection by repressive means. Weyler still believed he could prevail militarily by pushing his zone of destruction eastward from Havana, but by the summer of 1897 his power base in Spain was becoming more and more eroded. Spanish Liberals were openly opposed to Weyler's repressive acts, especially because it was evident to them that the general's severity was no more effective against the insurgents than his predecessor's more restrained approach had been. In the United States, popular opinion was increasingly outraged by the Cuban carnage.

The general was incensed at the failure of the United States to prevent sympathizers from illegally providing the Cuban insurgents with arms and supplies. Despite supposed Spanish military superiority, the celebrated Captain "Dynamite Johnny" O'Brien was able to unload his filibuster cargo for rebel General Rodrieguez within a mile of the Morro Castle at the entrance to Havana harbor.

One night Rodrieguez held up a train three miles outside Havana. The next night he made an attempt on Weyler's life by mining the railroad track.

Using remote controls, he blew up the train Weyler was supposed to be on, just ahead of the one on which the general was actually riding. The insurgents had a large quantity of American dynamite and plenty of experience with its military and naval use.

The railway incident gave Weyler another and more personal reason to blame the United States for Cuban access to ammunition and explosives. Yet the violations of the law against filibustering were being accomplished despite opposition from Washington officials. The Navy Department alone spent $1 million trying to prevent the export of munitions. Although United States warships, including the powerful *Maine* and the fast cruiser *Montgomery*, patrolled the Florida Straits regularly, the Atlantic and Gulf shorelines were too extensive to be policed effectively. The cost of keeping an unproductive watch along the coast irked the United States almost as much as the artful filibustering annoyed the Spaniards.

In August 1897 Conservative Premier Canovas del Castillo who had appointed Weyler was murdered by an Italian anarchist. During this period when Weyler was without a powerful sponsor in Spain, the U.S. government demanded that he be replaced. After a number of caretaker ministries, the Liberals under Práxedes Mateo Sagasta came back into power in October. One of the first acts of the new government was the recall of Weyler. The general departed for Spain, still claiming that if he had been given only six more months, he would have stamped out the rebellion. He blamed the United States for all his difficulties, saying that it was the arms sent illegally from there that had enabled the insurgents to continue. In the end, however, Weyler's most important impact on the island was on his junior officers whose dreams of recaptured Spanish glory he had falsely inflated.

Premier Sagasta promptly instituted a more realistic dual policy of slowly putting reforms into effect in Cuba and at the same time organizing a coalition of European powers to compel the United States to relieve its pressure on Spain. He claimed that his government was sincerely attempting to meet the rebels' demands. While the insurrection remained stalemated, with indecisive conflicts around Spanish outposts, Sagasta tried to smooth over both his Cuban and United States problems.

In November 1897 General Ramón Blanco y Erenas was sent to Havana as governor general in Weyler's stead. Since repression had failed, Blanco's mission was to pacify the island with concessions. He offered home rule under the Spanish flag, similar to the arrangement Great Britain had reached with the Dominion of Canada. This was a generous grant of authority by European standards, even though an autonomous Cuban government would be able to take no act contrary to Spanish policy. Any wider tender of home rule would have given Cubans more freedom than Spaniards had in Spain.

In contrast to Weyler, General Blanco was a proud Spanish don of mature years—tall, with a white goatee. He appeared to be gentle, soft-spoken and polite, proud, barbered and accoutered in the relaxed manner of a gentleman. He was remote as an executive, and in contrast to his charismatic predecessor, he inspired no personal allegiance.

Blanco was an experienced diplomat sent to Cuba to compromise, not fight. His mission was to get along by going along with the rebels, the Cuban civilians, the Weyler adherents who remained in the army and navy, the Conservative Spaniards in Cuba, and the United States. His purpose was to tone down hysteria about the rebellion, to defuse the fighting as an issue, and to gain time to allow the slow-moving consensus among European nations to solidify. On the Continent there was animosity toward what was seen as United States bullying of Spain, but unanimity among the nations awaited Great Britain's decision.

Blanco withdrew Weyler's order for the concentration of Cuban peasants, but his well-intentioned act was too late to save lives. In the words of the U.S. consul general in Havana, Fitzhugh Lee, "These people have no place to go to, so they stick right in the edge of the town, just like they did."

Next, Blanco granted autonomy to Cuba as of the end of 1897, but the reform never had a chance to succeed. After years of fighting, the concessions to the insurgents concerning home rule were insufficient and overdue. Even after an offer of amnesty, the insurgents would accept no less than full independence, without Spanish control. "Cuba *libre!*" was the only cry the rebels recognized.

The Spanish Conservatives in Cuba also opposed autonomy. Despite their loyalty to Spain, those who had been born in the mother country were to be excluded from the autonomous Cuban government. They considered the Cubans to be radicals who might legislate against conservative interests in the management of the island's economy.

Finally, with Weyler back in Spain and ready to seize power for himself if the monarchy was ousted, his disciples among the Spanish army officers stationed in Cuba joined the forces against autonomy. The Weylerites saw the compromise as a dishonorable acquiescence both to the Cuban ragtag rebels and to the hated "Yankee" meddlers they blamed for the fall of their leader. Coupled with the opposition from the insurgents and the Conservatives, this was the death blow to home rule, although Blanco kept the fiction of its possibility alive.

Only in the United States did the Spanish initiative toward moderation in Cuba appear to have any impact. Although the American press was critical of Spain because the heralded Cuban autonomy was less than had been anticipated by a democratic society, Spanish Minister Plenipotentiary Dupuy de Lôme reported to his government from Washington on December 2, 1897, that "the political situation has never been better since May 1895 and, I am informed by the McKinley administration, all motive for irritation has disappeared. Having never believed that belligerency would be declared or that rupture of relations would be provoked by the United States, much less do I believe it now. Congressional action will not take place, unless something unforeseen occurs."

Two weeks later the veteran diplomat added: "There is absolute quiet and lack of news. The president scarcely concerns himself with the Cuban question."

When Spanish Minister of State Pio Gullon in Madrid received a December 20 note from U.S. Ambassador Woodford to the effect that the desire of the United States was for peace with Spain, Gullon was unable to hide the great satisfaction he and the rest of the Spanish cabinet felt. Complacency was the order of the day. Gullon believed that relations between the two nations had finally become harmonious, but the truth was to be very different when Dupuy's "something unforeseen" did occur.

OUR MAN IN HAVANA

Toward the end of the 1890s three countries claiming to spring primarily from the same Teutonic/Aryan origins were in competition around the globe. Great Britain was the established naval power. Fledgling Germany was challenging its naval strength, determined to match the doughty British Empire in order to contest the colonization of Africa. With a growing agricultural and industrial economy, the United States was building a new Navy and assuming an essential role as an exporter of foodstuffs and raw materials. Widespread crop failures abroad had provided the far-off United States with the opportunity to serve as the granary of nations.

The United States had begun to take a small role in diplomatic affairs, too, having arbitrated a territorial dispute between Great Britain and Venezuela. In addition to pressing Spain over Cuban independence, the United States was taking steps toward the annexation of Hawaii.

Our man in Havana was Fitzhugh Lee. A nephew of the Confederate hero General Robert E. Lee, Fitzhugh Lee had gained his own niche. He had graduated from West Point only forty-fifth in a class of forty-nine, but before he was twenty-eight he had risen to Confederate major general in the Civil War. Fighting was his forte, not schoolbooks. After twenty years of private life as a farmer, he had been elected governor of Virginia in 1885 and was later appointed collector of federal revenue in Virginia.

Lee was named consul general for Cuba by the peace president, Grover Cleveland, in April 1896. His job was to investigate military, political, and economic conditions and to carry on relations with the Spanish authorities on the island. Cleveland chose the now portly Lee as consul to please the Democratic South despite the disadvantages that the former cavalryman spoke no Spanish and knew nothing of the history or culture of Spain or Cuba. Lee was impulsive, preferring military solutions to diplomacy. He also sought opportunities for personal gain through investment in a liberated Cuba. He distrusted Spaniards instinctively and was the wrong man for a delicate peacetime position.

In July 1896, after only three months in office, the jittery Lee requested that a warship be stationed at Key West, Florida. He wanted the vessel to be available to protect the Havana consulate and the lives of U.S. citizens on the island. Cleveland did not see any immediate danger. He refused.

Four months later Lee reported that Weyler was preparing for hostilities with the United States. He claimed that Spain had only two alternatives, a humiliating surrender to the demands of the rebels or a war with the United States in which Cuba could be lost with honor. Washington feared an additional possibility, that Spain might cede the island to Germany or Great Britain to save face.

When a few U.S. citizens in Cuba were jailed by the Spanish authorities in February 1897, Lee asked for a promise from outgoing President Cleveland that warships would be sent to Havana to back up his ultimatum to the Spanish officials. Otherwise, Lee threatened to resign. Cleveland refused again. Lee remained on the job, but Cleveland warned his successor McKinley that the militant consul general was a ringleader among American jingoes. He was clearly unreliable as a dispassionate observer. Lee's bias led to an openly negative view of all Spanish proposals and also to his call for warship diplomacy. This in turn made the Spanish authorities dissatisfied with his performance as the U.S. representative.

Despite Lee's obvious unsuitability, McKinley requested that he stay on as consul general. Enlisting a Democratic Southerner in the Republican administration was seen as politically unifying.

In response, Lee resumed his gloomy forecasts, stating that the rebellion would continue until Spain was exhausted physically and financially or the United States intervened. He saw no hope of Spanish compromise with either the rebels or the United States. A new Cuban regime would suit Lee's personal plans, too. In the midst of these intricate government-to-government dealings with Spain, he was attempting to put together a consortium of American financiers to build a street railway in Havana after the Spaniards were driven out.

When Spain recalled Captain General Weyler in the fall of 1897 and Blanco was appointed, Lee nevertheless reported that the ultimate course of events in Cuba was unchanged. He sent the new secretary of state maps and charts of the peacetime Havana harbor. He also disclosed a $1,200 emergency fund granted by Cleveland to maintain a secret network of spies to protect Americans from any surprise political crisis in Cuba. The fund was discontinued.

McKinley was a frugal president but he was humane. Before the end of 1897, his first year in office, he led two separate nationwide drives for contributions for the relief of the starving Cubans. McKinley is often appraised as a front man for unregulated business interests and a cautious executive in his negotiations with Spain. In his December 1897 address to Congress, however, he departed from the noninvolvement policy his predecessor had adhered to.

Instead, McKinley went far beyond Cleveland's gentle warnings. He referred back to Weyler's "cruel policy of concentration. This policy Spain

justified as a means of cutting off supplies for the insurgents. It was exter-
mination." The President stated baldly that the United States could not remain silent if conditions on the island did not improve. His position received
the support of the American press and of public opinion.

Meanwhile, our fidgety man in Havana was again reporting Cuban unrest
and asking for at least two warships at Key West to be responsive to his signal.
In early January 1898, however, the Cuban issue was fading from the headlines of U.S. newspapers as the Blanco policies went into effect.

Only the unheralded movements of the battleship *Maine* indicated
that the United States government agreed with the gist of Lee's disturbing
prophecies.

The New U.S. Navy

★ ★ ★ ★ ★ ★ ★ ★

THE HOLLOW VESSEL

During the Civil War the Union Navy had numbered an impressive 700 ships. Some represented the most advanced designs in the world. When the war was over, however, the Navy faced the usual peacetime pressures to reduce its size. In six years the number of warships in commission fell to 185. Ten years later, in 1881, the Navy was down to 139 ships. Thirty met the minimum standard of seaworthiness. Only four of these vessels had iron hulls, and they were among the smallest. The rest of the hulls were made of wood.

This meager U.S. fleet of 1881 offered pleasant outdoor jobs for several thousand sailors. Along with their officers, they had the opportunity to see foreign ports. The fleet upheld the tradition of showing the U.S. flag overseas, but the ships were almost useless for warfare. Besides, maintenance was poor. The vessels supposedly available for cruising were never all in service at the same time.

The Navy had no shipyard capacity to build its own warships in 1881. Even the initial engineering was done in Great Britain where all the steel plates and big guns were manufactured. Some of the propulsion machinery for the ships was made in the United States, but the saying was that domestic machinery was "one cylinder behind the practice of the rest of the world." In addition, some secretaries of the Navy who authorized shipbuilding were ignorant of battleships. One ended a ceremonial tour of inspection of a squadron by evidencing severe disappointment in what he had discovered. "Why," he lamented concerning the largest vessel, perhaps in jest, "the darned thing is hollow!"

The ultimate insult for patriotic citizens who wanted suitable warships for their country came in the early 1880s. The war between Chile, Bolivia, and Peru proved that the Chilean navy, with ships recently constructed in Great Britain, was bigger and more powerful than anything the United States had to offer.

Twenty- to thirty-year-old ships and outmoded armament were not the Navy's only problems. Fewer ships meant fewer sailors, and for officers, fewer opportunities for advancement.

The benefits of the Navy as a home for young men of "the governing class" were extensive. The membership was as exclusive as the British nobility, plus some advantages. The fact was that "the British peerage shows sour stomach for a generation or two after swallowing a rich brewer or a Hebrew banker, but the greenest Yankee in America can be made into a polished naval gentleman in six years. Or, if he cannot, he can be cast out."

The Navy did not pretend to be a democratic institution. Social background counted for much in gaining rank, especially where a family boasted generations of officers in the service. In the peacetime year of 1881, however, there was no way for a junior officer to advance more rapidly than the death and retirement of senior officers permitted. Officers were free to serve for forty years or until they reached age sixty-two. As a consequence, there was one naval officer for every four enlisted men. To ease this top-heavy ratio, the number of Naval Academy graduates who were commissioned was sharply reduced. Only a small percentage of those who entered the Academy in 1881 would receive commissions by 1887. The rest were released from their obligation to serve.

The professional careers of these junior naval officers were seriously threatened. When the young men discussed the conditions of their service, they compared themselves to the deteriorating ships on which they served. The U.S. Navy's vessels and personnel were both in a precarious state.

The reversal of this naval policy began in 1881 when President Chester Arthur declared in his first message to Congress that "every condition of national safety, economy, and honor imperatively demands a thorough rehabilitation of the Navy." A survey of naval needs undertaken by an advisory board recommended that the old wooden ships be replaced by 70 modern vessels.

In 1883 Congress began appropriating funds for these warships, authorizing the construction of three cruisers. Four more ships were provided for in 1885 when the whole U.S. Navy amounted to just 90 vessels. Only 25 were seaworthy.

In 1886 Congress appropriated money for two warships, the largest to be built until then. They were the inspirational *Maine* and her sister ship the *Texas*, each to be 6,000 tons displacement. The same legislation provided that all major components of these modern warships and their armament had to be of domestic manufacture. Construction was held in abeyance while capable contractors were sought.

In 1890 Congress authorized the building of three large seagoing battleships, all more powerful than the *Maine*, and in 1892 provided for one huge seagoing battleship, the *Iowa*. Between 1883 and 1897 a concerned Congress commissioned the construction of 9 first-class battleships, 2 second-class battleships, 2 armored cruisers, and 64 smaller vessels. The recommendations of President Arthur's advisory board had more than been met.

The actual construction, however, was much slower than the rapid legislative enactments. The *Maine* did not undergo its final steam trials until 1894. And in the summer of 1897, despite the apparent danger of war with Spain, Congress halted the progress toward a new Navy. The reason was that the nation had to rely on these expensive warships for its protection, but the vessels had never been tested under demanding conditions. Eight big new ships were in service in the Atlantic and their performance in maneuvers was sometimes unreliable.

The mere authorization of construction of big modern ships had brought hope of promotion to all the Navy's officers, but advancement could come only after time had corrected the substantial overpopulation of senior officers. Junior officers were naturally the most anxious about their career prospects. Their contributions to the creation of the new Navy had been outstanding.

French Ensor Chadwick was an example who became a central player in the mystery of the *Maine*. He had been sent to Europe as a lieutenant commander in 1877 to spy out details of current shipbuilding. In 1882 he was appointed the Navy's first attaché for overseas duty. He directed the initial group of United States Navy cadet engineers studying ship construction at the British Royal Navy schools in Greenwich, England, and Glasgow, Scotland. These cadets became valuable assistant naval constructors when they returned home.

The competition for promotion constantly pitted aggressive young officers against entrenched superiors. The traditional organization for officers was the Line Officers Association which had always been governed by senior officers. In 1895, however, the more numerous junior officers took over leadership. They were supported by a few senior officers, including Chadwick who had by then been promoted to commander, and his friend Captain William Sampson, another principal player in the *Maine* mystery. Most of the senior line officers dropped out of the old association to form a new group, the Naval Association. Commander Charles Sigsbee was one of the first members. He was to become the hero of the *Maine*.

Senior officers also took tours of duty in Washington where they managed the naval establishment. The new U.S. Navy had some modern ships, but the old organizational structure of the Navy Department had been retained. All the chiefs of the various bureaus reported directly to the Secretary of the Navy. Most important to the *Maine* were the Equipment, Ordnance, and Construction bureaus. The chiefs of the bureaus of Equipment and Ordnance were line officers like Chadwick and Sampson. Engineers headed the Bureau of Construction.

THE BIRTH OF THE *MAINE*

The legislation that committed the *Maine*'s funding was the Public Act of August 3, 1886. The ship was intended to become the star of the modern U.S. Navy.

The cost of the *Maine* was limited to $2.5 million, the price of a launch a hundred years later. Speed was to be at least 16 nautical miles an hour. The double-bottomed vessel was required to be built of steel, with armor, engines, boilers, and machinery to be of domestic manufacture. Obtaining major components made in the United States demanded the creation of an armor-plate mill as well as a foundry capable of casting large gun barrels. That meant delays, but attaining the national goal of independence in building warships was deemed worth the wait.

Previously U.S. warships had regularly been repaired in the country's navy yards, but no battleship had ever been built in one. In the judgment of the Forty-ninth Congress, however, the United States could never become an international naval power like Great Britain without the ability to design and construct warships in its own yards, as the British did.

The Navy's Chief Constructor Theodore Wilson directed the planning of the *Maine*'s hull. He faced a built-in conflict concerning the warship. The superior speed that Congress had sought was not compatible with the substantial displacement and heavy armor that had been specified. The speed was appropriate for a cruiser, while the formidable weight, armor, and armament were correct for a small battleship. As a consequence, the embryonic warship was initially given no name but was designated generically as ACRI, that is, an armored cruiser first rate.

Constructor Wilson and his staff had no technical experience with heavy armor. They turned to Great Britain for the preliminary concept. There is, however, no record of a purchase of the design. The story at the time was that the overall plans were secured from the British by a clever naval attaché such as Chadwick.

The 1880s were a period of eccentricity in ship design because of the rapid improvements in armor, armament, and coal-fired propulsion. The design of the *Maine* was no exception. The ship was initially supposed to be powered by a combination of canvas and coal. Wilson was of the old school of naval architects who continued to believe in the advantages of the clipper ship. In Wilson's first design there was provision for a tremendous expanse of sail. The more than 7,000 square feet of canvas was intended to enable the ship to stay at sea longer than would be possible with coal power alone.

The rig was to be either bark or barkentine, depending on the final decision concerning the placement of the mainmast. The conservative Wilson savored the idea that the great sail area of the big vessel would demand a crew of seamen of the old type, able to lay out and pass what he referred to as a "weather earing," or fastening line for the sails. Like other old-timers, he had no appreciation for the numbers or needs of the engineers who would run the propulsion plant on this most modern warship.

Soon, however, progress overtook the ACRI's sail plan. This was the end of the era when graceful wind power could even supplement the less aesthetically pleasing coal-fired steam power. Constructor Wilson was forced to redesign the ship's structure to eliminate the provision for canvas and one of the three masts. The two masts that remained were for military uses, not sails.

While the ACRI had been classified as an armored cruiser in the official Navy Register, her sister ship, the *Texas*, had been given a state name appropriate for a battleship. Both vessels met the contemporary test for battleships of having more than 5,000 tons displacement, so the ACRI was soon retitled the *Maine*. As a compromise, she was designated a battleship of the second class like the *Texas*.

After Wilson's changes in the plans, their English origin was forgotten. It was announced proudly that the *Maine* was to be of domestic design throughout. The Navy Department believed that no enemy ship of her size would be capable of standing up to her guns for an hour. The British Navy had 225 cruisers and gunboats, they boasted, and the *Maine* would be able to destroy any one of them in a fight. In reality, however, the *Maine*'s intended role was only as a small coastal-defense battleship, not as a seagoing vessel like the *Iowa*.

The ship's design was completed November 1, 1887, and bids were taken on the materials by June 4, 1888. For both armor plate and gun barrels, the quotation of the Bethlehem Iron Company was accepted. The armor was specified to be made of plain steel, oil tempered and annealed. The engines had been designed by the chief of the Bureau of Steam Engineering, Commodore George W. Melville, who later participated in the *Maine* controversy as an expert commentator.

The keel was to be a compound structure of horizontal outside and inside plates separated by a vertical plate running lengthwise along the center of the bottom of the vessel. After a violent early morning thunderstorm, the keel was laid October 17, 1888, at Brooklyn's New York Navy Yard. Considering that this was the largest vessel ever undertaken by the Navy, there was little ceremony.

The hull was to be built of a mild steel, soft and malleable. Except for the bow and the stern, the ship had a double bottom that was fastened to the keel and the frames. The outer bottom plating was half an inch thick, the inner bottom only five-sixteenths of an inch. In what seemed like a nautical miracle to civilians, more than 12 million pounds of steel warship were kept afloat by this thin skin.

There were to be 20 coal bunkers, 10 on each side. Most of the bunkers were set against the hull to absorb the impact and explosiveness of enemy shells and torpedoes before they could penetrate to the magazines containing the *Maine*'s gunpowder and shells. The capacity of the bunkers was 825 tons of coal, enough to steam 7,000 miles at a slow ten knots.

The armament was to be four breech-loading rifles with bores 10 inches in diameter. From these guns a charge of 250 pounds of powder would throw a 500-pound shell nine miles. The primary battery also included six 6-inch rifles taking a powder charge of 100 pounds. The secondary battery was to be seven six-pounder and eight one-pounder rapid-fire guns plus four Gatlings. There were also four Whitehead torpedoes.

Projecting from the bow was a beak for ramming and sinking an enemy vessel. This added a pugnacious appearance to the *Maine*. The designers said the ram would make matters unpleasant for the enemy in any battle at close quarters.

The *Maine* was to be the pride of the Navy, a homemade ship. Her hull was designed by the Bureau of Construction, her engines by Steam Engineering, and her guns and magazines by Ordnance. Equipment furnished the coal. Her materials came from domestic mines, furnaces, and rolling mills, and she was being built in a U.S. navy yard.

Constructing the *Maine*

★ ★ ★ ★ ★ ★ ★ ★ ★

THE NEW SCIENCE OF SHIPBUILDING

The era of wooden shipbuilding was ending when the construction of the *Maine* was authorized by Congress. In the old days naval constructors had directed the fabrication of a ship on the spot. They had supervised the rough assembly of the timbers for the vessel's hull until it was ready for the master shipwright. He was the craftsman who shaped the wooden curves and angles by rule of thumb. As an art, he shaved, sawed, or chopped the pieces to make them fit. A few inches of wood one way or the other was of little consequence.

In the new science of steel shipbuilding in the year 1889, however, there was no place for handicrafters. The constructors and their naval architects evolved ship designs on drawing boards. They made complex calculations by hand, employing long columns of figures. They were not in the construction shed at all, but on the second floor of a big granite building nearby. These designers furnished the drawings to model-makers in the molding loft where prototypes of finished parts were formed from thin strips of wood for every different frame, plate, and longitudinal. The length, width, and even the curvature of the steel were anticipated in the wood.

In its essence, though, the basic procedure for constructing a steel ship was similar to the way a wooden ship had been made. First came the laying of the keel, wood or steel, and then the fabrication of the frames which were the vertical ribs. When joined to the keel, these frames were the start of the principal horizontal support of the vessel, "the girder." On October 5, 1889, the girder of the *Maine* was in place.

The huge shed where the work progressed had been erected during the Civil War when its dimensions seemed extensive enough for the longest ship that would ever be built there. Inside this big building, however, nearly three hundred men were now at work. The bow of the oversized *Maine* with its menacing ram stretched many feet beyond the end of the shed.

The keel plates had been delivered a year earlier, laid in place in an unbroken line from stem to stern, and then assembled with rivets. Next the frames had been lowered from cranes and attached transversely to the keel. They were braced with steel longitudinals running fore and aft, parallel to the keel.

The contract with the Bethlehem Iron Company for the preliminary fabrication specified only the delivery of given quantities of flat plates by size and thickness. The contouring, bending, angling, and rivet-holing were all to be performed in the navy yard shops, to correspond exactly to the wood patterns.

An incoming plate might go to the roller shop where it would be passed back and forth between two great iron cylinders to smooth the surface and give it the proper angle. Then the plate would go to the punching shop where holes were drilled for the riveting. The holes in the plates had to correspond precisely with those in the frames. Fourteen plates were spoiled by improper drilling and were returned to Pennsylvania for salvage.

Other plates would first be taken to the forge. When white hot, they were rushed up to the bending slab, a great raised floor of heavy steel perforated with measured holes. The shape of the model had been chalked on the floor. The plate was formed to the model by pry bars wielded by brawny workmen who were pressing or pulling on command while the leader of the group put big steel pins in the right holes in the floor to keep every curve secure once it was formed.

At last the smoothed, bent, and punched plate arrived at the construction shed for assembly. The workmen there had only to raise the plate into place, jiggle the fit until the holes in plate and frame corresponded, and drive the rivets home.

The engineers were proud of a radically new source of power used for the work on the *Maine*. This was the first application of electricity to assemble a hull. Assistant Constructor Joseph Woodward explained that previously, "Sending the power aboard a ship being constructed was by a wire rope coming from a steam engine on the dock, the rope turning a complex system of shafting and belting. In the present method, dynamos for generating power are set up in the tool shop." The engineers reported that the technique "gives good promise so far."

Electricity was even more helpful in carrying out the intricate work involved in compartmentalizing the ship within the double bottom. The purpose of the steel skins braced one over the other was to keep the vessel seaworthy in the event of an accident to the underbody of the ship. If the *Maine* were to strike a rock and tear the flimsy outer skin, the only injury would be to admit water into an isolated area between the two skins and give the ship a little lower set in the water.

If she were to run upon a mine or be hit by a torpedo, however, it was feared that the double hull might not save the ship. Even then, though, the watertight compartments might minimize the flooding and keep the massive ship afloat.

In the drafting room of the sentimental chief constructor, there remained a small model of the *Maine* as she would have looked as a handsome bark-rigged sailing vessel with "everything clapped on." Instead, the modern *Maine* would be coal-fired and its assembly would have been accomplished with the aid of a promising new energy source, electric power.

THE CEREMONY OF THE LAUNCH

By the fall of 1890, four busy years after Congress had authorized construction, the *Maine*'s hull had been completed. The compartments were bulk-headed and the main deck was in place, but there was no superstructure, armor plate, or armament. The sides of the hull had been painted a dull red as an undercoat for rust-proofing. At this juncture the Secretary of the Navy Benjamin Franklin Tracy set high noon on Tuesday, November 18, 1890, for the traditional launching of the great warship. Tracy was a lawyer in President Benjamin Harrison's cabinet.

Monday night was stormy. The uneasy constructors at the navy yard in Brooklyn looked frequently at the turbulent skies for a good sign from the ocean gods. At midnight the prospect was still bad. The yard maintained a routine of four-hour duty watches, as if on shipboard at sea, and it was not until the morning watch at daybreak that fair weather was assured for the gala event only hours away.

The ceremony was open to the public. Special guests received formal invitations from the Secretary, still referring to the battleship as the U.S. Armored Cruiser *Maine*. In addition, the illustration on the invitation reproduced the original design with three masts and fore-and-aft sails. Even after the ship was sunk, sails appeared on some drawings of it.

As the largest warship ever built in the United States, the *Maine* was an odd sight. Besides the bow projecting far beyond the shed, the forty-foot depth of the hull was so great that the flagstaff which a vessel customarily carried at the stern during launching could not be erected within the building. At the moment the stern passed from under the shed, quick hands would be needed to set up the staff while the ship was sliding down the ways.

The public arrived early, ready to watch the spectacle with an enthusiasm never before seen at the yard. The grounds in the vicinity of the *Maine* were comfortably full by 10 A.M., two hours in advance of the scheduled ceremony. By eleven the yard was crowded. At noon the area was packed with twenty thousand visitors. Most of them had never seen a warship, let alone one so large.

The final preparations for the event began at eleven, before the official party had arrived at the launching platform. Chief Naval Constructor William Mintonye mustered his disciplined team of hundreds of workmen and prepared to lift the warship from her keel blocks into the grasp of the launching cradle.

Gangs of men on each side of the inclined ways were furnished with oak timbers. There were six men to a pole, their muscular arms swinging the eighty poles with tremendous force against the wooden wedges in the ways. Gradually the huge hull responded, rising from the keel blocks that had borne the weight. Slowly a hairsbreadth of space under the keel widened to a full half inch.

Before noon the ship was clear of the blocks and was resting entirely in the cradle. Only the solid blocks remaining at the bow restrained the vessel from speeding down the gravity railroad to the waiting water. Meanwhile thousands of eager spectators crowded about the red hull of the giant battleship, on the decks of all the vessels assembled nearby in the channel, and on the roofs of the adjacent buildings.

Secretary Tracy had been in court all morning. He did not arrive until a few minutes before the time set for the launch, the moment when the tide would be at its highest. As his carriage sped to the main gate, he was met by stately old Rear Admiral David Braine, the yard commandant, and his staff—all in formal attire. A tiny pennant was run up the peak of the yard's flagstaff as a signal to the gunners on the receiving ship *Vermont*. A salute of nineteen cannon shots reverberated through the grounds. There was also a military salute given by the marine battalion stationed at the yard, followed by cheers from the thousands of civilians present.

The Secretary responded to all these honors. He stood erect in his moving carriage and lifted his hat while the procession ahead of him was led by a score of crimson-coated marine musicians.

The launching platform at the bow of the battleship was draped lavishly with bright flags and flowers. Dignified Secretary Tracy mounted the steps and joined a party of women. His thirteen-year-old granddaughter, Alice Tracy Wilmerding, was the center of attention. The young girl wore a heavy black jacket over a cream white skirt as protection against the November chill at the waterfront. Her long hair was in a braid that fell gracefully down her back, escaping from her large dark hat with its light feathers. Modestly she stared at the enormous red bow of the battleship.

Miss Wilmerding's soft hands held a demi-bottle of San Bernardino, California, champagne to be broken over the bow in the traditional christening of the ship. Afterwards she would retain the pieces as a keepsake.

The pint bottle had been decorated into what she called "a pretty thing— quite too pretty to be offered up to so unfeeling a monster." The glass container was covered first with a network of fine cord and then was wound around its full length with a ribbon bearing a painting of the *Maine* in gold with the ubiquitous sails. From the base of the bottle hung a tie of varicolored silk pennants ending in a gold tassel. Around the neck were two more long ribbons edged in gold lace, one ribbon white and the other blue. At the end of the wide white ribbon was "Alice Tracy Wilmerding, November 18, 1890." At the end of the blue was "U.S.S. *Maine*."

At the stroke of noon Secretary Tracy gave the word to start the launching. The high point of the day had arrived.

"Are you all ready, men?" shouted Constructor Mintonye. His assistants, Woodward and Capps, looked on anxiously.

"All ready, sir!" came the response from the long lines of foremen and the last blocks at the bow were knocked loose.

Often a ship set to be launched would start down the ways on her own, especially where the runway had been coated with five thousand pounds of Mintonye's special mix of tallow, soap, and oil, as it was here. But the *Maine* remained motionless. Tackles were then hooked onto each side of the hull and straining workmen tugged at the ropes. Long minutes elapsed before the great mass of the battleship started almost imperceptibly down the ways. "She moved!" burst from the crowd, along with another hearty cheer. Miss Wilmerding's clear girlish soprano was heard above the background noise declaring, "I christen thee *Maine.*" She smashed the bottle of champagne against the ship's steel bow, shattering the glass within the wrappings. The sailors in the stern sprang quickly to their feet to be ready to raise the ship's flagstaff and her pennant.

Meanwhile the big red hull gained momentum with every foot of the downward slide. Just two and a half minutes later, at 12:50 P.M., the battleship was at rest in the Wallabout Channel, riding the calm waves gently and buoyantly. She had no list and showed no sign of stress or inward or outward evidence of scrape or scar. As launched, the displacement of the *Maine* was only 1,700 tons. The light weight had facilitated the safe slide. The draft was just a slight seven feet forward and seven and a half feet aft, down a little at the stern.

In the channel the waiting tugs took charge of the fledgling warship, fetching her easily alongside the yard's wharf where she was tied safely to the piles. There gangways were put in place and she was promptly boarded by the impatient crowd. The visiting went on until nightfall.

During the afternoon a reception was given for distinguished guests at Admiral Braine's residence. Other festivities took place at the Ordnance Bureau's quarters in the yard and on board the cruisers *Chicago* and *Boston* and other naval and private vessels lying off the yard for the day.

Everyone was aware that the *Maine* symbolized the splendid new U.S. Navy, but no one could have realized the extent to which the nation was in the course of becoming an international power of consequence—in part because of the misadventures of the *Maine.*

THE COMMISSIONING

After the launching the *Maine* remained at the New York Navy Yard for the installation of her superstructure, armor plate, and armament. The original specifications for the armor had been for the usual oil-tempered steel. As coal had replaced sail propulsion during the ship's construction, however, the materials available for armor were overtaken by improved methods of formulating and treating steel. Unfortunately, the advance in the armor was too late to upgrade the steel that had gone into the hull.

Before the first scheduled delivery of the armor plate in the fall of 1891, however, the plans were redrawn by the constructors to make radical changes in the specifications. Nickel steel was called for, along with novel reforging and face-hardening processes. This new method of treating the surface of the plate was a U.S. invention called Harveyizing, and carrying it out took time. Consequently the armor plate was not delivered until 1893.

When completed in 1895, the *Maine* was easily distinguishable from other warships. Instead of one continuous superstructure, there were three separate superstructure segments rising from the main deck and there were two "winged" turrets for the heaviest guns. One turret was placed on each side of the ship, aligned with the space between the superstructures. As in the *Texas* and in some European designs, each turret gun had a clear if narrow field of fire across the ship.

Above the forward superstructure was the foremast. Aft of this superstructure was an open space with the forward gun turret pointing toward the starboard. It was also capable of rotating toward the port side. This unique disposition of the turrets extending from the sides was controversial. Some experts said it was doubtful if that portion of the *Maine*'s design would ever be repeated. It was not.

The midships superstructure featured two fore-and-aft funnels. Two small-boat cranes were at the sides. At the forward end of this central superstructure was the conning tower, the armored pilothouse. The crew was to be berthed in both the forward and midships superstructures as well as in the same forward and central locations on the berth deck, underneath the main deck.

Between the midships and the after superstructures was the after turret, extending over the port side. Above the after superstructure was the mainmast. Inside was the captain's quarters. The other officers were berthed on the lower deck.

The 180-foot belt of Harveyized nickel-steel plate ran for four feet below the waterline to protect against torpedoes and shells. To save weight, no armor plate was installed at the bow or the stern, where there was no essential machinery or large magazine.

At the forward and aft ends of the armor belt there were V-shaped bulkheads to keep enemy projectiles from penetrating from the front or rear. The protective deck safeguarded the vital parts in the hold of the ship from shells entering from above. Below the hold was the double bottom extending upward from the keel to the armor-plate shelf. The thin low-strength steel of the bottom was the most vulnerable point of access to the machinery and the magazines in the hold.

Measured in the water, the *Maine* was 324 feet long, 57 feet wide, 21 feet mean draft, and 6,682 tons displacement. The ship was designed for a complement of 31 officers and 343 enlisted men. The total cost of construction was $2,484,503, just within the budget set by Congress.

The statement of mean draft was a composite figure and misleading. When the *Maine* was stowed with stores and supplies for the first time, the constructors discovered that a substantial error had been made in their loading plan. The ship drew three feet more water forward than aft, giving the appearance of permanently plunging at the bow.

To put the ship in balance, forty-eight tons of cement were poured near the stern as ballast. Even that amount was not quite sufficient—the ship still drew five inches more forward than aft. The captains of the *Maine* learned to consume the coal in the forward bunkers first, to dress the balance on their own so the ship was not always "down by the head."

With the draft adjusted, the *Maine* was a handsome example of the new Navy. Her peacetime colors were white for her fifteen small boats, for her hull up to the rail, and for the bow anchors. The funnels, masts, and superstructures were a dark straw color and the pilothouse was varnished mahogany. Only the searchlights and guns were black. The *Maine* never received her war paint.

The final ceremony for the completed *Maine* was a celebration bigger than the laying of the keel in 1888, yet much simpler than the public launching in 1890. This was the ship's commissioning, a ritual set for the New York Navy Yard on September 17, 1895. Nine long years had elapsed since Congress had authorized construction.

The crew was called to muster at 2 P.M. They formed into ranks behind a marine guard on the port side of the quarterdeck, the upper deck behind the mainmast. The officers assembled on the starboard side, facing the enlisted seamen and the marines.

Captain Frederick Rodgers was the current commander of the yard. He turned to Captain A. S. Crowninshield, saluted him, and said, "I turn the *Maine* over to you, sir."

Crowninshield was part of the progressive group of science-oriented naval officers, a friend of Sampson and Chadwick. He read aloud the orders from the Secretary of the Navy directing him to assume command of the ship. When he finished reading, he added "and now I will expect every man to do his duty."

The executive officer, Lieutenant Commander Adolf Marix, then nodded to the commander of the guard. The marines presented arms smartly. The drum gave three low ruffles and the bugle sounded colors. The captain's pennant and the national flag with forty-five stars were hoisted. The men saluted and the *Maine* was in commission. The bugle sounded and the ceremony was over. The flag hung limply from the staff in a light breeze. The secondary battery had yet to be installed, though the crew took their sea bags and hammocks aboard on September 21.

The *Maine* "lit off her boilers and stood out to sea" for her shakedown cruise on November 5, 1895. On November 29 the *Maine* was under way for Newport, Rhode Island, to meet the President of the Board of Inspection and Survey, Captain George B. Dewey who was there to supervise the ship's final trials. He witnessed the *Maine*'s maneuvers in Newport Harbor and pronounced her acceptable despite the freezing of her hydraulic gun controls.

The *Maine*'s sister ship, the *Texas*, was commissioned one month later. Both were soon overshadowed by larger and more powerful battleships such as the *Indiana*, authorized in 1890 but commissioned only a month after the *Texas*. The public lost interest in the *Maine* once her bigger successors were completed.

THE *MAINE* HOODOO

Although any new vessel will have its share of problems, the *Maine* was truly a bad-luck ship. The freezing of the hydraulic gun controls during her final trials was typical of her troubles.

Believers in the occult claimed that right from the start the stars had fore-told the destruction of the *Maine* in "a violent and unexpected end, by fire from beneath, from the acts of an enemy." During the battleship's launching in 1890, her horoscope read in Gypsy storefronts was inauspicious. The heavens allegedly portrayed her as ill starred even then.

In the summer of 1891, while the hull of the *Maine* was lying at the dock, a fire broke out on board. Oil-soaked cotton waste had ignited from the heat of the midday sun. Before much damage was done, the blaze was extinguished by a bucket brigade of marines stationed at the yard, supported by the Brooklyn Fire Department.

Years later some experts theorized that similar spontaneous combustion may also have caused the catastrophe in Havana harbor.

After the three extra feet the *Maine* drew forward had been partially corrected with ballast aft, the result was a greater draft than her design had specified, forcing her to live with the inconvenience of finding slightly deeper anchorages. The designers also feared that the excess weight would be a permanent handicap, rendering the engines less efficient and causing them to run rough.

The constructors next discovered that two torpedo boats intended to be carried on the deck were too large to fit. The little boats that had cost $80,000 were quietly taken away.

On her shakedown cruise the *Maine* had cast off from the coal wharf at the yard and started down the East River with a harbor pilot in the conning tower. Two hours later the steam-steering gear broke down, necessitating hand steering with the wheel. This was like driving a 6,000-ton truck without power steering.

When Captain Crowninshield pointed the *Maine* down the bay to test the ship's compasses, the vessel became befogged for three days. The wet decks kept the officers and men imprisoned below. The chief engineer who was stationed below had his problems, too. The dynamos heated excessively and eventually quit. The revolution indicator did not function at all.

With her faults supposedly "shook down," the *Maine* headed for Newport for her trials before the Board of Inspection and Survey. The trials were postponed, however, to the day when the hydraulic controls malfunctioned. Next the disappointed Crowninshield set a course for Portland, the principal seaport of the ship's namesake state. He wanted the silver service every sponsor presented to its adopted vessel.

Expectations were high. The citizens of San Francisco had given their namesake cruiser a thirty-two-piece silver service, including the customary punch bowl and goblets. Every large piece was decorated with a California grizzly bear cast in solid gold. The service cost $7,500, and the officers of the cruiser used the silver cups frequently.

To the officers of the *Maine*, San Francisco was only a city, not a state. Its ship was a cruiser, not a mighty battleship. Unfortunately, Maine was a prohibition state and parsimonious as well. The silver service was a large but prosaic soup tureen with accompanying vegetable dishes. The result pleased only the ship's abstemious chaplain.

In February 1896 the *Maine* was attached to the Navy's North Atlantic Squadron, then commanded by Rear Admiral Francis Bunce. While at sea during her first maneuvers, she behaved so poorly that Bunce reported to the Secretary of the Navy that "her pitching and rolling is excessive, and is attributed to faulty design and to placing too much weight at her extremities." The admiral was referring to the cement aft and the winged turrets port and starboard. He added that "the main battery could not be used in the manner intended." That is, the 10-inch guns could not be turned 180 degrees to shoot safely across the ship.

While at Key West with the squadron in July 1896, the *Maine* ran aground on a small coral head alongside the coral dock. Her bottom plates were slightly injured.

A year later the bad luck began to affect the crew. On February 5, 1897, the *Maine* was steaming down the Carolina coast with the squadron when a furious storm struck without warning and great waves dashed over the decks. Apprentice First Class Cogel was killed when he was smashed against a gun turret. Before his mates could reach him, Cogel was washed overboard. Seaman John Brown and Marine Private A. B. Nelson jumped into the sea to rescue the apprentice, not knowing he was already dead. They were swept away from the moving ship, soon lost to sight, and drowned.

A moment later Charles Haskell, a sailor on his first voyage, was swept into the sea. His friend who was on the poop deck saw Haskell go overboard and sprang after him. Two life buoys were thrown to them. Haskell caught one and held on to his intended rescuer until they could be saved.

The *Maine* put about to search for the five men overboard. A lifeboat with Naval Cadet Walter Gherardi and a crew of six capsized as it was lowered into the sea. The boat was lost, along with another torn from the davits by the waves, but the cadet and his men saved themselves by grabbing the life lines.

Only four days afterward, the fleet was off Charleston. A one-pounder gun in the *Maine*'s secondary battery was being loaded when the cartridge exploded accidentally. First Sergeant Wagner was seriously injured. Another crewman was also hurt.

This is not to say that the *Texas* and the other ships in the squadron did not have their own mishaps. In maneuvers in January 1898, the boiler tubes in the battleship *Indiana* leaked so badly that the cruiser *New York* had to take her in tow. In addition, the *Indiana*'s gun turrets jammed in practice against moving targets. One of the accompanying torpedo boats broke her propeller shaft. The *Iowa* ran aground for a second time and stuck fast.

The *Maine*, though, had more than just a comparably troubled record. She was called a hoodoo ship. No other vessel could match the scope of the *Maine*'s woes. When Captain Charles Sigsbee took the *Maine* over from Crowninshield on April 10, 1897, as part of the regular rotation of officers, he had been hand picked for the command by the Navy Department. Sigsbee's assigned task was to shape up the *Maine*, but compared to his problems, Crowninshield's had been small indeed.

The Captain of the *Maine*

★ ★ ★ ★ ★ ★ ★ ★

EAST RIVER EPISODE

For three months after Captain Sigsbee took command of the *Maine*, there was no evidence of bad luck. The ship's jinx appeared to be broken. Then on July 28, 1897, the *Maine* left her berth at New London, Connecticut, steaming routinely for the man-of-war moorings off Tompkinsville, Staten Island. At evening, the big ship prudently dropped anchor in Long Island Sound to avoid the hazard of night cruising in crowded tidal waters.

Early the next morning the *Maine* hoisted her anchors and started again for Tompkinsville. Sigsbee disliked using harbor pilots and was on the bridge himself. He had qualified to act as his own pilot through years of service in the United States Coastal Survey.

At 11 A.M. the *Maine* was heading slowly down the East River, aided by a strong ebb tide. This lower part of the river, with the navy yard astern and the Brooklyn Bridge ahead, was unusually busy with commercial vessels. Sigsbee was nursing the battleship along gently. He was a very large fish in a small pond, feeling his way through the traffic and keeping well to the right toward the Manhattan shore.

At 11:10 A.M. the *Maine* was at "ahead slow" on both engines. Sigsbee was cautious as the ship approached the bridge. Proceeding a little ahead of her and slightly toward port and midstream was the Mallory Line Steamer *Colorado*. The steamer was not under her own power but was being towed by the tug *J. Jewett* in the same direction as the *Maine*. Also going downstream ahead of the *Maine* but still farther to midstream was *Transport Tug No. 5* of the New York, New Haven and Hartford Railroad Company, with a large freight-car barge lashed to each side. All three vessels were on the Manhattan side of the river.

Coming upstream along the Brooklyn shore was a fourth vessel, an excursion steamboat named the *Chancellor*. She was a double-decker loaded with convivial members and guests of the F. J. Kelly Association of Jersey City. Aboard the steamer the Irish flag snapped in the brisk breeze and there was a fiddle band playing bouncy jigs in honor of Kelly himself, a now long-forgotten patron of Jersey politics.

Off the foot of Jefferson Street, the *Chancellor* was about to pass *Transport Tug No. 5* when the strong current changed the *Chancellor*'s direction. She was diverted to midstream, toward the *Transport Tug*, the *Colorado*, and the *Maine*, and finally into a collision with the tug. The excursion boat struck the tug's port barge a glancing blow, tearing away her own hull above the waterline from the paddle box to near her stern. The passengers panicked but the *Chancellor* was deflected safely toward Brooklyn and out of the tangle in the congested section of the river.

Transport Tug No. 5, however, veered toward the Manhattan docks and in front of the J. *Jewett* and her tow, the *Colorado*. This new bearing forced the *Jewett* to alter course closer toward Manhattan, narrowing the opening for the *Maine*, which was closing ground to the extreme right.

Captain Sigsbee ordered his engines stopped. He tried to swing clear of the *Colorado* which was now positioned broadside to the current, blocking four hundred feet of river. Sigsbee calmly headed the drifting battleship still closer to Manhattan. He did not believe he could turn to port and the relatively clear water in midstream because he was boxed in by the *Colorado*, and beyond her by *Transport Tug No. 5*.

Suddenly, into the tangle of whistling, turning, and colliding vessels there blithely steamed a new factor. This was the excursion boat *Isabel*, heading upstream and hugging the Manhattan shore, directly in front of the approaching *Maine*. The eight hundred members of the Alligator Club of Newark, mostly women with children, stampeded toward the *Isabel*'s rails in terror while the band struck up the strains of "The Star-Spangled Banner." The steadiest hand on the *Isabel* was her captain who plowed straight ahead at the *Maine*, leaving Sigsbee to make the life or death determination. The situation that had been merely annoying for Sigsbee was now highly dangerous.

Sigsbee saw his options as limited. He could either slam into the bow of the *Isabel* or he could crash into the Manhattan shore, perhaps finishing both the *Maine* and his naval career. The *Isabel* kept coming at him and he could see unsuspecting workmen on Pier 46 loading another railroad barge. His first command in the emergency was to order the engines full speed astern, but he was unable to make sternway against the swift current.

Then, with a last warning blast of the *Maine*'s whistle, his choice was made. He shouted, "Send the call to collision quarters." Slowly the big battleship swung to her starboard. There was a deafening crash as the *Maine*'s fighting ram pierced the pier while the *Isabel* steamed safely past, the brave band still playing the national anthem.

The stern of the barge being loaded at the pier was sliced clean off without touching the workmen or even the ten freight cars. The *Maine* hit the pier's pilings so hard that the battleship rebounded back into the river while the sailors were running below to close the watertight compartment doors. The only injury to the *Maine* proved to be a few dented plates and a slight loss of white paint on the ledge where the bow anchor rested. Sigsbee continued on to Tompkinsville.

Considering the possibilities, the damage was slight all around. The dock fared the worst. The entire outer end was wrecked. The planks were ripped up and the barge with its cars sank before the stevedores could remove the contents. The *Chancellor* was not seriously damaged and proceeded to land her Kelly partisans at City Island. The *Isabel*'s Alligator excursionists quieted down and had a lifetime to tell tall stories about the near miss with the big battleship.

The question that remained was the correctness of Captain Sigsbee's split-second judgment. Although there was nothing in the Navy Regulations requiring the use of a commercial pilot in a busy harbor, his detractors claimed he was remiss in not having engaged one. They pointed to an incident that had occurred to the USS *Concord* during her trials in 1890, the year the *Maine* was launched.

The *Concord* had left the New York Navy Yard in the afternoon with the members of her Board of Inspection as observers. As the vessel swung into the mass of traffic on the East River, the steering gear jammed. There was no time for hesitation. Pilot Francis Bell kept the engines going. He worked the indicator calmly while calling, "Full speed port engine," "Back her," and

"Ahead full speed," to guide the *Concord* into the Hell Gate opening. Steamers observing the *Concord*'s plight stopped while she glided past the dangerous gate. The ship's commander exclaimed, "Well done, pilot! That is the first time a vessel was ever taken through Hell Gate without a rudder." The pilot had special skills as well as long experience in the specific locale.

The point was that Captain Sigsbee's action was the only alternative he saw in the emergency, but perhaps it was not the only alternative there had been. A professional pilot might have avoided the crash altogether by reacting sooner, by choosing a different course, or by picking another time.

A naval board of inquiry was convened to investigate the East River episode. The board found that "the serious disaster which might have resulted from the collision with the *Isabel* leaves no doubt in the minds of the Board that the judgment of the commanding officer of the *Maine* was correct and that he probably avoided serious disaster and loss of life to the *Isabel* by taking the course he did." Sigsbee's quick reaction and his pluck were approved by his peers.

The board implicitly ratified the Navy Department's wisdom in promoting Sigsbee to the captaincy of the *Maine*. Assistant Secretary of the Navy Theodore Roosevelt wrote him a letter of commendation saying, "You have reflected credit upon yourself and upon the Service to which you belong."

Maybe the luck of the *Maine* had improved. If there had been loss of life or if the ship had sunk, Sigsbee might have received a harsher judgment. Instead no one had been injured and the ship was undamaged. In any event, Sigsbee's own prospects were certainly enhanced. His East River reaction was high among the reasons officially expressed for sending him to Havana six months later.

RECOGNITION FOR CAPTAIN SIGSBEE

The background, the experience, and even the peculiarities of Charles Dwight Sigsbee are discernible from his record.

Sigsbee was born on January 16, 1845, in Albany, New York, alongside the Hudson River but far from the ocean. There was no history of naval service in his family, yet in 1859 while he was still a schoolboy, he was appointed to the Naval Academy by Erastus Corning, the Democratic congressman and industrialist. He was at the minimum age for admission as an acting midshipman. His extreme youth led to his being "turned back" a year in 1860, or "bilged" as they said in Annapolis. He remarked much later, however, that he nevertheless "had arrived very young for an officer in the American Navy." For that reason he was senior in rank to officers like Chadwick who were older than he.

After graduating from the Academy in 1863 in the midst of the Civil War, he was promoted to acting ensign and assigned to a steam sloop. The next year he was transferred to the cruiser *Brooklyn* and fought in the battle of Mobile Bay. The following year found him on the *Wyoming*. His war record under Vice Admiral David Farragut was brilliant.

Sigsbee's rapid progress in the Navy continued after the war despite the lessened opportunity for advancement. He was transferred to the Asiatic Squadron and was promoted to master in 1866 and to lieutenant in 1867. He was commissioned lieutenant commander when he was twenty-three, a distinction without parallel.

During two years as an instructor at the Naval Academy he initiated a course in nautical drawing. He had sold sketches to the New York newspaper the *Daily Graphic*, but he refused an offer of employment as a cartoonist to remain in the Navy.

His specialty became the peripheral field of marine science, not a discipline directly connected to the Navy's primary business of fighting at sea but one regarded as glamorous by his peers. While Sampson became an expert in Ordnance's guns and explosives and Chadwick specialized in ship construction and equipment, Sigsbee turned to charting the ocean floor and surveying the coastal ledges. He was at ease with civilian naturalists and geologists.

In 1871 Sigsbee was assigned to the Hydrographic Office of the Navy, and in 1874 to the Coastal Survey. He commanded the steamer *Blake* from 1875 to 1878 and gained worldwide recognition for his improvements in deep-sea sounding. He was in charge of the U.S. team that explored animal life on previously untouched ocean bottoms. The famous zoologist Professor Alexander Agassiz said the group's success was due not only to Sigsbee's concern for scientific investigation but also to his numerous inventions of apparatus for deep-sea sounding and dredging.

The most remote valley in the Gulf of Mexico is officially named "Sigsbee's Deep," and the scientific designation *Sigsbeia murrhina* is for a rare specimen of ocean-bottom fauna. Near Morro Light off Havana, Sigsbee also discovered new kinds of sea lilies in an exploration of the Cuban shore that aided him twenty years later.

The question for the naval authorities, though, was whether Sigsbee's involvement in this exciting but in a practical sense irrelevant field would diminish his capacity for command. The novel way he handled the *Blake* in a tropical storm was the answer.

In 1876 the *Blake* was caught in a hurricane in a West Indian port. Despite her anchors, the little steamer was drifting onto a coral reef where she would have been pounded to pieces within minutes. To save the *Blake*, Sigsbee scuttled her. He deliberately sank the ship in the shallow bay by opening the sea cocks. After the storm had passed, the *Blake* was dewatered and put back in commission. The subsequent comment from the Navy brass was, "Sigsbee is a man who absolutely does not know what it is to lose his head. There isn't a man in the Service who doesn't envy him that trait. He has nerves of steel."

Sigsbee's accomplishments in hydrographics brought him international acclaim as a scientist. His deep-sea sounding machine was exhibited by the Navy Department at the Philadelphia Centennial Exposition in 1876. His treatise *Deep-Sea Sounding and Dredging* was published in 1880, winning him the double red eagle decoration from Prussia and a medal from Great Britain. Sigsbee also invented a parallel rule for mechanical drawing.

Apart from his being "bilged" at the Academy, the one possible blot on his otherwise outstanding record occurred in 1886 when he commanded the old *Kearsarge* on the European Station. A naval board of inspection reported dirt in the ship, along with a failure to comply with ordnance regulations and a laxity in drilling the marines on board. Sigsbee presented a defense that cited the age of the Civil War ship and the bad weather he had recently experienced. The charges were dropped. They were never again mentioned in the Navy.

In March 1897 Sigsbee was promoted to captain. The next month at Hampton Roads, Virginia, he was given his seventh and most impressive command, the *Maine*. His pay was increased from $3,500 to $4,500 a year. The *Maine*'s officers said Sigsbee looked like a college professor with his affable manners and the spectacles he wore to correct his one physical defect, astigmatism.

In receiving this command, he had been advanced beyond some of his seniors. One of them complained gently to the Secretary of the Navy, "Sigsbee, that admirable fellow, got the *Maine* within three weeks of promotion," when he was a very junior captain. The department had plans for Sigsbee, however, that others might not be able to handle.

This consummate naval commander, deep-sea explorer, inventor, illustrator, and mechanical draftsman was also an author. A selection from his book on the *Maine* shows his perceptiveness and kindliness, in the context of the racial attitudes of the nineteenth century.

Sigsbee wrote that "the colored cabin steward good old John R. Bell had been in the Navy for 27 years. . . . He had not much merit as a chef, excepting that he could always find delicate lettuce. He was honest and true to his duties. I could object to his acts only by delicate suggestion or subterfuge. Periodically he would make me a pound-cake. I would cut from it a single slice, which I would secretly throw away. The cake would then adorn my sideboard in its remaining integrity for many days, to Bell's evident pride. His range of desserts was small. When he felt he had run through his gamut and needed time to think, he would make me an apple-pie, a colossal monstrosity I abhorred. I would eat of his apple-pie—the same pie—day after day, until it neared its end, when immunity would be claimed on the ground of its extreme richness. No man can do more than his uttermost best, and that old Bell did habitually. . . ."

For his time, Sigsbee retained both humility and a sense of humor. These are qualities not found in every hero.

Sending the *Maine*

★ ★ ★ ★ ★ ★ ★ ★

SIGSBEE ON HAVANA WATCH

One of the last assignments of the *Maine* while A. S. Crowninshield was captain was the pleasant duty of representing the Navy at the New Orleans Mardi Gras in February 1897. Crowninshield engaged a river pilot to head up the Mississippi and anchor off Canal Street.

The *Maine* was welcomed in the city. The battleship was big enough to impress the sightseers who came on board and small enough to navigate the river channel without danger to herself. When the ship left on March 11 for Port Royal, South Carolina, the reluctant parting was with the promise of a return to New Orleans in mid-February 1898 for the next Mardi Gras.

Soon after Sigsbee took command, the *Maine* and the other ships of the North Atlantic Squadron anchored at the man-of-war station off Tompkinsville on the eve of another celebration. This one was the dedication of Grant's Tomb in Manhattan. At 9 A.M. on April 22, the Spanish cruiser *Maria Teresa* appeared in the harbor, bound for a North River anchorage to join in the ceremonies.

To avoid friction with the Spanish military authorities in Cuba, no U.S. warship had been sent to Havana since the start of the 1895 rebellion. Nevertheless Admiral Bunce who was in command of the squadron ordered the *Maine* to welcome the Spanish warship. The *Maine* lowered a small boat with an officer on board, but the *Maria Teresa* steamed past. Later that day a second Spanish cruiser, the *Infanta Isabel,* arrived in the harbor and also ignored the *Maine*'s greeting. Despite the Spanish government's stated policy of friendship with the United States, most Spanish officers hated anything

American. Neither Bunce nor Sigsbee was particularly surprised or offended. Each attributed the rebuff not to friction between the countries but to Spanish national idiosyncrasies that no one born in the United States could comprehend.

On October 8, 1897, the fate of the *Maine* was fixed. The battleship was unexpectedly detached from the North Atlantic Squadron and instructed to return to Port Royal, a harbor inconspicuously close to Havana. Lee was being listened to at last.

The *Maine* arrived at the South Carolina station on October 12 to await further direction from Secretary John Long. If U.S. citizens were endangered in increasingly perilous Havana, the *Maine* would be sent to the Cuban capital at once.

Havana was quiet for the moment, so the *Maine* was ordered to Norfolk, Virginia, to take on coal and to be put in shape for any Cuban emergency. At nearby Newport News the *Maine* was loaded with the highest grade of naval fuel, bituminous coal from the Pocahontas mine. Next, the *Maine* was drydocked on Assistant Secretary Roosevelt's instructions for a thorough scraping and repainting of her bottom to increase her speed and maneuverability. In view of the continuing need for the ship, Roosevelt directed that the *Maine* be refloated no later than December 10. That schedule was met.

Also at Norfolk, Lieutenant Commander Marix was succeeded by Lieutenant Commander Richard Wainwright as the *Maine's* executive officer. The switch was as much to ready the *Maine* for the Cuban expedition as were the coaling and the maintenance. Marix was an able administrator but Wainwright had a flair. He was among the most competent and conscientious of the officers in his grade. He was hand picked for the *Maine,* just as Sigsbee had been.

On December 11, the *Maine* was ordered to Key West, Florida. Only ninety miles from Havana, the Key was the U.S. port closest to the Spanish island. The *Maine's* orders were confidential, locked by Sigsbee in a drawer in the sideboard in his quarters. The gist, though, was reported widely in the press and was immediately available to Spanish spies. When called upon by Lee, Sigsbee was to "aid in the removal of endangered Americans from Havana, giving them asylum on board the *Maine.*" This was President McKinley's first acquiescence to Consul General Lee's repeated requests for a warship to be placed so as to have the captain available to cooperate with him.

Moving the *Maine* to Key West marked a decided change in U.S. policy. General Blanco's control of the Spanish army in Havana was now recognized as having been made precarious by the refusal of the Weyler partisans to accept autonomy for Cuba. McKinley thought the presence of the *Maine* in Key West might intimidate the Weylerites and stabilize the Blanco administration. He also increased the indirect pressure on Spain by instructing Secretary Long to announce to the press that sailors in the European Squadron whose enlistments were running out would be retained involuntarily during the Cuban crisis.

The *Maine* arrived in Key West on December 15. The only regular communication between Lee and Sigsbee was over an open cable line monitored by the Spaniards. No code could be arranged by cable so Lee sent Sigsbee a simple signal in a letter delivered by an officer of the commercial steamer *Olivette* which ran frequently between Havana and Key West. On the receipt of a cable from Lee including the words "two dollars," the *Maine* was to obey the "two" by making ready to dash for Havana in two hours. The *Maine* was not actually to start for Havana, however, until the receipt of a second message from Lee. The sentence "Vessels might be employed elsewhere" was to be the trigger.

Like boys playing war games, Lee and Sigsbee tested the Havana cable service with meaningless daily messages to make sure the Spaniards had not interfered with communication between them. Sigsbee felt that "things in Havana are very tense, the Spaniards quarreling among themselves and are hot heads. They may do foolish things at any time."

Nevertheless, he maintained his reputation for nonchalance. He gave "very nice" luncheons for guests on board, featuring "about 40 cents worth of flowers for ornament. Also olives and salted almonds. The bill of fare was, Consomme in cups, broiled pompano, tongue with chopped mushrooms, French chops with French peas, lettuce salad" in the *Maine*'s silver service, and "homemade ice cream with tea cakes."

On January 12 the first shoe fell. At 6 P.M. Sigsbee received the preliminary "two dollars" message, directing him to be ready to leave for Havana in two hours. He complied by getting up steam. The unruffled captain had planned to attend a dance on shore that night. He kept the appointment, concerned that a cancellation might reveal to reporters in Key West that there was an emergency in Havana. His private instruction to Wainwright was that if the second coded message arrived from Lee, a gun was to be fired as the signal to bring him back to a *Maine* ready to sail instantly.

Despite Sigsbee's precaution, the yellow-press New York *World* reported the inflammatory "Three Warships Sent to Havana. The battleship *Maine* has been ordered to sea immediately." The staid *New York Herald* had the story straight: "The Battleship *Maine* at Key West under Orders to be in Readiness/She May Go to Havana/General Lee Will Cable Whether Needed."

For three days Sigsbee maintained the preparedness of both his own ship and two smaller warships under his command. He told his wife that "the *Maine* goes shortly," but the second message from Lee never came.

On January 18 the *Maine* was being coaled to the brim once again, this time at Key West before rejoining the North Atlantic Squadron. Sigsbee did not believe he would be removed from his crucial listening post. "I have doubts about our going" with the squadron, he maintained. "In certain events the *Maine* is to be the chosen of the flock. I'm a Fitzsimmonsonian desperado"—Fitzsimmons was a resolute heavyweight boxing champion—"on the wild seas hereabouts. Events in Havana are and will continue to be very critical, and I have been and will continue to be, probably, very much in the swim." An admiring Rear Admiral Montgomery Sicard had earlier suggested that Sigsbee leave the *Maine* to take command of Sicard's flagship the *New York*, but Sigsbee had declined. He preferred the excitement of facing the Spaniards on his own in Havana harbor.

Notwithstanding Sigsbee's reservations about leaving Key West, the *Maine* was instructed to meet the squadron. The shorthanded battleship was to make her final preparation for Havana by taking apprentices from the other warships. Sigsbee turned his Havana watch over to Lieutenant Gleaves of the torpedo boat *Cushing* which was to remain at Key West to receive any cable from Lee. The message was to be forwarded to Admiral Sicard for Sigsbee via the recently commissioned torpedo boat *Du Pont*. This presumably secret arrangement was reported at once in the *New York Herald*. The revised warning signal to come from Lee was "pay nothing."

While these arrangements were being made feverishly, Sigsbee continued to demonstrate his poise. He sent his wife as "something in your line" the recipe for "Stuffed Tomato Salad. On each plate, a few leaves of lettuce dressed with French dressing. In the center a skinned tomato with the seeds removed and in their place a Filling. On top of the Filling a lump of Mayonnaise. This gives as colors yellow, red, and green or greenish white. The Filling: Take equal parts of chopped English walnuts and mashed French peas. Rub them up with a little Mayonnaise and enough very finely powdered cracker dust to give cohesion to the mass. It is good and novel."

Sigsbee was not as equable with the detested harbor pilots. When the *Maine* entered the station at Key West on December 15, he had asked for a civilian pilot because of "the frequency with which coral heads are discovered by vessels striking them." Unhappily, the pilot did not meet Sigsbee's standards. When Sigsbee was ready to leave on January 23, the Board of Pilot Commissioners of Key West insisted that he accept the same pilot who had brought the ship in. Sigsbee refused, pointing out that the responsibility for his vessel was his alone so he should be able to choose his own pilot. "We couldn't come to terms," Sigsbee explained, "so I diplomatically told them to heat themselves where fires were cheapest. I took the *Maine* out myself, thereby knocking the pilots out of $149.50." As a captain in command, he earned less than $90 a week.

The *Maine* met the squadron at 11 A.M. and took her place in the column of eight vessels. The fleet came to rest alongside the reefs for the night. The next day the fleet steamed to the Dry Tortugas in the Gulf west of the Keys. After anchoring at 6 P.M., Sicard directed the *Indiana* and the *Texas* to transfer the fourteen-year-old apprentices intended for the *Maine*. The *Indiana* ferried 39 boys to the *Maine*, but before the *Texas* could move her 18 boys, a signal went up from the *New York* instructing the *Texas* to defer her transfer until the morning.

The word about the *Maine*'s dramatic assignment on Havana watch had just spread among the ships in the squadron. The boys retained on the *Texas* were disappointed to have to pick up their sea bags and hammocks and return below.

Later Captain Chadwick of the *New York* went aboard the *Maine* to relay confidential oral directions from Admiral Sicard. When he was leaving, Chadwick joked, "Look out, Sigsbee, that those fellows over there don't blow you up."

"Oh," replied Sigsbee, "don't worry. I've taken precautions enough against that."

"Those fellows over there" were the dissident Spanish officers in Havana. The idea of the *Maine* being blown up by the Weylerites was in the air.

THE WEYLERITE RIOTS

The feeling in the United States at the beginning of January 1898 was that General Blanco's offer of compromise with the Cuban rebels was generous enough to end the insurrection. Cuba was not in the headlines in the New York City newspapers.

People such as Lee and Sigsbee who were close to the Cuban scene, however, knew that the Weylerites were a constant danger in Havana. The fractious Spanish officers still loyal to the deposed general were frequently on the verge of going out of control.

Lee could not be sure which direction the underlying rage would take or against whom violence would be aimed. That was why Lee wanted the *Maine* on the alert in Key West. He was looking for a way out of Havana on short notice if trouble came.

The most ardent of the pro-Weyler factions in Cuba was the *Voluntarios*, the Spanish home guards who constituted a significant percentage of the military forces resisting the Cuban insurgents. The disaffected officers of the *Voluntarios* were the leaders of the unorganized and unstable opposition to the authority of Blanco and the regular Spanish troops in Cuba.

The rioting led by the *Voluntarios* began in Havana on Wednesday morning, January 12. Two pro-Blanco newspapers in Havana had added to the philosophical insult of praising autonomy by accusing the Spanish Volunteers of abuses in the handling of army funds during the Weyler administration. The cumulative effect of the perceived insults was unbearable.

A hundred incensed officers led a mob of thousands of Spaniards to the publishing offices of *La Discusion* and *El Reconcentrado*. There they destroyed the printing presses, smashed furniture and windows, and pummeled the unresisting employees. The rioters shouted "Long live Spain!" "Death to Blanco!" "Long live the army!" "Long live Weyler!" and "Down with autonomy!" There was no anti-American cry as yet.

The Spanish authorities had been prepared for trouble. For days they had been trying to unravel rumors of various conspiracies against Blanco. At the bullfights, the place where revolutions sometimes began in Latin countries, extraordinary precautions had been taken to prevent an outbreak. Nevertheless the intensity and breadth of the rioting were not anticipated. The military police were alert. They tried to disperse the rioters gently, but they were powerless. Blanco was afraid that if an order was given to fire on the mob, it would not be obeyed. Spanish soldiers would not fire on other Spanish soldiers.

The mob rallied again in the afternoon and once more in the evening, shouting "Long live Weyler!" "Down with autonomy!" and "Death to Blanco!" The officials began to fear a civilian revolt in the city along with a mutiny among the military.

Apprehension spread to the United States Embassy, so called although Lee rated only a consulate. The headline in the *New York Journal* was "Soldiers Riot in Havana Streets/Liberal Newspaper Offices Gutted by a Military Mob." The *New York Herald* reported anxiously that the utterances of the mob showed the emotions to be equally bitter against the Spanish government and the United States. The *World* reported that "Rioting May Imperil Americans."

As consul general, Lee was properly alarmed at the inability of the Blanco government to maintain order. He knew that the Weylerites blamed the United States for the failure of their idol to put down the insurrection. Consequently, his first step was to send a cable to the State Department, startling the administration by advising that rioting was in progress in Havana. His second step was to send the cable to Key West that put the *Maine* on alert.

In the evening Lee sent another message to the State Department, still referring to "excitement which may develop into serious disturbances." There was no threat expressed against U.S. citizens in Havana, however, despite reports to the contrary in the yellow press. Lee retained his composure and never sent the dancing Sigsbee the second coded cable.

The following morning Blanco achieved some preliminary control over the city, but it took four more days for Havana to come under full constraint. Sixty of the ringleaders were placed under house arrest. None was court-martialed or otherwise punished. Blanco did not dare discipline these officers despite their call for his death. Instead, he found pretexts for releasing them from custody after a few days. He returned them to their commands while penalizing the Liberal press on the basis that the newspapers had impugned the honor of the Spanish army.

For the Weylerites, the riots had served their purpose by making a powerful protest against autonomy. As a practical matter, autonomy had already failed after only two weeks of existence.

The same morning Blanco regained partial control, January 13, Lee cabled the State Department that "the presence of ships may be necessary, but not now." The famous *World* correspondent Sylvester Scovel credited Lee with having averted war by not summoning the *Maine*. Scovel believed that bringing in the *Maine* at this juncture would have been seen by every Spaniard as a hostile act. The presence of the warship would have united all factions against the United States, perhaps causing the shedding of American blood that had been averted so far.

While Lee was reporting "all quiet" to his superiors, however, the Congress took as gospel the articles in the yellow press declaring the riots to have been inspired by anger at the United States. The members were debating immediate recognition of the rebels as the truly constituted government of Cuba. Congressional Republicans informed McKinley that they would insist that his pledge in the party platform be fulfilled by declaring Cuba to be independent of Spain.

McKinley was becoming persuaded that apart from the danger from the Weylerites, sending the *Maine* to Havana would be desirable on all counts, including quieting Congress. He was slowly being convinced that Spain could never establish autonomy, and he welcomed a suggestion from Lee that the last week in January might be the best time for the *Maine* to visit Cuba. Two German warships were due to be in Havana then, so the *Maine* would not be the only foreign vessel. Alternately, Lee recommended that the *Maine* enter the harbor by subterfuge, pleading an exhausted coal supply incurred while chasing filibuster boats. Lee did not know that Sigsbee would never risk taking on Cuban coal that could be booby-trapped.

In contrast, the Liberal government in Madrid hoped to postpone the *Maine*'s visit by persuading McKinley that the goals of Spain and the United States were the same: compromising with the Cuban rebels and suppressing the Weylerites. The Spaniards had just uncovered a Conservative plot to overthrow the monarchy by bringing on and losing a war with the United States. Anarchic conditions after the projected defeat would allow Weyler to become dictator.

In turn, Weyler was quoted as saying that the statements of the American jingoes made it obvious that the United States would intervene in Cuba. Only his return to command, he claimed, could prevent a take-over of the island.

Because of all the ominous signs, the Blanco government remained apprehensive. Yet Havana was quiet again. No indication of ill feeling toward Americans had been expressed. Blanco himself cabled the New York *World* to say that the riots had been brief and that Americans had not been affected at all. The *New York Herald*'s correspondent finally acknowledged, "Although I have been present at every collision between the troops and the people, I have not heard a single anti-American outcry."

Nevertheless, everyone in Havana—Liberal Spaniard or Conservative Spaniard or Cuban or American—expected that something more serious was going to happen soon. The question was whether the upheaval would be initiated by the uncontrollable Weylerites or by the cautious McKinley or by both.

THE REASONS FOR SENDING A SHIP

To this point, the reasons given for dispatching a United States warship to Havana were to protect American citizens and property, mollify Congress and other jingoes, and intimidate the Spanish war party.

President McKinley's own excuse for sending a warship to Cuba was as a gesture of American friendship for Spain. The visit, he claimed, was to be in recognition of Spain's supposed success in pacifying Cuba by providing autonomy and by putting an end to reconcentration. Since a Liberal Spanish government had come to power, amity was said to be the mark of the new relationship. In Havana, the *Maine* would serve as the symbol of the good will and peace that both countries wanted.

The explanation was an obvious distortion of the truth, a candy coating to make the presence of the *Maine* more palatable to Spanish honor. Autonomy had already failed. The reality of peasants still starving in camps could not be hidden.

In fact, the rebels were growing more confident. They were battling in city streets. Key Spanish targets were damaged by dynamite bombs. In view of the insurgent successes, sending the *Maine* could be looked at as an attempt to preserve the island for U.S. commercial interests rather than as a friendly gesture toward Spain. If McKinley waited too long to intervene, the Cuban rebels might seize the island before the United States could take over. The rebels might well turn out to be as resistant to U.S. exploitation as they had been to the Spaniards' brand of imperialism.

McKinley's decision to send a battleship to Havana had not been arrived at in haste. The belief of the administration had always been that President Grover Cleveland committed an enduring mistake by catering to the Spaniards. The McKinley Administration secretly set a contrary course when it took office in March 1897. The aim was to place a warship in Havana harbor the first instant that friction and risk could be minimized. United States pride in maintaining free naval intercourse in foreign ports carried more weight in Washington than soothing Spanish honor. Little thought was given to the possibility of the incendiary incident both Cleveland and the Spanish government had feared.

According to McKinley, the faulty rationale for the Cleveland policy of keeping American warships away from Havana was that the United States and Spain were on unfriendly terms. Such enmity, he maintained, did not exist. American commercial vessels serviced Cuban ports regularly. Two Spanish cruisers had taken a cordial role in the dedication of Grant's Tomb. Moreover, on the few occasions when U.S. warships had entered Spanish ports out of necessity, the underlying Spanish antipathy had always given way to good manners.

McKinley's scheme was to gain entrance to Havana harbor by stages. The first step was to have Secretary Long announce that the North Atlantic Squadron would resume the pre-Cleveland practice of holding its winter training on the traditional drill grounds near the Dry Tortugas. Although McKinley saw the move as putting great pressure on Spain, the announcement was received with equanimity in an observant but noncommittal Madrid.

The next step was to order United States gunboats to cruise the Caribbean. Spain raised no objection there, either, and so all that remained to restore the old custom was to send a battleship to Havana. The January riots in Havana delayed dispatching the *Maine*. Riots meant risk.

McKinley's decision concerning the *Maine* was supported by naval advocates such as Captain Alfred Mahan and Assistant Secretary Roosevelt. The expansionist policy that had led to the new U.S. Navy represented by the

Maine herself called for overseas bases where the warships could be refueled and repaired. In addition, since the United States could not afford to maintain big fleets in both the Atlantic and the Pacific, expansionist theory required a Central American canal to give U.S. warships access to both oceans. The canal would in turn require protection against attack. More bases would be needed, on Cuba in the Atlantic and on Hawaii in the Pacific.

Also significant was the long-held doctrine of preventing foreign powers from gaining colonies in the Americas. Germany had its own imperialist stratagems and was exercising its considerable weight in the Caribbean, seeking a coaling station for the German navy. The Kaiser was known to favor Spain over the United States. A Spain sure of losing a war against the United States might save face by selling Cuba, perpetuating the nearby island as a foreign colony.

In January 1898 there were four German warships in the Caribbean. Two of them were to call at Havana. If it was natural for Germany to send warships to Havana, McKinley insisted, it was equally natural for the United States. In the face of such a display, Spain would back down by lightening its heavy hand on the Cubans. Spain's hope of beating the rebels through starvation had disappeared when Weyler was recalled. Blanco had inherited a Spanish army unfit to conquer by arms.

Congress believed in the potency of the United States and the weakness of Spain. Any nation that considered itself a great power, the jingoes claimed, would have to send warships abroad to protect its citizens. Just talking about ordering the *Maine* to Havana quieted legislative moves to recognize the rebel government.

McKinley was more fearful of his own countrymen than he was of provoking the Weylerites. If he failed to send the *Maine*, U.S. citizens might be killed in Cuba. He would then be held responsible for their deaths. In contrast, few would blame him for dispatching the *Maine* to Havana.

On the other hand, there were negatives for McKinley to consider. First, there was no emergency in Havana after the Weylerite riots ended. The excuse of safeguarding lives and property was not timely.

Second, McKinley had handed control of the *Maine* over to Lee. The consul was relishing the applause he had received for not ordering the *Maine* from Key West. Lee was now asserting that if warships ever did become necessary, he wanted at least three battleships to disarm in advance any foolish assault that might be made against the *Maine* if she were alone. McKinley had no intention of making that large a commitment.

On January 24 the President conferred with Secretary Long and Judge William Day of the State Department. Justice Joseph McKenna of the Supreme Court and General Nelson Miles of the United States Army joined them. The primary discussion was about whether Spain could legally turn the *Maine* away from Havana and how the United States would respond militarily if the *Maine* was fired on. The negatives to sending the *Maine* in the first place were never explored with equal vigor.

In Madrid the report that U.S. warships might be coming to Cuban waters caused great excitement. The newspaper *Imparcial* published a violent article that concluded, "We see now the eagerness of the Yankees to seize Cuba." *El Heraldo* wrote on January 16, "If the Government of the United States sends one war ship to Cuba, a thing they are no longer likely to do [because the riots had subsided], Spain would act with energy and without vacillation." In the U.S. press, rumors circulated that in response to talk about sending the *Maine*, Lee had been assassinated and extra guards had been placed around the embassy.

If McKinley had thought the situation through, he would have seen that dispatching the *Maine* to Havana could turn into an indelible error. Even if the port were friendly, sending a warship bristling with big guns was a provocation. The *Maine* could only become a hostage in the harbor. Loyal Secretary Long had misgivings, but he restricted his doubts to his diary while his published interviews claimed the *Maine* was in no danger at all on this "friendly call."

The final word from President McKinley to Secretary Long was that the *Maine* would definitely be sent to Havana at the first opportunity. In truth, the dispatch of the battleship would be for bogus reasons founded on fake friendliness, whether the Spaniards liked it or not. The *Maine* was being sent to satisfy U.S. public opinion, not the Spaniards.

CHOOSING THE *MAINE* FOR THE MISSION

To make the entry into Havana harbor where the ship would be alone, exposed, and probably unexpected, the *Maine* was picked on the grounds of medium size, expendability, and personnel. She was suitable for the mission as a good but not too boastful example of the expanding U.S. fleet.

Naval progress had quickly overtaken the *Maine*. She was currently considered to be a modest vessel, a second-class battleship not much more powerful than one of Spain's own armored cruisers. Her displacement was relatively light, so she would not be as apt to hit bottom in shallow Havana bay as would the deeper-draft battleships. Besides, she was more expendable than a newer and bigger ship would be.

Secretary Long believed that any initial Spanish attack on the *Maine* would come from the shore batteries and the Spanish warships in the harbor when the *Maine* approached the outer channel. The ship would make a strong defense against those Spanish guns before turning back. If the *Maine* was allowed to enter peacefully, the Secretary expected the next danger to come from the Spanish authorities or the Weylerites. He thought that any potential enemy would, however, be overawed by the ship's 10-inch guns.

Thus the *Maine* fit the need. She was small for a battleship but not tiny, powerful but not overwhelming. If the *Maine* was to be an insult to the Spaniards in Havana, the affront would be moderate.

In addition, the captain who was chosen was an overachiever, as if he had been trained specifically for the task of commanding the *Maine* in an emergency. McKinley and Long had confidence in him, particularly because of the East River episode. Sigsbee would be able to cope with any crisis. His coolness, tact, energy, and intelligence were the reasons for placing great discretionary authority in his hands. His decisions could be the difference between war and peace with Spain.

Although Sigsbee spoke no Spanish, few native-born Easterners did, and he was an international figure in maritime circles because of his deep-sea-sounding inventions. Moreover, he was one of the most popular officers. His less fortunate seniors would acquiesce to his being picked for the Havana mission.

Besides, he was eager to go. He had been to the gates of Havana before and he called himself Fitzsimmons, a heavy hitter.

The *Maine* Arrives

★ ★ ★ ★ ★ ★ ★ ★

DIPLOMACY AND DEPARTURE

Because of his anti-Spanish attitude and aggressive nature, Consul General Lee was a festering thorn in the Spanish side. On January 19 when the *Maine* was still on alert at Key West and autonomy was not quite three weeks old, Spanish minister Dupuy de Lôme was in Washington. He complained to his superior Pio Gullon in Madrid that "the worst result of the events in Cuba is that General Lee has reported to the Government that autonomy has failed, the riots in Havana giving a show of truth to that opinion."

In reply, Gullon advised Dupuy to hint to McKinley that Spain would soon request Lee's transfer from Havana. When Spain did ask for Lee's removal, however, McKinley refused. The refusal was a highly irregular bit of protocol that the press played down as Spain being "miffed" at Lee.

Then on January 24, the McKinley Administration at last came to its decision concerning the *Maine*. Dupuy cabled Gullon that he had met with Assistant Secretary of State Day at 10 A.M. He had been told that McKinley had not departed from the attitude toward Spain set forth in his annual message. This meant to Dupuy that the Spanish government was at liberty to pursue its own policies in Cuba, including autonomy, despite Lee and without U.S. interference. That was the good news. The bad news was that McKinley intended to send warships on so-called friendly visits to Cuban ports.

Dupuy was enraged by McKinley's change in policy. His first reaction was to defy Day by threatening war. Then he backed down. When Day told Dupuy that U.S. warships would be going to Cuba on McKinley's orders in any event, Dupuy did not deny to the press that as Spain's envoy he had consented in principle to the coming visits.

The *Maine* and the rest of the North Atlantic Squadron had departed from Key West and were steaming for the Tortugas when Day requested that Dupuy return to the State Department that same afternoon. In the interim Day and Long held their meeting with McKinley, Justice McKenna, and General Miles. In addition to the legalities, they discussed the diminished risk of sending the *Maine* to Havana now they had Dupuy's grudging acquiescence. They had expected Dupuy to remain adamant in his refusal.

According to Dupuy, he conferred again with Day at 3 P.M. Day "told me he went to see the President. The result of our morning conference and the reports concerning the commercial negotiations have been so satisfactory that the President has determined to send the *Maine* to Havana as a mark of friendship. The President believes it has been a mistake not to have had an American war vessel visit Cuba in the past three years, because now what is a fresh proof of international courtesy is looked upon as a hostile act."

In keeping with the amicable mood of this second conference with Dupuy, Secretary Long remarked to the press that the Spanish minister had recognized the wisdom of sending an American ship to Havana in a friendly way, to resume the previous practice whenever the *Maine* was ready. No date was set. Day added that "the Spanish Minister here is fully informed of what is going on, and, so far as I know, he has not made the slightest objection." Dupuy agreed that the explanation of the purpose of the *Maine*'s trip was satisfactory. His understanding was that the *Maine* would not leave Key West until he consented to a specific time for the visit.

Consul Lee in Havana and Minister Stewart Woodford in Madrid were then advised by Day that "it is the purpose of this Government to resume friendly naval visits at Cuban ports. In that view the *Maine* will call at Havana in a day or two." The envoys were told to notify the respective Spanish authorities.

Foreign reaction to the news of the impending call was bad. First, there were bitter editorials in the Spanish newspapers in Madrid, complaining that the *Maine*'s visit meant U.S. intervention in Cuba and predicting violence against the ship.

Second, Lee's response to Day was: "Advise visit be postponed six or seven days, to give last excitement time to disappear." He was repeating the strenuous opposition of the Spanish officials in Havana.

Despite the negatives, McKinley seized the opportunity provided by Dupuy's limited assent and ordered the immediate dispatch of the *Maine* to Havana. In contrast with the homespun homily about treacherous dons and unsophisticated Americans, McKinley played Yankee trickster to Dupuy's gullible Spanish gentleman. McKinley's move was applauded in Congress.

Along with the President, Day and Long were toying with the Spanish government and with the truth. The objective of their game was to slip the *Maine* into Havana bay peacefully. Long, however, had his doubts. He confessed to his diary that "there is of course the danger that the arrival of the ship may precipitate some crisis or riot. I hope that everything will turn out right." New York newspapers also reported on "the danger of resentment being excited by the appearance of an American vessel in the harbor. Anything calculated to excite the people is extremely dangerous."

Dupuy went along with the McKinley Administration. He merely warned that "the only remote contingency which might lead to unpleasant consequences is some overt act on the part of the insurgents." He did not mention how outraged the Weylerites would be.

Day replied quickly to Lee's request for delay by cabling the conclusive "*Maine* has been ordered. Will probably arrive at Havana some time tomorrow, possibly early. Cooperate with authorities for our friendly visit." He betrayed his uneasiness, though, by adding, "Keep us advised by frequent telegrams."

Long issued the *Maine*'s actual sailing orders while the North Atlantic Squadron was steaming westward, approaching the Tortugas. At the same time Long was telling the press, "Notice has been given by the Spanish Minister to his people and by our Department to our Consul," despite the fact that Dupuy was not yet informed about the *Maine*'s imminent departure. The Spaniard was still saying that "even if the order sending the *Maine* were true, it portended nothing serious." He had not suspected how soon the *Maine* would be sailing.

The next morning, the Spanish Minister of State cabled Dupuy from Madrid. "Wishing to reciprocate," he announced, "we shall arrange that vessels of our squadron may visit the ports of the United States." Gullon was sending the warship *Vizcaya* to New York City to minimize the loss of face caused by the forced acceptance of the *Maine*'s visit. McKinley's deception concerning the *Maine* had been unnecessary. Spain would have agreed, given the chance. If McKinley had curbed his gamesmanship, the *Maine* might have entered Havana harbor as a welcome guest instead of as a bitterly resented interloper.

Early on the morning of the twenty-fifth, Lee did not yet have Day's cable that the *Maine* was en route. General Blanco was away from Havana but Lee had seen Acting Captain General Parrado. The consul rushed a message to Day, "Authorities profess to think United States has ulterior purpose in sending ship. Say it will obstruct autonomy, produce excitement, and most probably a demonstration. Ask delay."

There was no need for Day to reply. The *Maine* was already at her crisis point off the Cuban coast.

There was another, probably apocryphal story reported after the war about how the *Maine* came to be sent to her final destination. The first portion of the narrative about Lee's inflated evaluation of his own importance sounds true. The second portion about the revolver is unlikely.

Former Colonel John Caldwell was a *New York Herald* correspondent in Havana. A few days after the January 12 riots, his assistant overheard Spanish Secretary General Congosto tell Lee that the riots had been engineered by the Weylerites to upset the peace between Spain and the United States and that any additional anti-American threats would be just trouble-making by these dissident Spanish officers.

The one serious hazard Congosto saw was that the U.S. government might overestimate the strength of the Weylerites and unwittingly give them support by sending a warship to Havana. Congosto said the presence of an American naval vessel in the harbor might so enrage the ultra-Spanish element that calamitous results could follow. "I implore you," he urged, "not to allow a warship to be sent here."

Lee replied, "I believe you, and you need fear no such American interference. No warship will be sent here unless I ask for it, and at present I have no such intention." Lee knew that American citizens were in no immediate danger after the rioting had subsided. The Spaniards in authority feared offending the United States. The Weylerites seemed to be in check momentarily and the Cubans avowedly considered Americans to be their allies.

When Caldwell asked for permission to quote Lee, however, the consul urged the correspondent to postpone the article because Congosto might be accused of divulging Spanish secrets. Caldwell complied.

Like Lee, the correspondent had devised a cable code where seemingly innocent messages contained key words decipherable only at the *Herald* office in New York City. The code was used for news too controversial to pass the Spanish censor or too important to await the boat to Key West.

After the meeting between Congosto and Lee there was a brief period of calm in Cuba. Caldwell, though, feared for his personal safety in the event of further unrest. At his coded request, the *Herald* shipped him a revolver, but the bullets did not fit. He knew the censor would regard the need for bullets as bad press for Spain and would reject his message, so he used his code. On January 24 he cabled: "Camera received but not plates. Require special size. Send by next boat."

The telegraph agent at Key West where messages were rerouted was said to be a U.S. agent. He was aware Caldwell coded cables in emergencies and thought he had the key to a critical bit of news. He deciphered the message as the report of an attack in force against the American consulate in Havana. He so informed Secretary Day who advised McKinley.

The story is, the *Maine* was sent at once. At least that's what Caldwell said.

THE JACK AT THE FOREMAST

While newspapermen were questioning Day and Dupuy at 6 P.M. on January 24, the North Atlantic Squadron was anchored in the Gulf of Mexico, ten miles south of the Tortugas. Three hours later the lookout on the *Maine* sighted a small vessel to the eastward, heading toward the fleet at high speed. She was making frantic signals to attract the attention of the flagship *New York*.

From far off, Sigsbee recognized the approaching torpedo boat as the *Du Pont*. He realized that the *Du Pont's* signals had to relate to the *Maine's* Havana watch, so on his own initiative he ordered the boiler fires spread to enable his ship to depart quickly. The anchor chain was drawn tight and the gig was lowered onto the water. After half an hour the little *Du Pont* reached the flagship, which soon signaled, "*Maine* prepare to get under way. Commanding Officer repair on board the Flagship." The *Maine* replied at once, "All ready."

The impatient Sigsbee had climbed down into his boat before the message arrived and was being rowed toward the flagship. The night was now dark. The Gulf was rough and the tide was strong. Suddenly the *Du Pont* appeared directly ahead, Sigsbee recalled, "as if she had ridden up out of the sea." The searchlight almost blinded Sigsbee, but he got alongside the *Du Pont*, clambered aboard, sent back his own boat, and was taken toward the flagship. Another small boat rowed him to the *New York* after more tough work with the oars.

On board, Sigsbee—or "Fitzsimmons" as he privately named himself again in recognition of the heavyweight powers to be granted him—met with Admiral Sicard and was handed orders sending him south. The instructions read only, "*Maine* to proceed to Havana and make friendly call. Pay respects to the authorities there. Particular attention must be paid to usual interchange of civility." As Sigsbee put it bluntly, "I was left to act according to my own judgment, in the usual way. It was assumed I would know how to act, and it was intended to hold me responsible for my action. I volunteered the remark to Admiral Sicard that I should try to make no mistake."

Sicard was brief. As far as he was concerned, if Sigsbee made a mistake the error could easily be erased. Sicard had assembled off the Tortugas the most formidable fleet of armored warships ever seen in American waters.

The exhilarated Sigsbee hurriedly retraced his route from the *New York* to the *Du Pont* to the *Maine*. The battleship was quickly under way for Havana, less than two hours after the first sighting of the *Du Pont*. Sigsbee entered his cabin on the superstructure deck and wrote a long night order covering the many assignments to be fulfilled by his officers and men during the morning watch. Then he applied his personal discipline to retire to his bed and will himself asleep at once as the *Maine*'s prow cut through the rolling waves.

Sigsbee was awakened at six. While the *Maine* steamed southward through the Gulf Stream, the guns had been checked to make sure they were in working order. Ammunition had been brought to them. Gunners were hidden in the turrets. One sailor wrote home that "you would have thought we were going to war. Everybody was excited." Another said, "We had the decks cleared for action, and every man on board expected there would be trouble."

When the green hills of Cuba came into sight, the men were at their battle stations. The ship slowed. Not knowing what his reception might be, Sigsbee gave the *Maine* a last shaping up. When he finished, the ship seemed to be in proper peacetime condition to enter a friendly port. In reality, however, the vessel was set for a fight.

Sigsbee claimed that the *Maine* "was in such a state of readiness that she could not have been taken at much disadvantage had she been attacked, while presenting no offensive appearance." The crew believed that Sigsbee "thought we would be stopped, and he had orders to force his way in, if we had to," but there is no indication that Sigsbee's instructions went that far.

The ship's speed had been moderate all the way from the Tortugas because the Havana port regulations precluded entering the harbor before daybreak. In addition, Sigsbee's unstated mission was to impress the Spaniards with U.S. naval might, so he wanted to come into view when the city was awake. The *Maine* neared the coast to the westward of Havana at 9 A.M. on Tuesday, January 25. She steamed slowly along the shore toward Morro Castle while the windows in the buildings of the city flashed in the early sun. The officers were in frock coats and the crew was dressed in clean blues.

When the *Maine* reached the entrance to the harbor, Sigsbee had the small signal flag called the jack hoisted at the foremast. This was his formal request for a Cuban pilot to take the *Maine* in to the mooring. With his habitual aversion to commercial pilots, he insisted, "I could have taken the ship in myself, but I knew that the Spanish disliked the refusal of a pilot." As he saw it, his request was an evidence of good will toward Spain, although the battleship with her batteries of 10- and 6-inch guns was a formidable way to show amity.

At this moment the sobering realization came to Sigsbee that the *Maine* stood wholly revealed to the unseen Spaniards. In her vulnerable condition, the ship was well within range of the big guns of the Spanish coastal forts. Enough firepower was there to send the *Maine* quickly to the bottom of the sea.

In New York and Washington, the news of the *Maine*'s mission had just been published. The *New York Times* ran an editorial stating that the way to show American confidence in Spain was to resume the former naval relations, as the *Maine* was doing. The Congress was more honest in expressing militant American feelings. Senator Henry Teller of Colorado asserted, "I would like to see the harbor of Havana filled with American ships." More belligerent legislators charged that the *Maine*'s visit was concocted between McKinley and Dupuy de Lôme as a device to keep Congress quiet.

In New York City, the Cuban junta warned that the Spaniards would take the presence of the *Maine* in Havana as interference in Spain's internal affairs and that "we shall soon hear from General Weyler's subordinates in Cuba." The junta did not specify what form the "hearing" would take but the Weylerites dealt in violence.

In Madrid, *Epoca* described the dispatch of the *Maine* "as a sop to the American jingoes," and added, "We cannot suppose the American government so naive or badly informed as to imagine that the presence of American war vessels at Havana will be a cause of satisfaction to Spain or an indication of friendship."

In Havana a courier from the cable office handed Caldwell of the *Herald* a coded message indicating that the *Maine* had left Florida. Caldwell resided on the same floor as Lee in the Hotel Inglaterra. The reporter knocked on Lee's door and told him the *Maine* was coming. Lee gave Caldwell the same response he had given Congosto. "Nonsense," he asserted firmly. "The government would never send a Navy vessel here unless I requested it—which I have not done." Just then they looked through the window and saw the graceful *Maine* entering the harbor. White smoke was drifting from her battery that had saluted the Spanish flag flying over Morro Castle.

The portly, mustachioed Lee gave a gasp of surprise and then a deep sigh of relief. The coastal forts had allowed the *Maine* to pass.

ARRIVAL IN HAVANA

While the *Maine* had waited outside the harbor and under the guns of the Spanish forts to see whether she would receive a pilot or a broadside, every man was ready to spring to his loaded gun or other station. The spirits of the crew were buoyed during the moments of excruciating delay by the conviction that they had come to Cuba to protect their fellow citizens.

Nothing untoward happened. Finally the anxious men on the *Maine* saw a little pilot boat steam out of the channel leading from the harbor and approach the battleship in an everyday manner. The first crisis was over.

Sigsbee ordered the most obvious signs of preparedness for a fight to be removed.

In the absence of General Blanco and despite not having approval from a Madrid that did not yet know the *Maine* was in Cuban waters, the Acting Captain General had taken it on himself to allow the *Maine* into the harbor. The local Spanish officials were so shaken, however, that they forgot to ask for Sigsbee's papers. They did not realize that the *Maine* had left so fast, she was without the clean bill of health from Key West that was required to enter the port. If they had appreciated that the certificate concerning the absence of infectious disease was missing, they might well have turned the *Maine* away or put her in quarantine. That would have been disastrous to McKinley's political future.

Spanish policy, though, was to avoid friction. Blanco's presence in Havana would have made no difference. He too would have allowed the battleship to enter. He was soft compared to General Weyler. McKinley would not have sent the *Maine* to Havana if Weyler had remained in command.

The harbor pilot Julian Garcia Lopez had received the assignment to guide the *Maine*. When he came on board, Sigsbee asked him if the ship had been expected. The American captain professed to be surprised to learn that the pilots had known nothing of the *Maine*'s mission until the battleship appeared outside the harbor and the jack was raised. Sigsbee should have understood the government's strategy. If the news of a U.S. warship coming to Havana had been published with the day and hour of arrival, the fanatical Weylerites would have organized another riot. The American colony in the city might have been endangered. This way the Weylerites were caught unawares.

Sigsbee also asked whether the *Maine* would be well received in Havana. Garcia answered that Havana was a cultured town and Americans had nothing to fear if they behaved themselves. It was a put down for the sober battle-ready Sigsbee to have been assigned what he saw as a too casual Spanish pilot in a nondescript black suit who spoke accented English and gave Sigsbee the equivalent of parental advice. By then Garcia had taken control of the *Maine*. He set the course into the narrow entrance to the large landlocked harbor guarded by the menacing cannons of Morro Castle on the left and Punta Castle on the right.

The port was one of the most peculiarly shaped but safest maritime havens in the world. The outline of the shore looked to Sigsbee like the long neck and then the bowl of a huge glass laboratory retort. Ships entered the channel from the north-northwest. The shore was high and steep, and the passage for half a mile was only two hundred yards wide. At the end of the channel, the irregularly shaped and shallow basin was two and a half miles long and half a mile to a mile wide.

After passing the castles, Cabanas Fortress was on the left while the city was spread to the right. The *Maine* proceeded leisurely and majestically, the officers looking anxiously into the close-up faces of hundreds of Spanish soldiers and citizens crowding the forts, wharves, and shores. There was no cheering by the spectators. Instead, some were inquisitive, some were glum, and some were threatening. Sigsbee's main concern was that sharpshooters on the shore could assassinate the officers on the *Maine*'s bridge. There was, however, no overt demonstration against the Americans.

According to pilot Garcia, he was following standard instructions given to him for all foreign warships. He showed Sigsbee the location on the chart of mooring no. 4 which was vacant in the man-of-war anchorage. At thirty-six feet, this was the deepest mooring in the harbor. Sigsbee approved the choice and the pilot brought the *Maine* slowly into her place between the Spanish flagship *Alfonso XII* and the German cruiser *Gneisenau*, a school ship which was at mooring no. 3. Just before 11 A.M., the crew ran the chain through the ring on the mooring buoy, brought the end back on board, and shackled on. The *Maine* was at rest. Sigsbee complimented Garcia on his performance, although the lack of deference rankled.

After the pilot left, Sigsbee boasted to his officers that from the shore the battleship must have appeared to be a mile long and much more formidable than the Spanish and German men-of-war. "She looks magnificent," he declared. "Our coming was an awful 'call down' to the Spaniards." Sigsbee saw the *Maine* as what she was, a gloved fist and not an open hand.

Soon two Spanish naval officers and a German came on board. The first was Lieutenant Alberto Madrano, representing Admiral Pastor, Captain of the Port. Sigsbee observed that Madrano "was laboring under suppressed excitement. His hand shook and he simply looked whipped." Sigsbee, who considered himself to be a consummate diplomat, "treated him like a brother and gradually pulled him around." The second Spanish officer was a lieutenant from the Spanish flagship *Alfonso XII*, representing Admiral Manterola. The admiral was deprecated by Sigsbee because he flew his flag from the Spanish man-of-war while he lived on shore.

After having been an officer for almost forty years, Sigsbee was well versed in naval protocol. To him no form of etiquette was more stable than between naval officers. According to the ceremonials known in all ports, Lee as Consul General was entitled to receive the first visit. Then came the Spanish Captain General, the admiral in charge of the station, the Captain of the Port, and the captain of the *Alfonso XII*. Sigsbee was in full dress with cocked hat and epaulets as he moved about. He reported he "was everywhere received with courtesy."

Sigsbee started to pay his calls on the Spaniards rather than seeing Lee first. He wanted to avoid "letting the Spanish officers have a chance to brood over their wrongs before coming under my soothing influence." He sent his aide Cadet Holden to inform Lee that he would follow after completing his Spanish rounds.

The reality of these formal visits, Sigsbee explained, was that "you have no idea how hard it is to maintain a conversation with a man when neither of you knows any language understood by the other. Facial expression and the clicking of glasses have to do hard work." He assumed he was to remain in Havana only a short period before another warship took the *Maine*'s place so she could keep her appointment at the 1898 New Orleans Mardi Gras. He intended to make the most of his abbreviated experiences in Cuba.

The call on Admiral Manterola required going ashore in uniform for the first time. At the landing he walked through a crowd of loitering Spanish soldiers and sailors. He thought they looked sullen and angry so he held his gaze straight ahead, stopping only once to rearrange the sword at his belt in what he considered to be a bit of bravado. Spaniards saluted him with reluctance. He returned all the salutes he saw. In the evening he went ashore again to call on Lee. The consul told Sigsbee how pleased he had been when "the *Maine* came gliding into the harbor as easily and smoothly as possible."

"What is to come of all this cannot be foretold," Sigsbee mused. "The Spanish were greatly opposed to our coming, of course, and the Volunteers declare that we would do well to look out for ourselves."

The *Maine* had entered the port without incident, though. McKinley had gambled with the ship as a stake in his long-running poker game with the Spaniards, and he had won the first pot.

The *Maine* in Havana Harbor

★ ★ ★ ★ ★ ★ ★ ★

REACTION TO THE *MAINE*'S ARRIVAL

Sigsbee had anticipated a respite after entering Havana harbor and mooring the *Maine* at the man-of-war anchorage. Instead, he was immediately put in the position of a lion tamer in the circus. He had stepped into a cage where he was expected to hold deadly Spanish cats under unbroken control. The danger was constant and the outcome in doubt. Moreover, entry into the cage was only the beginning of the star turn. From then on, a continuous demonstration of agility and acumen would be required before the ultimate achievement, a safe exit.

The problem was that the *Maine* was paying what had been billed as a friendly call. Yet the entire mission was plainly meant to intimidate the Spaniards, particularly the Weylerites. The ship's aspect was intentionally bullying. There could be no unguarded moment between Americans and Spaniards under such contentious conditions. There had rarely been a less welcome guest in the harbor.

In asking Lee for postponement of the *Maine*'s visit, the Spanish officials had emphasized the warning about "obstructing autonomy and producing excitement." Now autonomy was passé because of the *Maine*. Beyond this blow to the regular authorities, the *Maine*'s presence was a challenge to the ultra-Spanish officers whose wild talk indicated their hatred of the United States. The Spanish officials recognized that this rage might produce an outburst that would precipitate war with the United States, a war they did not want.

As predicted, autonomy had been obstructed and passions aroused. That was what made Lieutenant Madrano's hand tremble and his bearing appear "whipped" when he made his formal call. He resented being compelled to practice polite naval formalities with an enemy. He was too proud to show his anger and too humiliated to respond amiably.

In contrast, Sigsbee was at ease in his diplomatic role. Tongue in cheek, he noted that the Spanish officers did not receive him with the cordiality that visits to other friendly foreign ports had engendered. He was baiting his hosts by making believe he was surprised to find resentment.

Lee knew the Spaniards better than they thought. He too was worried about what might happen to the *Maine* and to the U.S. colony in Havana. He made sure everyone comprehended that the McKinley Administration and not he had dispatched the *Maine* to Havana.

Until night fell on the twenty-fifth, Lee sent frequent cables to the State Department. First he wrote the hopeful "Ship quietly arrived 11 A.M. No demonstration so far." Second was the matter-of-fact "Salutes exchanged. All quiet." In the evening he reported the positive "Have just received visit of commander of the *Maine*. No disorders of any sort." Finally there was the poetic "Peace and quiet reign."

In Washington, McKinley had been informed of the favorable outcome of his bold move. He was greatly relieved. The evening after the arrival of the *Maine*, he attended a dinner for foreign diplomats where he singled out Dupuy de Lôme and spoke expansively about the good relations between the two countries. Unblushingly, he told Dupuy, "You have no reason to be other than delighted and confident."

McKinley did not know that the alertness of the Spanish authorities had probably saved the day in Havana. Acting Captain General Parrado was quite aware of the extent of the animosity aroused by the warship. He put the Weylerite ringleaders back under house arrest for the night and arranged for the police to patrol the consulate and the warship.

The following morning, however, visible excitement had disappeared. The agitated night talk of the angry Spaniards in the Havana cafés had died. The U.S. warship lying at her mooring seemed to attract no more attention than any other vessel.

Spanish newspapers were not restrained, though, in either Madrid or Havana. They played on the disruptive themes of U.S. intervention, loss of Spanish honor, and the potential for violence. Both the leading morning papers in Madrid expressed the hope that the Spaniards in Havana would abstain from acts that might cause a rupture of relations. *El Imparcial* accused the United States of wishing to provoke a hotheaded protest from Spanish patriots and prophesied that the indignant Weylerites would not be able to restrain themselves. In Havana, the Conservative press stated that the Blanco government had betrayed the Spanish cause by admitting the *Maine*.

Not unexpectedly, the *New York Journal's* January 25 headline warned Americans to "fear the Ultra-Spanish who would be stirred to aggressive acts. These Spaniards hate the sight of an American citizen and there is bound to be a mix-up. It will be almost a miracle if there is not some friction between the American sailors and the Spanish troops."

As a student of naval history, Sigsbee was well aware of past attacks on U.S. sailors in other hostile ports. He had the danger of fisticuffs in mind from the moment he moored in Havana. Though he complained, "We are cooped up here like chickens," he had decided that "the men will not be given any liberty whatever." The officers would not be permitted to go ashore, either, until Sigsbee himself had tested the depth of Spanish ill will.

Sigsbee observed that "we have passed the night without excitement. Evidently the *Maine* looks too formidable for trifling purposes." He did not know the Weylerites had been confined. Along with McKinley, he simply did not yet understand the difference between Spaniards like the officials who became impotent with repressed anger and the partisans of General Weyler. As nationalistic fanatics, the Weylerites were direct actionists who resolved grievances through the application of standards far different from what Americans were used to. They were the terrorists of the day.

MINES UNDER THE *MAINE*

At her mooring 500 yards from the Spanish powder magazine in the naval arsenal and 200 yards from the new floating dock, the *Maine* was a bit of official United States territory in the bustling harbor. For the crew of more than 350 men, though, the usual comforts were missing. The sailors were crowded into a poorly ventilated steel ship in a tropical climate without having the opportunity to go ashore.

Nevertheless, Sigsbee's order denying leave was appropriate. The precedent he followed was clear. In October 1891 the United States had nominally been neutral in a Chilean revolution. Surreptitiously, the United States had aided the government forces. The rebels won, and not surprisingly were antagonistic to Americans. When Commander Schley of the USS *Baltimore* blundered by giving his crew shore leave, two of his men were killed and seventeen injured in a fracas with Chileans.

On the other hand, President Cleveland dispatched four cruisers to the Rio de Janeiro harbor during the Brazilian insurrection in 1894, allegedly to protect U.S. shipping. No liberty was granted to the crews and there was no incident.

In addition to the frustrating prohibition against leaves in Havana, there was a significant health hazard for the men of the *Maine*. The harbor was polluted. Sigsbee observed that "the water of this harbor is comparatively less foul in winter than in summer but whew! how it smells when the ferry boats stir it up at night." Sailors believed that the filth an anchor brought up from the bottom was enough to breed yellow fever. Sanitary conditions in the city were even worse. Malaria and typhoid were prevalent in addition to the dreaded yellow fever. If seamen became infected with any of these diseases and the sickness spread, the *Maine* could be rendered defenseless.

Letters sent home by the *Maine*'s crew reflected the dangers on shore. The men were unanimous in accepting Sigsbee's denial of leave. Seaman Charles Dennig wrote, "If an American sailor went ashore he would not come back to his ship." In any event, "The Spanish shopkeepers would not sell us anything at all." Another sailor said, "We can't go ashore here, the Spaniards would kill us."

The primary worry of both officers and men, however, was the question of submarine mines under the *Maine*. Gunner's Mate Carlton Jencks wrote, "Our only real danger would be submarine torpedoes and mines that are pretty well distributed around the harbor bed." Another sailor complained to his mother, "I shouldn't be surprised if we should be blown up any day."

Seaman Frederick Paige's letter read, "I am ready to do my duty when called on, but I tell you it is not a pleasant feeling to sit here and think that the harbor is full of mines and that there are torpedoes on all sides. This is my first experience so close to war, but the old tars tell me that they do not trust the Spaniards, and would not be surprised if we had some trouble. But we are here, at anchor, and must stay to guard those we were sent here to protect."

Landsman Fred Blomberg was more concise. "We are in mortal terror of our lives. We expect to be blown up at any moment." Seaman Elmer

Meilstrup added, "The whole bottom of the harbor is covered with torpe-does." Both were reported missing after the explosions.

Torpedo was a generic name for underwater explosives, including mines. Whether the bottom was "covered" with mines or not was a decision for Sigsbee to make. If there was a mine under his ship, he had to move, defuse the mine, or satisfy himself that the trigger would not be activated.

The Navy Department's charts of Havana harbor did not show any mine installation, but the charts were not up to date and could not be guaranteed to be accurate. The apprehensions of Sigsbee's crew sprang from the concerns of his officers. The practical view among the officers was that the harbor was likely to be protected by submarine mines in the channel or at the moorings. The ports of all modern countries were said to be guarded by mines.

The harbor of Havana, though, was in daily use by the commercial vessels of many nations. Even if mines were present, they had to be under the control of the Spaniards. The possibility of an explosion of the devices was minimal while the countries involved were at peace. This mined-but-safely-so theory was also the opinion of most U.S. naval officers interviewed by newspapers in Washington.

On board the *Maine*, Lieutenant Friend Jenkins was the representative of the Office of Naval Intelligence, so Sigsbee delegated the matter of the mines to him. Jenkins' main sources were the American correspondents who claimed to know everything. He also questioned Lee.

After a quick investigation, Jenkins reported, "I am under the impression that the harbor has not been planted with mines, but it is impossible to be absolutely certain on this point. If any mines exist, it is probable that they have been placed in the channel, near the entrance of the harbor so as to destroy a ship attempting to force an entrance," rather than at the man-of-war anchorage deep in the harbor where the *Maine* was. "Situated here, the *Maine* is absolutely sheltered from the fire of all the forts and batteries and she holds the city absolutely at her mercy. Therefore, it is of course possible that the Spanish engineers may have taken into consideration the contingency of a vessel being able to force her way into the harbor as far as the man-of-war anchorage and they may have planted mines there. I am disposed, however, to think that this has not been done. If it has, all we can do is to keep a bright outlook and take our chances."

With Jenkins listing his impressions so fatalistically, Sigsbee had to come to his own decision. "I have given the question of mines the most careful consideration," he explained, "and my intelligence officer Mr. Jenkins agrees with me that it is improbable that mines are planted in the harbor, or, at any rate, in our vicinity."

After this unsubstantiated statement, Sigsbee added that the *Maine* lay with only five feet of water under her keel. If a mine were exploded under her bottom, he declared, she would sink only five feet. That would leave her main deck above water and would still permit her to fire her 10-inch guns to destroy the city. Therefore, he pointed out, there would be no benefit to the Spaniards from a mine explosion.

There was, though, a flaw in Sigsbee's reasoning. There were fourteen feet of water under the keel, not five. That was enough to sink the 10-inch guns and leave the *Maine* helpless. He had looked at the wrong position on the pilot's chart. If he had known the true depth, he might have come to a different answer about the possibility of mines.

However faulty Sigsbee's reasoning was, the conclusion did reassure his officers. "I with others had heard that Havana harbor was full of mines," Lieutenant John Blandin remarked, "but the officers whose duty it was to examine into that reported that they found no signs of any." He was satisfied.

The crew remained skeptical. In their letters home they continued to complain about the danger of Spanish mines.

READY FOR ANYTHING, ALMOST

Sigsbee's principal responsibility was to be available to answer an emergency call from General Lee, but that eventuality appeared to be remote in the quiet harbor. During the first evening the wharves had been crowded with peaceful citizens anxious to get a glimpse of the warship. The *Maine* had responded by playing her searchlights on the arsenal to make a light show for the spectators.

The correspondents who came on board wrote that they had never seen a more spick-and-span warship in such an obvious state of readiness. Small arms were stacked openly on deck to facilitate a rush to shore by the marines if they were needed.

Tactlessly, Lieutenant John Hood told newspapermen that the *Maine* was in the catbird seat, militarily speaking. He repeated Jenkins' observation that before the entry into the channel, the seacoast batteries could have sunk the *Maine* in minutes. Once in the harbor, however, the *Maine* commanded the city.

His advantage in firepower made Sigsbee cocky and at the same time a little nervous. The Spanish engineers must have prepared a hidden defense to overcome the clear advantage he had at the anchorage. Under the circumstances Sigsbee saw extraordinary vigilance as his best protection against this unknown threat. He did not anticipate destruction by a submarine mine. He did half expect the *Maine* to be attacked, but he had in mind a surprise cannonading by small guns from ship and shore during the night, to be followed by a huge boarding party to capture the *Maine*'s crew asleep in their hammocks.

Considering that the *Maine* was ostensibly on a friendly visit to an open port, the extent of the precautions Sigsbee did institute was enormous. Every possible protection against assault or treachery that was available to him was taken. In addition, he had the rest of the North Atlantic Squadron at the Tortugas as his backup.

He set sentries on the forecastle and high on the poop deck. A signal boy was also on the poop. The quartermaster and a second signal boy were on the bridge. The corporal of the guard was at the port gangway, alert against intruders. The officer of the deck and another quartermaster were at the starboard gangway.

Instead of the usual anchor watch in port where a few sailors would be on duty at night, a quarter watch was kept. One of every four men in the crew was on deck the entire night. The sentries were supplied with ammunition. Rapid-fire ammunition for the one- and six-pounder guns was at hand. Shells for the big 6-inch guns were on deck. To provide power for the 10-inch gun turrets, steam was maintained in two after boilers instead of just the customary one.

As if in a hostile harbor, the collision mat was ready to be hauled over holes made underwater in the hull. The officer of the deck was authorized to act on his own at once in any suspicious circumstance. During the day the master-at-arms and the orderly sergeant scrutinized every visitor. They followed to watch for packages that might contain explosives. After the visitors departed, the routes taken through the ship were reinspected.

Seaman Andrew Eriksen wrote, "We are standing watches every night and are keeping a good lookout for any small boat, for you can't tell what kind of mischief the Spaniards are up to." He died in a Havana hospital. Another sailor said, "We keep armed men on deck all night. We are all prepared for a moment's notice, and we have every rifle belt in the ship filled for firing. I do not think there will be any need, but we are all ready for them."

Sigsbee even refused to buy fresh food from sources on shore or to allow clothes to be sent to the city to be laundered. These luxuries, Sigsbee said, ". . . remain mysteries yet. I don't want these good people to burn our clothes or poison us." The only concession he made was to accept fresh water from a Spanish lighter, not to drink but to wash the decks after the ship's doctor banned the use of the filthy harbor water.

The catch was, the preparations Sigsbee could make were limited by his orders from Washington. The fiction of the friendly visit had to be preserved. The sentries he posted had to be as inconspicuous as possible. The harbor bottom could not be dragged for electrical cables that might be connected to mines. The bay could not be patrolled by the *Maine's* picket boats at night nor could searchlights be kept on after dark, except briefly for show. Despite Seaman Eriksen's letter, the sentries could not effectively challenge any small boat unless convinced that the intention of the occupants was hostile.

To keep the crew busy and vigilant in the absence of shore leave, an extra schedule of daily drills was adopted. The men were put through physical-development exercises both morning and evening.

The training routines of the naval arts were also used, except for "night quarters" where a crew simulated the defense against a night attack by rushing to battle stations. This was eliminated. The rush to stations might have alarmed the Spaniards. During the day the *Maine* lowered her small boats for trials under oars and sails. There was also gun-pointing practice. A launch steamed around the harbor as the purported target, although care had to be taken that the *Maine's* guns never pointed directly at the Spanish man-of-war, the *Alfonso XII*.

Sigsbee was pleased at the effect of the drilling on his crew, particularly because he never saw the sailors on the *Alfonso XII* take any exercise or training.

By January 27, life on the *Maine* was becoming routine. The Spaniards were relaxing their attention to the warship. There were still Cubans looking at the battleship as a curiosity, but the police boat that ran around the *Maine* at night, "watching us," Seaman Charles Fadde said, "like a cat watches a mouse," was discontinued. Fadde was reported missing after the explosions.

Sigsbee had been ashore several times, serving as the "red rag," as he put it. He observed that the Spanish naval officers were "simply paralyzed, stupefied by the visit of the *Maine*. We have called down their bluff completely. The Spanish officials are studiously polite and so am I." He sent out his laundry.

Lee, too, felt the risk of violence from the ultra-Spanish officers was over. Because the crisis had apparently ended, Sigsbee gave his officers leave to go ashore as they chose, night or day. The crew was still restrained, except for trusted petty officers on duty. As a gesture that was appreciated, Sigsbee ordered awnings put up on deck for the comfort of the men.

The first officer to venture ashore had been Jenkins, who roused the Spaniards' ire by going to the forts and drawing plans of them from the outside. Then he investigated Havana's water supply and found a vulnerable viaduct. Jenkins sent his reports directly to the Office of Naval Intelligence.

Sigsbee served as the eyes and ears of Assistant Secretary Roosevelt and the Naval Strategy Board in Washington. He transmitted all the data he could collect on the island's political and military conditions.

Through their supposedly clandestine actions, Jenkins and Sigsbee made it clear to the Spaniards that war would not be unexpected.

Quiet Weeks on the *Maine*

★ ★ ★ ★ ★ ★ ★ ★

TIME TO LEAVE

As a friendly gesture toward Spain, the *Maine*'s visit to Havana was a failure. Spanish officials were punctilious in the exchange of formalities, yet they remained unresponsive to Sigsbee's blandishments.

Although hundreds of people came in small boats to visit the *Maine*, they were all admiring Cubans. The *Maine*'s officers accepted scores of dinner invitations. They were, however, from the same Cubans. The Spaniards were courteous, but there was an understanding among them not to board the *Maine* or talk to her personnel other than officially. These recalcitrants were the authorities themselves, not just Weyler partisans.

The solitary exception was General Parrado, the Acting Captain General in the continued absence of Blanco. Parrado and his sister boarded the *Maine* socially on January 28. Sigsbee gave them champagne, not gleeful at the breakthrough in relations but grumbling to himself. When he was invited to Parrado's office, alcoholic beverages were paid for by the Spanish government. On the *Maine* the cost of extras was out of Sigsbee's shallow pocket.

When Sigsbee went ashore later and looked back at the *Maine*, the warship appeared to his proud eyes to be enormous, especially compared to the *Alfonso XII*. Spaniards like Parrado, though, were not impressed. They thought McKinley had sent the *Maine* because she was the most powerful vessel in the U.S. Navy and they knew Spain had larger ships. They ordered two of their big warships to Havana to neutralize the *Maine*'s commanding location at the man-of-war anchorage.

Lee's contacts reported that the Spaniards also believed their navy to be far superior to the United States Navy in discipline and marksmanship. Their gunners had been trained by French ordnance experts.

More to the point, the Spaniards understood the balance of naval power. While their navy might be numerically inferior to the U.S. Navy, the *Maine* was the key. With the *Maine* moored to buoy no. 4 inside the Spanish harbor, she was immobilized. She would be unable to exit past mines in the channel unless permitted to depart. Seaman Meilstrup wrote that the *Maine*'s crew recognized the peril. If the Spaniards did not let the *Maine* out of Havana, she would be unable to leave.

Moreover, the Spaniards were sure that the *Maine*'s crew was composed predominantly of foreigners who would desert in the event of war. Many of the sailors were Catholics who presumedly would not fire on the ships of a Catholic motherland. In the end, the Spaniards contended, the United States could not even defend its own seaports. If war came, the Spanish navy would seize the ports and exact tribute from the U.S. government as recompense for the blow to national pride resulting from the *Maine* affair.

Sigsbee recognized that these Spanish beliefs were wishful thinking. He was certain of the loyalty of his crew. All but eighteen were either U.S. citizens or permanent residents who had formally declared their intention to become citizens. Thirteen of the rest were registered as resident aliens. Only five were unregistered foreigners.

In contrast to the Spanish assessment of the *Maine*'s supposedly friendly call as a failure, Sigsbee saw the mission not only as wholly successful but as already completed. To him, the purpose had been penetration and intimidation, not amity. He was ready to leave for the next assignment.

"I trust we shall not stay here long," he remarked on January 29. "Having perpetrated all the deviltry likely to be in the case, I am now ready to seek other fields. Naturally I feel greatly honored at the continued confidence of the Navy Department in me as exhibited by sending me to Port Royal then to Key West and finally here. These things mark an officer favorably. When some fellows get nervous prostration simply through having been ordered to take command at sea, it follows that it helps other fellows who accept responsibility as an honor. I suppose I am thick skinned, but responsibility has never rested heavily on me."

The Spaniards would have been happier than Sigsbee to see the *Maine* leave. The Spanish Prime Minister himself continued to fear that the *Maine*'s presence in Havana might yet lead "through some accident or other, to a conflict."

The decision on moving the *Maine*, though, was not the Spaniards' or Sigsbee's to make. The arbiter was McKinley whose judgment was clouded by conflicting advice from the Navy and State departments. Secretary Long had intended to have the *Maine* leave Havana around the first of February because of the forced confinement of the crew and the danger of disease. The replacement was to be an armed cruiser.

One difficulty, however, lay in how to accomplish the physical switch of the ships. Bringing in a second warship to join the *Maine* before the day of the exchange would be substantially more provocative to the ultra-Spanish who seemed to be passive at the moment. Taking the *Maine* out of the harbor before the armored cruiser entered might be counterproductive if the Spanish authorities refused the cruiser access to the harbor on whatever pretext. Then there would be no U.S. warship in Havana.

According to the State Department, politics demanded that the advantage gained by having finessed the *Maine* into Havana be retained. As consul, Lee advocated that "a ship or ships be kept here all the time now. We are the masters of the situation and I would not disturb or alter it." The State Department did not want to give the appearance of backing down in Cuba. McKinley agreed, and so the *Maine* stayed on, despite the hazards of boredom, disease, accident, sabotage, and attack.

The monotony was not equally distributed among the personnel. The crew continued to be confined to the *Maine* at the end of January, yet the officers had as many social engagements as they wanted to accept. On the morning of the thirtieth, thirteen of the officers were invited to an elegant if late breakfast. At nine o'clock a steam tug came alongside the *Maine* to convey the officers to the Mariano Yacht Club to join Lee eight miles west of the city. "We steamed close along the shore," Sigsbee observed, "and saw all the western defenses of Havana." The time and place of the affair had been publicized, so the insurgents staged a raid nearby. They wanted to give the Americans a demonstration of their strength.

The main event of the day was attendance at an afternoon bullfight. Sigsbee's intention was not just to see the spectacle but also to indicate his right to go wherever other foreigners went and to gauge the Spaniards' feeling toward him while they were intensely excited. It was to be an extreme test, Sigsbee explained. Sylvester Scovel of the *World* had warned him that every Spanish revolution began at the bullring. If only one spectator shouted, "Down with the Americans," the whole place might attack him in an instant. Scovel concluded that the Spaniards would tolerate anything if they would stand having U.S. naval officers at one of their corridas.

A few days before the bullfight, Sigsbee had told General Parrado he was going to the event. The general replied that he would send tickets for a reserved box, with his compliments. Sigsbee considered the offer to be just another expression of meaningless Spanish politeness, but Parrado had the tickets delivered. There were six seats in the box. Sigsbee gave one to Lee, one to his own aide, and handed the remaining three to the officers' wardroom as prizes to be gambled for. Parrado also sent a case of sherry Sigsbee held for himself. In return, he presented Parrado with an autographed copy of his coastal-survey book.

The bullring was a high wooden structure with no roof. Boxes were on the top level. Sigsbee claimed that "as we took our seats, General Parrado bowed to me but he and his officers were nervous and avoided noticing us as much as possible. Occasionally when I would look up suddenly, I would catch some Spanish officers looking at me with an expression of hate. In front of our box on the seats below were a lot of armed Spanish soldiers and there were more plentifully sprinkled about. The moral atmosphere of the place was violence. I could feel it.

"When the fifth bull had been killed, General Lee decided that we should leave before that wild crowd could enclose us on board the ferry boat back to Havana. We filed out quietly and started through a dense crowd. Three of the party caught this boat but General Lee, [Lieutenant George] Holman, and I just missed it. We knew that the next ferry boat would be packed by the people from the bull ring so we hailed a sailboat and went to the *Maine* where I kept General Lee until the crowd could scatter on the Havana side."

Lee told Sigsbee they had been in great danger at the bullfight. There had been, he maintained, a volcanic atmosphere unusual even for the bullring, and they were lucky to have escaped injury.

Typical of the antagonistic Spanish attitude was a cartoon drawn on a blank wall off the promenade, El Prado. The sketch was a caricature of a strutting Uncle Sam unaware of the small female figure of Hispania slipping a banana peel under his foot. Cuba was an island of many banana peels, something the Spaniards themselves had learned.

THIRTEEN TWICE

Bullfighting was a Spanish sport, not Cuban. The Cubans preferred baseball, though they could not play ball because Weyler had banned the game as American.

Each Sunday when the last bull was slain, the Spaniards hurried to the ferry that took them back to the city. The lights were lit in Central Park and a military band played martial songs. Crowds strolled around the park, smoking strong cigarettes and occasionally stopping to eat ice cream at one of the cafés. All Spanish Havana enjoyed ice cream served in a dish with delicate little sugar wafers. By eleven o'clock the promenade was over. This Sunday, the Spaniards in the city dropped off to a sleep made fitful by awareness of arrogant Americans in their midst.

When the party from the *Maine* had reached Havana on its way to the bullring, a reporter brought Sigsbee one of the small printed circulars being handed out on the street. As Sigsbee informally translated the circular, "Viva Spain and death to Autonomy and the Americans was the song. The *Maine* was reviled as an insult to Spain and a demand was made to oust us and all that. Also the restoration of Weyler was demanded." Finally, the circular called for "the moment of action" by Spaniards against the Americans in behalf of "our brave and beloved Weyler." Since the arrival of the *Maine*, "Death to Blanco" had sometimes been supplemented with "Death to the Americans."

A second copy of the circular was mailed to Sigsbee with the warning handwritten at the bottom in English, "Look out for your ship!" The crude drawing of a hand was in the left margin with the index finger pointing to two underscored words in the text translated as "rotten squadron."

Sigsbee sent the warning home to his wife as another ultra-Spanish curiosity. He thought the violently anti-American handbill was commonplace. Lee had informed him that propaganda like the circular was received at the consulate every day and was ignored.

Some of the correspondents covering Sigsbee's appearance at the bullfight told him the professionally printed sheet was composed and distributed specifically to worry him. Real ultra-Spanish broadsides in circulation, they asserted, were shorter and typed or struck off on a hand press. Actually, the correspondents acknowledged, the Weyler partisans did not usually stoop to anonymous handbills. Like their role model, the general himself, they favored deliberate violence rather than threats.

Sigsbee paid no further attention to this warning about his ship except to joke about the passionate wording. No one present thought for a moment that the admonition was serious.

The last disturbance on January 30 was the only one directed against the *Maine*. After Sigsbee had returned to the warship with Lee, a ferryboat passed with fifty Spanish Volunteers among the throng on board. They shouted "*Viva Espagna*" and made derisive gestures while the ferry crossed in front of the American vessel.

Other Spaniards were indifferent. Soldiers and tradesmen ashore appeared to be disinterested. The harbor boats that sold provisions and souvenirs to sailors on anchored vessels kept their distance. The little passenger carriers moving about the harbor day and night seldom answered hails from the *Maine*. Sigsbee resented having the officers on the *Alfonso XII* see the boatmen "trifling" with his men. He had his image to maintain. He displayed his reserve even when writing to his wife. He signed himself with his initials *CDS* and not *Charles* or *Chas* or *Charlie*. When he felt particularly close to his wife, he signed with the letter *S* instead of *CDS*.

Because his wife's responses were sent via regular mail and not by State or Navy Department pouch, he warned her never to repeat anything he told her that might be of value to the Spaniards. One of her letters "was probably opened in the mails. The seal was broken and the flap open and showing indications of the rolling penholder trick." He protested to her that "the only remark they got was this, 'I am glad that things are quiet but I suppose you feel as if you were on the edge of a volcano.' *I never feel*, except that I rather like this situation [in Havana] where I am free to rise up to the level of my own conceit." Even with his wife, his training and his vanity required him to act the role of the self-possessed gold-braided gentleman the Navy had made him.

Sigsbee had become the symbol of the disliked Americans. Although he claimed that he was not a superstitious man, he did notice that the *Maine* had sent thirteen officers to the breakfast at the yacht club and that on the same day the box at the bullfight had been no. 13.

After a succession of quiet days, February 11 was busy. The first event was the unexpected but welcome arrival of the torpedo boat *Cushing* which had been part of the Havana watch in early January. The ultra-Spanish who resented the *Maine* loathed the combination of the *Maine* and the *Cushing*.

Both Lee and Sigsbee had been asking for regular torpedo-boat service to carry dispatches between Key West and Havana. That would make them independent of Spanish cable lines in the event of trouble. The Spanish authorities raised no objection, so the *Cushing* was ordered to act as a courier starting February 15. Because of an error in deciphering the coded instructions, however, the *Cushing* cast off four days early.

Sigsbee said the *Cushing* was the most vulnerable of the torpedo boats in heavy weather. Privately, he blamed the Navy Department for the death of Ensign Breckenridge who had been washed overboard and drowned en route. As the senior U.S. officer in Havana, Sigsbee had the body embalmed and encased in a metal coffin. The remains were sent by commercial steamer directly to the ensign's father, General Joseph Breckenridge, in New York City, rather than being returned to Key West on the *Cushing* the following day.

After dealing with the *Cushing*'s affairs, Lee and Sigsbee made a formal call on General Blanco who had returned to Havana at last. Sigsbee admired Blanco's distinguished bearing. He described the general as handsome and elderly, easy and pleasant, with a "good face." Later Sigsbee added as an indirect reference to Blanco that "It is difficult to grasp the Spanish character. They receive one with the most cordial grace and then one realizes that they probably dare not believe one word said to them. They are 300 years behind the times in their ideas—but they don't look it."

The incident that changed Sigsbee's opinion involved his invitation to Blanco to inspect the *Maine*. The general answered amiably that there was an official decree against captains general boarding foreign men-of-war because many years ago a captain general had been abducted while on an English warship. Sigsbee responded jokingly that "on merely personal grounds I would be glad to run away with" Blanco, as the English had with their captain general, "but I promised good behavior." Blanco still resisted gently but firmly.

Only afterward did Sigsbee comprehend that there was no decree against visits to foreign ships. General Blanco was the leader of the correct but inwardly hostile Spanish officers. Only Parrado had ever made a social call on the *Maine*. The truth was, Blanco was probably afraid to do anything that might further antagonize Weyler partisans. An official visit by Blanco to the *Maine* might well have precipitated another riot.

At the end of the day, February 11, Sigsbee attempted to repair a political omission that cost him a rare rebuke from his superiors. Despite his instructions to act in a manner conciliatory to the governmental and military agencies in Havana, he had failed to include an appearance before the new and therefore doubly sensitive Autonomous Council. In this he had reflected Lee's disdain for purported Cuban home rule. The Spanish authorities in Madrid, however, complained to the State Department in Washington that Sigsbee had not fulfilled the promise to recognize the council.

When Sigsbee made his belated call on the council, he was greeted with a lengthy speech in formal Spanish he did not understand. In reply, he declared, "I beg to express my admiration for the high purpose of your honorable body." Unwittingly, he went too far in praising official Spanish policy.

The day following his courtesy call, Long cabled him, "It appears you have now visited the civil authorities, as you were instructed to do on the first of February. The failure to comply has been a source of some embarrassment here." Long was not aware that in satisfying the Spanish government, Sigsbee had further enraged the ultra-Spanish army officers.

That was the pattern of the *Maine*'s entire visit, step by step offending Weylerite fanatics and pushing them to act.

A CANDLE ON A CASK

At an afternoon tea in Washington on January 25, Commodore Frederick Rodgers had happened to meet the forthright Mrs. Evelyn Wainwright whose husband was the *Maine*'s executive officer. Rodgers advised her that the *Maine* had been ordered to Havana the previous night. Impulsively, she replied that the dispatch of the battleship was "a foolhardy thing to do. You might as well send a lighted candle on a friendly visit to an open cask of gunpowder." Rodgers knew she was expressing her husband's opinion.

Before being attached to the *Maine*, Lieutenant Commander Wainwright had been head of the Office of Naval Intelligence. His wife was influenced by his awareness that the Spanish people were bitterly opposed to United States policy concerning Cuba. He had said the Spaniards were convinced that the United States meant to impose a war on Spain, and Spain expected to be ready. The form readiness would take was not known, he had told her, but it could involve violence against Americans and American property in Cuba.

Wainwright's Office of Naval Intelligence reports had consistently overstated Spanish preparedness, capabilities, and ship movements in the Caribbean. Spain was depicted as stronger and more hostile than she was. Wainwright's warnings might have motivated President McKinley to pursue a harsher policy toward Spain than the situation demanded.

In fact, the Liberal Spanish government was more conciliatory than combative. Dupuy de Lôme had already announced that sending the *Maine* to Havana would not be regarded as an aggressive act. Although Dupuy had not been given advance notice of the specific day for the *Maine* to sail, he had covered up U.S. deception by prevaricating. He said it was not customary for a foreign nation to notify Spain before its warship entered a Spanish port.

Two days after the *Maine* entered Havana harbor, Dupuy announced that the Spanish cruiser *Vizcaya* would soon be sailing to New York City to reciprocate. Spain saw the larger, faster, and more formidable *Vizcaya* as a trump to McKinley's ace. Secretary Long responded routinely though. He emphasized that Spanish warships frequently came to the United States on ceremonial occasions without contrary reaction and they were always welcome.

In addition to this cautious display of naval amity, preliminary negotiations for a new commercial treaty with Spain were completed on January 28. Permanent trade benefits were scheduled to accrue to the United States. The next day the U.S. press divulged that General Weyler might be prosecuted in Madrid for violating Spanish security. Relations between the powers were improving.

Apprehension concerning the fate of the *Maine* had turned to glee, and U.S. officials congratulated each other on McKinley's stroke of diplomacy. The longer the vessel stayed in Havana, the more secure Washington felt. In the Cuban capital, Sigsbee observed that British and German warships were coming to Havana, too. The Spaniards would see that the *Maine* was no more sinister than other nations' warships.

To capitalize on the *Maine*'s breakthrough in Havana, the Navy Department announced on February 3 that the cruiser *Montgomery* had been dispatched on a similar peace mission to the smaller ports of Matanzas and

Santiago in eastern Cuba. Secretary Long added that the visits were "to be friendly, and the department believes the result will be favorable, as it was in the case of the *Maine*." Consul Alexander Brice in Matanzas advised that "the usual courtesies" had been extended by local Spanish authorities. Brice became a key player later in the mystery of the *Maine*.

The next day the satisfaction of civilian officials in Washington was lessened by the Navy Department's mounting concerns. Assistant Secretary of State Day cabled General Lee, "Secretary of Navy thinks not prudent for a vessel to remain long in Havana: sanitary reasons. Should some vessel be kept there all the time?" Day expected an answer that would support McKinley's intention to leave the *Maine* in the harbor.

Predictably, Lee responded, "Do not think slightest sanitary danger to officers or crew until April or even May. We should not relinquish position of peaceful control of situation or conditions would be worse than if vessel had never been sent. Americans would depart with their families in haste if not vessel in harbor on account of distrust of preservation of order by authorities. If another riot occurs, it will be against Governor General and autonomy, but might include anti-American demonstration also. First-class battleship should replace present one if relieved, as object lesson and to counteract Spanish opinion of our Navy."

Newspaper correspondents confirmed Lee's statement about peaceful control by writing that Havana was *tranquillo*. Reports were of an untroubled scene in the colorful tropical harbor with the slim white battleship riding at its mooring. The Stars and Stripes was depicted as flying in a gentle breeze while launches chugged to the shore, ferrying smiling Cubans and out-of-uniform American officers. The officers were involved in a continual round of receptions, dinners, balls, and weekly bullfights. For some, the only regret was that the *Maine* might have to leave for the lesser festivity of Mardi Gras in New Orleans.

The Spanish authorities in Madrid, however, were not duped by McKinley, despite Dupuy's ingratiating remarks. On February 1, Minister Pio Gullon had taken a tough stance in responding to McKinley on American deadlines for further relaxation of restraints on Cuban self-government. On February 8, Gullon told his ambassadors in major European capitals about his misgivings concerning the continued stay of the *Maine* and the *Montgomery* in Cuban waters. He was again looking for European support to apply leverage against U.S. pressures. As Naval Intelligence had reported, Gullon believed

McKinley was covertly preparing for war and he expected to have Spain's forces ready by April.

The same day, February 8, the Cuban junta in New York City set back Spanish-American relations severely by revealing an inflammatory letter written by Dupuy de Lôme. The letter had been stolen by the junta's agent in the Havana post office. The career of the one Spanish diplomat who had held the junta in check through his access to McKinley was suddenly in jeopardy.

The following morning, a copy of the letter was published in the *New York Journal*. To a friend, Dupuy had confidentially described McKinley as only "a bidder for the admiration of the crowd." He also asserted that "besides the natural and inevitable coarseness with which he repeats all that the press and public opinion of Spain has said of Weyler, it shows once more what McKinley is: weak, and catering to the rabble, and, besides, a low politician." In addition, Dupuy had remarked that his government would "agitate the question of commercial relations even though it should be only for effect." After criticizing the President, he had recommended stalling tactics in an economic area where the Americans had not suspected trickery.

Although Dupuy's comment about McKinley was modest compared to the diatribes of American jingoes in and out of Congress, public passion was inflamed by the yellow press. Dupuy's usefulness in Washington was ended. He resigned.

The McKinley Administration played the gaffe to the hilt, demanding that the Spanish government both formally apologize for the insult and prove that the commercial accord was not just "for effect." The State Department did not close the incident until Spain expressed its official regrets through diplomatic channels on February 14.

While the Dupuy incident was not serious enough to let the American jingoes force a declaration of war, there was an abrupt cooling of relations between Washington and Madrid. Decreased U.S. patrolling of the sea lanes allowed the quantity of supplies reaching the Cuban rebels to increase. A big filibustering expedition left Tampa, Florida, on February 13 under the nose of Edward Gaylor, superintendent of Pinkerton's detectives in Spain's employ. The cargo included 5,000 rifles, 6,000 pounds of dynamite, and 200,000 rounds of cartridges. Insurgent General Calixto Garcia said the arms would last for months.

Even the ordinarily tactful Sigsbee voiced his anxiety about danger from anti-American Spaniards. He volunteered to a reporter, "I don't want to be obliged to take any coal aboard from Havana. It would be a risky experiment. Not that I suspect anyone in authority, but there is such an irresponsible rabble here, and it would be easy to get a couple of sticks of dynamite in the coal bunkers without our knowing it." The remark was repeated in the Spanish press. The "rabble" was assumed to be the Weylerites.

The picture was of once-proud Spain on her knees begging McKinley's pardon for Dupuy's indiscretion, combined with the presence of the *Maine*, the *Cushing*, and the *Montgomery*, Sigsbee's aspersion on the "rabble," and unrestrained filibustering. This was a heavy emotional burden for the ultra-Spanish officers in Havana to bear.

AS SIGSBEE SAW THE SETTING

The weather was clear in Havana harbor early in the evening of February 15. The constellation Orion the hunter was taking shape overhead, with the sisterly Pleiades near by. The air was soft in the tranquil tropical twilight. The winter sun had set at 5:36 P.M. and the moon would not rise until 2:49 A.M. The early part of the night would be dark.

During the next hour, the sky grew overcast. Thick low clouds heavy with rain were moving slowly through the harbor. The atmosphere turned oppressively hot and sultry for mid-February. The seamen who had shipped on sailing vessels still looked to the wind, but any breeze there was had fallen flat.

The *Maine* was heading in an odd direction this evening. Havana is in the region of the trade wind that blows from the northeast during the day. At sundown, the wind is likely to die down. During the night, there may be no wind at all.

At 6 P.M., however, the *Maine* was heading to the northwest, toward the naval "shears" near the admiral's palace. The watch officers said later that they had never before seen the ship pointing in that direction. The *Maine* was already in command of the harbor because no Spanish cannon covered her position in the man-of-war anchorage. Now the battleship was unexpectedly heading in the one direction where her starboard 10-inch battery bore on the harbor forts and the port battery faced the land defenses without needing to rotate her turrets. The *Maine* was unintentionally and unknowingly in the position she would have assumed if about to attack the city. She had trespassed into an unmarked zone that made her master of all the Spanish defenses and vulnerable to none that was apparent. The unfortunate consequence was an additional provocation to Spanish fanatics.

Unaware of the significance of his vessel's shift, Sigsbee was enjoying the relative calm in the harbor. A little earlier he had heard gay sounds from the city on this second day of the pre-Lenten carnival. He was provided with a taste of what New Orleans might have been like. El Prado was illuminated for the week of fiestas, bullfights, and merrymaking, and the streets had been full of good-humored throngs of grotesquely masked promenaders. Revelers in Havana drank to Spain despite the disease and starvation that were common eastward on the island.

At the man-of-war anchorage, the *Alfonso XII* and the smaller *Legazpi* were moored on the *Maine*'s starboard side. Other vessels to starboard were farther away. A Ward Line passenger ship, the *City of Washington*, had just arrived, and the Spanish pilot was mooring the vessel a hundred yards to port and astern of the *Maine*.

In the harbor, warships and larger merchant vessels did not tie up alongside wharves. They anchored to the southeast, as the *Maine* had. Cargoes and passengers were ferried to the ships by large lighters that were the trucks and taxis of the water. The lighters were constantly passing close to the anchored ships, night and day. They were especially active this evening, meeting the needs of the *City of Washington*. The bored sentries on the *Maine* were glad to have the lighters to occupy their attention.

Three uneventful weeks in the harbor had not jaded Sigsbee's delight at being on the *Maine*. To him, larger battleships were less pleasing. He considered all the quarters on his ship to be ample, although some of the compartments below were hot this sultry evening. His own quarters were the most spacious. The *Maine* had been designed to serve as a flagship, so there were separate admiral's and captain's staterooms across the passageway from each other in the after superstructure. In the absence of an admiral, Sigsbee occupied both rooms.

During the afternoon Sigsbee had entertained visitors in his cabin. After dinner, activities on board were carried on strictly according to established routine. At 8 P.M., everything was reported secure. All was quiet. In keeping with regulations, the 214 watertight compartments that were not occupied were closed for the night. The 328 members of the crew were all on board as usual. Of the 26 officers, 22 were present. Four were ashore on overnight liberty. One of the steam launches was in the water, riding at the starboard boom, broadside to the *Alfonso XII* as an additional precaution against unknown hazards.

Sigsbee was sitting with his aide Cadet Jonas Holden at the center table in his own cabin. Mess attendant James Pinckney had brought him a thin alpaca jacket to replace a heavier uniform blouse while the officers dealt with official papers. First, the captain responded to a letter from Assistant Secretary Roosevelt requesting an opinion on the existing practice of installing torpedo tubes above the waterline on U.S. warships. Sigsbee recommended discontinuing the installations. Then he freed Holden so he could take a final turn on deck for the night.

As the ship's bell struck twice at nine o'clock, Sigsbee returned to his quarters. Wainwright and Holden were talking in his cabin, so he moved to the after side of the table in the admiral's cabin which was a duplicate of his own quarters.

Except for the men on watch or on sentry duty, the crew had turned in at nine o'clock. Those who swung hammocks on the main deck escaped the hot berth deck below. The sailors on the quarter watch were dispersed more casually about the main deck. They were not on specific duty. Rather, they were free to lie down wherever within reason they could make themselves comfortable. Two men under discipline were also on deck as punishment, instead of in their hammocks below.

Most of the officers were half-dressed, reading in their rooms, asleep, or in the messrooms below. There was not much news to pass on in letters. Others were out on the main or the poop deck, near the officers' smoking area behind the after turret on the port side. Sigsbee's orderly, Private Anthony, was stationed in the passageway to the captain's cabin. Bill Anthony was a 45-year-old Marine with 28 years of service, starting with 14 years as a soldier in the West.

Sigsbee was alone in the admiral's cabin, which was brilliantly lit by eight electric bulbs in the chandelier. He was wearing his alpaca coat for the first time during the cruise. In a pocket he had found an unopened letter to his wife that he had accepted from one of her friends and had forgotten to deliver. He started to write to his wife, "feeling," as he said, "rather merry over the adroitness with which I believed I had apologized for having carried the letter for ten months."

The boatswain's mates shrilly piped down for the night. At ten minutes after nine, the "turn in and keep quiet" of taps was sounded from forward by Marine bugler C. H. Newton who was later reported missing. The notes echoed within the ship. The only visible movement was the pacing of the sentries on deck. The passing of an occasional lighter was the only noise.

At the familiar sound of taps, Sigsbee had laid down his pen to listen to the bugle's notes which were "singularly beautiful in the oppressive stillness of the night. The marine bugler who was rather given to fanciful effects was doing his best."

For the next thirty minutes, Sigsbee turned back to what had become a lengthy letter, like most of the communications to his wife. He signed with his initials on the last page and was in the act of enclosing the letter in its envelope at 9:40 P.M.

In Washington, the social season was at its height. The state of relations with Spain was not a live topic at dinner parties. In New York City, there was little about Spain in the news. Publisher Hearst had participated in laying out the next morning's regular edition of the *Journal*. The editorial in the *Tribune* was on the advantage of settling the Cuban question peaceably.

In Madrid, the holiday celebration was long since over. The hour was late and cafés were closing. Anti-American feeling was strong.

REMEMBERING FEBRUARY 15

Many Americans remembered for years what they were doing when Pearl Harbor was attacked or President Kennedy was assassinated. Similarly, the officers and crew of the *Maine*, witnesses on board nearby vessels, and observers on shore vividly recalled exactly where they were on the night of Tuesday, February 15, 1898.

The afternoon had begun no differently from any other in the preceding three weeks. Many of the *Maine*'s officers and men had noticed the peculiar change in wind direction. No one read any significance into it. Wainwright recollected that he had "directed the officer of the deck to set up the gallery target" for rifle practice. After a while, the officer reported that the ship had swung in an odd manner. Rifle fire aimed at the target would also be in the direction of the *Alfonso XII*. The officer asked Wainwright whether to continue the practice. Wainwright told him to stop the shooting because the Spanish officers might become uneasy.

When the *City of Washington* anchored on the port quarter, Wainwright observed that she was only 100 yards away from the *Maine* which was more than 100 yards long. He recalled thinking that the Ward Line ship "was too close to swing properly, only I knew that almost any vessel followed the direction of the wind, and there was very little danger of fouling." A prudent officer who was a stickler for regulations, he was watching the wind. Sigsbee had described him as "rather severe" on visitors to the *Maine* who wandered off limits, but Wainwright considered the *Maine* to be "in a position requiring extreme vigilance."

Lieutenant Jenkins was continuing to raise the hackles of ultra-Spanish officers. He had been sailing around the harbor all afternoon to gather information for the Office of Naval Intelligence.

The *Maine*'s chaplain, Father John Chidwick, had picked up a rumor from the crew that some great but unspecified event was going to happen in Havana that night. He thought there would be another rebel raid. The crew was more edgy. They still feared that the harbor was "honeycombed with mines."

Chaplain Chidwick had also noticed that the *Maine* was bow on toward the city. After reciting the divine office, he had climbed into his bunk to read "Facts and Fakes about Cuba" by the correspondent for *Harper's Weekly*, George Bronson Rea. The newspaperman was sympathetic to the Spanish side in the insurrection. He claimed to have seen no Spanish atrocity. This was in keeping with Chidwick's own feelings.

Cadet Watt Cluverius had received the petty officers' reports that the ship was secure for the night. He was relieved by Lieutenant John Blandin who walked to the rail and found everything as usual except that the ship had swung to take the position she would have assumed if about to attack the city.

"I was on watch," Blandin observed, "and when the men had been piped below everything was absolutely normal. I walked aft to the quarter deck, behind the rear turret, and sat down on the port side. Then I moved to the starboard side and sat down there. I was so quiet that Lieutenant Hood asked laughingly if I was asleep. I said, 'No, I am on watch.'" He was not the most alert lookout.

Marine Lieutenant Alburtus Catlin had gone to his room: "I had taken off my coat and had lighted one of the products of this country. The water and the sky were so peaceful that the very air had a certain stillness unfelt in northern waters. I was enjoying my cigar to the full."

Marine Corporal T. G. Thompson recalled that shortly before nine he was in the port gangway with twenty-five other men who wanted "a whiff of fresh air." He said he saw a small black boat circle the *Maine* several times and then disappear when hailed by Quartermaster Harris on the bridge. Afterward, Thompson heard the equivalent of "all's well" from the *Alfonso XII* and then the echo from the forts at the harbor's entrance. Thompson slung his hammock in the port gangway while Master-at-Arms Third Class John Load hooked his hammock outside the armory door underneath the middle superstructure. Thompson and Load were saved.

Coal Passer Jeremiah Shea was down on the berth deck. Fireman First Class Bill Gartrell was far aft on a mattress in the steam-steering engine room. The men doing punishment watch were on the port quarterdeck. Apprentice Ambrose Ham saw small boats several hundred yards away but none near enough to hail.

On the *City of Washington*, several of the crew and passengers were looking at the battleship. The assistant purser said sailors aboard the *Maine* had been singing and playing musical instruments. Before the final bugle call men were dancing to an accordion in the starboard gangway.

The second officer of the *Washington* remarked, frivolously for the circumstances, that "we were just commenting on the fact that the American naval officers were not making friends with the Spaniards very fast." The Spanish harbor pilot had passed on this bit of gossip.

Passengers Sigmond Rothschild and Louis Wertheimer were chatting. Rothschild had suggested, "Let us go to the stern and watch the *Maine*. We are under the guns of the United States. We are well protected and we can sit here." Passenger Mann was in the ship's saloon.

On shore, Francis Weinheimer had walked to the waterfront to cool off. "I was standing on the pier about 300 yards from the *Maine*," he recalled, "when I heard three bells [9:30 P.M.] struck on board. I looked toward the ship and could see men walking about the deck." William Carbin was in the Hotel Dominico overlooking the dark water of the bay. Like Thompson and Harris, he saw a small boat moving rapidly away from the warship.

On the stringpiece of the wharf abreast of the *Maine*, the steamship sailor Martin Bunting sat with a fireman who was also out of work. They admired the *Maine's* lines. Bunting told his friend he had overheard a Spaniard say the *Maine* would be gone in the morning. The fireman insisted that there could be no such departure. He knew the fireroom routine. The battleship did not have steam up.

Reporter Rea sat in a café with Scovel. It was Meriwether who had a standing order from his New York City editor to file the word *tranquillo* just before closing time if there had been no news that day. The editor would then know the line of communication was intact. Even the one word had to go through the Spanish military censor's hands so Meriwether went to the palace. He met the Associated Press man at the cable office which closed at nine. When they left, the Havana operator locked the door. The censor had gone off duty. No more messages could be sent that day.

Clara Barton was at her writing table in a quiet villa, taking care of the heavy clerical detail that was part of her job. Founder of the American National Red Cross, she was seventy-six. Distribution of aid from the President's Committee on Cuban Relief to the *reconcentrados* was her responsibility.

Food shortages in the provinces were acute, although supplies sponsored by McKinley were arriving regularly. Spanish authorities were cooperating because the drive toward unconditional Cuban independence might be eased if the scarcity of food could be remedied. Captain General Blanco himself had welcomed Barton. He told her plaintively, however, that "when your country was in trouble [in 1776], Spain was the friend of America. Now Spain is in trouble and America is her enemy."

Sigsbee had invited her to lunch on the *Maine*. His cutter picked her up at the wharf and she was received on board by the officers. The crew she described as "strong, ruddy, and bright" went through their drill for her entertainment. In the messroom she was impressed by the polished tables, glittering china, and cut-glass tumblers.

At night on February 15, her villa was quiet and the street noises were dying away. Later, she came to think of her luncheon on the *Maine* as her personal version of the Last Supper.

The Big Bang on the *Maine*

★ ★ ★ ★ ★ ★ ★ ★

THE EXPLOSION DESCRIBED BY THE OFFICERS

The battleship *Maine* was shattered by massive explosions at 9:40 P.M. on Tuesday, February 15, 1898, in Havana harbor. After the bursts came fire, smoke, mutilations, and drownings. Two hundred and fifty enlisted men and two officers were killed outright. Eight more men died soon after. The total was 260, according to Navy calculations, in one of the worst American naval catastrophes in peacetime.

Witnesses confirmed that the forward part of the ship had been wrecked without warning, but their detailed accounts of what happened were not identical. Part of the enduring mystery of the *Maine* springs from these different descriptions and from varying interpretations of the descriptions.

Newspapers reported relatively the same story concerning what had taken place. Most observers, both on the ship and off, told correspondents that there had been two distinct bursts of tremendous force. The first raised the forward part of the ship, they said. The second, even stronger explosion was from forward magazines set off by the initial burst.

In its lead article on the disaster, the yellow press *New York Journal* advised, "Officers Can Tell Little. Nothing is certain except that there was an explosion that lifted the *Maine*, immediately echoed by the explosion of the magazines on board." The conservative *New York Herald* wrote, "Two Explosions Were Heard. There were two distinct explosions, the first caused by something beneath the ship and the second from the forward magazine." The moderate Washington *Evening Star* concluded, "All officers agree that a double explosion occurred." The London *Times* printed the same observation. Regardless of the newspaper's political orientation, two separate explosions were reported.

Lieutenant Alburtus Catlin's recollection was typical. He said, "I heard an explosion that only perceptibly shook the ship. I rushed out in my shirt sleeves to see what was the matter. Then came the second—the terrific one that destroyed our ship and hurled to eternity so many of our brave sailors. It was like nothing I had ever heard."

Some of the statements of survivors were not as clear cut concerning the number, intensity, and sequence of the explosions as the newspapers made them appear. Wainwright had been across the passageway from Sigsbee. He remembered that "suddenly the lights went out, leaving the ship in intense darkness. The door banged shut, there was a heavy shock, a trembling and lurching of the vessel, a roar of immense volume, and the sound of objects falling on deck. I was under the impression, from the character of the noises, that we were being fired on."

Wainwright's observation was hard to categorize because of the wealth of visible and audible phenomena he provided. His statement could be read as describing two explosions, like the great majority of the observers, or as one. If there were two explosions, he did not hear the first, lesser burst that caused the lights to go out and the door to shut.

A few officers described the initial burst as more violent than the second. They claimed that the first explosion was unmistakably from a monstrous submarine mine under the ship near the forward magazines. This burst was followed quickly by another of lesser volume, they declared, evidently of small magazines ignited by the underwater burst. First the warship was raised out of the water by the detonation of the huge mine beneath the vessel. Next the ship was broken into pieces by the explosion of the magazines.

Another slim minority of the officers led by Sigsbee told reporters they heard only one explosion, a tremendous burst. Lieutenant John Blandin was an example. He told the press, "I remember only one detonation, from the port side forward. Then came a perfect rain of missiles of all descriptions, from heavy pieces of cement to blocks of wood, steel railings, fragments of gratings." He recalled only the one detonation. He had been hit on the head by a piece of the cement.

At first, hearing one burst was the code for saying a mine had been beneath the ship. There could have been no magazine explosion, proponents of one burst claimed, because the bow of the ship sank quickly. Water would have entered the forward magazines which could not then explode. Hence, there was no second burst.

In a letter to his wife, Sigsbee was not yet clear about the code. He wrote, "When the disaster came, there was an awful moment of trembling and roar, then a tearing, wrenching, crunching sound of immense volume, so great that you cannot conceive it: then falling metal, a great crunch and twist and a heeling subsidence of the vessel. There was instantaneous darkness and smoke filled my cabin. There was no mistaking it. I knew on the instant that my vessel had been destroyed." As he put it initially, there was first a moment of trembling and roar, followed by the crunching sound of immense volume. There were two events.

When he restated the experience, however, he wrote, "I was enclosing my letter in its envelope when the explosion came. To me, well aft within the superstructure, it was a bursting, rending, and crashing roar of immense volume, largely metallic. It was followed by a succession of heavy, ominous, metallic sounds of the overturning of the central superstructure and of falling debris. There was a trembling and lurching of the vessel, a list to port, and a movement of subsidence. The lights went out. Then there was intense blackness and smoke." He was describing one crashing roar from the large mine that blew up his ship. There was no magazine explosion.

Most officers believed, though, that the destruction was too complete and too widespread to have come from just one mine, however big. Magazines had to have exploded. When the divers discovered later that the forward magazines had in fact exploded, hearing one burst changed to code for the absence of a mine. If there was only one sound, it had to have come from the magazines. If there was no prior burst, there was no mine. This is one reason why the differences in descriptions sustained the controversy over whether there had been a mine under the *Maine*.

After Sigsbee understood this revision in the code words, he altered his story: "Many, both on board the *Maine* and outside, heard two different reports, first a short one and then immediately following a roar of greater volume and duration."

To give credence to the mine explosion, he returned to the way his officers had described the bursts in the first place. If he had agreed with them from the start about hearing two explosions, he might have forestalled much of the confusion about what had really happened to the *Maine*.

THE VIEW FROM THE CREW AND FROM OUTSIDE

Compared to the officers' thought-out statements to the press, the enlisted men's recollections of the explosions were sparse and relatively colorless. The officers had been aft, endangered just by water rising in the compartments. They had time to observe what was happening. Most of the crew were forward where the blasts and the fire were. Only a dozen of the scores of enlisted men who had been sleeping inside the ship escaped death. The few sailors who lived through the explosions were too astounded by their experiences to provide the correspondents with coherent explanations.

Just two men were saved out of all those who had slung their hammocks on the berth deck. Two higher decks had been between them and survival. Coal Passer Jeremiah Shea was one of these men. He must have been forced miraculously through a hole blown in the steel hull. "How ever did you escape, Shea?" Chaplain John Chidwick asked him.

"Indeed I can't say, Your Reverence," replied Shea. "I knew nothing until I found myself swimming, but in faith I think, asking Your Reverence's pardon, that I must be an armor-piercing projectile!"

The other sailor on the berth deck who survived "heard a terrible crash—an explosion. Something fell and then after that I got thrown somewhere in a hot place. I got burned. Then the next thing I was in the water." He had been dropped into the boiler room when the starboard side of the deck burst open. Water poured down on him before the second explosion lifted the deck higher and he escaped with minor burns.

Only sixteen of the surviving men were unscathed. They had little to add to the officers' accounts. In essence, what the men said was, "I was sound asleep and somehow when I woke up I was in the water." The seaman who had been in the yawl on the davits had the boat blown to pieces under him. He was thrown into the water uninjured. After he was saved, minutes passed before he could be convinced the whole episode was not just a bad dream. Two sailors had been in the launch that was tied to the boom, not twenty feet from the magazine. They were alive. The two men doing punishment watch came through unharmed. They were sinners spared because of their transgression.

On his first voyage, Landsman John White was "just getting asleep when I heard the explosion. It was an awful sound. Then there was a crash. I struck the water almost as soon as I heard the noise. I went shooting along at an awful rate. Suddenly I stopped, then I felt everything getting thrown around me. The water was horrible." He had been tossed fifty yards into the midst of debris from the ship.

Corporal William Thompson felt a shock like an earthquake just as he fell asleep. He was firm in stating there had been two distinct explosions and that the first which lifted the bow did not occur in the magazine. The crew had been afraid of Spanish mines. They naturally identified Spain as the culprit. When they talked together after the disaster they visualized the first quick shock from the mine as like lightning striking, followed by the equivalent of a huge clap of thunder, the magazines. They imagined chaos in darkness made more horrible by the shouts of their many mates unable to get out of the steel trap, the moans of those who realized they were doomed, and the death screams. The crew insisted on the mine story in part because they wanted vengeance.

In contrast, the observers on the *City of Washington* viewed the explosions more dispassionately. Their composite description of the catastrophe at its zenith was of "a vast column of flame and slate-colored smoke that was seen to shoot upward, with flying fragments, many of which were themselves aflame. At a height of 150 feet, the heavy column spread outward into a great rolling canopy of clouds which overhung the *Maine*, and from which descended a rain of fragments of ship and of bodies, some pieces falling half a mile from the *Maine*'s mooring."

Passenger Rothschild "heard a shot like a cannon shot. It made me look toward the *Maine*. I saw the bow rise a little. After a few seconds there came a terrible mass of fire and explosion, a black mass. Then we heard a noise of falling material. It didn't take a minute until the bow went down. There was a cry 'Help! Lord God save us! Help! Help!' The cry did not last a minute or two."

That was the consensus view from the *Washington*: hear a shot, see the bow rise, see and then hear the bigger explosion. Passenger Wertheimer agreed on "a minor report, in comparison with the greater report which immediately followed."

Passenger Mann in the saloon was startled by a loud detonation. The sound was muffled, like the explosion of a giant firecracker under water. He rushed to the porthole in time to observe an immense flash shoot up in the air with a tremendous burst that shook the *Washington*. He said, "My first thought was that war had been declared and hostilities had begun."

Captain Frank Stevens of the *Washington* was a most experienced witness. He declared, "There was the rumble of an explosion and the *Maine* seemed to leap into the air. The first report was instantly followed by a second and louder explosion, and the air became filled with missiles of all kinds. The *Maine* began to burn after the explosion."

Second Officer Sullivan affirmed, "There was the sound of an explosion. The Third Officer said, 'Hear that salute?' and then the second explosion came. The shock was so terrific that I thought at first our own vessel had blown up."

Assistant Purser Reynolds "heard the report and a moment later was almost blinded by a blaze of light. There was a deafening roar, and it seemed to me that the *Maine* had been literally blown apart." Again the pattern was, hear the first explosion, see the second explosion, hear the second explosion.

On the wharf, Francis Weinheimer heard "a crunching sound like the breaking of crockery. Then there was a terrific roar. Persons around me were almost thrown down by the force of the explosion."

Martin Bunting was also on the wharf: "We heard a shot that seemed to come from the *Maine*. The report was not loud. It was more like a gun fired a long way off, or the thump of a heavy plank dropping from a distance and striking the deck end on. Before either of us had time to speak, the second explosion came, with a report like thunder and a flash of fire in the dark. The shock threw us backward. From the deck forward of amidships shot a streak of fire as high as the tall buildings on Broadway. Then the glare of light widened out like a funnel at the top, and down through this bright circle fell showers of wreckage and mangled sailors."

In the city, there was a sound like the discharge of a heavy gun, followed by the prolonged roar of a great explosion. Windows were broken and doors were shaken from their bolts. The sky over the bay was illuminated with an intense brilliance. Above it all, innumerable colored lights resembling rockets were seen. After hearing the explosions, Consul Lee rushed to his window. He could see flames leaping from the *Maine* as she sank.

Clara Barton was still at work "when suddenly the table shook from under our hands. The great glass door facing the sea blew open. Everything in the room was in motion. The deafening roar was such a burst as perhaps one never heard before. And out over the bay, the air was filled with a blaze of light, and this in turn filled with black specks like huge specters flying in all directions."

Correspondent Meriwether was entering a café when the city shook in a shattering explosion. The lights went out and there was a rush to get to the street. "What is it?" everyone was asking. Some guessed that the insurgents had blown up the palace. One man yelled that the arsenal at Regla across the bay had been exploded. A squadron of cavalry went by at a gallop. Meriwether said a tall Englishman told him the casualty was the *Maine*.

According to these initial newspaper accounts of the disaster, substantially all the eyewitnesses on the *Maine*, the *Washington*, and the wharf described two explosions. The first was like a cannon shot. The second, some said, was cataclysmic, like the beginning of a war.

ESCAPE AND RESCUE

From the start, Captain Sigsbee thought the *Maine* was being attacked by the Spaniards. He knew the ship was sinking rapidly and feared she would capsize to port, dragging him underneath. He had to extricate himself before responding to the enemy.

First he hurried up the slanted floor of his starboard quarters to look out a porthole. The night was so black he could not distinguish anything. His initial idea was to escape through the porthole. At once, though, he abandoned such an unseemly wriggling through the small opening in favor of a slower but more decorous departure through the door to the passageway leading forward. Thirty-five years as an officer had conditioned him to act with propriety even when alone in the dark under the greatest stress of his life.

Night-blinded after the bright cabin lights were extinguished, he groped and stumbled along the smoke-filled passage. When he turned to starboard near the exit, he collided with the tall figure of Private Bill Anthony who had been stationed at the outer door. Anthony murmured something apologetic in the blackness and then drew himself up at attention. He saluted and said calmly, "Sir, I have to inform you that the ship has been blown up and is sinking."

Sigsbee followed his orderly to the quarterdeck. As he came out of the companionway, two sailors heard the captain say to himself, "The Spaniards have blown us up at last!" Although tears were streaming down his face, the men saw him as determined-looking. He was oblivious to danger while preparing to establish a command post on the vessel.

For a moment he stood on the starboard side of the main deck, forward of the after superstructure. He peered at the huge dark mass amidships but could not decide what he was seeing. His watch had been left in a drawer so he asked Anthony for the time. "The explosion took place at nine-forty, sir," he was advised.

He left the main deck because the ship was sinking steadily, and he climbed to the poop deck. There, in the midst of total confusion, he gave a futile order for silence to avoid alerting the enemy he thought was at hand.

Father Chidwick had been in his stateroom, reading Rea. Unaccustomed to emergencies, he was next to last to reach the ladder to safety. As he ascended with dignity, the officer behind him addressed him irreligiously. "Hurry up," he implored. "For God's sake!"

Chidwick's impression was that "the war was on, the enemy had engaged us, and our deck would be swept with shells and bullets." Once outside, however, "the deck was clear" of enemy projectiles.

Lieutenant Catlin said he located the ladder by touch. On deck, the *Maine*'s own one-pounder and six-pounder ammunition was being detonated by the fire. "On ordinary occasions," he observed, "the explosion of one of these pieces would create a great commotion, but here they were scarcely noticed."

Lieutenant Blandin remembered that "the quarter deck was awash but the poop was above water."

The sailors had death-defying tales to tell each other about their rescues. After being drawn down into the water, Landsman White "tried to swim up" to the surface "and found I was caged in. I went up again, and the same thing happened. I thought I was a goner. I kicked out once more and I seemed to shoot through an opening" in the debris. "I could hear the shrieks and cries of the men near the ship. I hung on until I was picked up."

From the poop deck, Sigsbee could not yet make out the men in the water. He continued to believe the explosion had come from a mine as the start of an all-out Spanish attack. Wainwright was already on the poop and Sigsbee directed him to post marine sentries about the ship to repel boarders. The captain's first hint of the immensity of the disaster to the crew came when Wainwright reported that he could find few marines or sailors to post and no defensible place to post them.

Sigsbee moved to the starboard rail to peer forward over the awning. He could distinguish only the wreckage folded back across the middle of the ship. The bow could not be seen. Then fire broke out amidships, providing a little light. Wainwright thought the flames were from a wooden hulk the Spaniards had set aflame and run alongside to ignite the *Maine*. For an instant he had forgotten that this Civil War tactic became obsolete once hulls were built of steel.

Because the fire made another explosion seem imminent, Sigsbee gave orders to flood the forward magazines. Wainwright advised him that the whole forward part of the ship was under water, as were the after magazines. The deck cocks could not be reached.

Next Sigsbee directed Wainwright to use hoses to put out the intensifying fire in the central superstructure. Wainwright went forward, then returned shortly to report that the water ducts had been destroyed. The hoses were useless, even if there had been enough men to handle them.

Only then did Sigsbee comprehend the full extent of the damage to both his ship and crew. As his eyes became better adjusted to the darkness, he made out for the first time a smokestack lying in the water almost directly under him. The poop deck where he stood was the last foothold on the ship. The officers and men with him comprised most of the able bodied.

There had been no chance to change clothes. Sigsbee was wearing the thin civilian sack coat, shirt, and trousers. Some officers were in uniform, some were partly dressed, and some were in nightclothes. Worse, they were defenseless. Efforts to obtain rifles from the armories below had failed because the ship was sinking so fast.

At last Sigsbee began to see the dim whitish bodies in the water and to hear faint cries for help. He was also aware of the chaplain shouting the absolution.

According to Chidwick, "The forward part of the ship was ablaze by now and up from the waters and from the ship came the heart-rending cries of our men, 'Help me! Save me!' From the quarter deck, I gave them absolution and, climbing to the poop deck, I saw and heard the Captain who was moving up and down, shouting his orders above the terrible din. I called on the men to mention the name of Jesus, and again and again I repeated the absolution," asking the men to resign themselves to the Almighty. "I was happy afterwards to hear that my voice was heard far toward shore. I only hope that our men heard it."

The water around the ship was dotted with the bodies of the men. Most were injured and clinging to floating wreckage in a mass so dense that others were trapped beneath. More were dead, torn apart by the bursts.

Once he saw the bodies, Sigsbee ordered the after boats to be lowered to rescue the living. Of the fifteen boats on board, only the gig at the stern and the whaleboat at the mainmast were undamaged. The officers outnumbered the sailors on the poop and handled the tackle themselves. They were startled to find that the boats were waterborne when they dropped just a few feet. Officers and crew manned the boats jointly. Sigsbee remained on the poop with a few officers and one seaman with a broken leg.

The captains of the *Alfonso XII* and the *Washington* came to the aid of the *Maine*'s sailors at once, despite the danger of further explosions. They also feared that the *Maine*'s stern might pitch and go under, creating a suction that would drag their small boats along.

The lifeboats from the *Alfonso XII* were first to reach the *Maine*. They carried 37 men back to the Spanish ship. The *Washington*'s boats took 24 from the water. Nine more of the severely injured were transferred by the Spaniards to the *Washington* because the men were afraid to be left in the hands of an enemy they believed to have blown up their ship. The *Maine*'s two boats also handed over to the *Washington* the few sailors they saved. There was an unspoken consensus to avoid dead bodies and pieces of bodies. Severed legs and arms were in the flotsam, although ten men were able to swim unaided, despite wounds, through the remains to the Machina wharf. Some of the men who were rescued died later.

On shore, people were rushing down every street leading to the harbor. They had been shocked by the explosions and drawn by the sight of the flames feeding on the cellulose waterproofing in the ship's ends. Horse-drawn fire engines were descending the same narrow streets to no apparent purpose, while lighters were leaving the docks to take newsmen to the scene.

Two incidents stood out. In one, Lieutenant George Blow was overcome by the sight of the casualties in the water and by a sudden awareness of the many more men who had been trapped in their hammocks on the berth deck. He sprang to his feet in the whaleboat and pleaded, "Put me aboard the ship again. I want to die with the men."

In the second, another officer in the whaleboat called out, "If there is anyone living who is still on board, for God's sake say so." The only response was the echo from shore, "For God's sake."

Because the *Alfonso XII* was in the forefront of the rescuers, Sigsbee realized that if the Spaniards had indeed blown up his ship, the attack was not being maintained. He no longer had to worry about a Spanish boarding party. The officers could speak in conversational tones, as calmly as if in a general quarters exercise. No one panicked, although there were thousands of pounds of gunpowder underfoot and spare ammunition was still exploding in the pilothouse. In the comparative quiet they could hear the weird sound of air whistling through supposedly watertight doors and hatches below. The bulkheads had sprung.

Sigsbee waited quietly. After fifteen minutes Wainwright reported that the whaleboat and gig had returned. All the wounded who could be found had been taken out of the water. He said the time had come to leave the *Maine*. The fire was getting hotter while Wainwright whispered to Sigsbee that the forward 10-inch magazine had been thrown up and was close to the burning mass amidships. The powder might explode devastatingly at any moment.

Sigsbee was at last satisfied that the *Maine*'s keel had touched the bottom of the harbor so that the confidential papers in his cabin were safely immersed. He ordered Wainwright to load everyone into the two boats, but there was a further delay because both Wainwright and Lieutenant Holman held back to offer their captain a hand to support him in stepping into the gig.

"The officers were very considerate of me," Sigsbee recalled, "and urged me to get into the boat but I declined and directed them to get in first. Of course I was the last to leave the dear old *Maine*. It would have been improper otherwise." He did not notice that his dog Peggy had found him in all the tumult. A sailor picked her up and handed her to a man in the gig.

The two small boats headed for the *City of Washington* while Sigsbee told the other craft nearby to leave the area at once because of the danger of further explosions. Correspondents were already at the wreck. The *World's* Sylvester Scovel translated Sigsbee's warning into Spanish.

Not all the Spaniards came to the rescue of the Americans. The captain of a ferryboat that had just passed the *Maine* refused to turn around to save the despised American sailors. In addition, two engineers from the British steamship *Olivedene* were on the wharf watching while Spaniards there danced with glee, exclaiming "Ah, *Americanos, Americanos!* They bring dynamite here in filibuster boats to blow up Spaniards and now they get it themselves!"

Sigsbee claimed he could hear the shouts of exultation coming from the shore. "A battleship which had cost $2,500,000 and had occupied seven years in the building was now a sunken pile of impotent metal," he lamented, "along with the grievous death of our men."

Statistics varied a little, but of 329 crew members, one was at Key West under reprimand. Sixteen escaped uninjured. Fifty-four of the wounded survived, making a total of 70 enlisted men saved by official count. The number of men killed was 258, not quite four-fifths of those on board. This figure was arrived at by subtraction because many bodies were not identifiable. Two of 26 officers were killed. The total of the dead was 260, according to the Navy's calculations.

Another seven, including Blandin, died later from injuries received on the *Maine*. They were never added to the Navy's list.

The *Maine* Destroyed

★　★　★　★　★　★　★　★

SUSPEND OPINION

Captain Sigsbee stepped out of his gig alongside the *City of Washington* and onto the gangway. At that instant, the rain that had been threatening began to fall. Calmly, schoolmasterish Sigsbee explained that the precipitation was caused by the effect of the explosions on the moisture in the clouds. The men who had been rowing felt he was "cool but changed. He looked ten years older."

On board the liner, Sigsbee struggled to overcome his dejection. As he put it, "No one can ever know the awful scenes of consternation, despair, and suffering down in the forward compartments of the stricken ship, scenes of men wounded, or drowning in the swirl of water, or confined in a closed compartment gradually filling with water."

Twenty of the rescued sailors who were injured had been carried to the *Washington*'s dining saloon and placed on mattresses where they were receiving medical attention. The clothes had been blown off some of them, resulting in burns all over their unprotected bodies. The smell of blood and the sound of moaning was overwhelming.

For fifteen minutes Sigsbee visited compassionately if briefly with each man. Then he ordered Wainwright to conduct a muster of the *Maine*'s crew on the *Washington*, the *Alfonso XII*, and the shore. Father Chidwick was sent to find out whether men had been picked up by lighters from the wharf. The chaplain declared he "did not yet know but that the war was on. I had visions of being taken a prisoner. However, when I stepped upon the pier, I found everyone very sympathetic."

Sigsbee walked from the *Washington*'s saloon to the starboard rail. He listened to the continuing detonation of ammunition on the *Maine* while he considered the ramifications of his situation and how to deal with his many problems.

As commander of the *Maine*, he was initially responsible for the loss of the battleship and scores of crewmen. He remained convinced that the explosion had been from a large submarine mine set off beneath his ship, but now he doubted his original assumption that the *Maine* had been attacked by official forces of the Spanish government. Who then had set off the mine? He was not sure, even at 10:30 P.M. when he turned away from the rail, entered Captain Stevens's cabin, and began preparing his statement for the Navy Department.

Sigsbee wrote the report in pencil in a firm hand on a letterhead of the New York and Cuba Mail Steamship Company, James E. Ward & Co., Agents. He knew what he wanted to say. Only one inconsequential clause of the message was scratched out and rewritten.

"Secnav/Washington, D.C." was the heading. "*Maine* blown up in Havana harbor at nine forty to night and destroyed. Many wounded and doubtless more killed or drowned. Wounded and others on board Spanish man of war and Ward Line Steamer. Send Light House Tenders from Key West for crew and the few pieces of equipment above water. No one has clothing other than that upon him. Public opinion should be suspended until further report. All officers believed to be saved. Jenkins and Merritt not yet accounted for." The signature was "Sigsbee."

Though it was composed under pressure, the report was a model of clarity and forbearance. Sigsbee said he "intended to temper public feeling in the United States" because he realized that a direct accusation of Spain would be inflammatory. He also modified the implied indictment of "*Maine* blown up" rather than "blew up" with the request that "public opinion be suspended."

Sigsbee chose the word "opinion" deliberately. He wanted people to "suspend" a belief before it finalized, rather than coming to a "judgment," a firm conclusion. He asked the public to withhold even the preliminaries to a decision as to guilt. Besides, he said later, the use of "judgment" might have provoked a negative reaction from the censor. That was unlikely, though. The shading was more in his eyes than it was real.

He knew he was probably whistling down the wind. The newspapers would inevitably compete for circulation by sensationalizing the circumstances of the disaster, yet he took it on himself to make a national appeal for continued peace. He was successful. The McKinley Administration was able to seize on his one short admonitory sentence to prevent the jingoes from insisting on an immediate declaration of war against Spain.

As Sigsbee closed his report, General Solano came aboard the *Washington* as General Blanco's representative to express official Spanish condolences. The Spaniards who accompanied him asked what the cause of the explosion had been. Sigsbee replied that he would not decide until further investigation. He observed that "while the Spanish officers were extremely cautious, I could not but note that they were *very* much *concerned* to know our estimate of the cause."

Sigsbee then excused himself to return to the captain's cabin, strike out his signature on the report, add "Many Spanish Officers including representatives of General Blanco now with me to express sympathy," and sign his name again. He did not mention that Blanco had remained in his residence.

Soon Consul Lee arrived. He agreed with the intent of the supplemented report to Secretary Long. Next Sigsbee read the message aloud to Secretary General Congosto to induce him to reopen the cable office, pointing out that the message would have a soothing effect in the United States. Congosto muttered that the report was "very kind," but he was ungracious, as if annoyed that the *Maine* had selected Havana harbor in which to blow herself up. He consented, however, to open the office and assign two extra censors to handle press accounts of the disaster.

Sigsbee had also composed a dispatch: "[Commander] Forsyth—Key West. Tell Admiral [Sicard] *Maine* blown up and destroyed. Send Light House Tenders. Many killed and wounded. Don't send war vessels if others available." The message was written on the face of an upside down envelope of the Ward Line, matching the stationery used for the Navy Secretary.

Newspaper correspondents had followed Sigsbee aboard the *Washington* and were frantically interviewing any officer or enlisted man who was able to talk. Because Sigsbee could not leave his Spanish guests, he stopped George Bronson Rea who was heading for shore to file a story for *Harper's Weekly*. He handed Rea the two messages and asked him to take them to the cable office.

Sigsbee had always been friendly with journalists and considerate of their needs. In return, he had their cooperation. Now he understood that as a potential defendant in an inquiry on the sinking of the *Maine*, he would be at their mercy. Trusting Rea with the official messages rather than using his own aide was an ingratiating gesture.

Rea, however, took advantage of Sigsbee. He proceeded to the cable office by lighter and cab, reaching there a little after 11 P.M. The office was open, as Congosto had agreed. Both Sigsbee's reports were written in the clear because the cipher books were at the bottom of the bay, so Rea transcribed the messages onto regular cable forms. He included the contents of the reports in his story as a little news scoop and he held on to the two originals. The next morning he mailed them to the New York *World* which he also represented. The historic report to "Secnav" was reproduced there in a photoengraving ten days later. Rea was paid for the usage.

After Sigsbee had handed the cables to Rea, he went back to the waiting Spanish officials. General Solano gave his word "as a man, as an officer, and as a gentleman" that the Spanish authorities had known nothing about the cause of the catastrophe. Sigsbee responded with a "ready acceptance" and the Spaniards departed, pleased at escaping what could have been a nasty bit of recrimination.

At this time Wainwright returned with the dismaying results of the first muster. Only 102 officers and men had been saved. Ten of them were not expected to live until morning. The wounded who had been picked up by the *Alfonso XII* had been taken to the Alfonso XIII and San Ambrosio hospitals in Havana. The move was made without Sigsbee's approval and rankled him, but Chidwick advised that the Spaniards had done the best they could in the emergency. He said the Spanish officers had acted more humanely toward the *Maine*'s wounded than they would have behaved toward their own ordinary seamen.

A sympathetic Lee remained with the *Maine*'s officers all night. Sigsbee was left to his somber musing. He went on deck and watched the smoldering *Maine*, still thinking about the events of the day and what they might mean to him. Police launches sped up the bay as if searching for culprits, but came back out of the darkness without any prisoner. The *Alfonso XII* slackened her mooring lines and tugs moved her farther from the burning *Maine*.

At 1:30 A.M., Sigsbee retired to the stateroom assigned to him. He was nauseous and could not sleep. The air was hot and the bunk was harder than his bed on the *Maine*. He had no nightclothes.

In addition, his cabin opened into the dining saloon where the wounded lay. The gasps and groans were just outside his door. There was a stench from the foul water of the harbor and from the blood. He knew he would need a clear head for the next day, still he managed to get only an hour of sleep before the morning came. It was a sorry night for him.

HAVANA AFTERMATH

When the cable office was reopened around 11 P.M., correspondents were told that it would close again at 1 A.M. With less than two hours left, Meriwether of the *Herald* organized his news gathering quickly. He instructed his Cuban assistants to "bulletin" the news by cabling each item separately while he hired a lighter to get to the *City of Washington* to interview the survivors. He was on the steamship taking notes when an assistant brought him the dispiriting word that Congosto had lived up to his sour demeanor.

The cable office had transmitted Sigsbee's two reports. The censors also received a 2,000-word article from the Associated Press correspondent, but they authorized dispatching just the first 100 words. The remainder was perceived to be anti-Spanish. The only other message sent was a note from Scovel that appeared to be personal but was actually coded. It was handed to the cable operator on a presigned form obtained illegally for use in emergencies like this one. The copy filed by the rest of the journalists was not released that night despite the pretense of putting two censors on duty. As poetic justice, Rea lost the advantage of having been the first to see Sigsbee's historic reports.

At 2 A.M., a last loud burst rocked the *Maine*. Francis Weinheimer left the wharf to rush back to his hotel to tell fellow Americans what he had seen. Spaniards were still congregating excitedly on Obispo Street. One group jeered at Weinheimer and bragged, "Send us another American warship and we will blow that up, too!"

At first light, Sigsbee awakened to face unrelieved gloom. After bathing from a bowl, he put his soiled civilian clothes back on and went to comfort the wounded. Then he moved to the rail to stare at the wreck. The poop deck had disappeared underwater as the keel slowly sank into the mud. Like the

Alfonso XII, the *Washington* had shifted berths during the night to get farther from the *Maine*.

Meriwether was visiting the injured men in the two hospitals on shore. He considered the maimed to be the real tragedy, writing that "Men that I took by the hand are this morning dead or will be helpless cripples for the rest of their lives. In cots were a sailor with his face half blown away and another with both legs so badly fractured he must lose them. At the end of the ward was a lusty marine crying, 'For God's sake, let me die!' The Spanish doctors were dressing the face of a fireman. 'There is something in my eyes. Wait and let me open them.' Both eyes were gone. 'Let me get up,' said another. Both his legs were broken below the knees."

Clara Barton concerned herself with the injured, too. As she left the hotel where she had breakfasted on the way to the hospitals, Lieutenant George Holman stopped her, asking, "Miss Barton, do you remember you told me on board the *Maine* that the Red Cross was at our service, because whenever anything took place with that ship, she was not a structure to take misfortune lightly. Someone would be hurt." Her presentiment had been realized.

She "proceeded to the Spanish hospital, San Ambrosio, to find 30 to 40 wounded, bruised, cut, burned; they had been crushed by timbers, cut by iron, scorched by fire, and blown sometimes high in the air, sometimes driven down through the red hot furnace room and out into the water, senseless. Their wounds were all over them—heads and faces terribly cut, internal wounds, arms, legs, feet and hands burned to the live flesh. The hair and beards singed, showing that the burns were from the dry fire and not steam from an exploding boiler.

"I thought to take the names as I passed among them, and drawing near to the first, I asked his name. He gave it with his address; then peering out from among the bandages about his breast and face, he looked earnestly at me and asked: 'Isn't this Miss Barton?' 'Yes.' 'I thought it must be. I knew you were here, and thought you would come to us. I am so thankful for us all.' I passed on till 12 had been spoken to. Their expressions of grateful thanks, under such conditions, were too much. I passed the pencil to another hand."

Meanwhile Sigsbee addressed his second report to the Secretary of the Navy: "Cipher code sunk with *Maine* but easily recovered by divers. For that reason American divers desirable. *Maine* was probably destroyed by a mine.

It may have been done by accident. I surmise that her berth was planted previous to her arrival; perhaps long ago. I can only surmise this."

Sigsbee could not send the message in the clear because of the accusation involving Spanish authorities, contradicting what he had told General Solano. He handed the report to an officer he was sending to Key West, where the encoding would be done. The report was not immediately published. The content was too sensitive and the McKinley Administration was not ready for war.

At 10 A.M. Sigsbee received the results of the second muster. Only 20 percent of the sailors and marines on the *Maine* had survived the explosion.

He cabled his wife, "*Maine* blown up last night, about 250 killed. I am uninjured but have lost absolutely everything but thin sack coat, trousers and shirt. Will borrow money of General Lee. Estimate my pecuniary loss $1,500." He was giving his personal loss more prominence than the wrecking of the *Maine* and the killing of the crew. Although Lee would have been a willing lender from the fund he had to aid indigent citizens abroad, Sigsbee never asked.

Lee's reaction to the loss of the *Maine* was surprising for a jingo whose judgment was suspect by the Spanish authorities. His first impression was that the explosion was an act of God, not the fault of the Spaniards. Contradicting Sigsbee, he cabled the State Department, "I am inclined to think it was accidental." He did not mean that a mine was unintentionally detonated under the Maine, but rather that the cause of the explosions had been within the ship in the form of spontaneous combustion or an overheated boiler.

In addition, Lee emphasized the sincerity of the Spaniards in expressing their sympathy: "Business suspended, theatres closed, and flags at half mast in Havana." He also wrote, "Suppose you ask that naval court of inquiry be held to ascertain cause of explosion. Hope our people will repress excitement and calmly await decision." In this he joined Sigsbee. He was confident that the court's findings would clear both Sigsbee and the Spaniards.

Congosto was allowing official United States cables to go through, though he was still blocking correspondents from dispatching speculative accounts. Aggressive journalists such as Meriwether, who had accumulated many pages of material concerning the *Maine*, were trying to find a way to evade the censorship.

"Suddenly," Meriwether exclaimed, "a light struck me!" He knew that the American passenger steamer *Olivette* was arriving in Havana that day. She was to take to Key West every healthy member of the *Maine* personnel who could be spared. In addition to the seriously injured, Sigsbee was retaining only nine officers and enlisted men: Wainwright, Chidwick, Holman, Paymaster Charles Ray, Dr. Lucien Heneberger, naval cadets Holden and Cluverius, Private Anthony, and Gunner's Mate Charles Bullock. Removing extra personnel would narrow his responsibilities at a time when he would need his attention for the continuing affairs of the *Maine*. Among other duties, he would probably be serving on the board of investigation to gather preliminary data for the court of inquiry.

The "light" Meriwether saw was that other correspondents were handing their uncensored copy to members of the *Olivette*'s crew for delivery to their newspapers' agents in Key West. None would be going to Key West. The *Olivette*'s seamen had performed messenger services previously and the newspapermen were afraid they might miss further happenings in Havana.

Meriwether perceived a chance for a news beat. He too had an illegitimately presigned censor's form he utilized to instruct his Key West agent to engage the telegraph wire that ran underwater to Punta Rassa and then up the mainland coast. The agent was to hold the wire open by sending any available text to New York City at the standard press rate of five cents a word.

Just before the *Olivette* sailed at noon, Meriwether hopped on board. During the six-hour voyage, he had the entire contingent from the *Maine* to himself. He interviewed some men and had others write their own accounts. When the *Olivette* reached Key West, his agent was sending an old Patent Office report over the telegraph wire. Meriwether had 12,000 words ready and he scooped the nation for the *Herald*. No one could break in on the wire. Even Sigsbee's second report had to wait.

Events were moving fast on this day after the disaster, February 16. In the early afternoon, the Light House Tender *Mangrove* and the Despatch Steamer *Fern* arrived from Key West in response to Sigsbee's first cable. The ships constituted a U.S. naval presence in Havana harbor.

The *City of Washington* transferred the wounded to the *Mangrove* and resumed her commercial schedule. Wainwright moved to the *Fern* so he could be close to the wreck and to his friend Lieutenant Commander William Cowles. Wainwright believed the explosion of the *Maine* was attributable to the Spanish authorities, through design or negligence. He swore not to set foot on Spanish soil until the *Maine* was avenged.

He was not swayed by the care the Spaniards were giving the wounded in the hospitals. Sigsbee had seen a placard on the door leading to the injured, requiring all who entered to remove their hats as a sign of respect.

Warm feelings for the wounded were a Spanish characteristic, but there was no equivalent courtesy for corpses. At 4 P.M., when Sigsbee was rowed ashore, he saw to his dismay that nineteen of the *Maine* dead were lashed together like logs, uncovered and unattended in the water in front of Admiral Manterola's palace. No provision had been made for their disposition. Chaplain Chidwick was immediately assigned to care for the bodies as Sigsbee declared emotionally that he "could think only of the *Maine* and her people. A better and more docile and quiet crew no captain had ever had under him. Oh, the damnable cruelty of it."

Sigsbee had just what he "stood in, nothing else" when he moved into the Gran Hotel Inglaterra where Lee lived. The correspondents maintained there was no *gran* aspect of the hotel except the pretensions of the management and the prices, nor was there anything suggestive of England. The location served Sigsbee's purpose, however. He could rest and receive visitors and he had access to Lee.

That night General Blanco and the mayor of Havana went to the hotel to call on Sigsbee. Blanco offered his personal and official regrets and requested that the Spanish government be permitted to hold a public burial ceremony to demonstrate Spanish sorrow.

Sigsbee agreed. He had no choice. In this tropical climate, there was no time to transport corpses to Florida. Bodies were surfacing regularly and there were not enough embalmers or metal caskets in Havana to handle them all. In addition, although Sigsbee was out of touch with what was going on in America, he hoped that allowing Spain to show grief might "serve to quiet the wild feeling that must now reign in the United States—perhaps."

He was justifying the confidence McKinley and Long had placed in him. He wrote to his wife, "My position is very delicate as you may suppose. I haven't flunked and don't intend to." He cast himself in the hero's mold and he was picking his path carefully.

His complaint to his wife was, "I have had no letters for *three mails* from you. I mean, what is the matter? It has seemed very remarkable that in this place of more or less danger and where there is yellow-fever, small-pox and typhoid fever—a notoriously unhealthy place—and where the populace hate us, I should not have been remembered."

Even a hero needs support from home.

RECEIVING THE TERRIBLE NEWS

Captain Sigsbee's friend Martin Hellings was manager of the Key West telegraph office. Shortly before 10 P.M. on February 15, he had been sitting idly at the key when Havana signaled. The message had to be personal because the island operator Domingo Villaverde would have closed his office. Hellings responded automatically and then transcribed the following clicks as, "There has been a big explosion somewhere in the harbor." A few minutes later came, "The *Maine* has blown up and hundreds of sailors have been killed."

Hellings turned the instrument over to Tom Warren, the night man, and went to the torpedo boat *Cushing* which was moored at the Naval Station. The commander of the *Cushing*, Lieutenant Albert Gleaves, was about to retire for the night when the quartermaster announced Hellings's arrival. Gleaves went on deck at once and Hellings read him the two messages.

Gleaves doubted the veracity of the information, especially considering that the source was Hellings whom he suspected of being a secret government agent. Gleaves also knew that rumors about events in Cuba circulated in Key West every day. The "embassy" in Havana was supposed to have been overrun. General Lee was said to have been assassinated. This sounded like the same stuff, but to be safe, Gleaves took Hellings to the *Fern*. Her captain, Lieutenant Commander Cowles, was the senior officer on the waterfront. Cowles, Gleaves, and Hellings went to the telegraph office.

Nothing new had come in from Havana. Cowles was more cautious than Gleaves. He decided to wait. The messages might be a hoax. Even if they were correct, Cowles wanted to avoid being the bearer of such bad news.

Shortly after 11 P.M. the telegraph instrument began chattering again. Warren wrote down the text while Cowles, Gleaves, and Hellings looked on. What was coming in was Sigsbee's first report confirming that the

Maine really had been blown up. Warren started the relay of the cable to Washington.

Commander James Forsyth, commandant of the Naval Station, was asleep in his home. He was awakened by Cowles who handed him Sigsbee's cable. Forsyth dispatched a torpedo boat at once to bring the cable to Admiral Sicard who was still at the Dry Tortugas with the North Atlantic Squadron.

When Sicard received the dreadful news, he thought about ordering his whole squadron to Havana to confront the Spaniards without waiting for instructions from Washington. He was not well, however, and he was nearing retirement. Besides, Sigsbee had specifically requested Light House Tenders, not war vessels. Sigsbee was a reliable officer and on the spot in Havana, so Sicard had the *Mangrove* and the *Fern* made ready to depart in anticipation of Washington's orders. Some of the extreme jingoes criticized Sicard later for not sending big warships to demand instant satisfaction and instead dispatching little ships that minimized the impression of U.S. naval strength.

In Washington, society affairs were at their height at midnight. Helen Long, daughter of the Secretary of the Navy, was being escorted from a ball to the family apartment in the Hotel Portland at half-past one. She found a Western Union messenger waiting patiently in the hallway with a telegram addressed to the Secretary. She took the envelope, went into her father's room, awakened him, and handed him what turned out to be the report from Sigsbee.

Long felt "it was almost impossible to believe it could be true, or that it was not a wild and vivid dream." Nevertheless, he forwarded the telegram to Commander Francis Dickins, acting Chief of the Bureau of Navigation in the absence of Captain Crowninshield. "Dear Dickins," he wrote in pencil, "I have just received this terrible telegram. Please have request attended to at once by telegraphing in ordinary language, not using cipher." Long wanted to avoid delay in getting aid to Havana.

After sending the order for two small vessels to proceed quickly to Havana with medical assistance, Dickins reported to Long. The Secretary was sitting in a tiny room adjoining the hotel office, talking with two journalists who had approached him for confirmation of the rumor.

There is a spurious story that Long faced up to bringing the President the bad news himself. There had been telephones in the White House for twenty-one years, although no Chief Executive had ever allowed a telephone in his office, let alone in his bedroom. It was reported that Long telephoned the White House at 2 A.M. and asked the night watchman to awaken the President and bring him to the phone. For years afterward, it was said, the watchman remembered McKinley pacing the floor and murmuring, "The *Maine* blown up! The *Maine* blown up."

Long made no such call, however. Long and McKinley had ordered the *Maine* to Havana as a gamble. They had lost. Long did not want to be around if McKinley decided to pick a scapegoat. He directed Dickins to inform the President. Dickins was just a courier. No offense could be taken to him.

In the false dawn Dickins arrived at the White House and had the watchman alert the President. According to Dickins, "The President came out in his dressing gown. I handed him the dispatch [from Sigsbee] which he read with great gravity. He seemed to be deeply impressed with the news, handed the dispatch to me, and took it again, two or three times, expressing great regret that the event had happened, particularly at that time." McKinley acted as though the loss of the *Maine* had ended his hopes for a settlement with Spain.

Dickins told McKinley that in accordance with Sigsbee's request, the *Mangrove* had sailed from Key West at three o'clock with doctors aboard. So had the *Fern*.

As the wire services spread the account of the disaster across the country, editors of morning newspapers were remaking their front pages by headlining the few known facts. William Randolph Hearst had worked with the editors of the morning edition of the *Journal* until midnight. He was in a battle with Pulitzer's *World* for circulation.

When Hearst arrived at Worth House where he had an apartment, the conscientious doorman was waiting. "There's a telephone call from your office," the doorman told him. "They say it's important news."

Hearst rang his editor at once. "Hello. What is the important news?" he asked. He was advised that "the battleship *Maine* has been blown up in Havana harbor."

"Good Heavens," Hearst exclaimed. "What have you done with the story?"

"We have put it on the first page, of course."

"Have you put anything else on the front page?" Hearst queried. "Only the other big news you saw," was the reply.

"There is no other big news," Hearst declared. "Please spread the story all over the page. This means war!"

At dawn, the flag was raised over the White House, then lowered to half-mast. Long went to the Navy Department to direct that "colors be half-masted" on naval ships and stations "until further orders." Expressions of grief were the most widespread since President James Garfield was assassinated in 1881. All official functions were canceled.

A crowd gathered in the hall outside Long's office. Workmen opened the glass case containing the scale model of the *Maine*. They took the tiny ensign down from the peak and placed at the stern another little ensign that was at half-mast.

Reporting the *Maine* Disaster

★ ★ ★ ★ ★ ★ ★ ★

THE PRESS AND THE SHIP'S MAGAZINES

Starting with newspapers published on the afternoon of February 16, the American press presented an encyclopedic array of facts and features on the *Maine* and her principal officers, possible causes of the explosions, expert opinions, popular theories, a lineup of likely perpetrators, and histories of previous naval catastrophes.

As Secretary Long observed, though, the slant of the articles was determined by each newspaper's particular bias toward the Cuban question. There was a wide difference of opinion concerning the basic questions that still remain open: What happened to the *Maine*? How did it happen? Who was culpable, if anyone?

The conservative papers were sure an internal accident caused the explosion because the *Maine* had been guarded so tightly that no intentional crime could have been carried out by an intruder without detection. The Washington *Evening Star* speculated that spontaneous combustion in the coal bunkers might have overheated a bulkhead, exploding an adjacent magazine. The *New York Herald* also referred to the possibility of fire in the coal igniting gunpowder in a magazine.

On the other hand, the yellow press reflected the majority view by insisting that the elaborate precautions taken against internal hazards precluded an accident on the *Maine*. The explosions must have been deliberately set by Spaniards, official or otherwise. The exploration of the path to these opposing conclusions from the same premise of safeguards well taken provided the public with deep coverage.

Whether the cause was accidental or intentional, most experts agreed that some of the forward gunpowder magazines had exploded, at least in part. Detailed descriptions of the magazines were provided in the newspapers, starting with their location in the hold below the waterline to avoid enemy shells and torpedoes. Even though the newspaper articles were intended for ordinary readers, the language was a little technical, with *afts* and *athwartships* and *starboards*. Stated simply, however, the magazines were storerooms for gunpowder and shells. Only the forward magazines were involved in the *Maine* disaster and there were just five of them. The location of these magazines and the bunkers is shown in the diagram of the *Maine's* hold (see plates p. VIII).

The forward 6-inch magazine was closest to the bow. The magazine's ceiling was the underneath part of the platform deck. The floor was steel plating set above the keel because the room was forward of the ship's double bottom. Shells were stowed on the starboard side, the right side looking from the stern toward the bow. Gunpowder was on the port side. Ahead was a space for provisions. To right and left were water tanks.

The fixed ammunition magazine, also called the six-pounder magazine, was directly aft of the forward 6-inch magazine. This was the repository of ammunition for the one-pounder and six-pounder Hotchkiss rapid-fire guns and the rifles. Paymaster's stores were to port and starboard.

The other three forward rooms ran side by side across the ship instead of fore and aft. The partition above the keel divided this space into halves. All the starboard half was the 10-inch powder magazine. The port half was divided again. The inner quarter was the 10-inch shell room, the outer quarter the reserve 6-inch magazine.

In the two 6-inch magazines, forward and reserve, and in the 10-inch shell room, shells were stacked on wooden shelves. In the same two 6-inch magazines and in the 10-inch powder magazine, brown gunpowder was stored in long cotton bags the diameter of the intended gun barrel. Each bag was in a round airtight copper container because copper does not spark. The reserve magazine also held black saluting powder.

Outboard of the reserve 6-inch magazine was the first fuel compartment on the port side, coal bunker A-16. This large bunker filled the space between the magazine and the hull of the ship. Aft of the magazine was smaller coal pocket B-4. To starboard, coal bunker A-15 was between the 10-inch powder magazine and the hull. Coal pocket B-3 was aft.

There were no outside hatches for bunkers A-16 and A-15. Access was through the coal pockets which had to be filled after and emptied before the bunkers. The usual practice was to take coal from these forward pockets and bunkers first because the *Maine* would otherwise be down by the head.

The forward 6-inch magazine, the reserve 6-inch magazine, and coal bunker A-16 play parts in the mystery of the *Maine*.

THE YELLOW PRESS AND EXPLOSIVES

On the afternoon of the sixteenth, both the *New York Journal* and the *World* reported the disaster dispassionately. The *Journal* identified the probable cause of the explosions as a powder magazine. The *World* repeated Captain Sigsbee's request for suspension of opinion until an inquiry could be held.

The next day, however, Hearst's promotional proclivities took over. An extra edition of the *Journal* proclaimed, "Destruction of the War Ship *Maine* Was the Work of an Enemy. The *Journal* Offers $50,000 Reward for the Conviction of the Criminals. Naval Officers Unanimous Destruction Was on Purpose."

The first eight pages were devoted to fictional accounts of how "The War Ship *Maine* Was Split in Two by an Enemy's Secret Infernal Machine!" A fanciful illustration showed the battleship being blown up by a mine set off by an electrical impulse transmitted by wire from a station on the shore.

The *World* was almost as extreme. The headline asked, "*Maine* Explosion Caused by Bomb or Torpedo?" Either would have been set deliberately, because "Experts Report that the Wreck Was Not Accidental." Ordnance specialist "Captain Zalinski Says a Torpedo Was Used." Other headlines were, "Heard of a Plot to Blow Up the *Maine*" and "Dynamite under the *Maine*?" The words infernal machine, torpedo, and mine were used interchangeably.

These newspaper references to torpedoes and mines required an explanation of the nature of explosives and the workings of mines. The most exhaustive material was in the *New York Herald*. Explosives were defined as substances which may be violently converted by heat or shock into gases with many times the volume of the original substance. The gases burst containers.

The most familiar explosive was gunpowder which was a "low" form expanded into gas by heat. The oldest explosive was black gunpowder which went off like a flash when ignited.

In the early 1880s brown gunpowder was introduced to provide higher velocities for shells and lower pressures in gun barrels. The brown powder was formed into hexagonal wafers with a round hole in the center. Wafers were so slow burning, the *World* reported, they could be lit while held in the hand and then placed on the ground before heat reached the fingers. Even if thrown onto a fire, the wafers would be consumed slowly like coal and would not explode. To ignite brown powder for military use, a priming charge of fine-grain black powder was needed.

Smokeless gunpowder, made from the more dangerous high-explosive guncotton, was invented in 1886. Twelve years later, however, the *Maine* still employed the less efficient but safer brown powder. There was no smokeless powder on board for the big guns.

Both high and low explosives were commonly used to charge mines for naval warfare. The buoyant contact mine was the simplest form of explosive device for naval use. When fabricated in an arsenal, it consisted of a water-tight metal casing containing guncotton or dynamite and fitted with protruding pins. The mine was attached to a cable fastened to an anchor so it would float close to the surface. If an object like the hull of a ship touched a pin in the casing, a percussion cap was fired that detonated the explosive.

During the Civil War the Confederate Navy sank more Union warships through the employment of improvised mines than were sunk by gunfire. Any Southern sailor who knew about explosives could rig a mine.

If the contact mine was homemade in Cuba, the container was likely to be an empty wine cask or a wooden dynamite box given an extra caulking and then filled with 75 to 200 pounds of ordinary gunpowder. Regular black musket powder was sufficient, as long as it was kept dry. Better, dynamite would fire even when wet, and it was available to both Weylerites and rebels in one-pound packages. Less than fifty pounds of properly placed dynamite would blow a hole through a ship's steel bottom.

These homemade contact mines charged with gunpowder offered simplicity of design, easy access to materials required, and speedy assembly. They were handyman's specials that did the job, even though high explosives in fabricated mines were more potent.

For sophisticated applications, contact mines were inappropriate. They did not discriminate in their attack. Any solid object that hit a firing pin with sufficient force detonated the mine, whether the object was friendly or hostile. A contact mine would not be planted to defend a busy harbor like Havana unless a single ship was being targeted.

For deep waters like the channel to Havana harbor, bottom mines were developed with large charges of high explosives which were three to six times as strong as gunpowder. Bottom mines were held down with mushroom anchors. Electrical wires led from the explosive charge to the anchors and along the harbor bottom to the station on shore. When the vessel to be destroyed was over the mine, the explosion was set off by an operator closing a circuit with a key.

The sound of the explosion of a submarine mine was a dull roar, not the sharp detonation of a burst in air. The reaction to the explosion remained concealed below the surface for an instant. Then the sphere of gas began to rise with great force, and if not obstructed, carried before it a mass of water which erupted like a geyser.

In bottom mines where high explosives were the charge, the burst was more abrupt than with gunpowder. Fish were stunned or killed over a large area.

WERE MINES PLANTED IN HAVANA HARBOR?

Did the Spaniards in Havana have mines available to them? Were mines planted in the harbor? If so, when, where, and by whom?

The New York *World* and the *Journal* had no doubt. "How the Torpedoes Are Laid in Havana Harbor" was described imaginatively in the *World*. The *Journal* echoed this with "Blown Up from Outside" and "No Accident!" According to the yellow press, huge bottom mines had been planted by the Spanish government in the inner harbor, before the *Maine's* arrival, below her mooring.

From the start, the officers and enlisted men of the *Maine* had feared that the harbor was planted. The drowned intelligence officer Jenkins whose job it was to determine whether there were mines near the *Maine*, had come to ambiguous conclusions.

Despite Jenkins' waffling, Captain Sigsbee had decided there was no mine under the *Maine*. Consul Lee had agreed with him. Although Sigsbee never mentioned it and the story was denied later, a Navy Department official said that the captain had a steam launch drag a grappling iron around the ship the night the *Maine* arrived in Havana, to make sure no cable ran from a bottom mine to the shore. According to the story, nothing suspicious was found.

Sigsbee thought that Spain would not have planted mines in peacetime. A cable might break and a mine float loose to sink one of Spain's own ships. Captain General Martinez Campos had commanded the army in Cuba before Weyler. He declared, "I would not have thought of constructing mines in a port frequented by so many vessels."

Moreover, the Spanish government stated officially that there had never been a mine in the channel or inside the harbor. This assertion tallied with Navy Department investigations. Weyler himself had replied to a question from the *World*, "You ask me if any submarine mines were placed in Havana harbor during my command. Certainly not. I never had any mine laid inside the harbor of Havana."

Despite the official denials, however, it is likely that Spain did have mines in Havana, whether or not they were in the water. The Spanish naval attaché in Washington, Lieutenant de Carranza, unwittingly confirmed this when he argued, "It seems absurd that from the mere fact of Spain possessing some Latimer-Clark torpedoes, the imputation should be made that one of them caused the catastrophe of the *Maine*. Such defenses are not placed in position until the last moment, in case of hostilities."

The existence of Spanish mines in Cuba was corroborated by English engineer J. P. Gibbins who told the *New York Times* that he sold Spain a large number of electrical mines years before and that eight or ten of them were planted in Havana harbor. He believed that the *Maine's* initial explosion was caused by a bottom mine like his no. 2 which contained 500 pounds of guncotton. His mines, he claimed, could not explode accidentally. A complicated keyboard had been designed to prevent errors.

Next, Charles Crandall came forward to state in the New York *World* that in July 1897 he had laid the mine that sank the *Maine*. "My work was performed at night," he maintained, "assisted by five Italian laborers and two Spanish boatmen. When the work was finished, General Weyler ordered me to place an additional mine near buoy no. 4."

The normally moderate Washington *Evening Star* was convinced that the Spanish authorities were lying when they asserted that Havana harbor was not mined. The *Star* recalled that in November 1897 when the *Maine* was known to be on watch at Port Royal, a severe explosion had occurred in

Havana harbor. Apprehensive Cubans were assured that the blast was routine and not the outbreak of war with the United States. Spanish naval officers said they had been experimenting with explosives in the harbor and a mine had been discharged accidentally.

The *Star* regarded this mishap as "physical proof" of the mining of the harbor, adding that "the Spanish government has reserved a part of the harbor for the anchorage of men-of-war, as the only way to forestall any hostile act. Every buoy in this anchorage has a corresponding mine. The vessel is not allowed to anchor for fear of interference with the wires but is made fast to a numbered mooring designated by the harbor master." The reference to numbered moorings was true.

The statements of Gibbins, Crandall, and the *Star* were supported in the *New York Times* by Captain Gronmeyer. He said that three years earlier his commercial vessel was about to steam into the harbor when a pilot came aboard and ordered a delay because "engineers were planting mines."

There was thus a multiplicity of witnesses quoted in the newspapers. Gibbins provided mines, Crandall laid mines, and Gronmeyer waited while mines were being planted. These statements were not verified, however. None of the three was called to testify at the naval court of inquiry when it was formed. Then the Spanish-American War intervened, and after the war the evidence was moot.

There was even the kind of deathbed confession that was so convincing to Victorians in resolving anonymous crimes like the destruction of the *Maine*. The Englishman Julius Grieg dictated the story in April 1899 during his final illness, after his release from a Spanish prison. Publication was in a posthumous book with very limited circulation, so his experience was virtually unknown at the time.

Grieg worked as the foreman in a machine shop facing the harbor. On the morning of January 4, 1898, he was surprised to see uniformed Spanish officers in the shop. Grieg knew his employer, Sr. Carvallos, was a Spanish naval officer even though Carvallos wore civilian clothes. Grieg was ordered to build three Brennan submarine mines of a type he had worked on in London. He promised prompt delivery if he could make the casings octagonal instead of round because his Spanish workmen detested spheres.

In ten days Grieg had the mines completed. Each contained 500 pounds of guncotton equivalent to the huge Gibbins no. 2 spheres, with room for ballast and with projecting wires for connections. The buoyant mines were taken to a private dock and placed on board a tugboat, along with anchors and cables.

According to Grieg, the first mine was laid on the bottom of the channel. A small boat came alongside the tug with the firing wires which were fastened to the mine's connections. The mine and anchors were dropped overboard and the small boat started back, paying out wire. The tug turned toward the inner harbor where the other two mines were dropped. The land end of the firing wires was attached to a cable leading to a tower over the shop.

The next day, Grieg was ordered to make six steel rods with front and rear sights like rifle barrels. When the rods were finished, they were taken to the tower and fastened to window frames, in line with the mines. A telephone was installed in the tower.

The last week in January, Grieg observed a foreign battleship mooring in the harbor. That was the *Maine*. A guard was then posted in the tower to exclude visitors. On February 15, two small boxes were carried to the tower. Grieg said he noticed that the battleship had swung to the northwest.

After Grieg had tea in the late afternoon, two more Spaniards arrived with another small box. The harbor became dark. As lights from the ships cast streams on the water, Grieg managed an inconspicuous entry to the tower. The Spaniards had spread a chart on the table and messages were being received over the telephone. Following one long conversation, two small telegraph instruments were attached to the cables with fine wires.

There was a ring on the phone and Carvallos raised his hand as a signal. The Spaniard at one apparatus moved something. Another Spaniard touched his key and in a moment, Grieg said, his eyes were drawn to the open window where he saw two distinct flashes of fire. There was a terrific explosion that shook the building and rattled the windows.

The Spaniards ran out and cheered. Grieg could hear others rejoicing in the distance as Carvallo told him that the *Maine* had blown herself up. Grieg replied, "You have deliberately caused the destruction. You have fired one of the mines laid down in the harbor. It was murder!"

"Mr. Grieg," said Carvallo severely, "do you know whom you are addressing?"

"Yes," Grieg answered. "I know I have been speaking to an officer of high

rank in the Spanish navy." Grieg was imprisoned at once. He was not released until after the war.

The Grieg story dovetails with much that happened to the *Maine*. Details
like the direction of the wind and the two flashes were right. The mines
Grieg manufactured were big enough to have caused the damage and they
substantiated the findings of the first naval court.

Of course there were discrepancies, too, that were developed in later findings. In addition, it was difficult to reconcile Grieg's deathbed account with
the similarly unexplored statements of others who also claimed to have made
and laid mines near mooring no. 4 in Havana harbor.

Spontaneous Combustion on the *Maine*

★ ★ ★ ★ ★ ★ ★ ★

SPONTANEOUS VERSUS INSTANTANEOUS

Newspapers that attributed the *Maine* disaster to an accident characterized her as a bad luck ship. She had experienced many mishaps. The final eruption was just another calamity of internal origin. Besides, if the explosions were not accidental, Spain was guilty of an inhuman crime. That would mean an immediate war neither Spain nor the United States was ready for.

Even after the yellow press had suddenly switched to a Spanish mine as the cause of the catastrophe, conservative newspapers like the London *Times* were still reporting that "naval officers are all inclined to suppose an accident." The *New York Times* added, "Naval men tell of many ways in which the disaster could not have been guarded against."

The type of accident most officers mentioned was spontaneous combustion of coal in the bunkers next to the *Maine's* magazines. Experts pointed out that spontaneous ignition was a frequent event in the Navy. They provided a dozen examples of accidental shipboard fires supposedly self-started in coal bunkers on U.S. warships.

The self-ignition of coal was, however, a phenomenon that most naval officers did not yet understand fully. Newspaper readers were even less informed about the process. When they thought of spontaneous combustion, it was of an act of magic. The impression was of a raging fire somehow started instantaneously in a cold substance. To civilians, the effect was much like striking a match.

The reason for the lack of experience with self-ignition on shipboard was that coal fires were new to the Navy. In transitional warships where coal was first employed to supplement sail power, spontaneous combustion was unknown. There was plenty of fresh air circulating in the hold because there was no steel protective deck over the few boilers and bunkers. Steam pressures were low.

These simpler conditions were radically changed in the vessels commissioned into service after 1895. As in the *Maine*, sail power had become obsolete. Steam generating coal-fired boilers and adjacent coal bunkers were more numerous and much larger. The fitted protective deck retained heat in the hold. Temperatures in firerooms reached as high as 150 degrees F.

One of the Navy's authorities on spontaneous combustion was Lieutenant Commander Wainwright, the *Maine*'s executive officer. While he was head of the Office of Naval Intelligence, Assistant Secretary Theodore Roosevelt had him prepare a memorandum on the way European navies protected their men-of-war from coal fires.

Wainwright determined that the danger of self-ignition of coal in U.S. ships was primarily the fault of inexperienced naval architects. In the *Maine*, for example, coal bunker A-16 was separated from the reserve 6-inch magazine by a steel partition only one plate thick. The bunker had been placed outboard of the magazine to keep a projectile piercing the hull from reaching the gunpowder, but what was intended as a protection against external perils became a source of danger from the internal hazard of fire in the bunker. Even more unsafe flaws existed in other warships in the new U.S. Navy.

Wainwright's overseas agents told him that European constructors designed their warships' bulkheads specifically to control spontaneous combustion. The English used double walls around magazines and bunkers and stuffed the air spaces with asbestos which does not conduct heat. The French not only built double walls and floors lined with asbestos, they also circulated cold air through the magazines and wall spaces. The *Maine*'s more primitive layout was ridiculed by sophisticated European naval architects.

With Wainwright's revealing memorandum in hand, Roosevelt wrote Secretary Long on November 26, 1897, when the *Maine* was already in Norfolk on Havana watch. He recommended an investigation into the self-ignition of coal in shipboard bunkers. "It may be found," he suggested, "that some of our bunkers have their bulkheads too near the boilers and furnaces but that there is no danger from spontaneous combustion when the coal is not subjected to excessive heat."

Roosevelt was describing hot firerooms that facilitated spontaneous combustion in adjacent coal bunkers next to powder magazines. This was a three-part chain of hot-furnace–ignited-bunker-coal–exploded powder magazine, not the *Maine*'s two-part chain of outboard bunker–magazine. There had been no contiguous hot furnace on the *Maine*. Furthermore, the bunkers that were next to the *Maine*'s fireroom did not combust.

Long approved the formation of a Board of Investigation of the Spontaneous Combustion of Coal, but he limited the scope of the study severely. The board reported to the Secretary just three weeks before the explosions on the *Maine*. The findings were so sound, they remained the authority on the subject for many years.

The board pointed out that there had never been a fire on a ship using anthracite or "hard" coal, so consideration was confined to bituminous or "soft" coal. The chief cause of spontaneous ignition of bituminous coal, the board found, is condensation and absorption of oxygen from the air. This produces heating. The process is self-stimulating, the board observed, and is aided by four conditions: at least a moderately high temperature transmitted from a nearby origin such as a furnace; a newly broken state of the coal providing fresh surfaces for absorption; a high percentage of volatile combustibles in the coal; and a supply of air sufficient to feed the fire but not strong enough to dissipate the heat.

Fires in bunker coal are relatively few, the board wrote, and require an external heat source that stimulates the chemical reaction. In most U.S. warships, the function of the coal required that bunkers be adjacent to the boilers which produced elevated bunker temperatures. The board's conclusion was that there should always be double bulkheads between the heat source and the coal. This was Roosevelt's original supposition, along with the corollary that "there is no danger when the coal is not subjected to excessive heat."

According to the board, when the temperature outside the bunker is extremely hot and the bunker coal reaches 120 degrees F., there is a strong chance of ignition. The time frame is a few days for development of fire, however, not minutes or even hours. When bunkers are exposed to external heat, a daily examination for temperature rises, odor, vapor, and smoke was recommended.

The board asked rhetorically why anthracite coal was not used exclusively if free from spontaneous ignition. The answer was that hard coal is inferior for naval use. Even after the *Maine* explosion, 117 of 123 commanding officers preferred Pocahontas bituminous coal to the other thirty-four hard and soft varieties that were available. The reason was that Pocahontas produced the best steaming. New River was a distant second.

The board concluded that controlled naval use of bituminous coal was comparatively safe. The number of deaths that could be charged to spontaneous combustion on warships was nil at the time of the investigation.

Applying the board's findings to conditions on the *Maine* is another part of resolving the mystery.

SPONTANEOUS COMBUSTION IN U.S. WARSHIPS

Despite the unequivocal findings of the board of investigation, newspapers supporting the accident theory alleged that spontaneous combustion of coal was unavoidable in the new U.S. warships. Therefore, the *Maine* catastrophe must have begun as a self-ignited fire in the coal bunker adjacent to the magazine that exploded. The semiofficial *Army and Navy Journal* aided the accident theory by commenting editorially that "the public has a right to know every instance of spontaneous combustion of coal which has been reported in these new steel ships."

In addition to explaining spontaneous combustion erroneously, these conservative newspapers listed every catastrophe they could discover that was at all similar to the *Maine* explosions. The roster of supposedly comparable disasters began with the *Demologos* which had been built by Robert Fulton in 1814 as the world's first steam-powered warship. Her magazine—containing defective gunpowder held solely for salutes—blew up from a cause never ascertained but assumed to have been carelessness.

The *Missouri* was wrecked in 1885 by an unexplained eruption of her magazines while lying at Gibraltar. In 1891, the *Atlanta*'s empty coal bunkers exploded. They had just been painted and vapors had ignited in the closed compartments. This was not self-ignition of coal. These examples were not analogous to the *Maine* disaster, but they demonstrated that steam-powered warships were so complex, accidents of some kind were bound to happen.

In 1892, the *Philadelphia* was in dry dock in the New York Navy Yard while the *Maine* was under construction there. One sunny noon, a barrel of Japan paint drier exploded on deck. "The flames sped like a flash over everything," the captain recalled later, "and we were compelled to flood the magazines to save the ship. If this had happened during the night, the *Philadelphia* would have shared the fate of the *Maine*" because the crew would have been off duty. Despite the captain's conjecture, however, the ignited substance was not coal and the sun did not shine at night when the *Maine* exploded.

Captain Henry Glass remembered a more similar incident to the *Maine*'s on the *Cincinnati* in early 1896. The cruiser "was lying at Key West," he stated in the *Army and Navy Journal*, "and, the weather being warm, the coal in the bunkers took fire from spontaneous combustion, but since the compartment was airtight, an actual blaze could not form for lack of oxygen. The magazine was separated from the coal bunkers by a steel partition, same as on the *Maine*. After awhile, the bulkhead became red hot, generating an almost invisible stream of smoke which issued from a hatch leading to the magazine. A sentry noticed this, and without waiting to investigate, water was flooded into the magazine and bunkers. This was not a minute too soon. Could air have gotten into the bunkers, the ship would undoubtedly have been blown to pieces hours previously. Even as it was, many of the loaded shells had been charred by the heat."

The pine boxes that held the *Cincinnati*'s shells were almost completely burned. The Navy's ordnance expert, Professor Philip Alger, observed that the bunker fire had ignited the wooden fittings in the magazine, including the shelving holding the powder charges. His opinion was that "had the fire not been discovered at the time it was, it would doubtless have resulted in a similar catastrophe to the one on the *Maine*."

Alger did not mention that the *Cincinnati* had experienced previous instances of spontaneous combustion of bunker coal blamed on high temperatures in the adjacent fireroom. In recognition of the danger from this external heat, changes had already been made in the ship's ventilators. Once a ship had troubles with self-ignition of coal, however, makeshift improvements did not eliminate the occurrences. In contrast, the *Maine* had no history of fires. And the *Maine*'s bunker in question was outboard of the magazine rather than next to a fireroom that was not in use in any event.

Moreover, while heat from the *Cincinnati*'s bunker fire burned wood in the magazine containing brown gunpowder, the gunpowder did not ignite. This demonstrated the inertness of brown powder. Coal next to the fireroom ignited itself, wood in the magazine burned, shells charred, but the gunpowder was not affected. The accident on the *Cincinnati* was a testimonial to the stability of the brown gunpowder also contained in the *Maine*'s magazines.

On March 9, 1896, the cruiser *New York* had a sobering experience with self-ignition of coal. Captain W. S. Schley claimed the episode was "thrilling." Despite frequent inspections, "fire had started from spontaneous combustion in the coal bunkers which smoldered from 9 in the morning until 1 in the afternoon without being discovered. It was near a magazine bulkhead when finally checked."

Like the *Cincinnati*, the *New York* was discovered to be on fire when smoke issued from the magazine. The heat had blistered paint on the magazine's steel walls. Woodwork next to the coal bunker had charred. When the bunker was opened, the coal on top was cool. As the men dug into the pile, though, the bottom coal touching the magazine was red hot.

Schley was ordered to take explosive materials from the affected magazine at once because the adjacent bunker remained exposed to high heat from the furnace that had stimulated the coal fire. The constructors then removed the *New York* from service until the bulkheads involved could be doubled to provide air space as insulation.

Again, there was potentially catastrophic self-ignition of bunker coal, but the initiation of the fire in the bunker was due to external heat from the fireroom. To the constructors, the *Maine* was not in similar danger. Her firerooms were not adjacent to coal bunker A-16. She was not brought into the navy yard to have her bulkheads doubled.

After the *Maine* exploded, the Navy Department disclosed that there had been seven recent fires in the battleship *Indiana*'s coal bunkers. No solution had been found. The *Philadelphia* had another fire in 1897. The *Cincinnati* flooded its magazines again. There had been several fires in the *Brooklyn*. Since 1895, there had been four bunker fires in the *Wilmington*, three in the

Olympia, and one each in the *Oregon, Boston, Lancaster,* and *Petrel.* While no warship was destroyed by explosion from coal fire before or after 1898, ignition could be difficult to detect and structural improvement was not always successful.

Fortunately, spontaneous ignition was not in fact a common occurrence. Less than a dozen warships suffered coal fires of any size during the three and a half years when statistics were kept. The number of bunker fires was one in eight hundred coalings. Secretary Long's Navy was practical about these relatively few accidents. Even after the demise of the *Maine,* Long paid slight attention to spontaneous combustion on shipboard. It was the turn of the century equivalent of cost effectiveness.

In Europe, naval experts cited six naval disasters to substantiate the accident theory concerning the *Maine.* The HMS *Captain* had capsized, HMS *Vanguard* and HMS *Victoria* were rammed, HMS *Doterel's* and HMS *Triumph's* paint lockers exploded, and the German ironclad *Kurfurst* was also rammed. None of these episodes was remotely related to self-ignition of coal.

Apart from the Spaniards, British experts were the most vocal in favor of the accident theory. Nevertheless, five of the six catastrophes listed were in British warships. All involved negligent handling of ships or careless stowage of inflammable liquids, not self-ignition of coal.

In contrast to the acknowledged British culpability for carelessness, spontaneous combustion of bunker coal was regarded as a relatively blameless process in the United States. Self-ignition was treated as an act of God, not as negligence. No American captain had been censured for the self-ignition of coal on his ship.

Why Did the *Maine* Explode?

★ ★ ★ ★ ★ ★ ★ ★

SPECULATION AS TO ACCIDENT

During the week after the explosions on the *Maine*, the press continued to speculate about the cause of the disaster. Articles in conservative newspapers favored the accident theory, sometimes with contradictory explanations.

Scores of American and European officers were interviewed. The Spanish and British ridiculed the supposedly slack discipline on U.S. warships that allowed accidents to happen. In contrast, American officers boasted about the frequent and thorough inspections of coal bunkers and magazines in the United States Navy. Some of the same officers pointed out, however, that half a day had elapsed between the intensive morning examination of the *Maine*'s bunkers and the explosions at night. That was enough time, they argued, for a bunker fire to start and then involve the gunpowder in the next room. They still thought of "spontaneous" as "instantaneous" combustion, confusing chemistry with time.

At first, many Navy Department officials were reported to have accepted the bunker-fire hypothesis. They had seen self-ignited fires smolder for days in piles of newly broken coal in their own Washington Navy Yard. One official admitted, "I have been expecting such an accident to happen, and am only surprised that many such accidents have not occurred."

The New York *World* questioned U.S. naval officers on February 18. Twenty-six were said to have picked an accident as the cause of the explosion, while a firm twenty-two held for a mine. The figures were, however, suspect. Captain Sigsbee was misquoted as inclining toward the accident theory. Wainwright allegedly blamed an electrical short circuit, although both officers continued to believe that the *Maine* had been blown up by a Spanish mine.

To this point, however, there was no real proof of exactly what had taken place. Some officers suspected Spaniards simply because the explosions occurred in hostile Havana. The veteran Captain Wiley of Merritt Wrecking Company debunked this reasoning. He said, "I do not believe there is anybody who knows just how the unfortunate affair happened. From above water, I would say the *Maine* was blown up by an internal explosion. If the affair had occurred in an English harbor, not one man in a hundred would say external cause after looking at that wreck."

Lieutenant Philip Rounseville Alger was the unofficial spokesman for the accident theory. After graduating first in his Naval Academy class in 1880, he had been attached to the Bureau of Ordnance at the start of the steel and big-gun Navy. In 1890 he was appointed as a professor at the Academy. He was responsible for much of the development of U.S. naval ordnance.

According to the professor, he could prove the accident theory by a negative. "We know of no instance," he announced on February 18, "where the explosion of a torpedo or mine under a ship's bottom has exploded the magazine within. It has simply torn a big hole in the side or bottom." He cited Civil War ships that had been torpedoed without exploding their magazines.

"On the contrary," he added, "magazine explosions produce effects exactly similar to the effects of the explosion on board the *Maine*. We should naturally look, not for improbable causes, but for those against which we have had to guard in the past. The most common of these is through fire in the bunkers. Many of our ships have been in danger from this cause."

The "effects" Alger referred to were the fallen smokestack, the disappearance of heavy turret guns, and the overturning of decks that indicated enormous destruction in the vicinity of coal bunker A-16 and the reserve 6-inch magazine. Alger claimed that deducing from the best evidence, the ship itself, there had been no mine explosion. The agent had to have been an internal bunker fire similar to those that had self-ignited on the *New York* and the *Cincinnati*.

The bunker fire was Alger's final choice, but it was not his first pick or his second. He had stated with equal certainty on the previous day, "My theory is that the trouble was caused either by an explosion of the guncotton which was stored in the compartment furthest forward, or by an explosion of one of the forward boilers. Spontaneous combustion in the coal bunkers may also have caused the trouble, but this appears unlikely to me. The origin of the disaster will have been within the battleship."

The guncotton thesis attracted many supporters. Guncotton was essential for the torpedoes' warheads even though it could be unstable. Chief Engineer Melville who had designed the *Maine*'s propulsion plant agreed with Alger. Lieutenant Commander Marix also opted for the guncotton explanation. Captain Charles O'Neil of the Ordnance Bureau asked whether the *Maine* had gone into Havana harbor with warheads on her torpedoes. Shock could have detonated the guncotton if the warheads had remained in place.

The guncotton theory was dropped the next day. The warheads had not been mounted on torpedoes. They were secure in their own magazine—not forward where the damage was but aft and still unexploded.

Alger's second choice, the bursting of a boiler, was also a popular theory, especially with the Spaniards. It was General Blanco's idea, and there were Navy Department officials besides Alger who concurred. The *Maine*'s forward boilers were on the edge of the major damage and separated from the powder magazine by just four feet.

In Havana, however, only two boilers were lit. Both were aft, under low pressure, away from the damaged area. The forward boilers were not in service when the ship exploded. They were cold, and so was Alger's second choice.

Even more remote possibilities were explored. One was methane. Ventilating engineer Cleery claimed, "In the open air, gases from coal are carried off, but on ships the coal bunkers are tight as a safe." A mining engineer maintained that "fire damp effected the destruction." The two engineers said coal gave off odorless yet highly inflammable methane. This theory was scuttled because the transient gas would have disappeared before the coal reached shipboard.

While the English leaned toward spontaneous combustion of coal, the French looked to self-ignition of the new type of smokeless gunpowder they used. It was made from unstable guncotton and blew up French warships. The *Maine*, though, stocked the older brown and black gunpowder.

In addition, a Stanford professor pointed to a highly volatile paint on board as the agent. However, all the *Maine*'s explosive liquids were properly stowed. The last suggestion was that sailors were smoking below decks. The explosion occurred, though, after the ship was shut down for the night. Magazines were locked.

Señor du Bose, the Spanish minister who succeeded Dupuis, was encouraged by the *World's* poll of the officers. He also relayed to Madrid the official White House statement that information at hand indicated the explosion was due to an accident and that in the absence of contrary evidence, this should be taken as fact. Du Bose added that "as the explosion was wholly accidental, it could not have an adverse effect upon the relations between the United States and Spain."

He was transmitting the wrong message. The accident theory was losing ground, especially after Hiram Maxim of the Maxim gun manufacturers contradicted Professor Alger. Maxim asserted in London that "a torpedo exploded under the *Maine* would, if in contact, be liable to ignite the inflammables inside by concussion."

SPECULATION ABOUT THE BOYTON THEORY

British newspapers printed advertisements and personals on the front page. Their editors were shocked, however, at the boldness of both the lies and the headlines in the American yellow press. The sole praise was for "the steadiness of the American public" which "cannot be appreciated abroad except by knowledge of the insane provocations they resist."

By devoting eight and a half pages an issue to these "provocations," the circulation of the *New York Journal* rose from 416,885 on February 9 to 1,025,624 eight days later. Headlines such as "The *Maine* Was Destroyed by Treachery" and "The Whole Country Thrills with War Fever, Yet the President Says It Was an Accident" were in heavy black inch-high type running the width of the front page. Many newspapers across the country copied the *Journal's* editorial stand, and some its headline style.

The goal of the yellow press was to persuade Americans that the *Maine* had been blown up by a mine, detonated either by the Spanish government or by a fanatic through Spanish negligence. Hearst and Pulitzer wanted war. In the absence of proof that the Spanish authorities had set off the mine, the alternative was to show how easily one Spanish zealot could have done the job. The expert on such a feat was Captain Paul Boyton, the swimmer.

Boyton's fame had spread to Congress. A member of the naval committee, Congressman Amos Cummings of New York, used the captain as an example to prove that a mine could have been planted under the *Maine* by one man. During a period of strained relations between London and St. Petersburg, Cummings said, the Russian vessel *Strelok* had anchored in New York's North River. The *Strelok* was under surveillance by the British warship *Garnet*, which had placed her torpedo shield at the bow to ward off any Russian explosive. Despite British sentries, Boyton swam with an empty mine fastened to a rope, tied the rope to the end of the shield, and let the tide drive the dummy under the *Garnet*'s engine room. The *Herald* printed a diagram of the exploit.

A *World* newsman went to South Windham, Connecticut, where Boyton was a patient in Dr. Rose's sanatorium for reasons of health. The captain maintained that blowing up the *Maine* would have been easy for any Spaniard with his ability and experience. As Boyton put it, "I would use the method which, from what I can learn, was used in blowing up the *Maine*. I would take a long line, which would be fastened to the torpedo at one end and to a piece of plank at the other. These would be placed in the current and allowed to drift the width of the line apart, until the line struck the anchor chain, the torpedo passing on one side and the plank on the other, where they would remain until the current struck the torpedo and it would explode."

Whether or not the captain's reconstruction of the mining of the *Maine* in calm Havana harbor was accurate, his analysis hastened the switch away from the accident theory.

SPECULATION ABOUT THE JINGOES

Secretary Long was carrying out the McKinley policy of avoiding war by encouraging the accident theory. A finding of accident would also temper his personal guilt at having agreed to send the *Maine* into the hostile harbor. From an ethical standpoint, too, Spain was innocent until proved guilty.

On the other hand, the line officers who were Long's bureau chiefs had soon changed to the contrary view. A finding that a battleship had been destroyed by accident could demoralize the Navy. There might be mass desertions of enlisted men and there would certainly be repercussions in Congress. These line officers allied themselves with the civilian jingoes.

Long's Assistant Secretary, Theodore Roosevelt, was a leading jingo. He addressed an unsolicited letter to Long the day after the explosion: "It may be impossible to ever settle whether the *Maine* was destroyed through treachery on the part of the Spaniards. The coincidence of her destruction with her being anchored off Havana by an accident such as has never before happened, is unpleasant enough to increase the existing difficulties between ourselves and Spain. Captain Sigsbee and Consul General Lee advise against a warship going to Havana at present. They would not thus advise unless there was at least suspicion as to cause of the disaster."

Roosevelt wrote to a friend at Harvard the same day, "The *Maine* was sunk by an act of dirty treachery on the part of the Spaniards I believe; though we shall never find out definitely, and officially it will go down as an accident."

The *Journal* printed the headlines, "Long and Roosevelt at Loggerheads. The Secretary Maintains That the Disaster Was an Accident, but His Assistant Doesn't Think So" and "No Accident Says Roosevelt. Inspection of the Battle Ship's Magazines Renders an Accidental Explosion Nearly Impossible." Because of these headlines, Long ordered Roosevelt to suspend public utterances.

Professor Alger, though, was free to make statements Long agreed with. This time the professor was saying that Havana correspondents had described the sound of the explosion as sharp, a noise consistent with a concussion within the ship. A mine exploding under water would have produced a dull sound.

In response, Roosevelt wrote to Captain Charles O'Neil, Alger's superior. "I don't want to bring this matter before the Department," he asserted, "but don't you think it inadvisable for Professor Alger to express opinions in this way. He cannot know anything about the accident. All the best men agree that, whether probable or not, it certainly is *possible* that the ship was blown up by a mine. The fact that Mr. Alger happens to take the Spanish side, and to imply that the explosion was probably due to some fault of the Navy has nothing to do with the matter."

In his answer, the professor did not pick up details such as Roosevelt's unconsciously referring to the disaster as an accident. Instead, Alger denied taking "the Spanish side." Is it not better, he asked, to lose a ship to an accident that is correctable than to have a ship sunk by the enemy where there could be negligence? From then on, however, he was silent.

Captain Royal Bradford, Chief of the Bureau of Equipment, asserted that Alger was wrong in blaming the disaster on a bunker fire. He praised the quality of the fuel his bureau had supplied. The ship's forward bunkers contained coal from Pocahontas and New River mines. Both were between bituminous and anthracite in hardness, he maintained, and equal to Welsh navigation coal, the British naval standard.

Next, Chief Constructor Philip Hichborn stated that the bunkers and magazines were inspected at eight o'clock each morning. He understood that the bunker temperature on the fatal Tuesday was a cool 59 degrees F. Also, Navy records showed that 87 degrees F. was the maximum temperature of the forward magazines during the preceding month. He observed that these were safe levels. At least 600 degrees F., he said, would have to be applied for a measurable time to ignite brown gunpowder.

According to shipbuilder Charles Cramp, the mere fact that a bunker was adjacent to a magazine would not by itself mean that a bunker fire exploded the magazine. Jingoes like Cramp asserted that high-quality coal, low temperatures in the bunkers and forward magazines, and the stability of brown gunpowder ruled out spontaneous combustion as the cause and left only a Spanish mine as the deadly agent.

One initially arresting note was the *New York Times*'s disclosure that the *Maine* had an untold history of self-ignition of coal. A private citizen had been at a dinner on the *Maine* in August 1897 when an orderly entered and whispered to Captain Sigsbee and then to Executive Officer Marix. "Both men became agitated. Marix uttered 'My God!' as he left the room. After awhile the orderly said, 'Gentlemen, the barge is ready to take you ashore.' When they were in the barge, the Captain leaned over the rail and said, 'Gentlemen, you have had a narrow escape to-night. The coal bunkers were on fire, and the fire was put out with much difficulty.'"

The story had not, however, been verified with Sigsbee. The quotation ascribed to him was not accurate. Instead, a refrigeration machine had overheated and was smoking. There was no bunker fire, although the prudent Sigsbee had the nearest bunker shoveled out to make sure.

In Havana, Sigsbee and his principal officers were aware they would be facing a naval court of inquiry on the disaster. They were careful about what they said in public. Other Americans in Havana were not as reticent. A government employee wrote, "There is little doubt in the minds of any of us now that the explosion was not the result of accident, but was a piece of black treachery."

The *World* reported that Spaniards had sworn to blow up the *Maine* "as soon as she showed any sign of preparing for action." A tourist, Dr. Pendleton, explained that the Spaniards were excited by the *Maine* swinging in the wind so her guns pointed at Morro Castle. A Spaniard had threatened, "If the *Maine* ever attempted to level her guns on Morro, she would go up in the air like a balloon. We have enough submarine wires under and all around her to blow her to hell whenever we choose." Even the Madrid government feared that the disaster might be traced to these uncontrollable fanatics.

Working with the yellow press, the Cuban junta in New York was also trying to make the Spaniards appear guilty. Treasurer Garcia remembered "the case of the *Virginius* during the ten years' war in Cuba. Dr. Gallardo a rabid Spaniard and a professor made an attempt to blow up the American ship." In Cuba, even educated Spaniards were dynamiters.

The Cuban junta was counting on the sinking of the *Maine* in a Spanish port to stampede the American people toward war. The Cubans admitted that their objective was to make Americans see Spain's hand in the calamity and cry out, "This is all of a piece with their devil's work in Cuba! Let us end it once and for all."

As the English press had observed, however, the surprise was that the American people had honored Sigsbee's request to withhold their opinion about the *Maine* as long as they had. In matters concerning crime, due process was the tradition in the United States, despite lies in the yellow press, outrage expressed by jingoes, and manipulation by the junta which was connected to both the yellow press and the jingoes.

WHO WERE THE MISCREANTS?

The ultimate question for the newspapers was whether the culprits responsible for the explosion of the *Maine* could be identified. The first step was to examine the physical evidence. Some correspondents again quoted experts who believed the destruction was so complete, no malefactor would ever be named.

Most journalists, however, reported that the facts would be clear when American divers looked at the wreck. Hiram Maxim stated that "the character of the hole in the bottom of the ship would show whether the primary explosion was inside or outside." This was expanded in the *Journal*: "If a mine was exploded under the *Maine*, [bottom] plates would be blown upward [and inward]. An explosion inside the vessel would bend the plates outward."

If the hole was outward, the determination would be accident or sabotage. There had been instances of U.S. sailors on other ships inexplicably finding their way into a magazine. A disgruntled or crazed sailor might have sabotaged the *Maine*. There was, however, no evidence of such an act.

If there was an accident, the cause was presumably self-ignition of coal. The initial malefactor would then have been the deceased Chief Constructor Wilson who had designed the bunker and magazine with only the single plate between them. Also, the current Chief Constructor Hichborn should perhaps have doubled the bulkheads in question after he was put on notice by bunker fires in other U.S. warships.

The secondary wrongdoer would be Captain Sigsbee. General Weyler charged that the *Maine* was a dirty ship. Sigsbee had been in command and so would be the principal defendant at the court of inquiry. Naval courts were tough. Sigsbee would have to answer the accusation that he negligently allowed the start and spread of a bunker fire.

Roosevelt volunteered his support of Sigsbee: "I am glad, if the accident had to occur, that it should occur on a ship with a captain and executive officer whose names are guarantees that everything right was done." Sigsbee's reputation as a strict captain would be to his credit, but his position on the cause of the disaster was cloudy. Despite all the evidence to the contrary, he was again quoted in the *World* as saying that "the powder magazines were in perfect order." He still contended that the entire damage had come from a huge Spanish mine rather than from the combination of a mine and magazines.

If the explosion was the result of a mine, either by itself or involving a magazine, there were many possible culprits. The Madrid newspapers accused McKinley. They wrote that a complete American war plan had been published in the *New York Herald* two days before the explosions. This proved that "the catastrophe was simply a pretext skillfully utilized by the Americans for launching themselves into the fight, and that the war was one of the secret aspirations of the United States." The indictment was not taken seriously. If McKinley had wanted to provoke an incident, he would have countermanded Sigsbee's order and allowed the *Maine*'s crew to go ashore.

There were American jingoes who wanted war badly enough to have sacrificed the *Maine* and her crew. The historian Henry Adams was at Aswan on the Nile when he heard the news. He felt relief, not horror, because now "Spain must bust!"

The most influential American warmonger was the *Journal's* William Randolph Hearst. When his illustrator Frederic Remington complained that there was no war in Cuba in late 1896, Hearst replied, "You furnish the pictures. I'll furnish the war." He had been searching for an incident with Spain to boost circulation. After the disaster, his coverage was "the orgasmic acme of ruthless, truthless newspaper jingoism." Sigsbee was convinced that Hearst had at least known in advance about the plot against the *Maine* and had not disclosed what he knew.

Last among the possibly guilty Americans was again Sigsbee. He had been responsible for vigilance. Saying "it was necessary to trust the Spanish authorities for protection from without" was not enough. He did, though, have four sentries on planks extending from the bow, stern, and sides of the ship. He had his crew on quarter watches during the night. His effectiveness was confirmed by Captain Puri of the Havana harbor police, who noted that any time his patrol boat approached within fifty yards of the *Maine* after dark, he was promptly hailed by an alert sentry. His boat was a noisy steam launch, however, with running lights.

Cuban rebels were more likely suspects. They wanted to involve the United States in war with Spain, some said, and might have blown up the *Maine*, knowing Spain would be blamed. Or, conceivably, they could have attacked the *Maine* by mistake, thinking they were destroying the adjacent *Alfonso XII*.

The rebels had the capability. In January 1897, they had blown up a Spanish gunboat on the Rio Cauto, using a submarine mine connected to an electric wire leading to a station on the wooded shore. They had plenty of dynamite, courtesy of American filibuster boats. Moreover, the Spanish authorities showed by their actions that the rebels might have had access to Havana harbor. After the *Maine* explosions, Spanish warships employed picket boats and searchlights at night. They appeared to suspect the rebels of sinking the *Maine* and acted as if they feared an attack on the *Alfonso XII*.

On the other hand, the Cuban rebel leaders claimed they did not want U.S. intervention. Rebel General Maximo Gomez regarded the United

States as an enemy because its policy favored Spain simply by being neutral. Militant Cubans were looking to free the island themselves, with United States aid but not United States troops. They would not trade Spanish imperialism for an American brand. The strongest point in their favor was that if they had been able to destroy warships in Havana harbor, they would have blown up Spanish warships, not American.

After a few weeks, U.S. public opinion reached a consensus, holding Spain responsible for the calamity. The yellow press insisted that Spaniards were treacherous or careless, and guilty either way. They could have moored the *Maine* over a mine or planted a mine under her. They could have accidentally tripped the key that exploded the mine or they could have let a mine get loose and drift into the *Maine*. Through negligence, they could have given a fanatic a chance to set the mine. They caused the burst or they allowed it to happen.

Newspapers emphasized that Spanish moral standards varied from American. Spaniards who could cause the deaths of hundreds of thousands of Cuban peasants were capable of choosing an hour for the *Maine* explosions that would be late enough to trap the crew asleep in their hammocks and yet early enough so the spectacle would afford amusement for Spaniards on the shore.

The Emperor of Germany was sure the explosions had been a Spanish attack even though the U.S. ambassador in Berlin reported that the disaster was accidental. At a dinner for his North Sea commanders, the Emperor asked for opinions on the cause of the *Maine* disaster. The officers said the catastrophe had resulted from an accident, but the Emperor insisted he knew how great powers functioned. Sinking the *Maine* appreciably depleted the U.S. Navy.

Yet the most knowledgeable Americans proclaimed the innocence of the Spanish authorities. Secretary Long wrote, "General Lee is of the opinion that the Spanish government had no connection with the disaster." Sigsbee himself said, "It was my official duty to entertain suspicions, but as to condemning the Spanish government, I rejected all that."

Other naval officers stated, "There is an unwillingness to believe that so atrocious an act could have been sanctioned by people who have manifested such signs of respect for the unfortunates," meaning the injured sailors in the Spanish hospitals and the dead who were buried reverently in the Havana cemetery. Even after "there was irrefutable proof that the disaster was caused by an external explosion, there was no connivance on the part of the Spanish government."

Two incidents were taken as circumstantial evidence of Spain's innocence. The Spaniards had dispatched the cruiser *Vizcaya* to New York City in response to McKinley's finessing the *Maine* into Havana. The Madrid newspaper *Imparcial* argued that the Spanish government would not have blown up the *Maine* at the moment the *Vizcaya*, "a far more valuable vessel," was reaching New York "where reprisal would have been easy."

Second, General Blanco was sitting with General Marinas in the cool corridor of the palace on the night of the disaster. When Blanco heard the explosions, he jumped up, exclaiming, "At last, they have put a shell in the palace!" He thought the insurgents were firing at him.

Logically, the Spanish government would never have committed an atrocity so apt to bring U.S. troops into Cuba. Blanco's efforts had been to compromise. The *Maine* catastrophe was the worst blow the Spanish government could have suffered in Cuba.

THE WEYLERITE AVENGERS

If the Maine disaster was man-made, the most likely perpetrators would have been drawn from the hundreds of Weylerites in Havana. U.S. newspapers speculated about the culpability of these young Spanish Loyalists who were junior army officers. The Washington *Evening Star* called them "avengers of General Weyler." The *Nation* described them as "insane," the *Herald* as "anti-American and anti-autonomist," the *Journal* as "rabid Volunteers," and the *St. James Gazette* of London as "Spanish conspirators." The Spanish government had little to no control over them.

The *Evening Star* printed a detailed indictment. These were the officers who had laid submarine mines in Havana harbor before the *Maine's* arrival. They had drawn plans showing the location of the mines and they had access to the electrical keyboard. They were Weyler's vindicators. They looked after Weyler's interests in Cuba. They were inspired by his animosity toward Americans, Cuban patriots, and liberal Spaniards.

They were incensed when Weyler was removed from Cuba at the insistence of the United States government while McKinley would not recall

Consul Lee. They resented Weyler's abasement before the Queen to defend himself against U.S. criticism.

They had led the January riots, the *Evening Star* added. They helped block the Spanish government from accommodating McKinley. In common with all Spaniards, they abhorred the *Maine's* presence in Havana. The ship was a menace, ready to kill Spaniards in the event of war. She showed no sign of ever leaving the harbor. She had even been joined by the *Cushing*.

These partisans, the *Evening Star* continued, had read about the forced resignation of Dupuis de Lôme. Sigsbee's visit to the Autonomist Cabinet was anathema to them. They refrained from violence as long as the *Maine* might be frightened into leaving Cuba. They circulated handbills warning Sigsbee about dangers to his ship. They sponsored the elderly Spaniard who appeared at the United States consulate every day to admonish, "Send the *Maine* away!" They restrained the bumboatmen from approaching the *Maine*, depriving the isolated crew of small comforts. They hissed at Americans in the streets, the cafés, and the theater. They had prayed aloud for the sinking of the *Maine*.

Above all, they wanted war with the United States. They believed Spain could land an army in undefended Florida and march to capture Washington while the Spanish navy exacted tribute from seaports. They wanted to destroy the *Maine* and substantially diminish American naval power as an act of patriotism. The sinking of the *Maine* fit every plan they had.

In addition to the mines they had installed for the Spanish government, the *Evening Star* reported, the Weylerites had access to materials needed for any number of homemade mines. They had the knowledge to build a mine or to have one manufactured in a naval shop and they had the means to plant a mine under the moored *Maine*. The *Times* and the *World* ran similar articles. Placing the mine would have been "comparatively easy," the *Journal* wrote, because "boats of all descriptions were continually crossing in all directions."

When the *Maine* exploded, the Weylerites were not under police surveillance and had not been for weeks. After the burst, there was no roundup of suspects. The Spanish government feared that the Weylerites might have been responsible for the tragedy and that Spain would be held liable. Blanco made no arrest. He hoped the disaster had resulted from an accident, yet he could not be sure.

While higher Spanish officials in Havana made protestations of their grief over the *Maine*'s destruction, the Weylerites reacted with unconcealed jubilation. They responded with jeers, not sympathy. They foresaw the war they wanted. Blanco and the Liberals had been discredited. Weyler would become dictator of Spain.

Officers of the Volunteers said, "We have carried out our purpose that the *Maine* should not leave the port!" In an anti-American restaurant on Lamparilla Street, *sopa del Maine*—"*Maine* soup"—was on the menu for two days.

In Washington, Secretary Long ordered that the "colors no longer be at half-mast" after four days of mourning.

In Havana, Consul Lee was advising Americans to ship their families home. He was afraid that if a court of inquiry found Spain guilty of blowing up the *Maine*, Weylerites might attack Americans. He could no longer send for the *Maine* to quell a riot.

The Inquiry on the *Maine*

★ ★ ★ ★ ★ ★ ★ ★

FORMATION OF THE SAMPSON COURT

In the early days following the *Maine* explosions, U.S. public opinion was still divided concerning the cause of the catastrophe. Congressional views reflected the public division.

In the House, Chairman Robert Hitt of the Foreign Affairs Committee asked that people suspend judgment until the reason for the disaster was found. That was the administration line.

In the Senate, Chairman Eugene Hale of the Naval Committee stated that "it was an accident." Then, to the consternation of the navalists, he went beyond McKinley's position to add, "A battleship is little less than a volcano under the most favorable circumstances, and I always feel that a war vessel may prove to be almost as dangerous to those on board as to those it might engage in conflict." Senator Francis Warren agreed, complaining that "our naval vessels cannot make any move, cannot go up or down a stream or go out to sea, without grounding or having some other accident befall them." "Go down a stream" was a snide reference to Sigsbee's episode in the East River.

In opposition, New York's Congressman Amos Cummings echoed the jingoes. He insisted, "It was more reasonable to suppose that the *Maine* had been blown up than that for the first time in our history, one of our ships had blown up without external agency."

Despite their willingness to render these premature opinions, congressmen knew that Navy regulations provided for appointment of a court of inquiry to resolve questions of fact and responsibility whenever a warship like the *Maine* was lost. The problem was a general lack of confidence in naval courts. According to the *New York Herald*, a court considering the sinking of the *Maine* would merely direct Sigsbee to provide a confidential report concerning the disaster. His assessment would be read to a closed hearing in the presence of the court's members, the captain himself, and the surviving officers and crew.

There would be just two interrogatories, the *Herald* maintained. First, the court would ask the captain standing alone, "Is your narrative a true statement? Have you any complaint to make against any of the surviving officers or crew?" Following the receipt of satisfactory responses from Sigsbee, the court would ask the officers and crew as a group, "Have you anything to object to in the narrative? Have you anything to lay to the charge of any officer or man?" After the expected mass denial, the court would announce its finding that there had been no negligence attributable to Sigsbee, the surviving officers, or the crew. The *Herald* claimed that the court would then conclude the investigation without taking further testimony.

The *Herald* description was not entirely accurate, yet it indicated the kind of whitewash that Congress anticipated concerning the *Maine*. Senator William Mason of Illinois warned that "the people are coming to the conclusion that the real situation is being concealed from them." He was certain the "treacherous" Spaniards had bombed the battleship. Senator Hale of Maine added, "The American people are sick of these investigations behind closed doors. Are we to have a few distinguished naval officers in executive session hear testimony and give out as much of it as they like? The time has come when people want to know whether that ship was blown up by the enemies of the country or destroyed by spontaneous combustion."

The critical Congress was thus advising the reticent Navy to avoid secrecy, bias, and evasion. If the inquiry was held in camera to clear Captain Sigsbee and the Spanish government along the lines the *Herald* suggested, Congress would swiftly follow with its own investigation. The congressmen admonished the Navy that their hearings would be held in public, regardless of the outcome, and the whole world would listen.

To restrain Congress, Secretary Long acted quickly. He telegraphed Admiral Sicard at Key West to appoint a court of naval officers. The regulations provided that the court was to be composed of three members and a judge advocate to serve as prosecutor. At least one member was to be superior in rank to the officer being investigated. The New York *World* editorialized that "no Court of Inquiry has ever been burdened with a responsibility so grave, for upon its findings a declaration of war may be made."

Sicard was oblivious to the political significance of the inquiry. Instead of considering how closely scrutinized his appointments would be, he casually selected Captain French Ensor Chadwick, executive officer Lieutenant Commander William P. Potter, and two lower-rated officers. All were from Sicard's flagship and all were junior in rank to Sigsbee.

Because the composition of that court would clearly not have satisfied Congress, Long promptly overruled Sicard. The McKinley Administration wanted a finding that the explosion had been caused by self-ignition of coal. Nevertheless, the members had to have stature and had to appear to be without preconceptions. Chadwick who was an internationally known naval authority met those standards, as did his subordinate Potter. They were influenced, however, by their service on the spontaneous-combustion–prone *New York*. They had already indicated privately that in their opinion the *Maine*'s demise had been the result of a bunker fire.

The two officers of lesser rating had to be replaced, though, in favor of officers whose seniority would give the proceedings greater credibility. Sicard himself was too ill to serve. The obvious choice for president of the court was his heir apparent, the *Iowa*'s Captain William T. Sampson who appropriately ranked Sigsbee.

The final appointment was to be Lieutenant Commander Seaton Schroeder of the *Massachusetts* as judge advocate. The elegant Schroeder could also have been counted on to espouse the accident theory at this time, but Long recalled that Schroeder was unsuited to decide Wainwright's guilt because Wainwright was his brother-in-law. In Schroeder's place, Lieutenant Commander Adolph Marix was selected. Marix was just concluding his service as judge advocate in a routine Washington court-martial.

Long was sure that Congress would accept the members of this court. Sampson and Chadwick were beyond reproach. Nevertheless, he knew that three of the four members favored the accident theory and the fourth, Sampson, was one of the few senior officers on the scene who was not committed to the mine theory. Long felt he had the court stacked with the best officers to achieve McKinley's goals. The Secretary was considered to be honest, though he was a practiced politician who even tailored his nightly diary entries to fit his aspirations.

The jingoes had ears in Long's office in the person of Theodore Roosevelt. Yet they did not suspect the private views of the members of the court. Instead, they objected because the members were all line officers. There was no specialist in combustion or construction. The jingoes and the yellow press would have been happier with the inclusion of Captain Bradford and Constructor Hichborn who openly refuted the accident theory.

The Madrid government was also wary of the court. The Washington *Evening Star* reported, "Spain Distrusts Us" and "Madrid Papers Advise Surveillance," but the Spaniards had no reason to doubt Long. Their interests coincided in this matter.

The Secretary gave lip service to the jingoes and the Spaniards. In civilian trials, he pointed out, a judge may be guided by expert witnesses without himself being an expert. Here, Sampson was familiar with armament, armor, and explosives. Chadwick knew about construction and coal. Potter and Marix understood shipboard routine.

The preliminaries began with the appointment of the board of investigation headed by Sigsbee, assigned to recovering bodies and gathering evidence for the court. Meanwhile a precept was issued by Sicard on February 19, directing the members of the court to convene in Havana. They were to ascertain what the cause of the explosions had been, whether negligence occurred, and if so, who was responsible. The court was to report testimony taken, facts established, and whether further action against defendants was appropriate.

A second precept named Sigsbee, Wainwright, Lieutenant George F. M. Holman, the *Maine*'s ordnance officer, and the ship's chief engineer, Charles P. Howell. They were advised of their right to be present at hearings, to cross-examine witnesses, and to offer evidence. A third precept stated: "If it shall appear that others [outside the Navy] should be entitled to appear as defendants, they will be informed of their right as above." The reference could have been interpreted to include representatives of the Spanish government, but they were never told they were privileged to appear at the hearings.

The operative word was "defendants." That in effect was what Sigsbee was. His brilliant naval career was at risk before a court which Long had selected to find an accident that could well be charged to Sigsbee.

WHO WAS WHO ON THE COURT

Sampson was a man of conservative yet quick judgment who kept his own counsel. Admired "as a son of the plain people," he was born in 1840 on a modest farm in upstate New York. Although his schooling was regularly interrupted by farm chores, his intelligence and character were so outstanding that his congressman appointed him to the Naval Academy. He was typical of many poor young men who attended service academies because they were not otherwise able to afford higher education.

Sampson was elected student leader despite a lack of social connections. He graduated first in his class. After his initial cruise, he returned to the Academy to teach science. Younger men like Chadwick and Sigsbee deferred to him. Toward the end of the Civil War, he was executive officer of the Federal monitor *Patapsco* when the ship ran into a Confederate mine in Charleston harbor. "My first impression on hearing the explosion," Sampson reported, "was that a shot had struck the hull below the water line, but the column of smoke and water which immediately shot upward convinced me of the real nature of the explosion."

After the war he gained a reputation as "the most brilliant officer of his time." In 1867, he was reassigned to the Academy to create a Department of Physics and Chemistry. He taught advanced science, including the chemistry of explosives. Later he developed improvements in explosives as head of the Torpedo Station, was Superintendent of the Naval Academy, commanded the new cruiser *San Francisco*, and was ordnance inspector at the Washington Navy Yard where he procured the nickel-steel armor plate for the *Maine*. The officer he replaced at the yard said, "We talked of little else than ordnance."

Sampson was Chief of the Ordnance Bureau for four satisfying years. Then in June 1897 he was advanced over seventeen senior captains to command the battleship *Iowa*, the biggest vessel in the new Navy. He was a short man, though his erect bearing made him seem taller. His eyes were blue and there was gray in his hair and beard. "Provoked" was the most extreme emotion he ever expressed. On shipboard, he was a martinet, respected rather than loved.

No one would ever think that Sampson could be part of a kangaroo court.

He was a proud man who cared too much about his own reputation to be that considerate of others. Besides, he filled the bill for the *Maine* hearings. He had been blown up by a mine, explosives were his specialty, he was uncommitted, and accident-minded Chadwick was his friend.

Where Sampson was revered, Chadwick was admired. Both were representative of the new breed of scientific officers. They were not intimate with the more popular Sigsbee. When they spoke to him, they addressed him by his surname.

Four years younger than Sampson, Chadwick was born of pioneer ancestry in West Virginia. He entered the Naval Academy in 1861 and graduated fourth in his class. Beginning in 1878, he served in Europe. While naval attaché in London, he had a hand in procuring designs for the *Maine*. He was such a successful diplomat that Navy Secretary Tracy commended him.

As an official of the Society of Naval Architects and Marine Engineers, he was familiar with ship construction. In 1891 he was inspector of ships at the New York Navy Yard when the *Maine* was being built there. Two years later he was Chief of the Bureau of Equipment, supplying coal and other commodities to warships while Sampson was Ordnance Chief. Chadwick was given command of the flagship *New York* in 1897, a job Sigsbee had turned down. He was tall, burly, and imposing in appearance. His manner was direct and forceful.

Potter, the third member of the court, was an administrator. He was placed on the court to follow Chadwick in finding an accident.

Judge Advocate Marix had been born in Germany. He became a U.S. citizen, graduated from the Academy, served as executive officer of the *Maine*, and was attached to the Judge Advocate General's office. Most important to Secretary Long, he was known to favor the accident theory, like Chadwick and Potter.

REACTIONS AT HOME AND ABROAD

February 17 was a busy day in the United States and Cuban capitals. By then President McKinley, Secretary Long, and Consul Lee had joined Sigsbee in pleading for patience concerning the *Maine*. Long cabled Admiral Dewey in Hong Kong, "*Maine* destroyed at Havana by accident." The administration was trying to prevent "the inflammation of popular passion against

Spain," as former Secretary of State Olney put it in a letter to ex-President Cleveland.

The same day, the Spanish cruiser *Vizcaya* arrived off New York City to return the *Maine*'s visit to Havana. Her captain was unaware of the *Maine* disaster. Police patrolled the harbor shores and police boats circled the ship, but there was no demonstration. The conservative press saw the *Vizcaya*'s presence as a token of the Spanish government's innocence.

Also on the seventeenth, the city of Havana staged an elaborate funeral for the *Maine* dead. Sigsbee reported that "no greater showing of sympathy could have been made." He was relieved. He would have preferred sending the bodies to the United States if there had been an alternative. In the tropics, however, the dead had to be interred quickly. Embalmers were scarce and there were few metal coffins.

The first 19 of the 25 bodies that had been recovered were taken to City Hall and placed in wooden coffins covered with ornamental crowns made of woven silk ribbons. Cards bore expressions of sympathy. The coffins were shut because most of the dead had been mangled in the explosion.

Sigsbee had asked Chaplain Chidwick to get permission from the Bishop of Havana to have Protestant prayers read over the Protestant dead instead of the Roman Catholic service. However, no Protestant minister could be found. To ease his conscience, Sigsbee read the Book of Common Prayer to himself in his carriage on the way to the ceremony.

Interment was at five o'clock in the afternoon. Flags on public buildings were at half-mast. Private homes were draped in black. Five thousand Havana residents had walked behind the coffins in the funeral cortege while 50,000 lined the streets. Blanco did not participate. He cited ancient Spanish laws, but Sigsbee thought Blanco feared antagonizing the Weylerites.

Sigsbee's personal concern was that he had no uniform. An officer who owed him $45 paid by check and he remembered he had a week's supply of underclothes at a Havana laundry, yet he was compelled to attend the ceremony in a cheap civilian sack suit. He was perturbed to learn that reporters for the Havana newspapers mistook the uniformed William S. Cowles of the *Fern* for the captain *"del Vapor Maine."* The Spanish press questioned how all his uniforms could have gone down with the ship as he claimed if he had appeared in one of them.

U.S. citizens working in Havana expected to lose their jobs because of the coming war. They took a dim view of the cortege, considering it to be too ostentatious for sincerity. They maintained that "dead Americans were carried in a sort of triumphal procession through the streets for the edification and enjoyment of the Spanish population, to whom the occasion afforded as much pleasure as a bull fight."

The rest of the *Maine* dead would be buried with briefer ceremonies because the Spanish authorities were taking sole responsibility. Forty more bodies were brought ashore on February 17, and by the evening of the eighteenth, 135 bodies had been recovered. The corpses were in bad condition. One coffin held legs and arms that had belonged to ten different sailors.

In Washington, Navy Department officials were awakening to the disquieting thought that the United States currently had only six big warships in service in the Atlantic compared to seven in the Spanish fleet. The naval advantage was now with Spain, but even if the two fleets had been evenly balanced, no American army could invade Cuba. Retired Captain Alfred Mahan, a leading authority on naval affairs, emphasized that "it would be foolish to land in the islands, men we might be compelled by an unlucky sea fight to abandon there."

In addition, Roosevelt was concerned because the Speaker of the House and the Chairman of the Senate Naval Committee were advocating a halt to the construction of more battleships. The commitment for ironclads had been $35,000,000, they complained, and the *Maine* had not even survived peacetime explosions. Roosevelt believed that the loss of the *Maine* was merely one price the United States had to pay to become a great naval power.

Like Roosevelt, Captain Mahan saw that congressional doubts had to be overcome. He insisted that "there are risks in battleships which have to be taken. Naval officers are accustomed to living over a magazine and eating their meals within a dozen yards of the powder, but the remoteness of danger is understood by them and precautions are taken. Because the effects of an explosion are fearful, you cannot assume that the danger of an explosion is great."

Mahan added that "the present battleship is not a sudden invention but the outcome of evolution over forty years. Development has been governed by experience, showing defects or suggesting improvements." What would be learned from the *Maine* disaster would go into the planning of new ships.

The jingoes' position prevailed. The naval budget had been cut early in

February. Now, though, Congress rebuffed the Speaker and the chairman to loosen the purse strings. As part of a new appropriation, $200,000 was allocated for recovery of bodies and for raising or otherwise working on the wreck.

The shallowness of Havana harbor favored raising the *Maine* despite the fact that no submerged battleship of her size had ever been dewatered. The *Texas* had sunk at her dock, but because there had not been enough water to cover her, dewatering had taken only a day. Salvaging the smaller British ship *Howe* in Cadiz, Spain, had consumed more than six months.

Two methods of raising the *Maine* were discussed in the newspapers. Using derricks was said to be hopeless. The wreck was too heavy. Alternately, wreckers might be able to pass chains under the keel from pontoons on one side to the other. Getting chains under the wreck would require months, however, and might be impossible.

Secretly McKinley had already acknowledged to his cabinet that war was probably coming. Long admitted years later that "it was manifest that the loss of the *Maine* would inevitably lead to war, even if Spain were innocent. Time was necessary, however, to enable completion of our preparedness for combat." Faced with imminent hostilities, Long would not initiate any long-term project such as trying to raise the *Maine* in Havana.

At the moment, the American people were more involved with sentimental trivia about the *Maine* than they were with serious matters. As an example, an apprentice on the *Texas* who had been scheduled for transfer to the *Maine* observed, "Chaplain, if it had not been for Providence, I might not be here now, as I see every boy that left the *Indiana* but two are missing, and maybe our crowd would have suffered a similar fate." The Chaplain remarked that the experience "made different boys of them all."

The press ran countless features concerning the *Maine* disaster. In a *Times* article headed "Touching Scene in Court," an old man was excused from jury duty because his son had "Gone Down on the *Maine*." The *Journal* noted that the Hewitt "vegetable party" of New York socialites was not postponed. Rich men costumed as plants danced while poor mothers mourned the *Maine*'s casualties.

In Havana, Tom, the big tabby cat that was the pet of the *Maine*'s crew, was found on the wreck three days after the explosions. He had been too frightened to move from his hiding place. Similarly, Sigsbee was quoted as saying that his dog Peggy "trembled with fear long after she had been taken off the *Maine*."

SPAIN'S RESPONSIBILITY

Within a few days after the catastrophe American newspapers were speculating about whether the Spanish government was legally responsible for the loss of the *Maine* and her crew. The issues involving monetary damages as well as criminal charges did not have clear sailing through the murky waters of international law. Experts agreed that the *Maine* had entered Havana harbor in compliance with Spanish port regulations. Also, the *Maine* was entitled to protection as an extension of United States territory. From then on, conclusions were conflicting.

The most quoted lawyer was Robert Todd Lincoln, the oldest son of the wartime president and a former Secretary of War. His opinion was that Spain was not responsible unless a Spanish agent brought about the disaster. "Assuming the cause was a mine exploded by a fanatic or by accident," he stated, "that would be the end of the affair." Lincoln presented what Roosevelt would have called the Spanish side of the question.

The most eminent dissenter was Professor Hermann Von Holst of the University of Chicago, who declared that "culpable negligence" would be enough to find Spain guilty. The Spanish authorities were responsible for "due diligence," even where Spain did not act through an agent. An instance of "due diligence," according to the *Times*, was the protection the *Vizcaya* had received in New York City. In comparison, "there was no patrol on guard" in Havana.

Modern jurists look to whether the cause was external or internal. If the *Maine* had been destroyed by Weylerites or insurgents, Spain would be responsible because it failed to protect the warship from external threats. On the other hand, if the *Maine* had exploded due to an internal accident, Spain had no liability.

The problem was to find the facts. In this search Spain rushed to the front, a hare to the American tortoise. Less than an hour after the explosions, Admiral Vicente Manterola ordered his aide, Captain Peral y Caballero, to investigate the disaster. Peral was on the scene examining Spanish witnesses while the *Maine* was burning and Secretary Long was asleep in his hotel.

The next morning, the Spanish Minister of Colonies cabled General

Blanco that "it would be advisable to prove the *Maine* catastrophe cannot be attributed to us." A passenger on the *City of Washington* sneered that the Spaniards could arrest a couple of Cubans, convict them on perjured testimony, and shoot them. The passenger did not understand, however, that Spain might still remain liable. Consequently, Peral was directed to prove that the explosions were the result of an internal accident. Then no one could charge Spain with responsibility.

To aid Peral, the aggressive Admiral Manterola confronted Sigsbee in the Hotel Inglaterra on the sixteenth. He told Sigsbee he had ordered a Spanish investigation. Sigsbee later recalled that he had responded candidly to show he was not concerned about negligence. According to Sigsbee, the admiral was interested only in proving that the cause of the disaster was an accident. He volunteered nothing about Spanish mines.

Manterola inquired first if dynamo boilers had exploded. Sigsbee advised him that the *Maine* had only the conventional round Scotch boilers. Manterola asked whether the steam boilers were near the forward magazines adjacent to the coal bunkers. Sigsbee explained that no forward boiler had been lit for months. Next, Manterola observed that modern gunpowders were unstable. Sigsbee responded that the *Maine*'s powder was the old brown prismatic kind. Finally, Manterola said the *Maine*'s plans showed that the guncotton magazine was forward, near the explosions. Sigsbee replied that those early designs had been changed. Manterola had admitted implicitly, though, that the Spanish government possessed the *Maine*'s official plans.

This was verbal fencing, with Manterola assuming the role of tough guy. Sigsbee was finding it hard to tolerate the admiral's steady probing, despite his resolution that "I must keep a stiff upper lip and sacrifice myself absolutely, root and branch, in every sense." When Manterola asked Sigsbee what his own views were concerning the explosions, Sigsbee was impolitic enough to reply that "a few persons of evil disposition, with conveniences at hand, could have blown up the *Maine* from the outside, if so inclined."

The direct response was not the discreet Spanish way. Manterola was visibly angered. While the Spaniard's aide and interpreter tried to soothe him, Sigsbee modified his statement slightly by saying, "Any investigation which did not consider all possible exterior causes as well as interior causes would not be accepted." The admiral acknowledged the concession courteously. Then he left abruptly.

The next day, February 17, Manterola began applying pressure. Sigsbee had requested the *Alfonso XII*'s captain to keep intruders off the *Maine*. That was done. This morning, however, the Spanish captain in charge of the patrol boat refused to allow Sigsbee to board the wreck to hoist the U.S. flag until he secured permission. The excuse was that Sigsbee was in civilian clothes, but the issue was much deeper.

The Spanish officer told Sigsbee that the order to deny him access to the wreck came from Manterola. Sigsbee knew enough maritime law to realize that Manterola was trying to establish that the Americans had abandoned the wreck. The crew had been removed. The flag had been lowered before the explosions. Although Sigsbee's own pennant was flying, Manterola maintained by his actions that now the *Maine* belonged to Spain.

Sigsbee could not request a pass because that would have acknowledged Spanish sovereignty over the wreck. Instead of arguing with Manterola, he asked Lee to make an immediate appointment with General Blanco. At the meeting, Sigsbee put on his lawyer's hat and "reminded Blanco that the *Maine* had entered the port with at least implied consent, that having so entered she was under the protection of the Spanish government and entitled to extra-territorial courtesy and to exemptions from local jurisdiction and control. While my pennant was flying at the masthead, Admiral Manterola had undertaken to say when I could visit my command."

All Sigsbee's rehearsed arguments were, however, wasted. Blanco had been waiting for him. The general indicated at once that the reason for denial of access was to show Sigsbee that the Americans needed Spanish cooperation. Blanco wanted to bring up a more serious matter in a receptive atmosphere. In return for access, what he was seeking was a joint investigation of the cause of the explosions. He visualized Spanish and American officers sitting as one court, with Spanish and American divers going into the wreck together. Spanish laws required a Spanish inquiry, he declared, and Spanish honor was involved.

Sigsbee was still smarting from Manterola's public restraint of his right to board his ship. He responded sharply that he "did not believe the United States would consent to a joint investigation, although the government would desire that Spain should have an opportunity to make an independent investigation." He was hoodwinking the old Spanish soldier by acting as if both sides had already agreed to the United States's retention of sovereignty over the *Maine*. Then he applied that sovereignty to offer Spain access to the wreck under American rules. Everything outside the wreck was to remain under Spanish control.

Blanco accepted Sigsbee's interpretation. Controversy might have precipitated war. He ordered Manterola to allow the Americans to board the wreck in exchange for Lee's promise to refer to Washington the Spaniard's petition for a joint inquiry. Sigsbee saw he had won, so he quickly ended the meeting.

By restricting U.S. sovereignty to the body of the wreck, Sigsbee had relinquished only the right to examine the harbor bottom for wires from electric mines. Blanco gave up the whole game. He yielded dominion over the wreck without securing a joint investigation. Sigsbee had an American flag brought to the *Maine* right away, hoisted, and then hauled down to half-mast. There the flag remained until the last American sailor left Havana, just before the war, although the national ensign is usually lowered at sundown on U.S. warships and is not raised again until the next morning.

Lee did forward Blanco's proposal to Washington. Much to his surprise, the request was taken seriously. The McKinley Administration understood that allowing Spain to participate in the inquiry would make it more likely that Spain would be found innocent. The *Journal* reported on February 19 that "Spain has requested representation in the Court and among the divers. President McKinley, Secretary Long, and Judge Day have no objection, and naval officials say representation would be only fair because Spain is a suspect."

The *Times* observed that Blanco was correct when he said local authorities are required to investigate any wreck in their jurisdiction. If the *Maine* explosions were external, Spanish divers could not destroy the evidence. If the explosions were internal, Spanish officers would be glad to join in the finding.

Two jingoes gave the deathblow to Blanco's request. The first was Senator Mason who was to Congress what yellow journalism was to the American press. Mason offered a resolution to take the inquiry away from the Navy if Spanish members joined the court. He claimed that he would not be willing to serve on any joint body, "as he would not sit at the table with a Spaniard who might have a stiletto under his clothes."

To this emotional complaint, Roosevelt added reason. A joint court, he said, would be politically unwise. He told McKinley through Long that "we never could convince the people-at-large" of the accuracy of a joint finding for an accident. "Our critics would undoubtedly seize upon a joint investigation as an excuse for asserting that we were afraid to find out the exact facts."

Privately Roosevelt told Cowles, "I put in my oar with great emphasis as to the joint inquiry, and I think I was largely instrumental in preventing it being done." Even if a mine caused the explosions, he explained, the Spanish members would nevertheless claim the cause was accidental. To resolve the issue, the Spaniards would call for international arbitration which the United States would lose because of foreign prejudice.

On February 20, McKinley announced that in line with established governmental policy, Spain would not be permitted to participate in the U.S. inquiry. The statement came as a surprise to newspapermen.

McKinley then told the Spanish chargé d'affaires that he felt "it will produce a better effect on public opinion to have the Spanish and American reports published separately, although it is believed and hoped that both will be identical." The chargé thought he had "been successful in having Sigsbee and Lee afford facilities to the Spanish divers to examine the wreck, but independently of the Americans." He was led to understand that if the Americans discovered anything indicating an external cause of injury to the *Maine*, Spain would be given an opportunity to examine the evidence.

McKinley had lulled Spain into believing as he did that the court would find for an accident. The *Times* reported, "Spaniards Satisfied with Our Fairness." The *Journal* wrote that McKinley's announcement "gave general satisfaction."

Roosevelt was the only one who comprehended what a meaningful change he had accomplished in the probable outcome of the inquiry.

The U.S. Battleship *Maine* at Havana, Feb. 14, 1898. (From a painting by Henry Reuterdahl, copyright 1898 by P. F. Collier. Authors' collection.)

General Valeriano Weyler, "the most cruel and bloodthirsty general in the world." (Reprinted from Murat Halstead, *The Story of Cuba.* Chicago: The Werner Co., 1896, p. 89.)

General Ramon Blanco, "the proverbial Spanish don." (Reprinted from Charles D. Sigsbee, *The "Maine."* New York: The Century Co., 1899, p. 52.)

General Fitzhugh Lee, our man in Havana. (Reprinted from Charles D. Sigsbee, *The "Maine."* New York: The Century Co., 1899, p. 8.)

The frames of the *Maine*, a "made in the U.S.A." ship. (Reprinted from the cover of *Scientific American*, Oct. 5, 1889.)

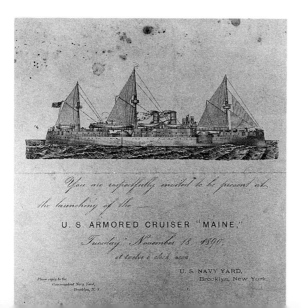

Formal invitation from the Secretary of the Navy erroneously referring to the *Maine* as a cruiser and reproducing the original design with three masts and fore-and-aft sails. (Reproduced from authors' collection.)

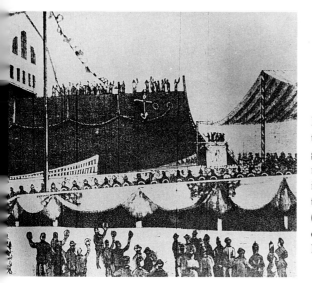

Miss Alice Wilmerding, the thirteen-year-old granddaughter of the Secretary of the Navy, breaking a champagne bottle on the bow of the *Maine*. (Reprinted from the cover of *Scientific American*, Nov. 9, 1890.)

The *Maine* started down the ways, and at 12:50 P.M. the battleship was at rest in Wallabout Channel. (Reprinted from the cover of *Scientific American*, Nov. 29, 1890.)

Executive Officer Lieutenant Commander Adolf Marix in his office on the *Maine*. (Reprinted from Charles D. Sigsbee, *The "Maine."* New York: The Century Co., 1899, p. 12.)

The *Maine* in drydock before leaving for Havana. (Reprinted from Charles D. Sigsbee, *The "Maine."* New York: The Century Co., 1899, p. 27.)

The Morro Castle, entrance to Havana Harbor. (Reprinted from W. Nephew King, *The Story of the Spanish-American War.* New York: Peter Fendon Collier & Son, 1900, p. 27.)

Lieutenant-Commander Richard Wainright who overstated Spanish preparedness. (Reprinted from Charles D. Sigsbee, *The "Maine."* New York: The Century Co., 1899, p. 168.)

Captain Charles Dwight Sigsbee in full dress uniform. (Reprinted from Charles D. Sigsbee, *The "Maine."* New York: The Century Co., 1899, frontispiece.)

"From the deck forward of amidships shot a streak of fire as high as the tall buildings on Broadway." (Reprinted from *Leslie's Official History of the Spanish-American War*, 1899, p. 70.)

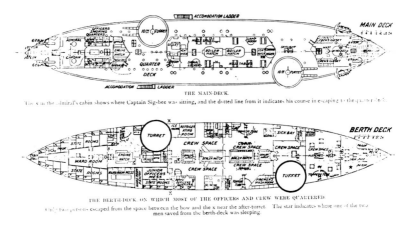

The crew quarters were on the berth deck and the officer's and the captain's quarters were on the main deck. (Reprinted from Charles D. Sigsbee, *The "Maine."* New York: The Century Co., 1899, p. 70.)

"There was the rumble of an explosion and the *Maine* seemed to leap into the air." (Reprinted from James Rankin Young, *History of Our War with Spain*. N.p.: J. R. Young, 1898, p. 31.)

The poop deck was the last foothold on the ship. (Reprinted from Charles D. Sigsbee, *The "Maine."* New York: 1899, p. 72.)

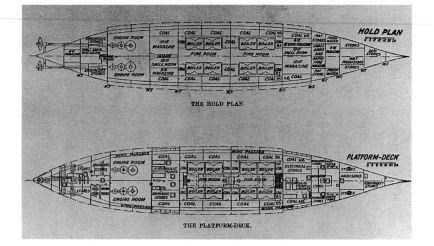

Left: "*Maine* blown up in Havana harbor," Sigsbee's report in pencil on letterhead of the New York and Cuba Mail Steamship Company. (Reprinted from Charles D. Sigsbee, *The "Maine."* New York: The Century Co., 1899, p. 76.) *Below:* Detailed descriptions of the hold plan were provided in the newspapers. (Reprinted from Charles D. Sigsbee, *The "Maine."* New York: The Century Co., 1899, p. 79.)

THE HOLD PLAN.

THE PLATFORM-DECK.

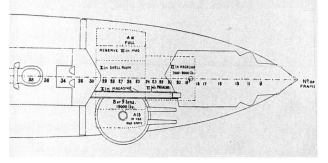

Only the forward magazines were involved in the *Maine* disaster. (Reproduced from authors' collection.)

Right: Members of the court of investigation on board the *Mangrove*: Left to right, Lieutenant-Commander Potter, Captain Sampson, Lieutenant-Commander Marix, and Captain Chadwick. (Reproduced from authors' collection.) *Below:* Sigsbee had an American flag brought to the *Maine*, hoisted and then hauled down to half-mast. (Reproduced from authors' collection.)

A wrecking boat lifting a great gun from the debris of the *Maine*. (Reprinted from *Leslie's Official History of the Spanish-American War*, 1899, p. 82.)

Left: Ensign W. V. N. Powelson busied himself with observing the divers around the wreck. (Reprinted from Charles D. Sigsbee, *The "Maine."* New York: The Century Co., 1899, p. 128.) ***Below:*** Sigsbee sent the divers for the shell-room key that hung on a hook near the ceiling at the foot of his bed. (Reprinted from Charles D. Sigsbee, *The "Maine."* New York: The Century Co., 1899, p. 131.)

Divers after a day's work. (Reprinted from *Harper's Pictorial History of the War with Spain*. New York: Harper and Brothers, 1899, p. 84.)

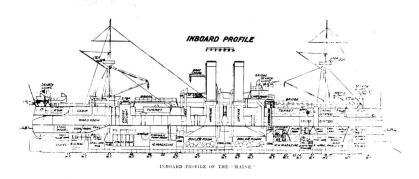

INBOARD PROFILE OF THE "MAINE"

The star near the foremast shows the height to which some keel plates were blown, and the dotted line shows the lifting of the keel. (Reprinted from Charles D. Sigsbee, *The "Maine."* New York: The Century Co., 1899, p. 67.)

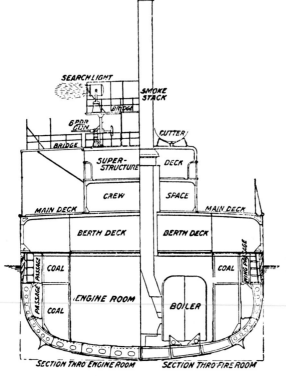

SEARCH LIGHT

SMOKE STACK

BRIDGE

6 PDR GUN

BRIDGE

CUTTER

SUPER-STRUCTURE DECK

CREW SPACE

MAIN DECK MAIN DECK

BERTH DECK BERTH DECK

COAL COAL

WING PASSAGE

PASSAGE PASSAGE

ENGINE ROOM BOILER

COAL

SECTION THRO ENGINE ROOM SECTION THRO FIRE ROOM

MIDSHIP SECTION.

Left: Cross-section view of the *Maine* showing wing passages. "I have never gone through [the wing passages] without putting my hand on to feel the temperature." (Reprinted from Charles D. Sigsbee, *The "Maine."* New York: The Century Co., 1899, p. 73.)
Below: Powelson's sketch of the elevated keel. (Reprinted from H. W. Wilson, *The Downfall of Spain.* Middletown: Wesleyan University, 1900, p. 26.)

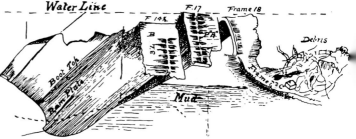

Water Line

F 17 Frame 18

F 14½

B 37½ 57½

Debris

Boot Top

Bottom Plate

Mud

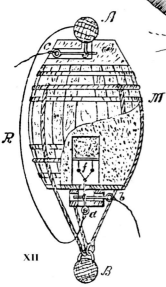

A mine of this kind could have been planted in broad daylight. (Reprinted from C. Sleeman, *Torpedoes and Torpedo Warfare.* Portsmouth: Griffin & Co., 1889, detail of plate 11.)

XII

Right: During the dewatering of the *Maine*, human remains were collected and mementos for patriotic organizations were chosen. (Reprinted from *Scientific American*, Sept. 2, 1911, cover.) *Below:* Vreeland board exhibit C1 showing damage. Decks and cabin floors were covered with three to five feet of mud, oyster shells, barnacles and coral encrustations; the stench was overwhelming. Human bones were scattered about. (Photograph courtesy National Archives, Record Group no. 80.)

SIXTY-SEVENTH YEAR

SCIENTIFIC AMERICAN

THE WEEKLY JOURNAL OF PRACTICAL INFORMATION

VOLUME CV.
NUMBER 10

NEW YORK, SEPTEMBER 2, 1911

10 CENTS A COPY
$3.00 A YEAR

This dramatic photograph was taken from the cofferdam wall, from a point dead astern of the "Maine," when the wreck had been partially unwatered. Captain —now Rear-admiral— Sigsbee and his officers were in this portion of the ship at the time of the explosion. It remains to-day structurally intact.

THE "MAINE," NOW PARTIALLY EXPOSED, ENCRUSTED WITH BARNACLES, AFTER THIRTEEN YEARS UNDER WATER.—[See page 216.]

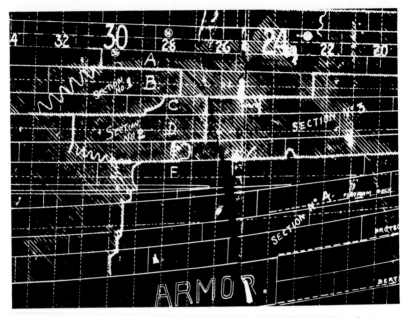

Detail of Exhibit G of the Vreeland report showing outer bottom plating from frames 34 to 20 with the breaks shown as solid lines and bends as wavy lines. (Diagram courtesy of the National Archives, Record Group no. 80.)

Vreeland board Exhibit D3 shows the plating over the center of B strake was twisted and the forward end displaced upward approximatly six feet above its original position. (Photograph courtesy of the National Archives, Record Group no. 80.)

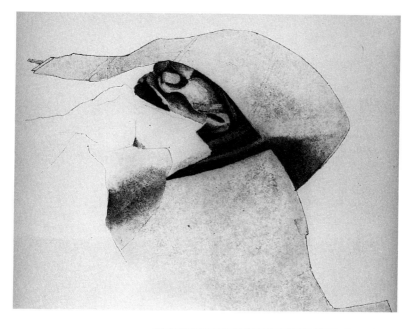

Above: Vreeland board Exhibit Q is a perspective sketch of the plating shown in Exhibit D3. (Photograph courtesy of National Archives, Record Group no. 80.) *Right:* "From the masthead floated the biggest navy ensign" ever seen. (Reprinted from *Scientific American*, March 30, 1912, cover.)

The last view of the *Maine*. She sank out of sight at 5:30 P.M. (Reprinted from *Congressional Record: Final Report on Removing Wreck of Battleship "Maine" from Habana, Cuba*. 63rd Cong., 2d sess., document no. 480, plate 68.)

Getting the Inquiry Started

★ ★ ★ ★ ★ ★ ★ ★

WHAT THE SAMPSON COURT SAW

On February 18 Blanco confirmed Manterola's appointment of Captain Peral y Caballero to investigate the *Maine* disaster. Through official channels, Peral then requested that Lee let him take testimony from the *Maine*'s officers and allow his divers to inspect the wreck. Lee never replied, although he knew Peral needed information from the officers to be effective. The Spanish divers would presumably be granted access routinely after the bodies and confidential documents were removed.

By the twentieth Peral was at a standstill. He released a preliminary report based on what could be seen from the surface, concluding that the *Maine* had been destroyed by an internal explosion. Not having heard from Lee, he asked Manterola how to obtain U.S. cooperation.

Spanish authorities were beginning to suspect they had been deceived. Americans in Havana were not living up to promises made in Washington. Madrid newspapers warned that in response to this breach, Blanco might refuse to allow American divers to descend without Spanish counterparts. At first Manterola did put petty obstacles in the way of the American divers, until a sharp protest to Blanco ended Spanish hindrances.

In Florida, the old lighthouse tender *Mangrove* had been readied for Sampson. The court's three members were in Key West, though Marix was not able to take the train from Washington until the eighteenth. The small steamer sailed for Havana with the full court at four o'clock in the afternoon of the twentieth, one day after the precept was issued. At sunrise on February 21, the tender anchored in the harbor between the *Fern* and the *Bache*. The

Fern housed the *Maine*'s officers, the *Bache* the divers, and the *Mangrove* the court. The three small vessels formed a modest American enclave around the wreck.

The *Maine* was the focus of all eyes and thoughts. She was no longer recognizable as the trim white battleship she had been. The keel had settled deeper into the mud. At the forward end of the wreckage, the deck had been torn loose from the port side and turned back in a tangled heap. The tremendous upheaval had thrown 10-inch guns into the bay. The big forward funnel had fallen onto what remained of the steel deck. From the funnel aft, the ship was relatively undamaged. The stern searchlight and one rapid-fire gun on the superstructure deck were in place.

The mainmast had stayed upright. In the bird's-eye view from the little platform fifty feet above the water, the superstructure deck aft was awash. Amidships was a mass of twisted steel. Forward, only the tips of three heaps of crumpled metal were visible.

A tour around the wreck in a launch showed the members of the court how massive the blast had been. The forward third of the central superstructure had been blown back and was bottoms up, with pilothouse, conning tower, and captain's bridge underneath.

Soon Sigsbee arrived from the Inglaterra. He provided the final orientation of the morning, pointing out that the *Maine* had never parted from her mooring. She had taken the buoy with her when the bow section sank. Sigsbee identified the broad white upper surface of the wreck as the ceiling of the berth deck where sailors had swung their hammocks. He thought he could see faint impressions that bodies had made when they were crushed to death against the ceiling.

He was depressed. He had been visiting the two hospitals on shore the previous evening. The few sailors who remained there were too seriously injured to be moved. He told the members that the wounded men had been delighted to see him: "One who was at death's door said to me, 'I'm sorry this thing came upon you, Captain.' I braced them with cheering words.

"Poor little Koebler the nicest Apprentice I ever saw and the most popular little fellow aboard ship was delirious but knew me away off. He kept calling for me, 'Captain, I don't think you ought to leave me here. I can go aboard ship to recover.' I said I would not leave him behind. 'But you are going to take the *Maine* to New Orleans and I am able to go in her.' I quieted him by saying that I would not take the *Maine* to New Orleans because two other ships were sent there in place of the *Maine*. Poor little fellow! He died at midnight."

Between the damaged and the dead, the court had a sobering introduction to Havana harbor.

ESTABLISHING PROCEDURES

To pacify Congress, Secretary Long indicated that the court's hearings would be open to the press. Naval courts, he remarked, are conducted in public view. As old Rear Admiral Henry Erben told journalists February 18, "Will the Inquiry be behind closed doors? I guess not. We don't do business that way. We have no secrets to guard. All we want is the truth."

The Secretary was concerned, however, about the leverage that other naval officers and jingoes might apply to members propounding the accident theory in open hearings. On the twentieth, Long announced that one of the court's first deliberations would be to determine whether the Spanish government was accountable for the disaster. He said findings about foreign nations had to be made in private. Congress did not object.

The next day Long declared that all proceedings would be "strictly secret." Naval regulations, he prevaricated, precluded publication of any testimony until the inquiry was over. Congress remained silent and the hearings were closed.

In Havana, the court was establishing its procedures. Sessions would be held in the commander's cabin on the *Mangrove*. Members were not in the formal dress they would have worn in open hearings. Rather, they wore regular workaday uniforms. In addition to members and the judge advocate, only defendants, witnesses, and the court reporter were admitted to the cabin. The reporter was to transcribe his shorthand notes when the hearings were adjourned for the purpose.

There was no timetable. Naval officers expected the investigation to last at least a month. Admiral Erben maintained that "it is useless to form any opinion until we hear from the divers. They will not be able to tell much because they will not be able to see well. The waters of Havana Bay are as black as coal. What is far better is to wait until the wreckers have examined the ship. You want to lift her out of the water and then look at her. You can go into the magazine and see just what did explode. Not until then can you determine with any degree of accuracy the cause of the explosion."

Despite the admiral's opinion, raising the *Maine* was not a possibility. There were a few divers on every warship, however, whose skills ran to examining a vessel's bottom and disentangling cables from propeller shafts in clear water. Half a dozen of them had been brought to Havana. Correspondents in lighters could see these divers descend one at a time alongside the wreck and then surface after long intervals. The first underwater assignment was to secure the Navy code book because Washington feared the loss of the ciphers to the Spaniards. Next the divers were directed to Sigsbee's "secret drawer for certain secret papers."

Sigsbee had side benefits from the search. He commented that his "watch was in the drawer and was recovered. This is the third time it has been down in salt water. Twice it has been under in Cuba. I have also recovered my gig's pennant. My decoration and gold medal have not yet been got up, but my bicycle has."

The *New York Times* reported that after reclaiming the official items, four divers were told to retrieve bodies. Not trained to go deeper than twenty feet, they suffered bad falls because of poor visibility and mud. They were not accustomed to creeping on slippery steel floors in the dark and groping for doors to narrow passages. The *Mangrove* supplied electric lights on long cords, but the divers said the appliances were unwieldy and a nuisance.

The twelve corpses brought up on the twenty-first were dismembered to get them out of the wreck. As portions of bodies rose to the surface, a Spanish patrol boat towed them to the barge where they were prepared for burial in the Havana cemetery. Reporters who went aboard the barge warned that the bodies were an increasingly sickening sight. They were in pieces, burned, and crushed. Few were identifiable.

Some divers gave fanciful details. One insisted that scores of corpses were still floating around sections of the berth deck. Many were twisted in hammocks with their arms extended upward. The diver claimed that the men had been startled and were reaching to unhook their hammocks when death came. He claimed that this confirmed there had been two explosions. The first made the men raise their arms and the second killed them in the act. The article was published as truth in the conservative *Herald* before any diver entered the berth deck.

The yellow press went further. The *Journal* reported a diver's word that new proofs of Spanish treachery had been found in magazines below. In fact, no inspection of the hold had been made. The public was led to believe in Spanish guilt before the inquiry began.

The divers were spared one horror. The Spanish warship *Sanchez Barcastegui* had been wrecked at the entrance to the harbor ten years earlier. When the crew jumped into the sea, they were attacked by sharks. Fortunately for the divers, the *Maine* disaster took place within the harbor and the explosions' magnitude frightened away any shark.

THE PENDULUM STARTS SWINGING BACK

The court began closed hearings on the day of arrival. From then on, correspondents had to search hard for fresh material or they had to create news. The man from the *Times* reported that he was handed Sigsbee's watch to be repaired. The second hand and part of the hour hand were missing, presumably from an earlier mishap, and the watch read twenty minutes after four. Such trifles constituted the day's news.

As president of the court Captain Sampson announced that every *Maine* survivor in Havana and Key West would be interrogated. The first witness was Sigsbee. At the end of his appearance, he told the *Times* only that he had answered all questions. He was equally cautious in his letters home, saying that "I gave my testimony yesterday. Not one thing has shown bad discipline, and everything shows great care. I cannot permit myself to state the cause of the explosion yet."

He acted confident, maintaining that "I keep a clear head," but he acknowledged being "very tired, having had a laxity of the bowels for three days. I think I am rather better today." The improvement in his health came after his testimony was given without any hitch that he could see.

Influenced by the high regard the Navy Department displayed for the fifty-three-year-old New Yorker, the U.S. press continued to treat Sigsbee as a hero. The *Times* wrote that he "conducted himself as an officer should. His tone is that of a discreet and level-headed man."

After interviewing *Maine* sailors in Key West, the *Times* also stated that "all stories of lack of discipline are without a shadow of truth. On the contrary, Captain Sigsbee was complained of by some for the rigidity of his rules and the strictness with which he enforced them. Moreover, the *Maine* never had a serious accident until anchored in [Havana] harbor."

To the Spanish newspapers, though, Sigsbee was the eternal enemy. *La Lucha*, the ultra-Spanish organ in Havana, printed the canard that he was not on the *Maine* when she was blown up. A *La Lucha* editorial charged the United States Navy with "unfairness in making Sigsbee the advisor of the Court of Inquiry when he was on trial himself and had no right to take an active part in the *Maine* investigation. In any other country, the first official proceeding would be to court-martial him." Spanish law did not allow equivalent latitude to a defendant.

In addition to his legal rights, Sigsbee made the most of his rank. In the evenings he no longer retired to the Inglaterra with Lee. He remained on the *Mangrove* to mix socially with the members of the court and with Marix who had been his subordinate. Sigsbee noted that the judge advocate brought him joyous tidings.

Marix had just passed through Key West where he talked to the *Maine's* officers waiting to be questioned. Sigsbee wrote that "Marix says the officers say good things of me, that he never heard any officer so praised. I'm glad of that, of course."

Also, "Marix says that Peggy is the sensation of Key West. I sent her over for safe keeping. Marix called on Peggy and found that she was having her picture taken for the New York *World*. When she returned she recognized Marix and was wildly glad to see him. According to report, she is being dreadfully spoiled." Sigsbee assumed his standing with the court was good if the judge advocate flattered his dog.

This happier time for Sigsbee was the last day of the Lenten carnival in Havana. The idea was beginning to get across that no blame would be attached to Sigsbee. His image in the United States was of a courageous captain who had insisted on being the last to leave his burning ship.

There was only one complaint against Sigsbee in the press. He now hinted that there had been a Spanish mine under the *Maine*. Why had he not been suspicious before the disaster when he could have sent a diver to search the bottom of the bay? The answer he suggested was that he had been satisfied there was no mine threat until after the explosions. His intelligence officer and Lee had misled him. Moreover, he had been on a peaceful mission, under orders to make the visit friendly. Setting up the pumping apparatus in the heavy diving boat would have antagonized the Spaniards. He implied that the McKinley Administration was to blame for misreading the dangers, not him.

In Washington, the accident theory some officials had espoused was fading. When Lee heard confidentially about the court's reaction to Sigsbee's testimony, he cabled the State Department, "Evidence beginning to prove explosion on port side by torpedo." He meant "by mine."

Also, Professor Alger's conclusion that an outside explosion could not detonate gunpowder in a magazine was being challenged by more experts than Maxim. According to an article in the *Herald*, the English had proved that twenty-five pounds of guncotton in a contact mine would burst through the double bottom of an ironclad. The energy developed in the burst would "react with enormous secondary effect upon other explosives in the vicinity." Thus, the concussion from a mine could blow up a magazine.

The war spirit was intensifying in the United States. Charles Cramp, the shipbuilder, declared that the American people would repudiate a court finding that the disaster was due to an accident. In Key West, the surviving *Maine* crewmen announced they would join the Cuban insurgents to fight Spain if the court cleared the Spaniards of complicity. If no action was taken against Spain, they maintained, "not a man among them would again pace the deck of an American man-of-war."

On the other hand, there were more volunteers to enlist in the Navy than there were vacancies arising from the *Maine* dead. In Passaic, New Jersey, ten-year-old boys armed with popguns and a small American flag formed a paramilitary company to search for Spaniards.

In New York City, the war scare caused a steep stock market decline. Newspapers played on readers' emotions. Scovel wrote an article in the *World* that produced nightmares. He reported that "I saw one vulture picking, with muscular jerks of his scaly neck, portions of the body of a man just risen." In contrast, the *Times* headline was, "Watches for Her Dead Brother." He had been a sailor on the *Maine* and she gazed all day at the *Vizcaya* in the bay. Another headline was, "Double Wedding Prevented." The *Maine* disaster had ended a tortuous story of lovers' quarrels and separations. One of the husbands-to-be was dead in the wreck.

The demand was rising for retribution against Spain. The pressure on the Navy Department to do something positive was becoming significant. Naval officers wanted the *Maine*'s hull raised and towed out of Havana harbor as a matter of pride. Reluctant Secretary Long was forced to start negotiations with a civilian wrecking company, although dewatering could not even begin until the court was through investigating the wreck.

Long's pace was not fast enough for the press. He was described as "Haggling with Wreckers While the Nation's Dear Are Without a Tomb." The *World* reported on the twenty-second that "the contract for raising the *Maine* and towing her to the Brooklyn Navy Yard has not yet been completed. This is despite the bodies of the entombed sailors and secure evidence upon which war may depend. The wreckers propose to remove all equipment that will come away and then the ship will be floated either by caissons or by pumping the water out of the compartments." Caissons were pontoons to be attached to the sides of the sunken *Maine* and pumped free of water so they would lift the ship without the need to drag chains under the keel. The wreckers were professionally optimistic. The chance of success, however, was slim.

The next day, February 23, the contract was signed. Sigsbee expected the wrecking crew to be under his direction but Wainwright received the assignment. Sigsbee never questioned the slight. He knew wreckers would be among the last to leave Havana. Wainwright would have to remain with them while he could depart earlier for a new post.

Identifying the *Maine*'s Keel

★ ★ ★ ★ ★ ★ ★ ★

ENTER ENSIGN POWELSON

A t this early stage of the investigation, the correspondents sensed that Captains Sampson and Chadwick still differed in their analyses of the cause of the disaster. From all indications, Sampson was leaning toward the mine theory while Chadwick firmly retained his preconception of an accident. They were open-minded men, yet neither had come upon the "clincher" needed to convince his friend to switch sides.

Both were aware of the view that the issue could be settled simply through observation of the *Maine*'s hull around the hole that sank her. According to expert opinion, the explosions came from inside the hull if the plates "bulged out." If the hull plates were driven in or up, a mine had burst beneath the ship. The hope of the two captains was to have the wreck raised so they could examine the hull themselves. If dewatering was impossible, they would reluctantly rely on divers' observations.

The first problem was to locate the one hole that was crucial in the widespread wreckage. From the surface, the focus was where the tremendous mass of decking was thrown up, near the reserve 6-inch magazine at about frame 30. Yet there was doubt that the initial explosion occurred there. The forward boilers were not lit at the time of the disaster. No significant amount of gunpowder seemed to have been in the reserve magazine. And the likelihood of spontaneous combustion was reduced by the absence of heat, odor, or smoke before the explosions in the forward sector.

Moreover, divers were finding unexploded 10-inch powder cans. The divers sent each can to the surface where it was rushed to the *Mangrove* and examined. Afterward, the can was marked as evidence and locked in the *Fern*'s tiny shell room.

The inference was that the largest forward magazine, the 10-inch, had not exploded. To Sampson's mind, there was too much damage to have resulted from an accident involving only the reserve magazine. The devastation had to have come initially from a more potent source such as a large mine.

In substantiation of Sampson's approach, the divers were also finding tremendous damage farther toward the bow, near the forward 6-inch magazine. This conflicted with the surface signs. The evidence was confusing as Sampson concentrated on the possibility of the detonation of a large Spanish mine around the forward magazine.

From Chadwick's standpoint, however, the explosions had probably occurred where the decking was thrown up. That was the obvious place, near coal bunker A-16 which had been filled in Norfolk in November 1897 with forty tons of bituminous coal subject to spontaneous combustion and not touched since. To Chadwick, conditions had been ripe for a bunker fire on the *Maine* similar to the ones that had struck his ship the *New York*.

From the start of the investigation chance played a big part. In response to Sigsbee's cry for help right after the explosions, Admiral Sicard had chosen the *Fern* from among many small ships in the squadron. The reason was mainly that the *Fern*'s steam was up. That was chance.

As another bit of luck, Ensign W. V. N. Powelson had been transferred to the *Fern* too recently to be fully occupied with regular duties. Because he had been interested in the *Maine* for years, he voluntarily busied himself with observing the divers around the wreck. Once Wainwright brought the ensign into the investigation, though, there was nothing serendipitous about his performance.

Wilfred Van Nest Powelson was born in Middletown, which made him another sailor from inland New York. The son of the city's district attorney, he was appointed to the Naval Academy in 1889 as a cadet engineer. After graduating first in his class, as Sampson had, he elected to go to Glasgow, Scotland, to study naval architecture.

He cut short his training as a constructor, a highly unusual step, because prospects were better for line officers. While waiting for a ship, he was stationed at the New York Navy Yard where the *Maine* was being readied for commissioning. He expected to be assigned to the *Maine*, so he examined the ship's structure in detail.

In Havana, Powelson watched Wainwright supervising divers at the wreck. Wainwright was uncomfortable with the uneducated divers and was unable to understand them when they described what they had observed below. Consequently, he had difficulty telling them what to do next. Seeing that Powelson interacted easily with enlisted men, Wainwright asked that the ensign be assigned to him for the duration of the investigation. Cowles was glad to comply. A cautious man, he had been irritated by Powelson's overzealousness.

Powelson's task was to interpret and direct the divers for Wainwright. He controlled the diving during the day, explained the divers' reports to Wainwright, and took soundings himself. Wainwright and he reviewed results each night and planned the next day's operations. They were dedicated officers who were sure the *Maine* had been destroyed through Spanish treachery. They expected to find evidence of a detonated mine.

Like everything else about the inquiry, Powelson's activities were supposed to be secret. The ensign was frank, though, with the divers, including Gunner Charles Morgan who had served with Powelson on the *New York*. The gunner was not as careful with the information.

At 10 P.M. on February 23, Morgan knocked on the hotel door of *Herald* correspondent Meriwether. He had met Meriwether during the reporter's service in the Navy. Morgan entered the room and the first thing he blurted out was, "I am in charge of the divers on the *Maine* and we have found the keel of the ship within 18 inches of the surface! We found it there to-night! Mr. Powelson was with me and he identified the keel plates." Even more startling, Morgan added, the bottom plates were above the surface of the water.

That was the end of the conversation. To Meriwether, the elevation of the *Maine*'s keel more than thirty feet above its original position signified only one thing. The bottom of the vessel had been driven inward and upward with tremendous force. Therefore, the battleship had been blown up by a large mine planted beneath the keel. The culprit had to be the Spaniards. This meant war!

Meriwether had received the biggest unintentional leak of vital information during the entire hearings. If he could get the story to his paper the next day, he would have a stupendous scoop. There was a dispatch boat waiting for him in the harbor although no vessel could leave until sunrise.

Fortunately, Spanish censors were on duty until midnight. Meriwether submitted the cable, "In important story which will be filed from despatch boat in Key West to-morrow, please note that main story is mine." Meriwether was advising his editor to prepare for a lead article on the *Maine*. The censor was a Spanish colonel. When he asked the reason for the unusual request, Meriwether replied that unless he took this precaution, the story might be credited to another reporter. "You can," the censor laughed, "tell that to your marines."

A different censor came on duty at eleven. Meriwether made a second try because he wanted the front page held for him. This time he was more inventive. At the Inglaterra newsstand he had bought a copy of *Life* magazine that contained the new Rudyard Kipling poem, "The Destroyers." He remembered the poem and handed the relief censor the cable, "Navy contingent left in Havana interestingly reading Kipling's poem current *Life*—especially last verse." The censor had been warned about Meriwether's subterfuges. He asked to see the poem. The last verse was, "The doom-bolt in the darkness free, The mine that splits the main. . . ." He too turned Meriwether down.

At daybreak, Meriwether went on board the *Herald* dispatch boat and spent the hours of the crossing writing articles. He filed enough sensational material from Key West to occupy most of the *Herald*'s front page on the twenty-fifth. He had his scoop.

Scovel learned the same news from a source he did not disclose. His dispatch boat, however, was in Key West. He had to depend on being more successful at the cable office than Meriwether had been. He wrote a feature story describing the gay crowds on the Prado, the brilliant sunshine, the heady sea breeze, and the shimmering bay. In the midst of the gushing verbiage, he tucked "the buzzards roosting on the keel of the *Maine*."

The clever message deceived the censor who saw only the complimentary references to his city. He approved the cable. The ruse also fooled the cable editor in the *World*'s New York office. He failed to observe the significance of the line about the buzzards, impugned Scovel's judgment in sending the cable, and spiked the dispatch for a future use that would never come. He realized his error the following morning when the *Herald's* exclusive account of the raised keel was published.

THE VISIBLE KEEL

Before Powelson's discovery, Sigsbee and Wainwright had feared that the extent of the damage might preclude the court from ever being able to pin the catastrophe on Spain. Cowles quoted the two officers to his brother-in-law Roosevelt as saying, "No one can tell yet what the cause of the disaster was. Even if it were due to Spanish treachery, it might be impossible ever to find out." The language was remarkably similar to Roosevelt's note to Long the day after the explosions.

Through the divers, the court had already established that both the forward and reserve 6-inch magazines had burst. As Cowles wrote, however, it was the reason for the magazine explosions that needed to be determined. The choices remained an internal accident such as spontaneous combustion, a deliberate internal act such as sabotage, an external accident such as a mine breaking loose in the harbor, or a deliberate external act such as the exploding of a mine under the *Maine's* keel.

Now Powelson's elevated keel confirmed Sampson's suspicions. Although the ship was demolished in the vicinity of the visible keel that still connected the bow to the stern, the mere presence of the upthrust keel was all Sampson needed to fix the cause of the disaster. He was convinced that the *Maine's* forward 6-inch magazine had been detonated by a large mine bursting under the keel, probably with Spanish involvement.

This reasoning was not available to the press. Despite the publication of Powelson's discovery, the rest of the evidence presented to the court remained secret. Meriwether had only Morgan's few words to go on. The balance of the story had to be elaboration and conjecture.

Meriwether filed the *Herald's* lead article from Key West on the twenty-fourth, emphasizing that "in the light of discoveries, there is no longer any reason to doubt that the explosion which wrecked the *Maine* came from underneath the vessel. Her magazines had nothing to do with the initial explosion, and played a smaller part in the disaster than was at first supposed. The forward part of the keel was stoved upward so far that parts of the shattered double bottom show out of the water."

Meriwether then added that "a plumb line dropped from a point just forward of the conning tower would have laid the lead exactly on the spot where the explosion occurred that drove the keel, plates, and ribs to the surface. The contents of the Reserve Six Inch Magazine were exploded by the initial blast."

Meriwether was logically though mistakenly combining two facts that were unrelated. On the one hand, he had Powelson's solid information about the elevated keel, but he had no indication of what part of the long keel had risen. On the other hand, he surmised that the location of the explosion was at the point of greatest damage as seen from the surface. He was writing the article on the dispatch boat. He could not know that the conning tower and reserve magazine he chose for the locus of the explosion were originally fifty feet aft of the visible keel. Eventually this reasonable if flawed connection plagued the court itself.

Meriwether concluded his article by responding to a question not yet asked: "If there was a mine beneath the *Maine*, no trace will ever be discovered, as the wreck in going down must have crushed any fragment that might have been left. The mud is very soft and the wreck is settling at a foot a day. The hull is now embedded to a depth of eight feet."

Scovel's subsequent article in the *World* took the discovery a step further. How did Powelson know the particular steel tangle projecting from the water was the bottom of the ship? As Scovel explained, "The *Maine* was clean on her bottom. She left Norfolk dry dock December 9. Her McGinnis green anti-fouling paint on bottom plates is still fresh, as seen in pieces of iron protruding from aft of the bow." The only green paint on the Maine was the McGinnis paint on the outside of her double bottom to discourage marine growths. When Powelson saw green, he was necessarily seeing bottom plates.

To Scovel, as it had been to Meriwether, that was proof of a mine explosion. Scovel started a list of nine points of "cumulative evidence" with the fact that the bottom plates were displaced upward. He ended with the sounds of the two explosions heard by the witnesses. The first report was the mine, he said. The second was the powder in the reserve 6-inch magazine. He too failed to notice the distance that had existed between the raised keel and the reserve magazine before the explosion.

The Washington *Evening Star* followed the lead of the New York papers, writing that "in Ensign Powelson's evidence the Court is confronted by a fact, not a theory. His exploit in discovering the green painted plates from the bottom of the *Maine* has been the sensation of the week. This points undoubtedly to an explosive force from the outside. The unparalleled upheaval of the decks and superstructure is consistent with the accident theory, but such explosion would have tended to force downward the plates from the ship's bottom and could hardly have resulted in an upward thrust."

The American press stampeded behind the story of the risen keel. The only doubter was the London *Times*, which was not widely read in the United States: "A rumor based on an alleged statement of Ensign Powelson appeared to-day in some serious papers. According to this, the forward keel of the *Maine* was blown upward, part now showing above water, painted green. If so, it is wonderful that it was not noticed before, but this story like others is unconfirmed." Debunking American explanations for the sinking of the *Maine* was to become an English cottage industry.

While verifying Powelson's testimony, the court recognized that the lack of a constructor as an expert witness was a weakness. Young Powelson was trained in naval architecture. None of the members was educated in the discipline, despite Chadwick's practical experience. The members were planning to take testimony from officers and men waiting in Key West, so Long directed Naval Constructor John Hoover and Carpenter James Helm to meet the court there. They had both worked on the *Maine* in the New York Navy Yard.

The *New York Times* reported that the constructors would also advise on whether the visible bottom plates were conclusive evidence of a mine or whether the exploding deck might have pulled the bottom plating with it. A few conservative newspapers like the *Times* still hoped for a finding of accidental cause. They were not optimistic.

INCLINED TO WAR

After Powelson's sensational disclosure and the inferences that were drawn to prove a mine caused the *Maine* disaster, Havana and Washington were quiet. The Sampson court continued its patient if relatively unproductive interrogation of every available American witness while Spain and the United States set their unspoken course toward war.

Madrid newspapers printed tirades against the United States. *El Correo Español* described how Spain benefited from the *Maine* sinking: "When American ships go to the bottom, Americans feel less inclined to go to war. The Spanish government ought to rejoice when these ships go down. The event brings peace about, for the ship has drowned the Yankees just as the army of Pharaoh was submerged in the waters" of the Red Sea.

After this ill-conceived allusion, *El Correo* asked a significant question: "If it were reported that the fine *Vizcaya* was blown up in the bay of New York, who would succeed in making Spaniards believe it was an accident, although there was no doubt about it?" A week earlier, the parallel to the *Maine* might have been meaningful. Now, following the discovery of the elevated keel, the argument was not persuasive.

El Correo also reported that Captain Eulate of the *Vizcaya* had admired New York City while exercising the greatest care in taking on coal. Every basketful was inspected by his officers. The only scare that Eulate had in New York was the sighting of a wooden barrel floating on the tide alongside the Spanish vessel. The seams were coated with tar, the side was painted red, and there was a red disk on one end. The barrel could have been a home-made mine, though it turned out to be a gunnery target that had escaped from a firing range for U.S. warships.

The *Vizcaya* left Sandy Hook February 25. After sundown on March 1 she entered Havana harbor to a wild welcome. Sigsbee said there were "prolonged toots, pyrotechnics, band playing, and all that. There were also shouts of 'Down with the Americans,' but officers on the cruiser seemed uneasy and kept her searchlight going until the moon rose well up." Eulate called on Sigsbee the next morning and gave him a warm hug.

Most American newspapers were less vindictive than the Spanish press. The *Nation* argued that the impediment to peace between the United States and Spain was not the *Maine*, it was a misunderstanding about the future of Cuba. The Spaniards thought American humanitarian demands were insincere and that the United States really wanted to acquire Cuba as a territory. In fact, the *Nation* contended, "We do not want Cuba at all."

Spain was right, however, to be suspicious. American expansionists saw a need to gain control over Cuba. The *New York Times* emphasized how easy a take-over of Cuba would be if the *Maine* disaster was officially attributed to Spain. The *Times* claimed Havana could not stand a siege of two weeks. The only real antagonist Washington perceived was powerful Germany. The

London *Times* reported the Kaiser's oath that "so long as William II is the German Emperor, the United States shall not possess themselves of the island of Cuba."

Meanwhile, bored correspondents in Havana joined the circle of the *Fern*, the *Bache*, the *Mangrove*, the commercial salvage tug *Right Arm*, and the Spanish vessels to watch the divers. In addition to bits of evidence, the divers sent up souvenirs. Some were grim. The *Maine*'s officers gave the less gory mementos to friends. A leg of the table where drowned Lieutenant Jenkins was sitting when the explosions occurred was handed to an American doctor. The little nickel number plates from officers' berths were treasured.

Veterans' organizations were not yet interested in *Maine* relics. Sigsbee said, however, that every mail brought him private letters pleading for pieces of the wrecked ship. Some letters enclosed payment in advance. Sigsbee turned down all requests. He was afraid that businesses might be seeking souvenirs to resell at a profit.

In his role as investigator for the court, Sigsbee had been at the center of the early diving activities. Because the harbor was polluted, the ship's doctor had recommended that recovered uniforms and paper other than official documents be burned. The unnamed exception was currency. When the divers brought up petty cash from Sigsbee's drawer, he made them a present of the money. This was a generous gesture for a man short of funds, if highly unethical for the defendant in an inquiry. Neither he nor the correspondents mentioned the gift.

The correspondents' most gruesome job was to describe the extent of the mutilation of the dead. The divers had entered the berth deck where sailors were asleep when the explosions occurred. In some sections, metal floors and ceilings had been ground together, reducing bodies to smears of flesh. Even in open areas, corpses had been pressed against the ceiling.

Diver McGee admitted to nausea when "we had to drag them to the hatchway with the boat hook, where they would bob to the surface." As pieces of corpses rose from the wreck and were towed to the Spanish "dead barge," superstitious fishermen who were passing in little boats dropped their sails and doffed their red caps. Despite this mute show of respect by the Spanish, another diver urged that "while God may be merciful to the men who blew these poor fellows to eternity, the United States should not!"

This was a sample of the strong feeling that limited President McKinley's options on the issue. He already knew what the outcome of the inquiry would be. The day after publication of Powelson's discovery, Admiral Sicard's chief of staff, Commander Clifford West, visited Havana in civilian clothes on a passenger liner to assess the situation sub rosa. Returning to Key West the same afternoon, he carried the message that a mine had undoubtedly caused the catastrophe. The identical conclusion was heard from officers in Havana, from Lee, and from correspondents.

The American public was also influenced by a March 1898 report on the visit of Senator Redfield Proctor of Vermont to the hard-pressed *reconcentrados* in Cuba. To avoid the war McKinley knew was otherwise coming, his plan was either to purchase Cuba from Spain or to force Spain to pay an indemnity for the loss of the *Maine*. Spain would not consider selling the island, however, so the administration turned to an exploration of the indemnity. The amount asked was $25,000,000. Spain refused.

The yellow press was outraged that the offer had even been contemplated. The headline in the *World* was, "Those Who Would Set a Price upon the *Maine* Shamed into Silence." Jingoes suggested sarcastically that instead of seeking a bribe to forget the *Maine*, the United States should apologize to Spain for carelessly blowing up the battleship in the Cuban port and then should offer to repair the damage by removing the wreck and dredging the harbor bottom for human and material remains.

These bitter responses compelled McKinley to change his tune. He dropped the appearance of compromise. At his suggestion, a bill was introduced in Congress on March 8 to appropriate $50,000,000 "for the national defense." The funds were to be withdrawn from the Treasury's cash balance of a substantial $224,541,637.

The Spaniards were stunned at both amounts. They had just bought two cruisers being built for Brazil in England. The Spanish Treasury was empty, so the government had to borrow more than $5,000,000 from French loan sharks.

The "$50,000,000 Bill" that passed Congress on March 9 was a deathblow to peace. The insurgents in Cuba would never accept anything less than independence once the United States was committed to intervention.

The President's Message

★ ★ ★ ★ ★ ★ ★ ★

AS SIGSBEE SAW IT

Lloyd's, the British carrier of marine insurance, announced on February 26 that the chance of hostilities between the United States and Spain was one in ten. Lloyd's should have checked with the U.S. officers in Havana. Most of them were looking for vengeance to be taken as soon as the Sampson court published its findings.

In contrast, an amiable Sigsbee was pleased by the arrival in Havana of newspaper articles that read valor into his actions under stress. "It was hardly possible," he reflected, "that a captain who had just lost his ship should look further than exoneration so soon afterward." Yet he was being praised. He gave the impression of being a courteous captain performing his duties on the investigative board by accommodating himself to the Spaniards.

When Navy divers arrived from Key West, he had ordered them to recover the cipher code and signal books. Next he sent them after the magazine and shell-room keys that hung on hooks near the ceiling at the foot of his bed.

Sigsbee told correspondents that when the first diver failed to find the keys in their usual place, he received more of a shock than he had from the explosions. That was an exaggeration, but missing keys meant that a perfidious sailor might have had access to the magazines. The public sympathized with Sigsbee's plight as a courageous commander in trouble not of his making. Along with Sigsbee, the country felt relieved when a second diver found that the keys had been lifted by a floating mattress.

Surprisingly, even active young officers like Powelson did not dive. Instead, they stood by while enlisted men were fitted into rubber suits, metal helmets, lead-soled shoes, and lead belts, then hitched to air hoses and life-lines. Encumbered by the unwieldy gear, the men were let down into the wreck by winches and told to grope in foul and muddied water through torn steel plates, unexploded ammunition, and trailing wires. Bad falls were common.

When divers surfaced, their reports tended to be vague. Officers blamed the failure in communication on the enlisted men's lack of education. Although the officers had no experience underwater, many complained that it would be a pity to rest the court's verdict on testimony from such inarticulate bumblers.

On the other hand, Sigsbee was openly impressed by the divers' efforts under Powelson's supervision. He claimed that the ensign had made common men into effective instruments to uncover obscured facts in a hostile environment—and the facts were coming down on Sigsbee's side!

Once Powelson satisfied Sampson concerning the cause of the explosions, Sigsbee believed he was in the clear at last. He soon became arrogant and contentious. He told his wife that "the wrecking tug is not of much use. The captain is a hopeless chap. Yesterday he began yelling that there was a body alongside his tug and he wanted it removed. I had managed to absorb all the vexations from the Spaniards I could assimilate without calling on my own countrymen for more, so I opened out on him in my highest style of indignation—you have seen it—and he is now without adverse views of any kind."

Despite Sigsbee's histrionics, the only problem with the tug's captain was his compassion. When he could not get the bloated and mutilated corpse of an American sailor moved from where his men were diving, he was understandably upset.

In a more telling incident concerning Sigsbee, the members of the court decided that once Powelson had discovered the elevated keel there was no longer any reason to prevent the Spaniards from investigating the wreck. According to Sigsbee,who had become uncompromisingly anti-Spanish, "It was suggested that I invite the Spanish authorities to begin. The Spaniards had previously assumed a dictatorial position in reference to my command. I therefore declined to move in the matter except with the express authorization of the United States government. This was given me and I was content."

In his continuing capacity as captain of the *Maine*, Sigsbee was reluctant to aid a Spanish inquiry that might somehow overturn Powelson's proof. He handed Captain Peral only the obsolete *Maine* drawings he knew Spain already had.

He also engaged in a foolish power struggle with General Blanco. The tug's captain asked him to obtain permission from the Spaniards for detonation of small dynamite charges that would enable divers to remove obstructions they could not cut by hand. This sounded reasonable to Sigsbee. Blanco insisted, however, that destroying evidence on which American conclusions might be based would be indiscreet. The general ordered the wreck to be left undisturbed at least until the Spanish divers finished their examination. Due to Sigsbee's foot dragging, the Spanish divers had only just begun.

Sigsbee grumbled that "the Spanish government is again showing the cloven hoof. It attempts to refuse me the use of dynamite to clear away wreckage. I lash my private sentiments up and put them away. Then I calmly repeat my request to use dynamite. I telegraph their refusal to the Navy Department, knowing that the censors will acquaint these people with the telegram. Then I quietly put in my second request." His ploy did not work this time. Secretary Long agreed with Blanco that Spanish suspicions made the use of dynamite inappropriate.

Sigsbee had changed, and was now seeing Spanish villainy in every sign. When the *Fern* was ordered to leave Havana early in March to bring a gift of food to *reconcentrados* near other Cuban ports, the cruiser *Montgomery* was dispatched from the Tortugas to take the *Fern's* place. Sigsbee had the *Fern* drop clear of her mooring to free the berth for the *Montgomery*, but the *Vizcaya* moved in first. Sigsbee protested to Monterola at once, demanding and getting the mooring for the *Montgomery*.

Sigsbee asserted that "I did not fancy the berth to which the *Montgomery* was to have been sent. It was remote from the wreck and I noticed that the Spanish men-of-war did not ride at it but *anchored* away from it." He thought the rejected berth was mined just as the *Maine's* mooring had been mined. He feared the Spaniards might blow up the *Montgomery* as he believed they had the *Maine*.

To be near the wreck and the court, Sigsbee moved to the *Montgomery*. The first night, a tapping sound in the hold was timed at 240 beats a minute. This was a multiple of 60 and therefore originated in clockwork of some kind. Sigsbee was convinced that a submarine mine controlled by a timer had been planted on the *Montgomery*. As ranking officer on board, he sent a boat to probe around the hull with an oar but nothing was discovered. Next, two boats swept the bottom of the ship with a rope, a safeguard Sigsbee had not practiced on the *Maine*. The sweep turned up nothing.

Once the *Montgomery* swung parallel to the *Vizcaya*, however, it was clear that the beat was being transmitted through the water by machinery operating on the *Vizcaya*. There was no mine. Nevertheless, Sigsbee dispatched the *Montgomery* to the Tortugas as soon as the *Fern* returned. He was afraid the cruiser was being "unnecessarily risked" in Havana harbor.

Sigsbee's irascibility was partially due to fatigue coupled with minor ailments. He told his wife that in the explosions, "I burned my fingers and got a thump on the thigh, but beyond being kept awake a little by the latter they were of no consequence." After "I recovered from my bowel trouble," he continued, "I have a nice bit of malaria—tired joints."

Sympathetic correspondents reported that "Captain Sigsbee is anxious to wind up work in Havana. His health is gradually failing since the *Maine*'s destruction, and now he is no longer sustained by excitement he fears a collapse. He seldom appears in the city, feeling unable to get about." When the Navy Department cabled to check on his health, he denied being ill. Despite his protestations, though, he wrote his wife a few days later that "I am rather under the weather again."

Through all his troubles, Sigsbee was considerate of members of the press. After he learned that Rea had sold reproduction rights to the historic cables, he told his wife that the correspondent whose name he spelled phonetically as Wray was "not to be trusted. Look sharp. If he calls, don't drop into any pitfalls." To Rea's face, though, he was pleasant and cooperative. He never let his "highest style of indignation" loose on a journalist. He bragged about dining "with two of the best newspapermen here—Mr. Johnson of the Associated Press and Mr. Low of the Boston Globe." He allowed photographer Jimmy Hare to take his picture. He preferred pose 66 and "ordered half a dozen of the number at 75 cents each."

Sigsbee explained that in dealing with "American newspaper correspondents, I never impugned their motives, nor denied myself to them when it was possible to see them, nor gave any correspondent 'the start in the running.' If I had news that could properly be given, I gave it. If what I knew could not be given, I informed them frankly. I could not give 'interviews.'"

When Sigsbee finally left for Key West on March 26, the *New York Herald* reported that "he stood on the *Olivette* surrounded by friends who had learned to love him. Outside tossed a barge with the coffins of Jenkins and eight more of the *Maine's* dead. Beyond, a tattered American flag floated above the wave-washed wreck. The newspaper correspondents sent Sigsbee a basket of flowers presented by General Lee 'expressing their whole souled appreciation of your unswerving fidelity to duty and your unfailing treatment of them as friends and newspaper men. Your conduct here as man and seaman has won the respect of all.'"

THE ACCIDENT THEORY KEELHAULED

Spanish diving began March 3. The search was independent of the U.S. investigation, as agreed, although Spanish and American diving vessels were anchored side by side. Sigsbee had watched the Spaniards derisively. Their approach was casual. While the Americans boasted that diver Olsen had surpassed the naval record for time spent underwater, Spanish divers had been down for less than five hours in four days. After each American diver completed his stint below, he was washed with disinfectant. The Spaniards took no such precaution. Sigsbee said the Spaniards never got wet enough long enough to need disinfecting.

Moreover, the Spanish divers explored the harbor bottom when they descended, not the inside of the wreck. The speculation was that their examination of the devastated forward area had quickly proved to be fruitless because they could not recognize what they were seeing on the blown-away port side. Few clues were left. On March 11, Captain Peral issued another preliminary finding that explained his divers' odd-seeming conduct. He listed the negatives they had substantiated, claiming that the state of the harbor bottom precluded a mine explosion.

"Our divers are hard at work examining the hull," Peral maintained. "Great difficulty is experienced owing to the deep mud and the condition of the wreck." The polite Peral refrained from blaming the United States for denying access until mud covered the ship's bottom.

"We cannot believe there was an external explosion of a mine," Peral added, "for the following reasons: 1. A mine must have blown a great hole in the mud. No hole was found." The crater was what the Spanish divers had been looking for.

"2. A mine must have thrown water into the air," Peral continued, "or produced a wave reaching other ships. No one remarked any upheaval or wave. 3. A mine always kills fish in the vicinity. No fish were killed. 4. To produce the effects noted in the wreck, a mine would have had to be of enormous size, fully 150 or 200 kilos [up to 440 pounds]. I am therefore of the opinion that the explosion occurred within the ship."

Peral concluded as diplomatically as he began: "I do not believe there was carelessness on the part of the officers of the *Maine*. I believe American regulations were observed, but some things which cannot be foreseen are bound to happen. I believe there was an accident. Our Court of Inquiry will decide."

To U.S. officers, Peral's reasoning was feeble. His four points were circumstantial. In addition, Peral must have been aware of the elevated keel. Scores of stories concerning the keel had been cabled through Spanish censors for two weeks. Yet Peral never mentioned the keel. The Americans said that by making no response, Peral proved their position to be correct.

Although the officers were sure that Spanish treachery was to blame for the disaster, they were required to restrain their feelings in public. Yet whenever they walked aft on the *Mangrove*, the telltale bottom plates protruded from the water as an infuriating reminder of the dead sailors still in the wreck.

Each afternoon the popular young daughter of the *Mangrove*'s commanding officer sat on a chaise under an awning on the deck, embroidering linen. The officers lifted their caps in response to the girl's happy greeting. Despite her presence, however, their smiles quickly faded. Less than a pistol shot behind her were the raised plates that called for revenge.

The officers' consolation was that they knew the end of the court's proceedings was in sight. Unfortunately for the *New York Herald* its correspondent had lost his private source and so was one of the few newspapermen not well informed. Since publishing Meriwether's scoop on the keel, the *Herald* had been denied confidential data. Meriwether believed that "never in the history of similar proceedings have such precautions been taken to guard facts from public scrutiny." The London *Times* man who was also without a source on the court agreed: "The nature of the testimony is unknown. I do not know whether the explosion was due to accident or treachery. Nobody knows, except perhaps the Court of Inquiry and they do not tell."

News was being leaked steadily, though, to other American papers. The *New York Journal* had disclosed Captain Chadwick's original view that the reserve 6-inch magazine had exploded due to coal heating in bunker A-16. Even after Chadwick was dissuaded by the unexploded powder cans divers found and by Powelson's discovery, he did not accept these facts as absolute proof of a mine. The Washington *Evening Star* reported that Chadwick was actively cross-examining Powelson. The *Herald* correspondent saw Chadwick board the diving floats with Constructor Hoover. To him, that indicated Chadwick's continuing ambivalence.

The jingoes suspected that the court was stalling because of orders from Washington, presumably to permit further overtures toward peace. In fact, the court was continuing with the investigation because a hasty judgment might be contradicted by better evidence than had been produced by divers its members looked on as unreliable. More time was devoted to questioning Powelson about diving than to any five other witnesses, apart from Sigsbee. In a flurry of last minute activity, the members were spending hours on the water. Sampson became ill from overexposure to the sun.

Criticism had to be anticipated. A slim hope remained that the wreckers might obtain more powerful apparatus such as derricks able to raise the shattered ship. Consequently, the court was waiting until the best evidence that could ever be secured was in hand. Then the finding would never be questioned.

COURT SESSIONS END

In Washington there was a brief sideshow involving Secretary Long and the *Maine* that distracted the public. Theodore Roosevelt summarized the contretemps in a March 2 letter to New York newspaperman Jacob Riis: "I am sorry about Secretary Long's interview. The *Sun* this morning says that he believes it [the disaster] to be an accident, and that there was no complicity of the Spaniards. What he meant to say, I am sure, was that there was no complicity of the Spanish government. No one can say definitely yet whether it was, or was not, an accident."

Immediately after the explosions on February 15, both President McKinley and Secretary Long had called the explosions accidental. Long maintained this pro-Spanish posture until he was silenced by the Powelson discovery which deprived the accident theory of its remaining support.

That was when Cowles told Roosevelt that "the opinion of the officers at Havana is nearly unanimous. There was no accident, but the ship was destroyed by a mine from without." At this point the press believed that if an accident had caused the disaster, court sessions would already have ended because the finding would favor the administration. McKinley would no longer need time to prepare for war. A silent court meant that a mine had been the cause and McKinley was delaying the announcement because business interests he represented opposed war. Just the threat of hostilities was depressing stock prices.

Long's public statement in early March reverting to an accident as the cause was a bombshell. The Secretary's remark was taken as McKinley's official position. That meant peace and the stock market soared. A firm of stock brokers who knew Long well made a $20,000,000 profit. Long was charged in the press with having influenced the market for his friends' gain.

Despite headlines such as, "How Long Stirred a Storm in Stocks" and "Long May Be Asked to Leave Cabinet," the controversy blew over in a day because of Long's sterling reputation. His excuse that his remark was a personal view and not McKinley's was accepted. Otherwise his replacement in the cabinet would probably have been the jingo Roosevelt.

At the same time, Spanish newspapers were erroneously reporting that U.S. investigators in Havana had found the wreck to be completely demolished. Determining the cause of the disaster would be impossible, they wrote, and there was no way the United States could blame Spain for the loss. Peculiarly, the visible bottom plates were never mentioned.

The Spanish chargé d'affaires in Washington was, however, cabling Madrid a truer story. He warned his minister that "reports from Cuba that the catastrophe was caused by a mine have stirred up agitation until even the most conservative men have lost their heads. All await with anxiety the American official report. If it declares that the catastrophe was due to an accident, the present danger will be over, but if it alleges it was the work of a criminal hand, then we shall have the gravest situation."

Finally Captain Sampson announced on March 15 that a unanimous court was leaving for Key West to formalize the findings. The court had received a confidential report from Constructor Hoover showing that the *Maine* had been sunk by a large mine and Chadwick had given in.

Hoover had also concluded that raising the *Maine* would be impossible. The wreck was too heavy for pontoons or derricks and no cofferdam could be built in the harbor because of the deep mud. The court possessed the best evidence that existed. The proceedings could end at last.

Madrid had resolved to postpone the issuance of Captain Peral's findings until after the American decision was published. If the Sampson court found a Spanish mine to be the cause of the disaster, Spain would demand international arbitration based on the accusation of Spanish guilt. When European arbitrators held for Spain, as seemed certain, members of the Sampson court would have to apologize for their wrongful assault on Spanish honor.

In its turn, the Sampson court considered ways to forestall an international review. The evidence that the *Maine*'s bottom plates had been pushed up was decisive as to cause, though no culprit had been caught red-handed. There was no proof that Spanish authorities had committed the crime. If the court avoided fixing blame for sinking the *Maine*, Spain would have no right in law or honor to demand an international investigation. As in a coroner's verdict, the miscreant would be a person or persons unknown.

Congress had allowed its impatience with the court to be known for weeks. Now the court would leave the naming of a guilty party to McKinley and Congress who would have the option of plunging the country into war or not. The court felt that such a weighty determination belonged with the Chief Executive or Congress, not with the Navy.

THE SAMPSON REPORT GOES TO WASHINGTON

On March 19, the members of the Sampson court were on the battleship *Iowa* off Key West composing their formal report. No surprise was anticipated.

In Washington, this was a quiet Saturday morning. Admiral Sicard had alerted Secretary Long that Constructor Hoover and three officers of the *Maine* were secretly bringing an outline of the report to Washington for review by the President. Hoover's public role was limited, although he had been a key persuader of Chadwick and a formulator of the court's reasoning. Now he was a covert liaison with the President.

The next morning McKinley disclosed the outline to his cabinet. Assistant Secretary of State Day cabled the advance findings to Ambassador Woodford in Madrid to try to nudge Spain toward granting Cuban independence. When the *World* printed the headline, "Report of Court of Inquiry Sent to the President/The Board Finds the Explosion Was from an Exterior Mine/Responsibility Is Not Placed by the Board," however, the cagey Long denied he had received the findings.

Sigsbee was at loose ends with activities winding down. He remarked that he "had no knowledge as to what the findings of the Court will be but I do not fear anything will reflect unfavorably on me." He "hoped something would be done to express continued confidence in me unmistakably."

While he expected to be exonerated from charges of negligence, his fear was that he would be returned home on waiting orders rather than on active duty. Waiting orders would reflect a lack of faith in him and also his pay would be reduced to $3,500 a year. He had lost uniforms, civilian clothes, and personal gear in the wreck and was considerably out of pocket. He warned his wife, "Don't forget that" in her expenditures.

When he was ordered back to active service, the correspondents saw it as another confirmation that the court would find for destruction of the *Maine* by a mine. Otherwise, the *Herald* speculated, Sigsbee would have been bound over for court-martial instead of being promised a new command.

The following day, the twenty-first, the court's findings were completed after twenty-three days. Marix took the formal report from the *Iowa* to Admiral Sicard on the *New York*, dramatizing the delivery for the benefit of correspondents on board. Sicard was ill. He was anxious to relinquish command of the North Atlantic Squadron, but he had to stay on until the inquiry was concluded because his probable successor, Sampson, could not approve his own findings.

Marix remained with the admiral in the ship's office for a long overnight conference. Newspapers described how the *New York*'s junior officers maintained an elaborate guard over the report after taps. The next day, minor alterations were made in the findings to delete references that could have been construed as accusations against Spain.

Sicard approved the revised findings on the twenty-second, claiming that the inquiry was the most peculiar in modern times. Never before, he insisted, had a vessel of one nation been destroyed in the harbor of another nation without responsibility for the destruction being resolved beyond dispute. He said that under the circumstances he would withdraw U.S. naval officers from Cuba. If Spain would not consent to dynamiting the *Maine*, the wreck and her entombed sailors might be abandoned.

Meanwhile Marix and three armed officers from the *Maine* took the night train for Washington. According to the *Journal*, "the exit of the famous document from Key West was as finely designed a piece of stage play as any Gilbert could have invented" for Sullivan to put to music in their comic operettas about the British navy. While Marix and the three officers were en route, the *Herald* claimed the country was "In the Whirlpool of a Niagara." Washington officials were nominally waiting for Marix with great anticipation, although McKinley had been making decisions for weeks on the basis of the expectation that the coming report would prove external cause.

On the train, the four officers stood continuous watches over the white canvas mail pouch containing the report. The bag and contents weighed more than fifteen pounds. Reporters envisioned endless pages of complex testimony and findings to be read and resolved by the President.

On the evening of Thursday the twenty-fourth an enormous crowd gathered in Washington's Union Station to wait for the Florida train. Shortly after 9:30 P.M., the travel-weary officers descended onto an unlit platform. Long had sent only a naval cadet to meet them. No carriage was provided.

Lieutenant Holman as the senior *Maine* officer carried the pouch under one arm. When the unrestrained throng jostled him, he put his free hand on the gun he wore at his hip. Lieutenant Blow grasped the butt of a revolver sticking out of his side pocket. The frightened crowd fell back. Marix, who knew his way around Washington, dashed across the railroad tracks and led the way to the hack stand.

The officers registered at the famous Ebbitt House for the night. The three from the *Maine* placed the pouch in the hotel safe and prepared to stand watches one last time. Marix gave a short interview to the press, admitting that "Spanish sources" were probably the perpetrators of the explosions even though the evidence was insufficient to fix responsibility. Then he too went into the room with the vault and closed the door.

McKinley was alone in his White House office, considering how to word his message to Congress on the Sampson report. Legislators were pressing him to recommend a declaration of war against Spain, while the Spanish government was requesting that the *Maine* report be withheld from Congress. The Spaniards insisted that "to place before an assembly, without explanation, a report which must meet with sentiment rather than reason, reveals an intention of allowing national enthusiasm to form a judgment not founded on proof." The Spanish prime minister asked that the *Maine* disaster remain a subject of diplomatic negotiation with the assurance that "Spain would do in this matter whatever is right."

McKinley was overtired. He resolved to transmit the report with no recommendation. His feeling was that Congress wanted the war. Let Congress declare it. As far as Spain was concerned, the plea for delay was not coupled with an offer to compromise. Spain was merely procrastinating again. The President waited for the Sampson report, prepared to abdicate his authority as a rebuff to both Congress and Madrid.

At 9 A.M. on the twenty-fifth, Marix was wearing civilian clothes when he delivered the pouch containing the Sampson report to his superior, Captain Samuel Lemly, the Navy's judge advocate general. Lemly and Marix went to Long's office. Long did not open the pouch. He talked to Marix for twenty minutes to give the President time to get ready.

At 9:35 A.M. Long and Marix drove from the Navy Building to the White House in the Navy brougham. They waited in the Blue Room until they were told to join the President in the library. Marix opened the pouch and put the report on the President's desk. McKinley did not read the report. He was familiar with the findings.

The cabinet met at eleven as usual. Marix was brought in to answer questions. He repeated Sampson's informal opinions on the explosive device and on culpability. As Marix left the meeting, McKinley was complaining that "we are still not prepared for war."

On Sunday afternoon, the twenty-seventh, McKinley began dictating his message to Congress on the Sampson report. A suspicious Congress requested in advance that his transmission include the verbatim findings.

The Associated Press reproduced the court's findings the next morning, before the President released them. No one doubted the validity of the court's conclusions. *Life* magazine insisted that "the grounds on which the *Maine* Board's findings are based are so easily verified that fair-minded readers in all countries are likely to accept its verdict that our ship was destroyed by a submarine mine."

PUSSYFOOTING

A great crowd stormed the Senate galleries early on March 28. Police estimated at least 6,000 visitors. Five thousand were turned away by 11 A.M. because the politicians could not cram the 6,000 voters into 1,000 seats. The overflow went to the Congressional Library. The senators had been harassed by more requests from important constituents than had been received in thirty years.

After the galleries were filled, the Vice President and the senators took their places. There was a signal at the door and a hush fell over the chamber. The Vice President rose as President McKinley's assistant, O. L. Pruden, entered. The *Herald* observed that "the more you study Pruden, the less you will know. He looks well groomed, and as if he had enjoyed his breakfast. With a Websterian dignity, he delivers a message from the President of the United States."

The message was read in its entirety by the Clerk of the Senate, who intoned the words in a round, magisterial manner. Each sentence fell firm and cold from his lips. There was no warmth in the enunciation, just as there was no passion in the message. Senators listened with profound attention. There was no noise in the galleries, either. The swish of a fan or the rustle of a feather boa would have been heard.

In his message McKinley summarized the court's short 1,800 word report. There had been two distinct explosions. The first was at frame 18, where a mine lifted the ship and forced the bottom plating above the water. In the second, decks were blown aft by explosions of forward magazines. The court found neither negligence of the ship's personnel nor evidence fixing responsibility on any other person. The President concluded by stating ambiguously that the Spanish government owed the United States what is due when the sovereign rights of one friendly nation have been assailed within the jurisdiction of another.

After the Clerk turned the last clipped-together page, he read the signature William McKinley and put the message down. The silence in the Senate continued. The President's message was anticlimactic and senators were chagrined at what they saw as pussyfooting. They said that the statement meant no more than "the Spaniards blew up the *Maine* but we could not prove it in a court of law."

After a pause, Minnesota Senator Cushman Davis asked for a reading of the court's findings. The text of the message had been typewritten. Ten copies were all the President's secretary, George Cortelyou, could accomplish during the preceding night. The findings, however, were still in Marix's hand and included interlineations arrived at with Sicard. They were the scrawls of a sailor on a ship with a rolling sea beneath him.

In attempting to read the findings, the Clerk spelled difficult words aloud. He studied the composition of sentences and tried one phrase after another to get the meaning. The *Herald* noted that his performance was "like walking barefoot through thorns" until a despairing Senator Davis moved that the reading be suspended. The troubled Clerk sat back, blushing while he mopped his forehead. The assemblage joined him in a sigh of relief.

Because McKinley had not recommended war, he was burned in effigy across the country. A fund was started in Durango, Colorado, to repay Spain for the gunpowder used in blowing up the *Maine*

Testimony Concerning the *Maine*

★ ★ ★ ★ ★ ★ ★ ★

SIGSBEE SPEAKS

When the court of inquiry's findings were published, the hundreds of pages of seldom-read testimony provided the only contemporaneous account of what the witnesses saw and heard.

The record of the first hearing took the focus back to the *Mangrove* in Havana harbor on Monday morning, February 21. Sigsbee was the witness. Although he was the primary defendant, he did not choose to be represented by counsel. Yet he was a controversial figure. Europeans insisted he had been responsible for a fatal lack of discipline on the *Maine*. In the United States, however, he was a hero.

At 1 P.M. the court adjourned for the day. In addition to giving the stenographer time to transcribe his notes, the members had a lot to consider. Marix had not hesitated at putting hard questions to Sigsbee. He asked about "coal too long in the bunker" in exploring spontaneous combustion as the cause of the disaster. He also brought up the hazard resulting from the single thin plate between bunker A-16 and the reserve magazine.

In his responses, Sigsbee implied that the Spaniards had directed his ship to buoy no. 4 because the mooring had been mined. This allegation was never amplified. Instead, he concentrated on his theory that a huge Spanish mine had destroyed his ship because "there was simply one overwhelming explosion." At that stage, "one explosion" was Sigsbee's code for a mine. Although the reserve magazine was at the center of the devastation, he claimed the magazine held too little powder to have caused significant damage.

In giving evidence, Sigsbee showed himself to be remote from shipboard routine and unfamiliar with the layout of his vessel. He was a poor witness in his own behalf. Nevertheless, the ship had obviously been well run. He testified that safety regulations concerning inflammables, paint, waste, electric wiring, and guncotton were strictly observed. Powder magazines and bunkers were examined according to regulations and temperatures were never near a danger point. Externally, Sigsbee said he had followed the extraordinary precautions in guarding the ship's perimeter that were described in the newspapers. He indicated that he had done all he could reasonably do under the circumstances to protect the *Maine*.

According to Sigsbee's testimony, there was no indication of negligence on the night of the explosion. There was nothing to suggest the possibility of an accident. The management of the *Maine* had been in good hands. Yet the *Maine* court of inquiry was Sigsbee's third court. If he had been seeking Lloyd's casualty insurance as a ship driver, he would have been classified as accident prone, regardless of fault.

On the second day the witness was Lieutenant G. F. M. Holman, the defendant who had been the *Maine*'s ordnance officer responsible for the magazines. Sigsbee attended the hearing, exercising his rights as defendant. Holman declared that when the explosions occurred, "I called, 'We have been torpedoed.' My [present] impression is that a very heavy mine went off under the *Maine*."

Next, Executive Officer Wainwright appeared as witness and defendant. The questions to him concerned regulations on closing doors and hatches, the report to Sigsbee at 8 P.M., scrutiny of visitors, lookouts, and watches at night. He also acknowledged that "frequently small boats came very close." In one example of the mine theory, the planting would have been done by a passing lighter.

Cadet W. T. Cluverius who later married Captain Sampson's daughter said he was in the junior officers' quarters: "My first knowledge was a slight shock as if a six-pounder gun had been fired. After that a great vibration, which was followed by a heavy shock."

This classic statement of the two explosions was confirmed by Sigsbee's aide Cadet J. H. Holden: "First, there was an explosion of considerable force, and about three seconds afterwards there was another explosion of far greater force." Although Holden and Wainwright had been together at the explosions, Wainwright had testified, "I only remember one very heavy shock." Wainwright was supporting Sigsbee before the court, despite his original statement to the press that could have been interpreted as two explosions. Marix did not question the contradictions.

On the third day, the witness was the final defendant, Chief Engineer Charles P. Howell, who was responsible for the bunkers. The judge advocate got right to the point: "Q. Have you had any sign of spontaneous combustion in the coal bunkers? A. None whatever. Q. When did you make your last examination of these bunkers? A. Every time I go through the wing passages, I pass right by the bunkers. I have never gone through without putting my hand on them to feel the temperature. I never found any signs of heating.

"Q. What was the condition of bunker A-16? A. It was full of coal. Q. Is it easy of access for feeling the temperature? A. Yes, sir. Outside, for temperature. On all four sides. Q. The inboard bulkhead of this bunker is against the magazine, is it not? A. Yes, sir."

Hands were the simplest and best practical test for overheating. Nevertheless, Captain Chadwick saw the flaw in Howell's assertion. The bunker was not exposed on the critical side, the magazine side.

In his brusque manner, Chadwick asked Howell, "How could you examine the temperature of that coal bunker on the outside where it abutted against the magazine? A. We did not examine it from the magazine. We examined it from aft and outboard. Q. This coal bunker is on the same deck as this magazine. How could you get at the outside of that coal bunker on this deck? A. Not on the deck shown here [the hold], but on another [platform] deck. Q. But the magazine is not on another deck." Howell could not have laid his hand on the bulkhead between the bunker and the magazine where any combustion would have been. He then withdrew as a witness and Holman was summoned again.

As judge advocate, Marix was no crusading district attorney. There was no need for him to be. His job was to help find the facts, not to prosecute. The pace of the hearings was slow. Marix could think about a day's testimony as long as he liked. He could call a witness back. No officer or man connected with the *Maine* was going any place until the court concluded the entire investigation.

In Holman's reappearance, he offered a change in the amount of black saluting powder in the reserve magazine: "I stated 200 pounds. On reflection, we must have had very much more than 200 pounds." A substantial quantity of volatile black powder would have been another significant hazard. The reserve magazine took on new importance. At that early stage, Chadwick's conviction that an accident had destroyed the *Maine* was strengthened.

POWELSON IS INTRODUCED

In retrospect, it is surprising that young Ensign Powelson could have become the guru of the mine theory, making the veteran Captain Sampson and later Captain Chadwick his disciples, but that is what happened for a while.

Powelson appeared as a witness on the third day: "Q. What duty have you been engaged on since you have been in Havana, regarding the wreck of the *Maine*? A. I have not been on any official duty in connection with the *Maine*." The ensign immediately caught the court's attention with his preciosity. He had not been assigned to help with the *Maine*. He had volunteered.

"Q. Have you not been present a great deal during the diving? A. Yes, sir. I have been on the *Maine* every day since the *Fern* has been here, and have been present most all day. Q. Will you please tell the Court, as far as you can, the condition of the wreck." If Marix meant "as far as you can" to excuse an ensign's limitations, he need not have bothered. Powelson's response was exactly what the court had been looking for. He was trained in ship construction so he could recognize details that escaped the members. He also expressed clearly what he saw. In a bravura performance, he spoke at length without notes.

At the end of his elaborate presentation he was far from finished. He asked, "Did you mean for me to say anything about what the divers reported? Q. What impression is produced upon your mind by the [divers'] reports? A. From reports alone, or from the appearance of the wreck?" Marix was getting the hang of Powelson's finickiness. "Either," he replied.

"Q. What weight are you giving to the statement made by the gunner, Mr.

Morgan, as to falling into a hole on the port side? A. No weight, sir, because I think he may be mistaken about it." Powelson's unwillingness to rely on uncorroborated evidence built confidence in the court.

"Q. Could you not tell by the divers? A. The divers do not seem to express themselves as to what they see below. I have not been able to learn much. Q. They do not know what they find? A. They see things, but they do not know exactly what they are."

"Q. How have you become so well acquainted with the *Maine*? A. I thought I was going to the *Maine* when she went in commission. I used to go through her, with an idea of learning. Then I was on the staff of Admiral Bunce, and made an inspection of the *Maine*. Q. How often are you on duty at the wreck? A. As I said, I am not detailed for duty there. I have days duty on the *Fern*, but I attend to work on the wreck, or anything Lieutenant Wainwright wants me to do." After this, whatever Powelson had to say would be treated by the court with the greatest respect.

By the fourth day, Sigsbee's board of investigation was able to produce a few witnesses who had been on other ships in the harbor at the time of the explosions.

Captain Frederick Teasdale was master of the bark *Deva* which had been at the Regla wharf, half a mile from the *Maine*. He heard two explosions, two seconds apart. In addition, Marix dutifully explored with Teasdale the Spanish court's negative defenses concerning the absence of waves and dead fish.

Although Captain Sampson had taught physics and was aware that the speed of sound differed in different media, he did not have each witness state the quality and sequence of the sounds to spell out whether that witness heard one explosion with two sounds or two explosions with two sounds. Based on the weight of the testimony, he and the other members of the court took it for granted that there had been two distinct explosions.

The next witness was crucial. He was Sigmond Rothschild, a tobacco exporter who had been on the *City of Washington* a hundred yards from the *Maine*. His testimony repeated his remarks that had appeared in newspapers. First, he heard a sound like a shot. Second, he saw the bow rise. Third, he saw the fire. Fourth, he heard the violent explosion. The shot and the explosion had to have been different events because in between them he saw the fire from the explosion. Light travels faster than sound. If the shot and the explosion had been from one phenomenon, the light would have preceded both.

DIVERS COME UP TO TESTIFY

The divers began their testimony on the afternoon of the fourth day. It was easy to see why Powelson was needed.

Gunner Morgan from Chadwick's ship the *New York* was first. He had been down only once. "Q. It has been stated that you fell into a hole. What about that? A. There is a space where it is deeper. That is where the soft mud is. Q. But you did not touch the edge of this hole? A. It is simply an incline, but nothing to make a round hole." As Powelson had implied, Morgan was not a reliable witness.

Chief Gunner's Mate Andrew Olsen from Sampson's *Iowa* had been down four times for eight hours. He was an intelligent and perceptive man, until pressed. "Q. State to the Court your experience while under water. A. I went down forward of the crane on the port side [frame 40]. Part of her bottom plates are turned up. Then you follow the bottom from there up and the plates are blown outward. At the top and underneath the bottom they are blown inboard—blown in. The skin of the double bottom is curled over like a sheet of paper inboard."

The court's first charge was to ascertain whether the hull and bottom were bent in or bent out. Here the bends were described as both in and out. Simplistically, the *in* would be a mine from the outside and the *out* a magazine from the inside exploding as a consequence of the mine burst.

"Q. Where did you find the skin of the double bottom turned up and in? A. A little abaft of frame 30." The description appeared to be the answer to the court's quest. Olsen had found the double bottom bent in at the point of greatest damage. This was precisely where experts who had examined the wreck from the surface expected the telltale hole in the bottom to be.

Because the testimony substantiated the mine theory, Chadwick became involved and asked, "Was it a hole blown into the ship? A. No, sir. It is no hole. It is a curve. The plate is warped. Q. You did not find a hole? A. No, sir. No hole, not in that part." If there was no hole, the find was not significant because penetration of the ship's bottom was necessary to have detonated the reserve magazine.

Wainwright attended the session as a defendant. He too took up the questioning about the bent bottom plates. Olsen became rattled as the interrogation continued.

On the fifth day, February 25, the witness was Gunner's Mate Thomas Smith from the *Iowa*: "Q. Please state exactly what you found under water. A. Yesterday I went down where the crane was. The skin of the ship looks in good condition there until you walk out to where the Six Inch Shell Room [Reserve Magazine] starts [at frame 30]. The plates are bent from outside inboard. They are all ragged edges."

Marix asked, "You said there were plates blown inboard. Describe where those plates are. A. They are coiled up from out inward. One of them is coiled right over, just as if you took a piece of paper like that (indicating). Q. What do you think it is? A. It is the ship's bottom. Q. The outside skin of the ship? A. Yes, sir. Q. You place that about the middle of the Reserve Shell Room [Magazine]? A. Yes, sir."

The fourth diver was Seaman Martin Reden of the *Maine*. He had been a professional diver for eight years before enlisting. "Q. Tell the Court all you saw down there. A. I struck one bottom plate in the mud, and the plate is bent in this way, and up that way (indicating)."

Chadwick stepped in. "Q. In what part of the ship would you say that bent plate was? A. About ten feet forward from the break in the superstructure." That was about frame 30. The divers were relatively consistent in their placement of the bent-in plate.

The most convincing of the divers was the last, Gunner's Mate Carl Rundquist of the *New York*. "Q. Please describe what you saw. A. I was rolling along in the mud when I happened to strike my hand against something. I felt the green slippery piece of steel. I put my face close to the plate and I could see it was this green paint. I followed that some eight or ten feet and I came to the raggy edge of it, and there at the edge it was standing in this direction, like (indicating). It looked to be inboard, bent over—more rolled up than anything else."

Then came the ultimate question: "How did you think this hole was made in the bottom of the ship? A. I believe that she was blown up from the outside, because there was no explosion from the inside could make a hole like that. There may have been an explosion from the inside afterwards, but in the first place there was an explosion from the outside."

The court's main precept appeared to be satisfied. According to the divers, the bottom of the *Maine* was blown in at about frame 30. Rundquist testified that the green paint on the outside of the skin was visible from inside the ship, so the blast had penetrated the double bottom. Presumably that meant a mine had burst under the *Maine*'s reserve magazine, setting off the powder in the magazine.

The only response of the judge advocate was, however, "What strikes me is this, that you did not examine enough of that edge [of the inboard hole] to form an opinion." Marix spoke for the court.

What more did the members of the court want? They could not see the bottom of the *Maine* with their own eyes, yet as elitists they did not credit reports by these divers who were uneducated common sailors. They were in a bind. They would not be satisfied until they had an airtight explanation from someone they trusted—such as a fellow officer.

The Telltale Plates

★ ★ ★ ★ ★ ★ ★ ★

POWELSON FINDS THE BOTTOM

Powelson was recalled as a witness on the afternoon of the fifth day. He gave what proved to be key testimony in the inquiry, startling the court by beginning with "I have succeeded in identifying part of the protective deck."

His procedure had been to examine the visible plating in the middle pile of debris showing above the water forward of the overturned superstructure. When he found frames in the wreckage, he measured the differing spaces between them to locate them on the ship's plan: "My conclusion is that the plate [in the center pile] comes from cellulose compartment A-36, forward of [and a deck above] the Forward Six Inch Magazine."

That was a master stroke in detection, but the best was still to come: "I have also succeeded in identifying part of the bottom plating, which is now about four feet above water, twelve feet abaft the piece of protective deck I have just referred to."

His technique was the same as for the protective deck: "The distance between the frame that is highest out of water and the frame next below is three feet six inches. The distance between this frame and the one below is four feet. There is only one place in the [forward half of the] ship at which such spacing occurs. That is bulkhead 18, the space between 18 and 19 being four feet and between 18 and 17 being three feet six inches."

The members listened intently. "Forward of frame 17, the outside plating has been split, forming a V [inverted]. Frame 17 is the apex. The bottom plating [was originally] almost directly under the forward port edge of the Forward Six Inch Magazine, between frames 18 and 21."

Belatedly, the mention of the raised plating alerted the judge advocate: "Q. Then the appearance of that V-shape you saw makes you convinced that the bottom of the ship was thrown up? A. Yes, sir. Q. And not [the sides blown] out? A. Not out." Marix knew that the *Maine's* elevated bottom would lead ordnance experts to assume the cause of the disaster was a mine.

Here Chadwick entered the discussion: "Q. How much has that [bottom plating] been raised? A. It would have been lifted 38 or 39 feet from its original position when the ship was floating." Powelson figured that the *Maine* was in 35 or 36 feet of water. The bottom plates rose 35 plus 4 feet or about 39 feet.

"Q. Was there paint on the outside of that bottom plating? A. The outside of the bottom plating is covered with greenish paint." Diver Rundquist who was now forgotten had prepared Powelson to recognize the color of the anti-fouling coating.

Chadwick continued, "Mr. Powelson, you have not come across any portion of the decks above the protective deck, have you? A. Yes, sir. There is a part of the berth deck which was thrown 20 feet forward of the protective deck, but as to just where that was on the berth deck, I am unable to determine." This was the third pile of wreckage hurled forward. Each pile was located relative to its original position in the ship, with the ship's bottom, which was deepest, ending up closest to the overturned superstructure. The protective deck was next and the berth deck was farthest away. Powelson had identified all three piles, but typically he held back on the berth deck because he did not have all the answers.

Captain Sampson then cautioned Powelson about disclosing matters pertaining to the inquiry. The ensign had already, however, confided in Gunner Morgan, who had in turn imparted the information to Meriwether. For his indiscretion, Morgan was removed from diving, but Meriwether's scoop made Powelson famous. His picture was taken by press photographers while he posed on the flat of the elevated bottom plates as if standing on water. Newspaper interpretations of the significance of the risen keel enraged the country against Spain.

THE MAN OF TWO MINDS

Sigsbee was recalled as a witness on Saturday, February 26, to introduce his June 30, 1897, report to Washington on powder and shells then stowed in the *Maine*. Contrary to earlier testimony, the report showed a large amount of gunpowder in the reserve magazine, including 3,400 pounds of black saluting powder.

"Q. What changes were made since June 30th? A. I think there has been considerable change in the Reserve Magazine because we have done a good deal of saluting. I also understood there was very little left in that magazine. It [the 6-inch tanks] was probably put in the regular six inch."

Sigsbee was losing credibility because his self-serving tactic was to minimize damage that might have been done by magazines and maximize mine damage. To resolve the issue, Wainwright was recalled. He contradicted Sigsbee by stating that few 6-inch charges had been removed from the reserve magazine. He was not asked how much saluting powder was left, but the quantity was assumed to have remained substantial.

Next Powelson returned. "Q. Have you done anything toward verifying your testimony in regard to thickness of the plates you referred to? A. I do not think I mentioned thickness of the plates." The ensign was as persnickety as ever.

Wainwright and Powelson had taken the divers away from exploration of the obscured inboard hole at frame 30 to concentrate on something the officers could see, the inverted V made by the raised bottom plating at frame 17. After Powelson testified to his usual minutiae, the judge advocate asked him, "What do you deduce from this information? A. I think that an explosion occurred on the port side somewhere about frame 18. Q. Would you put 18 as the center of impact? It seems to me that has to be taken in connection with other injuries." Marix was concerned about the origin of the devastation at frame 30, but Powelson's response was an unequivocal, "Yes, sir."

Marix would not let go of the frame 30 destruction: "How do you account for the immense damage abreast of the Reserve Magazine, where there is nothing left, whereas between frames 16 and 18 you have found damaged plates? A. My idea is that after the ship was raised at frame 18 [by the mine], the magazines, one or all of them, were exploded, for some powder tanks were exploded while others were not."

This was the ultimate answer. Powelson was asserting that a mine had exploded beneath the *Maine* at frame 18, forcing up the bottom plates and partially detonating the forward 6-inch magazine. The reserve magazine had blown up in a chain reaction, causing the devastation at frame 30.

As the press accurately reported, Captain Chadwick was not convinced. He asked a tough question: "Do you think that this same means [the mine at frame 18] carried away the forward part of the Reserve Magazine?" He was talking about the mine doing all the damage rather than through a chain reaction of the magazines. Powelson hesitated: "That question, sir, brings in so much conjecture. If anything were known about the amount of powder [in the mine], you might draw some conclusions."

Chadwick continued the inquiry: "If there were a big hole driven up through the ship at frame 26 [frame 30], is it not likely that the same force would be the force that lifted the ship at frame 18, 30 feet away?" Rather than contradict the domineering captain, Powelson began to hedge: "I think a very heavy explosion farther aft than frame 18—as the ship was much weaker forward of frame 24 than aft—could well have produced" the damage at frame 18. "Q. Is it not likely there were two outside forces?"

The hearing deteriorated into an informal discussion. Chadwick cautioned Powelson, "Then I think I would not say definitely that it was at that particular place [frame 18]." Sampson added, "Yes. He is basing his opinion now on what he has seen [from the surface]. When you come to take in the big hole [aft], that may have been produced by still another mine."

An intimidated Powelson acknowledged that "where the bottom plate was thrown up, it would seem to me the force was communicated some distance through the water, because this thing [bottom plate] was lifted up instead of being battered in. It was a force that was cushioned in some way. So, this explosion may have occurred aft."

By then, the time was 5:15 P.M. An irresolute court was ready to adjourn. Sampson was thinking about two mines. Chadwick was not convinced there had been any mine. As the result of forceful questioning by Chadwick and Marix, Powelson had backtracked from his concept of a mine at frame 18 as the primary cause of the damage. Instead, he was acquiescing to the suggestion that the primary explosion might have occurred near frame 30, where the cause could equally well have been a mine or spontaneous combustion.

The clever young officer who was to become celebrated as the identifier of the *Maine*'s risen bottom plates was of two minds concerning the meaning of what he had discovered.

SPIKING IN KEY WEST

Because there was nothing constructive to do in Havana for the moment, the court moved to Key West where the rest of the survivors were. Sigsbee remained in Havana on the understanding that Marix would cable him if his interests as defendant were threatened.

There had been no meeting on Sunday, so the inquiry's seventh day was Monday, February 28, in the United States Courthouse on the Key. Both officers and enlisted men testified.

One witness was Frederick Bowers, the first assistant engineer: "Q. Give the history of the coal inside bunker A-16. A. That bunker contained soft coal, Pocahontas, I think. If it came from Norfolk, I inspected it."

Soft coal was Chadwick's focus: "Q. Did you have the usual thermostats in the bunkers? A. Yes, sir, but they didn't work very well. Sometimes they rang when there was no coal in the bunker. Q. You never had a fire from spontaneous combustion in that ship, did you? A. No, sir." Chadwick knew that a ship which had never had a coal fire was unlikely to experience self-ignition, but faulty thermostats favored the accident theory.

The next witness was Assistant Engineer John Morris: "Q. You were on duty the day of the explosion? A. Yes, sir. Q. When did you inspect the bunkers? A. It was some time during the forenoon. I think between 10 and 11 o'clock. Q. Can you remember making a careful inspection of bunker A-16? A. There was no heat perceptible, more than just the temperature of the hydraulic room." The heat was only at the low level that was usual in the room on the deck above the reserve magazine.

Then came the crucial point: "Q. Had you any occasion to go in coal bunkers B-4 and B-6, adjacent to A-16? A. Yes, sir. The [last] inspection was at 7:45 P.M. Q. You did not go into B-4? Q. I looked inside. There was nothing unusual there. I simply had the door closed down, as it was night inspection. I did not enter B-6."

Self-ignited coal fires were not instantaneous. Yet Morris had been in the vicinity of bunker A-16 two hours before the explosions. There had been no smoke, smell, or overheated air, and no surface was hot to his hand. For Chadwick, the possibility of spontaneous combustion had suddenly diminished. Morris spiked the accident theory just as Powelson had boosted the mine hypothesis.

During the early afternoon of the ninth day, Marix informed the court that he had no more testimony to offer at Key West. In the presence of the court, all the ambulatory survivors were assembled in the army barracks. As a unit they declared under oath that they had no fault to find with any officer or man belonging to the *Maine*, either on the night of the destruction of the ship or previous to that night. This was the group ceremony the press had deprecated before the inquiry began, but the joint oath proved to be only a minuscule part of the investigation.

COMPLETING THE FACT FINDING

Back in Havana for the tenth day, First Officer George Cornell of the *City of Washington* testified he was looking at the *Maine* at the moment of the explosions. He "heard a rumbling sound and saw the *Maine* raise up forward. We saw her raising by her lights. After that the explosion occurred." He saw the lights raise before the second explosion because the second explosion put out the lights by destroying the dynamo.

Captain Frank Stevens of the *Washington* "heard a dull, muffled explosion like it was under water, followed instantly by a terrific explosion, lighting up the air. My first impression was that it was a gun or a shot, but then it flashed across my mind that there was dynamite under the bottom of that ship."

The evidence favoring the mine theory was mounting as Powelson submitted a sketch of the devastated forward part of the ship, based on divers' explorations while the court was in Key West. In addition to the plate curled like paper at frame 30, the divers had discovered several other plates they claimed were pushed in. Faced with this multitude of possibilities, the officers could not determine what was real. In contrast, the inverted V above the surface of the water was hypnotizing.

The members of the court had intense discussions at dinner and while sitting on deck in the evening. Sampson was not wholly reconciled to Powelson's original premise, yet he was convinced that no accident had occurred. Chadwick was weakening in his support of spontaneous combustion, although he did not trust Powelson's analysis. According to the sketch, the greatest damage to the *Maine* was in the forward area that was most critical in determining the cause of the explosions. Only heaps of debris remained. There was no structure left that could be raised in one piece.

The time was right for the court to comply with its precept. Substantially all the information that could come from the wreck was at hand. What was needed now was interpretation, confirmation, and decision.

EXPERT WITNESSES

At Captain Sampson's request, Secretary Long sent Constructor John Hoover to appear as an expert witness on the twelfth day. His influence on the court was considerable, though off the record.

On the fifteenth day the court turned to Commander George Converse of the *Montgomery.* He had served at the torpedo station in Rhode Island for eleven years, was familiar with explosives, and had frequently observed the detonation of mines. Like Powelson, he was available as a witness only because his ship happened to be in Havana, substituting for the *Fern.*

Chadwick took up the questioning: "If one or more of those magazines [on the *Maine*] should explode, would such an explosion lift the forward body of the ship out of the water? A. I don't think it would." This was a warm-up question. Experts agreed that a magazine explosion could not raise a ship and that the detonation of a submarine mine might. Besides, Sampson and Chadwick had already privately discussed the subject with Converse, so the nature of Converse's response was no surprise.

From the tenor of Chadwick's questions, it was apparent that he was discarding the coal-bunker theory: "Q. What is your experience in the explosion of a submarine mine, as to what becomes of the case? A. I have rarely seen any considerable pieces of mine. They are almost invariably ruptured and lost. They are blown up." Europeans were claiming that there had been no mine under the *Maine* because no casing had been found. Converse supplied a logical response.

Chadwick continued the examination: "To what kind of explosion do you attribute this bending of plates and keel [at frame 17]? A. I am of the opinion that it could be produced by the explosion of a submarine mine containing a large amount of the lower explosives—gunpowder—not in contact with the ship, but perhaps on the bottom [of the harbor]."

"Q. Could that portion of the keel which has frame 18 on top, and the bent plates forward of it, have become so distorted from an internal [magazine] explosion alone? A. I do not think it could. Q. Do you think then, necessarily, there must have been an underwater mine [at frame 18] to produce these explosions? A. Indications are that an underwater explosion produced the conditions there."

Chadwick then relinquished the interrogation to Marix who asked the hardest question of all: "Would it be possible for the forward ten inch and six inch magazines to have exploded [by accident], torn out the ship's sides, and leave that part of the ship forward of frame 18 so water-borne as to raise the after portion of the ship, drag it aft, and bring [bend] the vertical keel into the condition you see?" He did not mean "drag it aft" but draw the after part of the ship forward the ten feet the ship was foreshortened according to Hoover's measurements.

Marix was asking whether the inverted V of the keel at frame 17 could have been caused merely by the settling action of the two segments of the sinking ship, without any mine explosion at frame 18. The answer was, "It is difficult for me to realize that that effect could have been produced by an [accidental] explosion of the kind supposed." That was less than a direct response, but it was one typical of Converse.

Marix continued, "Could a mine causing the distortion of the plates forward of frame 18 also set fire to the magazine?" This was still in dispute among ordnance experts. The conservative Converse replied, "I am unable to answer that question," even though he offered no other explanation for the devastation at frame 30.

Finally, Marix presented a personal opinion. If a mine exploded beneath the ship and penetrated into a magazine, letting in water while detonating the powder, only a partial explosion of the magazine would be likely. Wet powder would resist explosion. If an accidental explosion occurred inside the magazine, however, the powder would be dry and all would be likely to explode. The *Maine* had both exploded and unexploded 6-inch powder cans. Therefore, Marix believed that the *Maine*'s magazines had been detonated by a mine.

THE COURT DELIBERATES

Converse reappeared on the seventeenth day: "Q. Supposing the initial cause of the disaster had been by such a mine as you have described, and that this explosion had exploded the forward magazines, what would have been the result caused by this second explosion? A. The explosion of a magazine, entirely or partially flooded, would tend to blow open and back the sides and deck of the ship. An explosion of this kind would be progressive, until all obstacles were removed. Much of the explosive material in the magazine would be scattered without exploding." This description of the results of a mine explosion detonating a magazine tallied with what had apparently happened to the *Maine*.

On the eighteenth day, March 15, Powelson made his eighth and last appearance. He was the discoverer of the raised bottom plates, yet his testimony had lost its luster for the court. Sampson had conscripted Hoover and Converse to draw conclusions from Powelson's find rather than relying on the ensign. To the public, however, Powelson remained the most ingenious American officer in Havana.

The court moved to Sampson's battleship *Iowa* at Key West, where no stenographer was present to take notes of the discussions. The members deliberated in closed sessions until the twenty-third day of the inquiry, Monday, March 21.

The Sampson Findings

★ ★ ★ ★ ★ ★ ★ ★

EXPLOSION AT FRAME 18

A dmiral Sicard's February 19 precept had called for findings by the court on facts established by the evidence, the cause of the explosions, and whether there was fault by the *Maine*'s officers or men or by others not part of the United States Navy.

When the findings were completed March 21, they were devoted mainly to demonstrating that there had been no negligence on the *Maine*: "The state of discipline was excellent, and all orders and regulations in regard to the care and safety of the ship were strictly carried out." Sigsbee and his officers were pronounced free of wrongdoing. There was no equivalent declaration of the innocence of the Spaniards who were the "others" in the precept.

The description of the disaster and the determination of the cause were briefer: "There were two explosions of a different character, with a very short but distinct interval between them, and the forward part of the ship was lifted at the time of the first explosion. The first explosion," the court continued, "was in the nature of a report like that of a gun, while the second explosion was more open, prolonged, and of greater volume. This second explosion was caused by the partial explosion of two or more of the forward magazines."

Thus the impartial testimony of the witnesses on the *City of Washington* was accepted as factual. The finding was implicitly that the first explosion was the mine, the second the roar of the magazines. The court could have listed three or more magazines instead of two. The forward 6-inch magazine at frame 18 necessarily exploded. So did the reserve magazine at the point of greatest damage. These two magazines were connected by the fixed ammunition magazine. All three were demolished.

Next the court turned to the wreck's forward section near frame 30, which was obscured by the mud on the harbor bottom: "The evidence bearing upon this [section], being primarily obtained from divers, did not enable the Court to form a definite conclusion as to condition."

This was a gratuitous slap at Powelson and the divers. The court had lost confidence in the ensign. The implication was that he had made no contribution to the investigation apart from his identification of the elevated keel. The services of the divers could have been spared. The inboard hole they discovered in the ship's bottom near frame 30 was not mentioned.

The court went on to describe the crucial forward part of the ship that could be seen above the water: "At frame 17, the outer shell of the ship has been forced up about four feet above the surface. The outside bottom plating is bent into a reversed V shape." This was not in dispute.

Then came the principal finding: "In the opinion of the Court, this effect could have been produced only by the explosion of a mine under the bottom of the ship at about frame 18 and on the port side." This was an expected if incomplete judgment. Nothing was said about the mine's size, type, explosive content, distance from the ship, or source.

Finally, the court claimed to have been "unable to obtain evidence fixing responsibility for the destruction upon any person or persons." The indication was that the mine was of Spanish origin, although members of the court agreed privately that the Spanish government was not involved. Fanatics were presumably culpable, but the court did not say so.

This evasive closing paragraph aided American jingoes by encouraging the belief that the Spanish government was at fault for the deaths of 267 sailors and the loss of a fine battleship. The surge toward war with Spain was accelerated by the court's failure to extend its precept and expressly state the innocence of the Spanish government as it had for Sigsbee.

DOCTRINE OF CHANCE

Before the court of inquiry issued its findings, *Harper's Weekly* editorialized that "we may never know the mysterious cause of the loss of the *Maine*, but we may rest assured that the report of the Sampson Board will be conclusive.

When that is published, we shall know all that will ever be discovered of the cause."

After the court's findings were released, the *Weekly* confirmed that "every decent citizen in the country accepted the report as final judgment on the disaster. In American minds, the report is conclusive."

The *New York Herald* described Wainwright and Powelson as "reading the report with delight" in Havana because "the Court's deduction was drawn chiefly, if not solely, from the structural evidence." Powelson was praised as the protagonist in the inquiry, the only twenty-five-year-old listed in *Who's Who in America* for 1898: "His testimony before the Court, proving the *Maine* was blown up by a mine, was widely and favorably commented on by scientific journals."

Conservative newspapers applauded the court for what they called dedication to fair play. They reported that from the day the keel was identified, there had been no question but that the explosion was external. The court had been under tremendous pressure because of public prejudgment of Spanish guilt, yet Chadwick had led a determined hunt for contrary evidence that was never found. The members had leaned over backward to reach an unbiased verdict. To the court's credit, the conservatives wrote, Spain was not specifically indicted.

The yellow press was not satisfied, however, with the court's avoidance of the issue of Spanish guilt. These papers reported falsely that "some of the most sensational testimony accumulated by the Court has been withheld from the public. There were two witnesses who furnished startling facts showing the culpability of certain Spanish officials." The *Journal* specified that "two persons crossing the bay one night suddenly had their boat caught by a wire which became entangled on the rudder." The wire was supposed to have been the electric cable to explode the mine, even though detonating wires would have run along the bottom of the harbor.

The *Journal's* accusation was, "Suppressed testimony shows Spain is guilty of blowing up the *Maine*." Secretary Long denied the charge. He announced that the printed report contained all the evidence except for one witness' name that was withheld for the man's protection. In the course of Long's denial, the anonymous witness was unintentionally disclosed to be Havana resident Señor Brondi. What happened to Brondi as the consequence of the revelation was not mentioned.

Sampson remained characteristically silent about the findings. Instead, the court's reasoning was clarified by Marix and Chadwick. According to Marix, the court "did not feel a particle of doubt as to how the *Maine* was destroyed" once the elevated keel was discovered.

Marix maintained that "we know the *Maine* was blown up by a mine as surely as a physician knows a man was poisoned when he finds the effects of poison. The evidence was circumstantial, in that we did not find any remnant of the mine or the person who caused the explosion, but it was conclusive. The keel was blown upward, plates were blown inward, and nothing except a mine could have produced that. The wreck of the *Maine* was mute, incontestable evidence, and, after exhausting all available evidence, the Board has so reported." By "plates blown inward," Marix meant the bottom plates that were displaced upward with the keel.

When the *Herald* shielded Marix as an "unnamed source," he spoke freely concerning the unresolved issue of responsibility for the disaster: "The investigation proved that the mine was too big and too well suited to the purpose to have been secured or made by an ordinary conspirator or fanatic, but could have been got only through the connivance of someone whose business it is to manufacture, guard, or direct the use of government mines. It does not mean necessarily the complicity of the Spanish government, but simply that an employee of the government may have used his position to aid the dastardly plot." Marix added that the explosive was probably a large quantity of gunpowder, as Converse had suggested.

Chadwick wrote about the disaster in various publications over a period of years. As background, he repeated that "the presence of the *Maine* was regarded by the Spanish in Havana as a threat. She dominated the city. It required but a fanatic to combine the serious weakening of an enemy's power, revenge for supposed injuries, and a dramatic stroke dear to such a temperament. That the Spanish government was responsible, except through want of precautions, was not supposed."

Chadwick claimed he had been uniquely qualified to sit on the *Maine* court because he "was intimately acquainted with her construction, as her inspector during building." He knew that her "scantling [framing] was heavier than any other ship in the service." When he was told "the bottom of the ship in the vicinity of the upheaval was terribly rent," he decided it was "rent in a way no other explosion [than a mine] could have caused."

"The wreck was gone over with the greatest care," he asserted. "Part of the ship's bottom was [more than] 34 feet above its normal position, and this fact was the determining cause of the Board's finding. It was inconceivable that the bottom could be lifted by the explosion of magazines alone.

"The only question was whether this lifting [of the keel] could have been caused by the descending of the ship. The ship's bottom was a very powerful girder only 14 feet above the harbor bed. I cannot conceive that it should have been doubled upon itself until first weakened by an exterior explosion. Moreover, the after body of the ship sank so slowly in the shallow water that no such effort could have bent the heavy girder."

Chadwick also stated that the *Maine*'s "arrangements were much freer from danger through spontaneous combustion than most ships. The bunkers next to the magazines adjoined wing passages through which men were constantly passing, and in which any unusual heat would have been noticed at once." He pointed out that "spontaneous combustion is not an instantaneous process. It is a gradual heating. The temperatures of bunkers, magazines, and shell rooms were taken daily. I would regard her as a perfectly safe ship."

In addition to logic, Chadwick stressed "the doctrine of chance. That a ship peculiarly safe and with a crew in a special state of watchfulness should have waited until her arrival in Havana to undergo accident aboard, seems to transcend the bounds of probabilities to such a degree that this is almost sufficient of itself to settle the question against interior accident, apart from the reasons which seemed to the Court to be conclusive. However, this doctrine of chance did not occur to me at that time." The court, he was saying, acted on rational grounds, not probabilities, although the *Maine* was "the only ship in our Navy which has ever been so destroyed."

Finally, Chadwick recognized that the naval court would inevitably be attacked as biased because the members were investigating fellow naval officers. He insisted that "the Board was aware of the delicacy of its position and the importance of its finding. There was no unkindly feeling toward Spanish officials. The Board would not allow itself to be hurried. The members had begun with taking for granted that the explosion was wholly interior. The conditions shown as the examination proceeded convinced us otherwise.

"To ask whose hand dictated the finding is silly. The Board was left absolutely free, and felt itself so. The members would welcome an examination of the wreck by a complete exposure [dewatering]. It could only result in substantiating the description by the Court."

That was the explanation of how the Sampson court arrived at its conclusions. The court believed that the *Maine* had been sent to an enemy port where a foreseeable disaster occurred. Members of the court were familiar with the ship and able to ascertain her condition after the calamity. The elevated keel was the key to the finding that a mine had been detonated beneath the ship. The keel could not have been bent in that manner by magazine explosions or by lurching of the ship after the explosions.

Further, the *Maine* had been a safe and well-run ship. There was insufficient time for spontaneous combustion of bunker coal to have developed after night inspection. If there had been ignition, the fire would have been discovered.

Besides, there was the doctrine of chance. Who could believe in an accident in a hostile harbor on the eve of war when no such disaster had ever happened any place before in the long history of the United States Navy?

A NEGLIGENCE SO GROSS

Both the court of inquiry and President McKinley had relinquished the finding of Spanish guilt to the Senate Foreign Relations Committee. Nine of the eleven members of the committee were undisguised jingoes and the chief witness was to be the militant Sigsbee.

As soon as the Sampson court left Havana, Sigsbee had asked Powelson to prepare a private report on the disaster. Powelson was thorough as usual, even though some of his ideas had already been rebuffed by the court. Sigsbee remarked that Powelson's "report convinced me I could accept my own views. I never believed any other theory than that the *Maine* was blown up from the outside." Actually, a liberated Sigsbee had started flaunting his previously guarded hatred of the Spaniards after Powelson's discovery of the elevated keel.

When he appeared before the Senate committee on March 31, Sigsbee testified that from the outset he knew his ship was sunk by an outside explosion. He described the mine as big but no larger than could be planted near the *Maine* in broad daylight by one of the small boats that were always passing. By his calculations, twelve men would have been needed. He was not certain whether the fatal mine was Spanish or homemade, but he knew fanatics "could make a mine out of an old hogshead or even a wine pipe."

Sigsbee revealed that while socializing with Sampson and Converse during the hearings in Havana, he told them how a Spanish lighter could have laid the mine. "They admitted the plan was feasible," he recalled, "and when I pointed out a lighter passing ahead of the *Montgomery*, each admitted that if she were then dropping a mine, we could not detect her in the act."

Next, he recycled his court testimony about the mined mooring and the rare variation in the trade wind. Then he added a bit of uncorroborated gossip: "The *La Gasca* came out and anchored at that buoy the day before we went in. She has torpedo tubes and was General Weyler's dispatch boat. The captain of that vessel never called on me. I permitted myself to suspect him [of laying the fatal mine], but I never had any proof." No one else ever mentioned this.

The rest of Sigsbee's statement dealt with spontaneous combustion of coal: "There was but one thing to be taken under suspicion in the *Maine*. There was a bunker alongside a magazine, but there is not the slightest suspicion of that bunker besides its existence there." He emphasized that the coal in the bunker had been untouched for three months and so was particularly stable. At last he was learning his lessons about the routine on the ship that had been run well by his officers.

The Senate committee welcomed anything Sigsbee said that would pin guilt on Spain. The members cheered when he ended by declaring that after the explosions "I had no more confidence in the [Spanish] people. Treachery had been shown us." The press reported Sigsbee's testimony as concluding that the engine of destruction was a submarine mine of the Spanish government, exploded by men who wore the Spanish uniform, but without the knowledge of the Spanish government. The *World* reduced this to "Spanish officials blew up the *Maine*, according to Sigsbee."

Consul General Lee was also a witness. He pictured himself as an insider at the court: "I do not suppose there was a day they were there that I did not see Sampson and Potter and Marix." He did not mention Chadwick who had been the holdout.

Lee's theory of planting the mine corresponded to Sigsbee's: "The *Maine* was anchored to a buoy. A vessel swinging gets all around the circle. Anybody could go in front of her on a dark night and drop one of these submarine mines of 500 pounds."

Correspondent Honoré Laine of the *Journal* presented the only new material. He showed a copy of a January 1898 letter supposedly from General Weyler to a Cuban friend: "I have read the Americans are sending one of their warships to Havana. During my command in Cuba they did not dare to dream of it. They knew the terrible punishment that awaited them. I had Havana harbor prepared for such an emergency. If the insult is made, I hope there will be a Spanish hand to punish it as terribly as it deserves." After the *Maine* exploded, Laine was in Havana. He told the committee that all he said in public was, "Someone followed Weyler's advice," and he was arrested by the Spanish police.

Weyler denied the letter's authenticity even though the phrasing had a ring of truth. Many people believed Weyler had planted the mine that blew up the *Maine* and that one of his fanatical disciples had detonated the charge in his behalf. The *Journal* reported that Weyler had bought dynamite in London and Philadelphia and that Manterola had ordered electric cable.

Out of these tidings of doubtful validity, the Senate committee perfected the findings of the court of inquiry. On April 13, the committee observed that "there was in Havana an expressed hatred of the United States among officials who had been adherents of Weyler." The conclusion was "that the destruction of the *Maine* was either by the official act of the Spanish authorities or was made possible by [Spanish] negligence so willing and gross as to be equivalent to positive criminal action."

The deliberations of the jingo senators were serene compared to similar hearings in the House of Representatives. Because the Speaker of the House was opposed to a Spanish war, "Men fought, the charges 'liar' and 'scoundrel' were bandied, there were half-a-dozen personal collisions, books were thrown, and members rushed the aisles like madmen. Not for years had such a scene occurred."

Both Houses of Congress were swept along by the war spirit.

THE FISH STORY AND ALL THAT

The verdict of the Spanish court of inquiry was forwarded from Madrid to the State Department on March 26. The finding was not immediately released to the American public. Instead, it was tacked to the end of a published Senate document where it received little attention.

In the Spanish finding, Captain Peral argued that after the *Maine* blew up there was no physical indication of a mine explosion. He claimed that American divers had prevented a complete evaluation inside the wreck. Nevertheless, the Spanish divers had examined the hull and bottom as carefully as possible for two weeks. They reported no major damage. Hull plates were bent outward. The keel was buried in mud and was uninjured.

From a mixed bag of plausible Spanish witnesses and unreliable divers, Peral had evolved his conclusions. Beyond what he called the absurdity of the mine concept, the points he raised were essentially the same as in his preliminary opinion. They were serious considerations that demanded a thoughtful U.S. response they did not get.

First, Peral stated that the explosion took place while the battleship was motionless at a time of no thrust of wind or tide. A contact mine could not have been detonated. The mine would have had to be set off electrically, and no trace of cable or land station was discovered.

Next, Peral applied textbook principles to the disaster. In submarine explosions, he explained, the bursting sound is followed by a rising column of water. Quaking is noticed on shore and shock is felt on nearby ships. Also, he said, "great weight should be attached to the [absence] of dead fish on the surface." Finally, he pointed out that "no case has been recorded where the explosion of a torpedo against the side of a vessel has caused the explosion of magazines." To support this statement that had originated with Professor Alger, Peral cited standard English treatises on torpedoes.

Peral then brought in witnesses to demonstrate the dearth of physical evidence. Although the witnesses testified that the harbor "abounds in fish and fishermen," he had examined the bay himself in the early morning of the sixteenth without finding dead fish. Whenever even a small amount of dynamite was used in harbor blasting, a great number of dead fish were found inside the hulls of sunken ships and floating on the surface.

Beyond mentioning that there was no crater in the mud, Peral ignored his divers just as the Sampson court had ignored the American divers. Instead, he emphasized the frequency of spontaneous combustion of bunker coal in U.S. warships. He professed astonishment "that powder magazines should still be placed in contact with coal bunkers," as in the *Maine*.

The 181-page Spanish finding concluded that "external appearances and lack of circumstances which necessarily accompany the explosion of a torpedo [mine] assert that the catastrophe was due to internal causes." Negative evidence precluded the existence of a mine and spontaneous combustion was what was left.

Peral was a knowledgeable investigator. Nevertheless, he weakened his conclusions by disregarding the raised keel. He was also handicapped by his superiors' desire to avoid conflict. Either the Spanish authorities were afraid a deeper search would turn up a Weylerite mine as the cause or they accepted the inevitability of war and no longer cared about causes.

The Spanish report's bitterest critic was Captain Sigsbee. When asked about the absence of dead fish in the harbor, he replied, "We regarded that excuse as rather peculiarly Spanish." Concerning the extent of the Spanish investigation, he remarked that "our people laughed at them. They did very little work on the wreck. The greatest point on our side was that we had Ensign Powelson. When military and naval men look at our report and compare it with their report, with the fish story and all that sort of thing, a military smile will go around the world."

Captain Chadwick was equally smug about the comparison between the two reports: "The incompleteness of the Spanish examination is shown by the statement of the principal Spanish diver that 'the keel did not appear to have suffered any damage,' a statement in complete disaccord with the facts."

Another attack on the Spanish report was that Manterola did not rebut the American insinuation that Spanish mines were planted in the harbor. Moreover, the Sampson court spent twenty-three days developing structural data on the wreck while Peral was doing his research in the library.

The Spaniards had allowed themselves to be buncoed by McKinley. They had expected the American court to hand down a verdict of accidental cause. When the finding was a mine as the cause, they were too surprised to react in a timely manner. They should have brought in international experts from the beginning.

Finally, Sigsbee pointed out the defect that "no American appeared before the Spanish Court." That was a major weakness in the Spanish report, but it was a flaw that Sigsbee himself had contrived.

Declaration of War

★ ★ ★ ★ ★ ★ ★ ★

THE MARCH TOWARD WAR IN APRIL

Captain Sigsbee was feted as a hero on his return to Washington the end of March 1898. He expected no less.

Congressman George Smith of the *Journal*'s Cuba commission had told Sigsbee that he was with the President on the morning after the *Maine* explosions. The President was disappointed to hear a report that Sigsbee was on shore when the disaster struck. Then came the news that Sigsbee was not only on board but had in fact been the last to leave the burning ship. Smith said that when the President learned this, tears came to his eyes.

Sigsbee was recognized on Washington streets. Passersby waved their hats at him and called out, "May God remember the *Maine!*" In the Navy Department his associates greeted him affectionately. Long took him to the White House where McKinley made flattering remarks and offered him a choice of receptions in a theater or at the National Geographic Society. Sigsbee chose the society because he was a member. Alexander Graham Bell was host at an evening affair the President attended on April 2.

When Sicard was allowed to resign, Sampson was named commander of the North Atlantic Squadron. He was promoted to rear admiral, without the presidential reception Sigsbee received.

Before assuming the position of Sampson's chief of staff, Chadwick sailed back to Havana on the *Fern* which was the shuttle from Key West. He was the senior member of a naval board of survey to determine the final disposition of the *Maine*. Despite the unrecovered bodies of scores of U.S. sailors, the decision was to abandon the destroyed ship. War was too near to permit extended salvaging. The commercial wreckers were instructed to leave Havana as soon as they could and Wainwright was ordered to return to the mainland on April 5.

Admiral Manterola assumed that U.S. naval personnel would depart with the wreckers. The day the wreckers were scheduled to leave, Manterola directed the Spanish lieutenant on guard at the *Maine* to haul down the tattered American flag that had been flying day and night. When Wainwright learned about the order, he issued a warning through his interpreter, "Tell the officer in charge of the guard that if any Spaniard touches the flag that flies from that wreck, there will be another wreck in Havana harbor. Tell him I will sink his barge myself!"

Wainwright had only the *Fern's* one one-pounder Roosevelt had wangled for Cowles in response to his brother-in-law's plea for any kind of gun. The rapid-firing Hotchkiss compared poorly with the heavy armament on the big Spanish warships anchored nearby. Nevertheless, Manterola recognized Wainwright as a brave opponent. The Spanish admiral sensibly relented when he was told that the Americans would be staying for only a few more days. Wainwright himself hauled down the flag and Sigsbee's pennant as his last act before quitting the harbor. He ceremoniously tore the pennant in half to signify official abandonment of the *Maine* to the Spaniards.

The Americans' departure from Havana was one more indication that war was near. As Spain floundered reluctantly toward accommodation with the United States, McKinley's demands became more stringent. On March 27, McKinley had finally insisted that Spain withdraw completely from Cuba as the price of peace. Spain was just then accepting McKinley's less onerous conditions set two weeks earlier. Spain never did catch up.

The U.S. ambassador in Madrid told McKinley that Spain was moving as fast as possible without provoking a revolution that could place Weyler in power. When Spain stalled for time on March 31, however, McKinley secretly put the United States on a war footing the next day.

Paradoxically, this was the moment when prospects for peace looked most favorable to foreign observers. Spain was openly offering to arbitrate while entreating the Pope to act as mediator. In contrast, McKinley was rebuffing the European powers' overtures in behalf of Spain and covertly warning United States consuls in Spanish territory to be ready to leave on short notice. Congress had given McKinley latitude to negotiate, but the Spaniards had no idea how little time was left for a bloodless resolution.

McKinley was now convinced that war was the only answer to the Cuban problem, even though his ambassador to Madrid was cabling, "You will win the fight on your own lines" if negotiations are allowed to continue. The President advised the ambassador that diplomacy was finished. He was already preparing a war message to Congress that was being delayed solely "to give the consul general at Havana the time he urgently asks to insure safe departure of Americans."

Meanwhile, Spanish General Beranger imprudently admitted in Madrid that Havana harbor had actually been mined. He had been responsible for mines as Minister of Marine in the Conservative government that sent Weyler to Cuba. Ensign Powelson was back in Havana on the *Fern*. When he poked around the flagless wreck to relive his triumphs, he was ordered off by the Spaniards. He rowed back to his ship without an argument.

Also in Havana, Consul Lee was hastily preparing to depart from the post where he had become the American most hated by the Spaniards. Before boarding the *Fern* on April 9, Lee called at the palace to bid a nostalgic if ceremonial goodby to his adversary, General Blanco. He was turned away with the word that Blanco did not wish to see him. When Lee left the palace, he was jeered by the guards. The reason for this display of ill will was a *La Lucha* editorial, "Without diplomatic relations being broken, Lee leaves in a hurry with his clerks, after alarming many American citizens. His departure has the appearance of an escape."

When Lee steamed out of Havana harbor on the *Fern*, thousands of Spaniards lined the shore of the channel to mock him. Unperturbed, the portly consul offered a champagne toast as the *Fern* passed Morro Castle: "Here is to the officers and men of the *Maine*, which was blown up by a Spanish mine."

Lee knew that he would be the hero of the hour in the United States because his unrelenting hatred of Spain fit the national mood. After he made fiery speeches in Washington, he was challenged to a duel by a hotheaded young Spanish naval attaché. Wisely, he did not respond. He insisted, "I think some of the Spanish officers were cognizant of the plans to destroy the *Maine*, but not General Blanco." He could afford to be magnanimous.

At the critical moment on April 10, the Pope's intervention met with success in Madrid. Spain agreed to an armistice in Cuba. The Spanish newspaper *Epoca* wrote, "It now lies with America to show whether she will cooperate with Spain for peace or whether she wishes to provoke a quarrel."

McKinley answered the question the next day. He sent the war message to Congress, asking that he be empowered "to use the military and naval forces of the United States" against Spain.

The President had given in to congressional pressure expressed as "Remember the *Maine* and to Hell with Spain." Militancy was widespread throughout the country. Children shrieked, "Remember the *Maine*." Women wore hair ribbons stenciled with the slogan. "Remember the *Maine*" was printed in red on white peppermint candies. The most popular American toy was a replica of the *Maine* that blew up at the release of a spring. Shop windows and family sitting rooms enshrined photographs of the sunken ship. The omnipresent exhortation was sung, recited, thundered, and sermonized. The story was released and then denied that "Remember the *Maine*" was being baked into the daily bread of the Army and Navy.

Congress passed a war resolution that was signed by the President on April 20. McKinley was directed to intervene in Cuba although any intention of assuming sovereignty over the island was disclaimed. On the twenty-first Spain severed relations with the United States.

At daybreak on April 22, Admiral Sampson's squadron sailed to blockade the Cuban coast. On the twenty-fourth, Admiral Dewey received orders to attack the Spanish fleet in the Philippines. Sigsbee left for Philadelphia to take command of the converted passenger liner the *St. Paul*. He called the ship an auxiliary cruiser, "the largest man-of-war ever." In his eyes, his rehabilitation was complete, but to the Navy the new command was a mockery.

On April 25, Congress enacted the declaration of war against Spain "since the 21st day of April, including said day" when Spain broke relations.

The New York *Sun* sighed, "We are all jingoes now, and the head jingo is the Hon. William McKinley."

WHY WAR?

After the Sampson report had been published in March 1898, war was said to be unavoidable because "not one American in 10,000 will admit the possibility of an accident" on the *Maine*. According to the *New York Times*, Spain was directly responsible for the disaster: "The *Maine* was deliberately moored over a Spanish mine. The Spanish officer who actually blew up the *Maine* was as indiscreet as Madrid newspapers which exulted in his deed."

That was the conservative view. The yellow press went further, promoting hysteria by contrasting Spanish treachery with dead American sailors. War was called a crusade for vengeance against perfidious Spain for the young heroes who had been plunged from sleep into a watery grave by a sneak Spanish bomb exploded under the *Maine*.

A year later when the war was over, the destruction of the *Maine* was still credited with having stampeded the American people into the conflict. The Senate committee's report fixing guilt on Spain for the disaster had inflamed southern and western populists who were hard-core jingoes. "Remember the *Maine*" had been printed on every surface. The barrage of rallying cries, editorials, poems, buttons, and badges had aroused deep patriotic emotions.

Cynicism, however, was already being expressed. McKinley's need for populist support to win the upcoming presidential election was also being given as a reason for the war. Some people labeled the hostilities "Hearst's War" because of the role of the yellow press. Heavily discounted bonds issued by insurgent Cubans to pay for U.S. arms were listed as another cause. Investors had lobbied for war because the bonds were to be redeemed at full value when the Cuban republic was established.

Ten years later, the allegedly reprehensible role of the Spaniards in the *Maine* disaster was down-played in favor of blander reasons applicable to any foreign involvement. Historians mentioned the humanitarian resolve to halt suffering on the island. There was also the excuse about protecting the lives of U.S. citizens and their commercial and financial interests. A dawning awareness of the absence of true menace to the peace and safety of the United States, though, signified that there had been no moral justification for the war.

By 1925, the loss of the *Maine* was regarded by historians as "a matter of small import" among the war's causes. The disaster merely supplied the peg the war was hung on. "It was the preceding and subsequent events that made the *Maine* the signal of a new era of national prestige." The construction of the big navy and the seizing of colonies were manifestations of the "new American era."

Twenty-five years later, the *Maine* catastrophe was seen as inconsequential among the "events which impelled the United States into war with Spain. The Spanish position in Cuba would have been untenable, regardless of whether the *Maine* exploded. Sooner or later, a mixture of idealism, nationalism, and strategic calculation would have brought about American intervention."

The modern view recognizes a more imperialist slant. The war is not perceived as just an embarrassing blip in the progress of a righteous American nation. Rather, naval preparations for a campaign against Spain had been going on for fifteen years. The underlying reason for the hostilities was neither the *Maine* disaster nor humanitarian feelings toward the Cuban people. Instead, the war can be looked at simply as a natural outgrowth of an expansionist U.S. foreign policy, especially as defined then by proponents of the new Navy.

From another viewpoint, the Spanish war was a consequence of the industrial revolution that flowered in the United States during the second half of the nineteenth century. There was a drive for overseas markets to sop up domestic overproduction.

In addition, lasting dislocations from the great 1893 depression had produced widespread discontent in the United States. By 1898 there was a compelling need to relieve pent-up frustrations. There was a desire to fight any foreign country—Spain, England, Germany, Japan, or Chile. The villainous Spaniards were within reach, and battling Spain would also achieve imperialist ambitions.

In this modern hypothesis, Americans were glad to "Remember the *Maine*" and to "*libre* Cuba," but the slogans were only side issues. The Spanish-American War is charged to the influence of American expansionists on national policy.

The View from the Other Side

★ ★ ★ ★ ★ ★ ★ ★

HISTORY WILL ACQUIT SPAIN

When war was declared, European newspapers sympathized with the Spaniards who were seen as underdogs against the United States. The London *Times* asserted that "war about the destruction of the *Maine* is manifestly premature when the act has not been traced to the Spanish government or anyone connected to it. History will assuredly acquit the Spanish authorities." English newspapers were taking the Spanish side in the conflict, whereas the British government was essentially pro-American.

The United States also received a bad press in Paris: "There is not a single Frenchman who supports the American government. Spain gave Cuba such self-government as, if it had been bestowed on George Washington's contemporaries, would have prevented the War of Independence." France was Spain's banker.

The leading paper in Berlin wrote that "to expel [Spanish] Satan [from Cuba] by [American] Beelzebub can hardly be described as the result of genuine philanthropy." Germany was looking for naval bases in the Caribbean and had its own eye on Cuba.

In Havana, Austrian and Italian naval officers were reported to have scrutinized the wreck from the surface. Their opinion was that the explosions had been internal. They had the *Maine*'s original plans and wrongly thought the cause was guncotton.

Despite the criticism in foreign newspapers, the respected United States magazine *Scientific American* reported that "the English technical press has given practically unanimous indorsement to the findings of the Court. The political aspects are subordinate to the scientific and technical side." This meant that English naval experts supported the U.S. findings, although there was severe overseas pressure to specify an accident.

Scientific American cited three British technical journals, two of them correctly. The magazine *Engineer* had written, "It is not possible to read what the divers have to say without arriving at the same conclusions as the Board."

Industries and Iron was the second source properly quoted. The magazine published a letter "from a distinguished English engineer" who concluded, "We believe the destruction of the *Maine* was premeditated, caused from the outside. Some of the French and Spanish engineers combat the mine theory by asking why no dead fish were found and why no water was thrown into the air. The mine was probably in direct contact with the bottom of the ship and when exploded it found vent through the ship."

Listing the journal *Engineering* as favorable was, however, a mistake. Instead of wholly supporting the mine theory, *Engineering* gently suggested that the decks might have been blown out by an accidental explosion. That was a disturbing supposition, even though the journal added the caution, "We only advance the hypothesis as possible rather than probable."

Engineering's contrarian view was expressed so discreetly that *Scientific American* missed the meaning. The English article agreed that "there can be little doubt that two explosions occurred. The point of importance was whether that first explosion took place outside or inside the ship. The Court had no difficulty in deciding on the former. But," the journal argued, "the existence of an outside source of explosion is not apparent."

"The Court was of the opinion," the article continued, "that the forcing up of the bottom of the ship could only be caused by the explosion of a mine beneath the vessel. However, the question arises, Would it be possible for the forward part in sinking while the after part was water-borne to so bend the thin bottom into the shape shown? The illustrations give more the idea of a bending rather than the distortion that would be caused by a vertically-acting force." This line of investigation had been expressly rejected by the Sampson court.

Second, "Whatever may be the faults of Spaniards, we have no right to conclude that their officers would commit as cowardly an act." This defense was popular in Europe. It was, however, a character reference, not a judicial opinion.

Finally, "Evidence was given that the ship lifted forward when the explosion took place. The point is of great importance, for it is difficult to attribute such a movement to an internal force. The evidence, however, is not very strong." The lifting was purely a question of fact. As the article acknowledged, "The Court had the advantage of being on the spot" to hear credible witnesses from the *City of Washington* in person.

A large number of readers' letters followed. Half wrote, "I do not think Spain has been given 'fair play.'" The other half complained that *"Engineering* is writing platonic editorials instead of analyzing the technical points."

An additional refinement was contributed by Fred Jane, the English naval engineer. He commented that "it might appear that if the plates around the hole were blown inward, it would be proof of an external explosion. The only clear point is that absolute proof of the cause is impossible." If the first explosion had been of a magazine, he explained, the soft bottom plates would be blown outward. When the water returned to fill the void at the point of explosion, the water pressure might then re-bend the plates inward. This was an explanation that survived over the years to attempt to make the accident theory possible.

The points listed by *Engineering* sounded as though the members of the Sampson court should have been placed on the defensive. Instead, they were blockading Havana at the start of the Spanish-American War they had helped to precipitate. The *Engineering* article was important mainly because it launched similar English critiques which eventually reached the U.S. public, first in generality and then years later in detail.

ENTER LIEUTENANT COLONEL BUCKNILL

The key player on the accident side of the *Maine* controversy was Lieutenant Colonel John Townshend Bucknill. He was an English ordnance specialist who wrote two texts on mines.

Bucknill entered the Royal Military Academy in 1861. As a lieutenant he engaged in experimental detonation of underwater charges. From 1873 to 1876 he was assistant secretary of the Royal Engineering Committee which carried out tests of high explosives detonated against HMS *Oberon*. The experiments were said to be the first involving a double-bottomed steel ship. In his informal report, Bucknill mentioned that fishermen "reaped a harvest of stunned fish after each explosion."

Following the *Oberon* experiments, Bucknill became Instructor for Submarine Mining in the School for Military Engineering. The long involvement with explosives deafened him in 1887 when he was forty-four, cutting short his Army career but not his feisty and implacable analyses. His rank of lieutenant colonel was honorary.

In retirement, Bucknill delighted in puncturing the U.S. naval establishment's linkage of the *Maine* disaster to a mine explosion. In a series of articles that followed the April 1898 issue of *Engineering*, he provided later critics with substantially all their arguments against the mine theory. Yet when he died at ninety-three, his obituaries did not mention the connection.

His first article in *Engineering*'s May 27, 1898, issue stated his goal: "If only we succeed in disproving the accuracy of the [American] Court's finding, it will be a good work, tending to remove much of the strong anti-Spanish feeling which dominates the people of the United States."

To this point, Bucknill was an English colonialist defending colonialist Spain against an expansionist America which coveted all foreign possessions in the Western Hemisphere, including Canada.

A JAR ON THE ANKLE BONES

In his second article, Bucknill excerpted the testimony of the witnesses before the Sampson court to classify them as having heard one explosion or two.

In his third article, he analyzed this testimony. He was forced reluctantly to agree with the court on the number of explosions because he could not ignore the seven reliable witnesses who swore to the two separate explosions: "The only way to reconcile these divergencies is to believe there were two explosions, that the first was not powerful, and consequently many others [witnesses] did not notice it."

In the fourth article, the condition of the wreck above water was described:

1. A great explosion occurred, forward of the conning tower [frame 30], which is also the location of [some of] the forward magazines.
2. The effects were greater on the port side.
3. Portions of the bottom of the ship near frame 18 were found at the surface.
4. The forepart of the ship had sunk, the only parts showing being wreckage in the neighborhood vertically of the magazines.

Ensign Powelson had testified to the origins of the three piles of wreckage.

In the fifth and final article, Bucknill got down to business at last. The question he put was whether the court's theory of a large mine at frame 18 was correct.

First, in an erroneous conclusion, he pointed out that "the theory appears to be quite impossible because any such initial cause of the disaster would have given a tremendous shock and explosion to which every survivor would have testified." However, Bucknill forgot his *Oberon* experiments. In one test explosion, he had remained on board. The only effect he reported was "a sharp jar on the ankle bones."

Second, Bucknill continued, "Assuming the finding of the Court to be correct, a mine capable of driving the keel 34 feet would drive the portion of the vessel above it into the air, including the magazines. But if the magazines were driven into the air, their contents would have exploded in the air, and no witness saw that. Rather, the evidence of the entire wreck proves that the magazines exploded when they were in the ship."

Unbelievably, Bucknill had successfully overturned the court's finding on its own evidence. The magazines had burst while they were still in their original positions, not above the ship where they would have been if a large mine had exploded at frame 18. The finding of the Sampson court was demonstrably wrong. Exactly what the court had tried to guard against had now happened because the members' elitist attitude toward divers' testimony had diverted them from conditions at frame 30.

Bucknill's third reason was a corollary of the second: "In the experiments against *Oberon*, the final 500 pound charge was submerged 50 feet. It broke the back [the spine] of the vessel, but the damage was confined to the bottom which was blown up while the sides were left. In the *Maine*, however, the sides are gone and part of the bottom remains. Consequently, the sides must have been blown out by the magazines when still inside the ship." As in Bucknill's previous explanation, the detonation of a large mine would have driven the magazines into the air before they could blow out the sides. The sides would have remained in place. Here the sides were blown out. That precluded the elevation of the magazines by a large mine.

Finally, "A mine capable of bending the keel and double bottom would not bend them into a sharp angle but would produce a dome shape. Other reasons might be given but enough has probably been said to raise a grave doubt on the accuracy of the finding of the Court of Inquiry." He was right.

"My theory is," Bucknill concluded in a full restatement of his findings,

"1. A small initial explosion occurred in or close to the Reserve Magazine—port side about frame 27." This was the major departure from the Sampson court's findings. According to Bucknill, the first explosion was small in size and it occurred in the area of greatest damage, well aft of frame 18. This was his theory. He did not provide proof, other than his interpretation of the condition of the vessel. He did not cite the testimony of Powelson's divers concerning an explosion at about the same frame 27 because they were documenting an external burst, the opposite of his theory.

"2. Contents of this magazine immediately became involved. The energy would be directed to the adjoining Ten Inch Shell Room and to the Six-pounder Magazine." These were the adjacent magazines shown on the hold plan.

"3. The pressure being increased, it would find a vent and involve the Ten Inch [powder] Magazine and the Forward Six Inch Magazine. The decks would be lifted." That accounted for all the forward magazines.

"4. Having found these vents, the cumulative explosion lasted perhaps three seconds and was described as 'the roaring of the ship.'

"5. The principal discharge [of the Ten Inch Magazine] being to port, the [aft part of the] ship was driven to starboard. The great final explosion would also drive the [forward] double bottom downwards, but the mud being so close, a reaction of recoil would ensue, tending finally to buckle the bottom upwards." This recoil was a third version of the reason for the inverted keel, opposed to *Engineering*'s lurching and the Sampson court's mine.

"Moreover, the after body would be subjected to water pressure driving it forward. The simultaneous motion of the after body to forward and to starboard would crumple and twist the remaining double bottom to bend the keel at frame 18 [17]."

"The cause of the [first] explosion," Bucknill speculated, "may never be known. I think it was due to Pocahontas coal heating in bunker 16. A powder tank in the Reserve Magazine lay against the steel bulkhead, metal to metal. In Her Majesty's Navy, powder magazines are always lined with wood and magazines are not next to coal bunkers. Comment is unnecessary." Implicitly, incompetent U.S. naval architects were at fault.

"Of course, the primal explosion may have been due to a small contact charge [at frame 27], but the only evidence in favor is an anonymous letter." Citing the extensive evidence supporting a mine did not suit Bucknill's purpose. He was defending the Spaniards, not providing an even-handed analysis.

Not surprisingly, the Bucknill articles evoked many letters to *Engineering* from other retired English engineers. Most were attacks on Bucknill for his "reaction of recoil" explanation for the elevation of the keel.

Bucknill's relocation of the original explosion from frame 18 to frame 27 was shocking. The Sampson court had made an inexplicably flagrant error. To those who were convinced by the Bucknill opinion, no finding by the court could be trusted. Thus, the disaster was purely accidental. The locus was definitely frame 27. There was no Spanish involvement.

The salvation for the Sampson court was that Bucknill's articles reached a limited audience in the United States. In addition, the rejection of his recoil theory concerning the bending of the bottom plates detracted from his more important conclusions, although not as much as the Sampson court's error was seen as invalidating its entire opinion.

MAVERICK AMERICANS

The purpose of Bucknill's articles was to undermine the court of inquiry's decision in order to vindicate the Spaniards. To accomplish this and to establish spontaneous combustion as the probable cause of the disaster, he had to move the location of the initial explosion from frame 18 to at least frame 24. The reason is that frame 18 and coal bunker A-16 were not contiguous. A look at the hold plan (see plates p. VIII)) shows that the suspect bunker was 24 feet aft of frame 18. Ignition in the bunker could not possibly have directly involved the contents of the forward magazine, the locus of the mine explosion according to the court. Instead, bunker A-16 began at frame 24 and shared a common bulkhead with the reserve magazine from frame 24 to frame 30.

To eliminate this physical limitation, Bucknill was able to prove, first, that the initial explosion was not from a large submarine mine beneath frame 18, and second, that the bending of the keel at frame 17 could have been from internal forces. He also theorized that the initial explosion was near frame 27. These determinations corrected both express and implied findings of the court.

On the other hand, Bucknill did not consider the extremist Weylerites. In addition, he could not prove that the initial explosion was accidental. There was no affirmative evidence to indicate internal cause. Only the capacity of Pocahontas coal to self-ignite under special conditions not present here and the proximity of the bunker to the Reserve Magazine were suspect. Moreover, Bucknill admitted that the initial explosion could have been external in the form of a small mine in contact with the Maine's bottom at frame 27.

A thoughtful reply to the Bucknill opinion came from Commander F. M. Barber, the naval attaché at the U.S. Embassy in Rome who was an expert on explosives. A covert agent of the Office of Naval Intelligence, he also acted as an international salesman for American munitions manufacturers.

Barber called the *Engineering* articles "most prejudiced. In his conclusions, Bucknill quotes only such evidence as will support his contention of spontaneous combustion." If Barber had checked the actual testimony, he would have found that Bucknill sometimes went so far as to rewrite quotations to heighten the force of his conclusions.

To make spontaneous combustion more likely as the cause, Bucknill had pointed out that "a powder tank in the Reserve Magazine lay against the steel bulkhead, metal to metal." Barber responded that "the colonel quotes the evidence of a gunner who had been relieved from duty and who was incompetent while he ignores the statement of the captain to the contrary.

"Commander Kimball, one of the ablest American experts, said the

Maine 'was probably blown up by an improvised torpedo [mine], planted just ahead of her, and fired [electrically] when she swung over it.'

"Twenty-five years ago, one of the frequent exercises of the officers under instruction at the torpedo station in Newport, Rhode Island, was the construction of improvised torpedoes. The operation consisted simply in taking an empty powder or fish keg, pitching it inside and out, filling it with gunpowder, inserting an electric igniter through a cork in the bung, lashing a stone to it, and putting the whole [thing] in a skiff pulled by two men, carrying it out a couple of hundred yards, heaving it overboard, running the wires ashore, and firing it off. The whole operation occupied two to three hours.

"In Havana, a mine of this kind could have been planted in broad daylight. It would have driven pieces of the bottom plating into the magazines with sufficient velocity to have set off the fixed ammunition at least. The reaction from the [harbor] bottom would bend the keel."

Barber was moving the locus of the initial explosion to a middle position under the fixed ammunition room, between the forward and reserve magazines. He agreed with Bucknill on the controversial reaction of recoil as the reason for the inverted V, but the Englishman was not pleased. His only rejoinder was, "I have re-examined Captain Sigsbee's evidence and cannot find the statement asserted by Mr. Barber." This was Bucknill at his stiffest. He knew that the witness Barber meant was not "the captain" Sigsbee but the more credible Lieutenant Holman, the ordnance officer. Holman had testified that "there was woodwork on that bulkhead," that is, that wood was in contact with the metal.

Despite Barber's jabs, Bucknill's assault on the Sampson court stood firm. There were, however, few maverick Americans to join Bucknill. One was Professor Robert Beggs, a Colorado scientist. His article, "The Mystery of the Maine," was published in the Boston *Transcript*.

According to Beggs, the Sampson court was prejudiced because "a war with Spain must be largely a naval war, full of promise for Sampson and his associates. As evidence of the bias of the Court, 52 lines of the finding are devoted to the exculpation of the officers and crew, while but seven are given to the explosion." Next, he calculated the number of explosions by the number of witnesses to each. He also had the ship shortened by 72 feet by hauling the forward portion aft when the measured shortening was ten feet and the bow remained fixed to the mooring.

The most formidable of the American dissenters was Captain George

Melville who had joined the Civil War Navy as an engineer. He did not attend the Academy. In 1879, heroism in Arctic exploration brought him worldwide attention. He was chosen Engineer-in-Chief in preference to forty-four more senior engineers. Propulsion machinery was designed, constructed, or installed under his guidance in 150 American warships. He designed the machinery in the *Maine*.

A poet said Melville needed only "a trident to transform him into Neptune riding over the waves." The picture titled *America* in Kaiser Wilhelm II's private portrait gallery was of Melville. In the Navy Department, he was a bulldog. The day after the *Maine* disaster he had asserted that the cause was accidental and once he made up his mind he seldom changed.

Melville began his article with another character reference: "There is a comity that exists between the personnel of the navies of the world. All resentment ceases when even an undesirable foreign vessel enters a port. Their duties bring naval officers in contact with the most cultured and refined of every nation. Eighteen hours from the time the request for the *Maine* visit was made, before consent to welcome the visitor, the *Maine* steamed into Havana. The Spaniards were too proud to show regret, but too humiliated to extend other than the most formal of official courtesies." They had lost their comity.

"Spanish officers were incapable of this crime. We have a higher appreciation of the character and manhood of Spanish soldiery." Melville described Spanish officers as gentlemen which was more than he said for the Sampson court.

He then restated what Bucknill had written. His errors of fact were numerous. He also listed unrelated naval disasters since 1829 to prove "there have been explosions of magazines which have been inexplicable. Such is probably the case with the *Maine*. Responsibility for explosions cannot be evaded simply by showing unusual care." That was a knock on Sigsbee.

As long as the Americans restating Bucknill's opinions were as illogical as Beggs and Melville, the Sampson court had little to fear from critics at home.

American Rebuttal

★ ★ ★ ★ ★ ★ ★ ★

THEY BLEW STRAIGHT UP

The Cuban part of the Spanish-American War was brief enough to be told in headlines: April 22, Naval Blockade of Havana. April 25, Congress Declares War. April 29, Spanish Admiral Cervera's Fleet Sails for Cuba. May 1, Dewey Victorious at Manila. May 19, Admiral Cervera's Fleet Reaches Santiago, Cuba. June 3, Lt. Hobson Sinks the *Merrimac* to Block Santiago Harbor. June 14, American Expeditionary Force Sails for Cuba. June 22, American Expeditionary Force Lands in Cuba. July 1, Land Battle of San Juan. July 3, Destruction of Cervera's Fleet at Santiago. July 14, Santiago Surrenders. August 6, Spain Accepts American Peace Terms.

The naval battle of Santiago took place July 3 when the Spanish squadron attempted to elude the U.S. blockade of Santiago harbor by fleeing along the shore. The Spanish ships were set on fire by American shells and driven onto the beaches. The flames ignited magazines that exploded on most of the vessels.

Three days later, Admiral Sampson appointed a board of survey to examine the wrecked Spanish warships. The stated purpose was to determine the effectiveness of U.S. gunners. In addition, Sampson asked the board to report on damage from the magazine explosions so results could be compared with damage his court of inquiry had found on the *Maine*. Bucknill's conclusions about the *Maine* disaster would also be put to the test.

The *Almirante Oquendo* had been an armor-belted cruiser similar to the *Maine*. She was shot to pieces and broken in two. A magazine explosion caused by fire forward had blown out the sides above the protective deck but not in the hold where the magazine had been located. The platform deck was thrown up against the protective deck. The bottom plating bulged outward only in the immediate vicinity of the explosion. Despite the detonation of the forward magazine and the breaking of the vessel into two sections, as the *Maine* did, the *Almirante Oquendo's* keel remained in place.

The *Vizcaya* which had visited New York City in happier days was a little bigger than the *Maine*, but in the identical battle class. She was the same age. Both forward and aft magazines had exploded, forcing up the decks and heavily injuring the structure. There was, however, little disturbance to the ship's bottom. The keel was not elevated.

A member of the board of survey remarked to the press, "Any doubt that the *Maine* was blown up by an outside explosion has been dissolved by an examination of the destroyed Spanish ships. Of four ships, three had been blown up by their magazines, and of these, one had every magazine exploded, yet there was no upheaval of the keel."

According to an officer of the *City of Washington*, "From an examination of the *Vizcaya*, I was more than satisfied that the *Maine* was blown up from the outside. In the explosion of the *Vizcaya's* magazines, they blew straight up in the air and did not burst the ship the same as the *Maine* explosion rent that ship, which is conclusive evidence."

The bottom plates on the wrecked Spanish ships had remained sound. So had at least the lower part of the sides. This was not an experiment like Bucknill's *Oberon*. These were actual magazine explosions in circumstances more similar to the *Maine* disaster, but with no displacement of the bottom plates or keel.

Bucknill did not comment on the stability of the Spanish bottom plating and lower side plates after the wartime magazine explosions. He might have repeated that the first explosion on the *Maine* was not caused by a large mine at frame 18 where the bottom plates were elevated, regardless of what happened to the Spanish ships. He might also have said that the *Maine's* raised bottom plates could still be explained as a possible consequence of the magazine explosions, but he did not. Just as he could not prove spontaneous combustion on the *Maine* by showing that there had been no large mine at frame 18, so the board of survey could not prove there had been a mine explosion at frame 18 by showing that the magazine explosions did not raise the keel in the destroyed Spanish ships. In both instances the positive connection was missing.

Another boost for the Sampson court came in the Russo-Japanese War. If there was doubt that a torpedo or mine could cause a magazine explosion, the proof was the destruction of the Japanese battleship *Hatsuse* and Russian Admiral Makaroff's flagship the *Petropavlovsk* off Port Arthur in 1905.

Furthermore, U.S. ordnance officers resurrected a Danish naval report from 1873, the same year as the *Oberon* experiments. The report concerned explosives tested against the double-bottomed steel warship *Foersigtigheten* at Carlskrona, Sweden. Appropriately for comparison with the *Maine* disaster, the explosives used had been both dynamite and ordinary musket powder. Similar explosives were readily available to builders of homemade mines in Havana in 1898.

The Danish report was couched in terms of whether the ship's bottom was breached. In applying these tests to the *Maine* disaster, the Navy's experts assumed that enough explosive to hole the bottom would also be sufficient to ignite gunpowder in a magazine directly above the bottom.

Test no. 12 involved 650 pounds of gunpowder placed in a mine set 23 feet below the ship's bottom. The vessel was lifted bodily and virtually destroyed. The sides were blown out. The hull was breached through a 64-square-foot hole in the outer bottom and a larger 71 square feet in the inner bottom.

This test was cited to substantiate the Sampson court's finding of the big gunpowder mine at frame 18, for the benefit of diehards who did not acknowledge the accuracy of Bucknill's conclusions. The results were somewhat similar to the *Maine* disaster in that the sides were blown out. There was, however, no raised keel.

The Danish report demonstrated that the optimum placement of a mine was in close contact with the ship's bottom. Test no. 7 was 33 pounds of dynamite set 4 feet below the ship, near enough to be called contact. The double bottom was breached by a 50-square-foot hole.

Test no. 11 employed 112 pounds of gunpowder, an amount approximately equal in force to the dynamite in test no. 7. With the mine set 5 feet below the ship, the hole was 72 square feet and the ship was full of water in five minutes.

These last two tests lent themselves to a face-saving excuse for the Sampson court's findings that some experts attempted by dropping the reliance on the elevated keel at frame 17. Officers like Commander Barber admitted that the raised keel could indeed have been an indirect product of the explosions, as Bucknill asserted, and that the initial explosion had really occurred about frame 27. That was approximately where Powelson's divers had discovered the inboard hole.

In this informal modification of the 1898 opinion, the cause of the first explosion would still have been a mine, as the Sampson court found. In order to conform to the Danish tests and to Bucknill's alternate conclusion, however, the mine was moved aft, made smaller, charged with gunpowder, and placed in contact with the ship's bottom rather than in the harbor mud.

As a foundation for this altered finding, the Danish report had established in a separate test that as little as 22 pounds of dynamite or 70 pounds of easily managed gunpowder would breach the double bottom of a warship of the period. Admiral Makaroff's sunken flagship showed that a mine breaching the double bottom could detonate the powder in a magazine. Bucknill had admitted that a small contact mine at frame 27 could have wrecked the *Maine*.

It all tied together. Captain Chadwick declared that no one had ever proved the Sampson court was wrong. There had been a mine under the ship, as the court had said, if not where the court had placed it.

REMEMBERING THE *MAINE*

During the war the American public was not aware of any debate concerning the cause of the *Maine* disaster. Spanish guilt was taken for granted. "Remember the *Maine*!" continued as a civilian rallying cry for military enlistments and for solicitation of contributions to patriotic funds.

In the Navy, however, employment of the phrase "Remember the *Maine*!" was prohibited. The "Christian President" McKinley had declared in his message to Congress that war was being waged for humanitarian reasons and not to retaliate against the Spanish people. In carrying out McKinley's policy, moralistic Secretary Long characterized the slogan "Remember the *Maine*!" as a sin because it expressed a desire for revenge. He directed that its use be forbidden in the Navy.

Consequently, there was no signal flag for "Remember the *Maine*!" in the

Navy. No United States warship flew a *Maine* pennant. When naval officers permitted this appeal for retribution to be voiced on their ships, they were reprimanded. Officially, the Spanish-American War at sea was fought without relation to the *Maine* disaster.

In fact, though, the phrase was an ineradicable part of the naval mystique. Long could not overcome deep-seated emotions by issuing paper orders. Captain Robley "Fighting Bob" Evans succeeded Sampson as commander of the *Iowa*. He bragged that his eager sailors were "swearing like pirates" during the sea battle of Santiago and calling on the memory of the *Maine* every time they fired a shot at a Spanish vessel.

On the *Indiana* the sailors scratched "Remember the *Maine!*" onto shells before running them into the breeches of the guns. When a shell struck a mortal blow on the stern of the fugitive *Vizcaya*, setting the cruiser on fire, the gun crew yelled in unison, "Remember the *Maine!* Remember the *Maine!*"

Lieutenant Commander Wainwright hated Spaniards openly. While in Havana supervising operations of the salvage company, he had lived on the *Fern*, refusing to set foot on the island until, as he put it, the time came when he could go ashore at the head of a landing party of conquering American bluejackets.

When his assignment with the wreckers in Havana was over, Wainwright requested sea duty. He was given command of the *Gloucester* which had been J. P. Morgan's luxury yacht, *Corsair*. By electing not to wait for armor to be installed on the *Gloucester*, he arrived in Cuba in time for the naval battle of Santiago.

During the fighting he ordered his unprotected yacht to attack two larger and more powerful Spanish destroyers, *Furor* and *Pluton*. His gunners sank one at close range and drove the other onto the beach, killing or wounding two-thirds of the Spanish sailors on board.

He could not forget the *Maine*'s destruction that had occurred less than five months earlier. While he watched flames leaping through the decks of Spanish warships, he exulted, "The *Maine* is avenged!" After the battle he effected the rescue of Admiral Cervera and two hundred Spanish sailors from the *Infanta Maria Teresa* and the *Almirante Oquendo*. His exploits were not publicized as much as those of some other officers, but he was one of the sailors' heroes of the war.

Captain Sigsbee did not fare as well in the hostilities. Sigsbee's command, the chartered passenger liner *St. Paul,* had been relegated to scouting duties.

In May 1898 Sigsbee became embroiled in a question of veracity with his senior officer Commodore Schley. Schley claimed he had relied on Sigsbee's erroneous scouting report that Cervera's fleet was not in Santiago harbor. Sigsbee denied making the oral report to Schley, but the commodore had witnesses. Luckily for Sigsbee, Schley soon had a much more critical confrontation with his superior Sampson that wiped Sigsbee from his mind.

Only ten U.S. sailors were killed in the entire war, compared to the 267 *Maine* fatalities. After hostilities were over, however, it was the Spanish peace commissioners who remembered the *Maine.* In December 1898 the commissioners proposed that a joint Spanish-American board be appointed to make the ultimate investigation into the cause of the *Maine* disaster. Despite Professor Beggs's statement that "nine-tenths of Christendom charged us with unfairness in our dealings with Spain," the United States refused to participate in a new inquiry.

Spain then announced her unilateral intention to form a nonpartisan international board to investigate the *Maine* disaster. *Life* magazine remarked condescendingly that "this illustrated anew the sentimentality of her disposition." In the end, however, Spain did nothing, illustrating her futility instead.

The mystery of the *Maine* was closed, or so most Americans believed.

Raising the *Maine*

★ ★ ★ ★ ★ ★ ★ ★

A WREATH OF GALAX

When peace was restored, the *St. Paul* returned to civilian cruises and Captain Sigsbee was given command of the *Maine*'s sister ship, the *Texas*. His luck was bad. A routine inspection of the battleship in March 1899 found dirt and rust. Some of the small boats were inadequately outfitted.

As a veteran of such accusations, an unrepentant Sigsbee told Secretary Long that "officers feel these things very much, because an officer of high spirit and love for the service prizes his record above all things of a personal character." He claimed he had been "on shore ill" during the irregularities and he obtained "documentary evidence" against "nearly every allegation contained in those reports."

The time was too close to Sigsbee's exploits in connection with the *Maine* disaster for him to be reprimanded publicly for sloppy housekeeping. Instead, he was advanced slightly in rank for routine services during the war. The truth was that he needed an efficient executive officer such as Wainwright to keep on top of his job.

Nine months after the inspection of the *Texas*, Secretary Long was instructed to have the bodies of the *Maine* sailors in Havana's Colon Cemetery disinterred for reburial in Arlington Cemetery. Appropriately, Long chose Sigsbee, the commander of the old *Maine* and of her sister ship, to bring the remains home.

By the time the *Texas* arrived in Havana, Cuban morticians had transferred the bodies into 150 new wooden caskets supplied by Washington.

That was too many for even a battleship to stow below, so Sigsbee had the boxes lashed securely on deck for the return voyage.

Early winter was the storm season in the Atlantic. Sigsbee worried about the coffins, but the ropes held despite a full gale off Cape Hatteras. He arrived in Newport News, Virginia, on December 26 and sent the caskets the rest of the way to Arlington by rail with an honor guard.

In midmorning on December 28, the caskets were arranged in rows inside a temporary fence defining a snow-covered circular plot newly dedicated on a cold and windy Arlington knoll. The bodies of the sailors were not identified. A U.S. flag was spread over each coffin and on top was an ornamental wreath woven with leaves of the evergreen galax. Through the mist rose the Washington Monument. The Potomac River and the city of Washington were visible in the distance.

Dismounted cavalrymen from Fort Meyer stood shoulder to shoulder around the far side of the fence. The yellow of their coat linings was a band of vivid color on the grim morning. To the right was a company of marines from the Washington Navy Yard. They were wearing spiked helmets and their capes were turned back to show the scarlet inside. To the left was a detachment of *Texas* "jackies" in navy blue.

The only personnel from the *Maine* were Sigsbee, in charge of the ceremonies, Father John Chidwick, promoted to lieutenant for his care of the crew, Lieutenant Commander Wainwright, Lieutenant Frederic Bowers, and Jeremiah Shea, the fireman who had miraculously been blown through the hole in the *Maine*'s side.

McKinley and his friend Long had been driven to the cemetery in the presidential carriage. They stood on a flag-draped platform looking over the rows of caskets. At the rear of the stand were the other cabinet members and a group of high-ranking Army and Navy officers, including Admiral George Dewey and General Nelson Miles. Hundreds of mourners who had braved the snow and the biting cold to honor the *Maine* dead were walking around the grounds.

At eleven o'clock, a simple religious service began in the calm air. Father Chidwick gave the sailors a Catholic burial in their home soil. No one objected to the denominational ritual as Sigsbee had in Havana.

The marines then marched farther to the right and fired three volleys over the dead. In the quiet that followed, the clear silvery notes of a bugle rang out the sailors' last good night and the ceremony ended.

A cabinet officer who was staring somberly over the coffins remarked, "The lives of these men from the *Maine* cost Spain her colonies." There was no other note of triumph in the sad farewell.

PRESSURES TO RAISE THE *MAINE*

By 1900, Americans no longer remembered the *Maine* with the same ardor that had possessed them two years earlier. The abnormal hatred of things Spanish had run its course and Americans were beginning to feel warmer toward Spain. There was an appealing nobility in a proud nation preferring certain defeat to giving up a long-held colony at the demand of an upstart.

There was appreciation, too, for the unfortunate Admiral Cervera y Topete who had been sent by the Spanish council over his protest to have his sailors slaughtered and his fleet annihilated on Cuban beaches. Demonstrably brave and chivalrous, he was the role model for the English when they said no Spanish naval officer would have detonated a mine to sink the *Maine* or have permitted anyone else to do so.

In addition, there was an awakening in America to the responsibilities of power. The bloody business of putting down the Philippine insurgents showed the new U.S. imperialists what it had cost Spanish imperialists to control a rebellious people.

In 1903, five years after the war, the same explanations for the explosions on the *Maine* remained in vogue, though the number of Americans who believed in the different theories was shifting. The first finding had been the Sampson court's determination that the *Maine* had been blown up by an unidentified mine, with no miscreant named. Specifics of the court's opinion had been overturned by Bucknill.

Second had been the pronouncement by the Senate committee that the *Maine* was destroyed by a mine planted at the bottom of Havana harbor by the Spanish government and detonated by a Spanish officer either under orders or aided by the government's gross negligence. The justification for the war had been the Senate's indictment of Spain, a conclusion formulated in a context of national hysteria.

Third was the European position: The explosion was accidental, probably from spontaneous combustion in coal bunker A-16. There was, however, no proof of self-ignition.

The fourth approach was that the extent of the destruction was so great, no one could tell what the cause had been. This explanation was acceptable to few because it resolved nothing.

In the more sympathetic postwar milieu, awareness was growing that the Spanish government had probably been innocent of detonating the mine beneath the *Maine*. Subordinate Spanish officers under the influence of General Weyler or insurgent Cubans were thought to have been responsible. An increasing number of bolder Americans were also considering the possibility that the *Maine* had blown herself up in the catastrophic accident Bucknill depicted.

One reason for the expanding belief in an accidental cause was the sense of having been let down by the Sampson court. All the drama of discovering and interpreting the elevated bottom plates was now acknowledged to have been a gigantic mistake. Scoffers said a court capable of committing that magnitude of error could hardly have been right concerning the explosion of a mine anywhere under the *Maine*. The whole episode could have been the Navy taking care of its own in a secret proceeding, just as congressmen had predicted when the inquiry was announced.

In addition, specific evidence that there had never been a mine under the *Maine* remained unanswered. As the Spaniards had pointed out, there was no upheaval of water after the explosion, no shock to nearby ships, no dead fish, no crater. Moreover, a mine explosion followed by a magazine explosion would have been two sounds. Some leading witnesses heard only one. The *Maine*'s sentries would have observed an attempt to plant a mine. The *Vizcaya* would not have been sent to New York City if the Spaniards intended to blow up the *Maine*, and so on. Clearly, precipitating the war had not been to Spain's benefit.

By 1908 the Navy's line officers were renewing the call to raise the *Maine* because they had lost credibility along with the Sampson court. They also said national prestige suffered from the abandonment of the remains of so many U.S. sailors. If the wreck could not be raised, they wanted the hull dynamited to eliminate the "visible reminder of the ill-fated ship in Havana harbor."

The Cuban government was asking for the removal of the *Maine*, too. The sunken vessel had created a shoal that took up valuable space and menaced navigation at the man-of-war mooring.

In addition, veterans and other patriotic organizations were petitioning

Congress to authorize funds to raise the *Maine*. They wanted the recovery of the bones of the entrapped dead as well as mementos from the wreck that could be enshrined.

A decade earlier correspondent Meriwether had broken the news of the elevated keel he then attributed to a Spanish mine. Now he asked, "Why has the American government not raised the wreck? Some say that only this will determine whether the ship was destroyed by an explosion from without or within, for this is a doubt which the neglect of ten years has permitted to arise. When the protest against this neglect, no less than against the theory that the American government is afraid to raise the vessel, had reached its present vehemence, the question of raising the ship was placed before Rear Admiral Chadwick."

Sampson had died in 1902 so Chadwick was the senior living member of the court. He replied that "my conviction to-day is as firm as ten years ago, that the destruction was primarily from the exterior. Whence has come opposition to raising the ship, if there is any, I do not know; certainly not from any member of that board. We did our duty to the best of our lights. So far I have seen nothing to alter my judgment."

Chadwick should have been aware that the naval bureaucracy was the real impediment, as charged. When Secretary of the Navy George Meyer reorganized naval operations under President Taft, his right-hand man for the complex task was Rear Admiral Wainwright. Meyer would never have reopened the Sampson inquiry voluntarily. He would be putting his associate Wainwright back at risk.

"A GLORY SEPULTURE"

On April 8, 1908, the New York *Sun* repeated a 1902 statement from departed Secretary of the Navy Long that continued as official policy on the *Maine* disaster: "The Department does not regard with favor raising the *Maine* with the view of entering upon another investigation. No reason is perceived why the former investigation is not sufficient." Trying the *Maine*'s top officers again for negligence might be the naval equivalent of double jeopardy.

The American people, however, were not satisfied. New York's Congressman William Sulzer spoke on May 12 during the Sixtieth Congress: "More than ten years have gone by since the *Maine* was destroyed. Public sentiment has demanded that the wreck be raised, but a bill pending in the Committee on Naval Affairs does not get reported [out of committee to the full House for action]. In the words of our poets, 'Down in that tropic, torpid bay,/In the slime and filth of the Spanish way,/Shall the hulk of the *Maine* forever stay?/Take the old ship out of her filthy grave/To the clear blue sea and the white-capped wave,/And there in the depths serene and pure/Give her a glory sepulture.'"

Sulzer also asked that "a few letters and newspaper comments" be inserted in the *Congressional Record*. Among the many he offered was a clipping from the April 13 *Sun*: "It is deplorable that the naval bureaucracy has been, in every matter that touched upon its own convenience or advantage, a packed jury. If Congress should decide to remove the hulk of the *Maine*, painful as that might be to the naval bureaucracy, it would probably settle some momentous questions. It has always, for instance, been difficult to understand how the Spaniards who blew up our man-of-war managed to hold their tongues. It is against human nature."

With the passage of time, this new reason had surfaced to substantiate Spanish innocence. If there were Spanish conspirators, they had been silent about the catastrophe for a decade and their reticence was said to be hard to believe.

On February 16, 1909, Sulzer was back in the *Record*, quoting Charles Magoon, Provisional Governor of Cuba: "The neglect to remove the wreck is attributed to the fear that its removal will disclose the fallacy of the belief that the *Maine* was destroyed by a mine. So generally does this opinion prevail that the Cuban government was deterred thereby from destroying the wreck."

As usual, the *New York Times* took the establishment side: "There is still a mystery of the *Maine*, but the mystery is how anybody can now affect a doubt. That was settled for good ten years ago and nothing would be accomplished by raising the wreck."

Ten days later, the poetic Sulzer was back again: "Raise the *Maine* from Cuban waters/For Columbia's sons and daughters/To the surface of the ocean/With a glorious emotion!"

In response, there was some congressional carping. William Douglas of Ohio maintained that "if this proposition be to improve the harbor, let the

Republic of Cuba remove the wreck. If it be a matter of justice [to discover guilt], let the Kingdom of Spain remove the wreck. As far as sentiment is concerned, there are no bodies left."

Sulzer countered with a *New York Herald* article by the author Rupert Hughes: "The day after the ship was sunk, you could hardly find an American who did not believe that she had been foully done to death by a treacherous enemy. To-day you can hardly find an American who believes Spain had anything to do with it. People have come quietly to believe, 'They will not raise the *Maine* because they are afraid to.'"

Sulzer had not endeared himself to the establishment. When the Navy Department finally acquiesced to congressional pressure and agreed to raise the *Maine*, Secretary Meyer endorsed a rival bill by Representative George Loud of Michigan. On March 23, 1910, in the Sixty-first Congress, Loud took the floor and declared, "I call up the bill."

To Sulzer's consternation, Loud then delivered his own metered salvo: "With fighting top and tangled wreckage still/Uplooming from the waters of the bay,/The fated *Maine*, abandoned to the waves,/Unhonored lies, while rust eats her away./Why is it thus? Where is our boasted pride?/Why has our Congress suffered this to be?/Are we so poor that we must let her lie/Year after year for scornful eyes to see?"

Sulzer was bested. He could only respond with a reprise of his favorite, "Down in that tropic, torpid bay." Both congressmen had exhausted their repertory of rhymes appropriate to the subject.

That being so, a vote was taken on the bill. There were ayes 115, noes 4. Accordingly, the bill to raise the *Maine* was passed.

NO SUCH COFFERDAM EVER

In addition to the removal of the wreck from Havana harbor, the bill Congress enacted provided: (1) The remains of the sailors in the ship were to be recovered for reburial in Arlington Cemetery; (2) The mainmast still standing was to be erected over the new graves; and (3) The wreck was to be exposed without disarrangement of the parts so as to provide the best leads to the source of the explosions.

Congress appropriated $100,000 for the removal on May 9, 1910, and added $200,000 the next month. On August 2 the Chief of Army Engineers,

General William Bixby, appointed a board whose members were qualified to plan and carry out the project. The senior member was Colonel William Black who was well known because of his part in the construction of the Panama Canal. Major Mason Patrick was an expert on harbor projects. Captain Harley Ferguson had experience in Cuba and would be stationed in Havana to supervise dewatering the wreck.

This was not a board to cover up for the Navy or condone a whitewash. On August 29 the members met to formulate a program. Spain was invited to participate, but the *Maine* was no longer of interest in Madrid. Whatever had caused the explosions was ancient and distasteful history.

The board considered two ways to raise the wreck. Either cables would be passed under the ship and attached to pontoons or a cofferdam would be built around the wreck. The cofferdam would be more radical. The concept had been discarded in 1898 because deep mud made the bottom of Havana bay unstable.

The board calculated that constructing a watertight enclosure around the 325-foot battleship would involve 3,200 steel piles, each 75 feet long and weighing $1\frac{1}{2}$ tons. The piles would have to be driven 38 feet, accurately enough to interlock. No interlocking cofferdam on such a scale in such a depth of water and into such a soft bottom had ever been built.

Nevertheless, the board of engineers proposed this untested approach on October 10. At best, cables would have lifted just the undamaged after portion of the ship. Dewatering was the only way to expose the whole wreck without disturbing the alignment of the parts. President Taft gave his approval three days later. Once committed, Congress appropriated an additional $350,000, for a total of $650,000.

Despite two hurricanes that roared over Havana in October, a floating workshop consisting of tugs, dredges, and scows surrounded the wreck by December 6 when the first piles were delivered. Pile driving began right away.

After four months spent constructing the enclosure, General Bixby reported in April 1911 that the planting of the steel piling had been completed although the interlocks were untried. The dam was elliptical and would have to withstand 4 million pounds of pressure after mud and water were pumped out to a depth of about 42 feet.

The wreck had continued to sink slowly during its thirteen-year immersion. According to board reports, all that was visible was the mainmast, the stern searchlight platform, the flopped-over decks amidships, and the isolated wreckage forward. Mercifully, there was no reference to Powelson's elevated keel.

Bixby had employed divers who determined that the undamaged portion aft had sunk to a depth of 50 feet. He recommended that after dewatering, the totally destroyed forward third be cut into manageable pieces for dumping at sea and that the undamaged portion be floated and sunk at sea. It was not his job to concern himself with investigating the cause of the explosions.

When pumping started June 5, Chief of the Bureau of Construction Admiral Richard Watt assigned Constructor William Ferguson to act as liaison with his brother who was the Army board's resident officer. During the dewatering Ferguson prepared preliminary records for the Navy investigation to come, collected human remains, and chose mementos for the patriotic organizations. He also took photographs of the wreck, built wooden models, and painted white frame numbers on the corroded hull.

Pumping was halted frequently to check for leaks and to adjust the pilings. By the end of June the cofferdam was fairly tight. Bixby visited the site, looked at the partially uncovered wreck, and announced that the origin of the explosions would never be determined.

The damage was much worse than had been anticipated, although the after portion of the vessel from the stern to frame 54 was relatively sound. Forward from frame 54 to frame 41, the main deck was torn loose and the hull was partly blown out on the port side. Forward of frame 41 the ship was destroyed for 60 feet. Farther forward there was only a twisted mass, out of line with the after portion, and bearing little resemblance to the bow of a ship.

Decks and cabin floors were covered with three to five feet of mud, oyster shells, barnacles, and coral encrustations. The stench of dead marine life, drying filth from the harbor water, and corrosion was overwhelming. Human bones were scattered about.

In early August, Secretary of War Stimson pointed out that the water within the dam had been lowered 24 feet without indicating whether the cause of the explosions had been external or internal. He recommended discontinuing the dewatering. Major Patrick, however, was optimistic. The part of the wreck where destruction was greatest was still buried in 17 feet of mud and water. He expressed the hope that the cause of the disaster might yet be found when the destroyed area was uncovered.

Influenced by the Navy Department, Congress resisted the appropriation of more money. In his August 21 message, however, President Taft agreed with Patrick, remarking that "the issue is not whether we ought to have begun this investigation but whether we ought to break it off for lack of a small additional appropriation. Nothing [must] remain undone to enable the world to know the original cause of the explosion." Thus motivated, Congress set aside another $250,000. The total authorized expenditure was $900,000.

In March 1912, London's *Engineering* magazine, which had been the nemesis of the Sampson court, published a progress report on the dewatering. While describing the original explosions in a casual reference, the writer who was again Colonel Bucknill commented, "The *Maine* was sunk as the result of one or more explosions."

The Sampson court had found at least two explosions, the mine and the magazine. After lengthy soul-searching for his 1898 response, Bucknill had agreed to two explosions, both internal. Implicitly, he had now changed his mind. One explosion could only be a magazine, precluding the possibility of a mine, large or small, submarine or contact.

The reference to one explosion was a tip-off that the colonel's shadow would hang ominously over a new naval board of inquiry, even before the membership was known to him.

THE EVE OF DELIBERATIONS

The board of engineers' *Final Report on Removing Wreck of Battleship "Maine" from Harbor of Habana, Cuba*, was issued in April 1913, long after the work was done. The report did not add much to the story. When the dewatering was completed, the remains of one officer and seventy-four enlisted men were still entombed in the wreck. Each shovelful of mud to be removed was washed through a wire screen to recover human fragments. Progress was as slow as on an archeological dig, yet it was impossible to say how many of the dead were recovered.

The report contained the first description of the wreck free of mud. Presumably, naval experts would be able to determine conclusively whether the reason for the explosions was external or internal.

The board's approach was directed toward removing the wreckage, however, not toward an investigation into cause. For the Army engineers, the dividing line in the ship was frame 41, between the forward and aft boiler rooms. The principal damage aft of frame 41 was above the water line. If the ship was cut off there, the open end could be sealed and the hull refloated.

This intact section of the wreck requiring the Army board's attention was remote from the locus of the explosions that would concern the Navy. Frame 41 was 44 feet aft of frame 30 and 92 feet aft of frame 18. The piles of debris forward of frame 41 were of little interest to the board. The material there presented no engineering challenge. When the Navy finished its inquiry, the debris would merely be cut into small pieces and dumped into the sea in accordance with Bixby's recommendations.

As exposed by the complete dewatering, the upper portion of the ship had been blown away from frame 41 to frame 30. The sides were thrown out while the ship's bottom was nearly whole. Between frames 30 and 18, only half the bottom was in place, mainly on the starboard side. Forward of frame 18, the ship had been destroyed above the level of the protective deck. What was left of the bow was nose down to port and lying on its starboard side in the mud.

The critical area immediately forward of frame 30 was hidden by the rubble Sigsbee had sought to dynamite. William Ferguson advised Admiral Watt that the front part of the rubble should be cleared away with recently introduced oxyacetylene torches. Watt's predecessor, Admiral Washington Capps, went to Havana and approved the cutting. The ship was then judged ready for inspection by a naval board appointed to determine cause.

The magazine *Scientific American* congratulated the Army Corps of Engineers for constructing the 350 by 170 foot cofferdam, calling the accomplishment "without parallel. The plan was the subject of much criticism from the day it was made public. Complete failure of the cofferdam was freely predicted by the engineering profession, yet it has done its work. Not only will the after portion of the ship be floated and towed away, but practically every part of the wreck will be made to yield its evidence in determining first cause."

On the eve of the deliberations of the naval board, however, *Scientific American* was not optimistic about an answer being found. According to the magazine, the Spanish government was above suspicion and the Spanish navy was too inept to make functioning mines. During the war, Spanish contact mines had not exploded when struck by U.S. warships. Cuban rebels were even less efficient. On the other hand, the possibility of spontaneous combustion was denied by the normality of shipboard operations.

The problem would lie in interpreting what was found in the dewatered wreck. "The mystery of the *Maine*," *Scientific American* contended, "is today as profound as ever. Every hypothesis presents insuperable difficulties."

The Second American Inquiry

★ ★ ★ ★ ★ ★ ★ ★

MEET THE VREELAND BOARD

The precept for the Board to Inspect the Wreck of the USS *Maine* (Old) was issued by the Secretary of the Navy on November 10, 1911. Sigsbee's sunken battleship had already been replaced in the fleet by a new USS *Maine*. The Spanish-American War had been over for thirteen years, time enough for a different generation of leadership and warship to emerge in the Navy.

The order required the board to "make an exhaustive examination of the wreck and state whether there is anything shown, or any new evidence developed, that would indicate the cause of the explosion." There was no additional instruction to consider culpability as the Sampson court had been charged. There was in fact no reference to the 1898 inquiry. The Taft Administration wanted it to be clear that this was an independent board, not an apologist for the Sampson court. The 1911 board was to come to its own conclusions based on the dewatered wreck, evidence that had not been available to the Sampson court.

In addition, the size of the new board was increased to five to make room for leading authorities in the relevant disciplines. This was in response to continuing criticism of the technical qualifications of the officers on the 1898 court.

The senior member was to be Admiral Charles Vreeland, the Navy Secretary's Aide for Inspections. His rank was a cut above Sampson's 1898 captaincy. Furthermore, his specialty was the conduct of investigations. He was the Navy's chief sleuth whose job it was to head consequential boards such as this one. There had been no trained analyst like Admiral Vreeland on the Sampson court.

The second member was another admiral, Chief Constructor of the Navy Richard Watt. A graduate of the Academy and of the Glasgow school of naval architecture in Scotland, he had been in charge of building U.S. warships since he was twenty-nine. Moreover, he was familiar with the dewatering of the *Maine* through William Ferguson, his contact with the Army Engineers. There had been no one with engineering qualifications comparable to Watt's on the 1898 court.

The third member was Commander Joseph Strauss, an internationally recognized ordnance expert with awards from Great Britain, France, and Japan in addition to the Navy's Distinguished Service Medal. While serving as Sampson's protégé he had invented double-decker turrets for battleships. He had been an ordnance inspector, had performed experimental work on mines, and had written articles on ordnance. There was no higher U.S. authority on naval ordnance, including mines, than Joseph Strauss. He would be promoted to admiral within two years.

As if these three were not eminent enough, President Taft ordered the appointment of an Army officer so no one could say this was just a Navy whitewash. Taft chose the noted Colonel William Black, builder of the Panama Canal and head of the board of Army engineers that supervised the dewatering of the *Maine*. The Vreeland inquiry had become a joint Army-Navy enterprise.

The fifth member was Commander Charles Hughes, the recorder. Known as "Handle Bars" because of his full mustache, his expertise was in naval equipment including coal.

These members assigned to the 1911 board were the most experienced and talented naval and military officers available. They had been selected carefully over a period of weeks. No pressure was exerted on them. There was no threat of war. Even the horde of special correspondents who had harried the members of the Sampson court was missing. Nothing hung in the balance other than ascertaining the truth about the cause of the *Maine* explosions.

The first meeting of the board was in Havana's Plaza Hotel on Monday, November 20, 1911. Heavy rain prevented the board from visiting the harbor. Instead, informal discussions were held with Major Patrick and Constructor Ferguson.

Rain was still falling on the second day. The tropical downpour dumped tons of water into the cofferdam, covering the wreck's bottom plates. Nevertheless, impatient Admiral Vreeland and his colleagues put on borrowed coveralls and rubber boots to descend as well as they could into the shattered section between frames 18 and 30.

Next, the board returned to the hotel to examine Ferguson's drawings, photographs, and models. They also discussed the Sampson findings in terms of the structural elements they had seen. Wary of becoming tainted, they kept their distance from anyone who had been involved with the 1898 court.

They were also more reticent with journalists than Chadwick and Marix had been. There was no leak of information concerning progress. The only word released was that the inspection would probably continue for ten days. Consequently, there was little news about the board in the Havana or mainland newspapers.

On the third day, the board went back to the wreck which had been pumped dry. An evening session was devoted to a comparison of the wreck with what the witnesses before the Sampson court had described. Despite the disrepute of naval divers in general and the refusal of the Sampson court to rely on divers' observations, the testimony of Powelson's divers had been accurate.

The board's pattern was established. The members were taken to the wreck every day and afterward they met at the hotel to discuss what they had observed. By the tenth day, November 30, they were formulating their opinion.

On the twelfth day, December 2, the board finished its inspection of the wreck, completed its report, and adjourned. Six days later, Constructor Ferguson began setting up his most elaborate model on a table in Secretary Meyer's outer office in Washington. This was not a priority project. Ferguson's labors were frequently interrupted by naval officers who gazed at the model with surprising dispassion.

In the afternoon, Vreeland and Ferguson tried to explain the board's findings to the Secretary although all parts of the model were not yet in place. For a layman like the Secretary, the presentation was difficult to understand.

The contrast with the theatricality of the 1898 delivery and publication of the Sampson findings was deliberate, but the down-playing of this report was overdone. Neither the Secretary nor the members of the Vreeland board nor Ferguson spoke to the few newspapermen who came to look at the model. The Secretary could not talk intelligently about the *Maine* disaster and the officers had been ordered not to talk at all. Consequently the public which had come to believe that the *Maine* disaster was an accident scarcely knew there was a Vreeland report.

A conscientious newsman from the *New York Times* was an exception. He prepared himself by rereading the Sampson report and the devastating Bucknill response. Then he wrote a long article based on what he could make of the model. His analysis, however, was still in terms of Powelson's inverted V. The board's findings had not been published and the model confused him. So did the negative attitude of the Navy Secretary.

"The model is encased in a wooden frame and can be transported with comparative ease," the journalist concluded. "Secretary Meyer would not permit photographs to be made, and said he did not know when he would permit them. The model may be taken over to the White House for the inspection of the President, or the President may go to the Navy Department. The report will not be submitted to the President until after Secretary Meyer has gone over it thoroughly with the members of the Board. The President is wholly occupied just at present with pressing business, and there is no hurry about this report. When he has examined it, it will be made public."

Meyer's attitude toward the report was disparaging. He never did allow photographs and soon had the model put in storage where it was lost. The President did not see the model. As Secretary Meyer said, Taft was busy. He was occupied with trying to get re-elected now that his former mentor, Theodore Roosevelt, had returned to politics.

SOME EXTERNAL FORCE DROVE IT

Despite the Secretary's casual air toward the Vreeland report, President Taft transmitted the findings to the House of Representatives for publication in less than a week.

In its report the board recited the history of the disaster and then provided a detailed description of the wreck based on what the members saw when the bottom plates were completely dewatered. As an example of how extensive the damage was, ten bulkheads had divided the forward magazines. After the explosions, only one remained attached and it had been blown down against the ship's bottom. The other nine were gone.

To establish that there were two explosions and to resolve the cause of the first one, the condition of the port bottom plating in the devastated area was critical. Not much remained. The board noted that part of what was left was displaced and distorted, both in and out. The full particulars took only four short paragraphs:

1. As figure 34 shows, the bottom plating ran in strips parallel to the keel the length of the ship, similar to a boardwalk. Each width of plating was called a strake.
2. The strake closest to the keel was the garboard strake, or strake A. Between the garboard strake, that is, the one next to the keel, and the bilge, at the outer end of the ship's bottom, there were four more strakes, B, C, D, and E.
3. After the explosions, tears along the strakes and breaks across the strakes separated this area of bottom plating into four distinct sections. Each section was attached to the ship at one end, where it was bent in or out.
4. Section 1 was an irregular 100-square-foot piece of bottom plating that was torn from strakes B and C. The plates were broken across the strakes at frame 28, bent aft at frame 32, and displaced upward and inward into the reserve 6-inch magazine. The section was folded back almost flat against inside bottom plates that had remained in their original position.

Thus, decks and sides had been blown up and out by the magazine explosion in the area of greatest damage. Some of the port bottom plating, however, was miraculously still in place. The sharp inward bend of section 1 was the Vreeland board's crucial bit of evidence. Completing the dewatering had proved to be worthwhile.

The indicia were being seen by experts for the first time, but the question was the same. Had there been an external explosion to ignite the black saluting powder in the reserve magazine? Or had the explosion been wholly internal through spontaneous combustion of bunker coal? The board had expressed no opinion this far in the report, although the emphasis on section

1 seemed to indicate a belief that an external explosion had driven bottom plates inward.

Moreover, a longitudinal piece of steel had been fastened over B strake as a support. This longitudinal was torn at frame 28, just as section 1 was, and its forward end was displaced six feet above its original position. Counting the inner plating of the double bottom, there had been three layers of steel at section 1 and they were all displaced upward into the reserve 6-inch magazine.

Section 2 was of interest only in comparison with section 1. Immediately outboard of section 1, this section was similar in shape, size, and location of breaks and bends. Section 2 was displaced downward and outward, however, unmistakably blown from the inside by the ignited reserve magazine.

Sections 3 and 4 were not in contact with section 1. Their displacement outward was of lesser importance.

Thus the Vreeland board described four separate but relatively similar sections of port bottom plating. One was blown in, the others out. There could be no argument with the facts. They were visible to the members of the board and they were documented by photographs, drawings, and models. The only issue could be in the interpretation of what was there.

Embarrassingly for the Sampson court, this displacement had been observed by the maligned naval divers and was recorded in the 1898 testimony. Diver Olsen had said, "I found the bottom bent in between frames 30 and 32, warped like some external force drove it in like that." Diver Smith had observed, "The plates are bent from out inboard, about the middle of the Six Inch Reserve Magazine." Diver Rundquist had advised, "The green paint was on the part bent inboard, rolled up. I believe she was blown up from the outside and in."

The Sampson court had trusted what they had seen for themselves, the elevated keel, rather than what was described to them, the obscured bottom plates curled inboard at about frame 30. In contrast, the Vreeland board was able to see the bottom plates.

A CHARGE BETWEEN FRAMES 28 AND 31

In its formal report, the Vreeland board of inspection found that "the injuries to the bottom of the *Maine*, above described [the inboard displacement], were caused by the explosion of a charge of a low form of explosive exterior to the ship between frames 28 and 31, strake B, port side." The mines the Spanish government had in Havana were charged with guncotton, not with a low explosive such as gunpowder, so the reference was implicitly to a fanatic as the miscreant, not the Spanish government.

"This resulted," the board continued, "in igniting and exploding the contents of the Six Inch Reserve Magazine, said contents including a large quantity of black powder. The more or less complete explosion of the contents of the remaining forward magazines followed. The magazine explosions resulted in the destruction of the vessel."

The board had ended its findings on the simplest possible note. Naval authorities quoted on the day after the 1898 explosion had insisted, Wait until salvagers raise the *Maine*. At that time the investigators will see the condition of the wreck with their own eyes and the source of the primary explosion will be clear. If the hole at the location of the greatest damage is blown in, a mine was the cause. If the hole was blown out, the cause was a magazine.

The hole that had been section 1 was blown in. Furthermore, the section was bent inward without being shattered, so the charge had to have been gunpowder with its softer force and not a high explosive that would have blown a clean hole through the bottom. Because the indicia of a large mine such as the geyser, shock wave, and dead fish were missing, this must have been a small gunpowder mine in contact with the ship's bottom. It could have been homemade.

The 1911 conclusion was similar to the theory if not the specifics of the Sampson court, which had determined that a large bottom mine had exploded at the forward end of the forward magazines. The chain reaction was then said to have proceeded aft. The Vreeland board located a small contact mine at the after end of the forward magazines and had the reaction proceed forward. That was one difference. The other difference was that the Sampson court was demonstrably wrong in its placement of the mine.

Nevertheless, the confusing similarity in theory was the basis for the casual reception of the Vreeland board's report, despite every effort to divorce the board from its 1898 predecessor. Nothing in the new finding looked to be novel or different. Making matters worse, the Vreeland board had issued a press release before its opinion was published, seemingly apologizing to the Sampson court for reconsidering its 1898 verdict. The board then prefaced its formal opinion by excusing the Sampson court's error because the wreckage had not been exposed in 1898.

Unintentionally, the dishonored Sampson court had been resurrected. Newspapermen read the Vreeland release and report as indicating that the Sampson court had been vindicated by a Vreeland board wholly supportive of the old verdict. There was little news value in what appeared to be a meaningless attempt to substantiate a discredited finding. Consequently, the Vreeland report received little publicity.

On December 9, 1911, the *New York Times* even questioned the economic value of the report: "With every frame and plate of the *Maine* laid bare for investigation, the Vreeland Board reaches a conclusion in all essential particulars identical with that reported by the original Sampson Court. Whether this was worth the money it cost depends upon how much weight one has ascribed to the doubts of some and the denials of others, in this country and abroad, of the accuracy of the Sampson Court's findings."

Despite the Bucknill proofs, the *Times* was still supporting the Sampson verdict: "Every doubt and denial had for basis, of course, only a willingness to ascribe incompetency or dishonesty to the naval officers of whom that Court was composed. That manifestation was comprehensive enough when shown by foreigners who resented interference by the United States with what they regarded as private affairs of a European monarchy. Its manifestation by a small but highly articulate group of citizens of this country is not so easy to understand."

The *Times* saw clearly the future of the *Maine* affair: "The chances are that neither the foreigners nor the Americans who had hitherto rejected the outside explosion theory will even now make public confession that they were wrong. They can still say, as the mine used has not been found, the cause of the explosion remains a matter of opinion, and that the mystery will not be cleared up until the identity of the man or men who fired the supposed mine has been discovered. This is in a measure true, but it is a demand for a degree of certainty which the circumstances of the case preclude."

In this manner, the Vreeland board's well-reasoned finding was relegated to obscurity because it was erroneously read as corroborative of the refuted report of the Sampson court. Most historians have commented that "a second Court of Inquiry upheld the findings of the first." Samuel Eliot Morison observed in 1965 that "this [Sampson] finding was confirmed by a careful examination of the wreck in 1911."

Other writers were less complimentary: "A second Court of Inquiry was called. Its findings were no more conclusive than those of the earlier Court." One never looked at the Vreeland opinion: "A second Court of Inquiry found that what the initial Court had taken as evidence of the detonation of a mine could as well have been an explosion in one of the ship's own magazines." Another erring scholar wrote, "In 1911, a thorough investigation showed the ship's bow plates buckled outward, which indicated the explosion had taken place within the vessel."

Captain Sigsbee was roused from retirement to declare, "A joint board reported in 1911, confirming the verdict of the Sampson Court except in the non-essential detail that the center of the explosion was a little farther aft." A self-serving voice from the past, he added that "I have never had a doubt that the *Maine* was blown up from the outside, but I have never expressed an opinion as to who destroyed the vessel and never will."

The *Times* might have noted that expecting to find bits of the mine casing in the wreckage after the explosions was like looking for a bubble after it burst in air. There would be no trace. Why Sigsbee, the Sampson court, and the Vreeland board avoided discussion of possible miscreants, however, was another minor mystery.

THE RETURN OF THE OBSTINATE COLONEL

Although the Vreeland board's report was a nonevent in the United States, the finding was a red flag to the uncompromising English sapper, Lieutenant Colonel Bucknill.

Bucknill had been in touch with General Bixby, the Chief of Army Engineers, early in 1911. Influenced by Bixby's pessimism, he had elected not to go to Havana to inspect the dewatered wreck. After all, he had been able to destroy the Sampson court's report based on its own testimony and exhibits in 1898. To help pass the long winter nights he expected to do the same to the Vreeland board's findings.

When he completed his new analysis, he wrote another article for *Engineering*. Over the years he had come to realize he had made a tactical mistake by acknowledging there had been two explosions. As a prisoner of logic, he had left open the loophole of a small gunpowder mine as a possible cause of the first explosion, the kind of mine the Vreeland board described. Without mentioning any alteration, he now stated that there had been only "one single great explosion." He was attempting to deny the mine theory right at the start of the analysis, not by reasoning but by surreptitiously changing the ground rules.

Next the aggressive expert claimed that the bending upward and inward of section 1 "could have been produced in many ways during the water turmoil following the great explosion of the magazines." Anything could have happened "when the water fell back," he maintained, but he did not specify what did happen, why section 1 reacted differently from sections 2, 3, and 4, or how section 1 came to be folded back almost flat against the inside plating.

By basing its finding on the incontrovertible physical existence of the inboard hole at section 1, the Vreeland board had presented at least prima facie evidence of the explosion of an exterior mine. Unless rebutted, the evidence would be final. In response, the partisan Bucknill merely gave his contrary opinion. He needed persuasive facts or authorities, and he had none.

His conclusion was, "As neither a large nor a small mine fits the case, any unbiased judge must regard the theory of an external explosion as a myth." If he did not win the decision through his arguments, he implied, it was because the judge was prejudiced.

The sapper who stung the 1898 court was only a gadfly in 1912.

The End of the *Maine*

★ ★ ★ ★ ★ ★ ★ ★

DOWN AT THE NOSE AGAIN

On December 16, 1911, the day after President Taft forwarded the Vreeland report to the House of Representatives for publication, Congressman Thomas Sisson of Mississippi offered an amendment to an appropriations bill to permit the hull of the old *Maine* to be sold at auction. Unsolicited offers of almost $1 million had already been received from showmen who wanted the truncated ship for exhibition.

Sisson's contention was that the government would have spent $900,000 on the *Maine* by the time the scheduled scuttling in the ocean was accomplished. A private sale of the historic wreck would eliminate the need for the sinking, more than cover the cost of the dewatering, and still allow Secretary Meyer to retain part of the wreckage for a memorial in Havana and for souvenirs to go to patriotic organizations.

Illinois Congressman James Mann put an end to debate on the auction. "I am surprised," he exclaimed sarcastically, "that the gentleman [Sisson] has not included in his proposition the selling of the bones of the seamen who died in the *Maine*."

Alternately, penny pinchers had suggested dynamiting the entire wreck within the dewatered cofferdam to avoid the cost of constructing the wooden bulkhead at frame 41 and refloating the hulk. They said that once the Vreeland board was through and corporal remains were removed, death by explosion was fitting for a vessel that had been sunk by explosion. The pomp-loving Navy, however, opted for the ceremonial burial that Congress had funded.

While the warship's fate was being resolved in Washington, the Army engineers had resumed control in Havana. The wreckage near frame 30 that the Vreeland board had interpreted as the locus of the mine was now just a pile of debris to the engineers. The rubble was broken up, placed on barges, and dumped in the ocean so work on the bulkhead across the ship could begin. Sluiceways were built into the bulkhead.

In addition, twenty-nine 6-inch holes were cut in the ship's bottom with oxyacetylene torches. Water was jetted through each hole to break suction with the mud below. Next, closed sea cocks with long stems were fastened in the holes to allow the gates to be controlled from the main deck for the scuttling. Finally, dynamite was placed inside the wooden bulkhead. If opening the sea cocks and sluices did not sink the ship, the dynamite would be detonated electrically.

The flooding of the cofferdam was started January 26, 1912, fourteen years and a day after the *Maine* was first chained to mooring no. 4. The hulk broke away from the mud and floated at 1 A.M., February 11, when only sentries were around. By February 15, the anniversary of the catastrophe, the cofferdam was full again. The draft of the ship was 21 feet to port and 17 feet to starboard at the blunted bulkhead end, so the conning tower was lashed to starboard to provide lateral trim. The draft was 26½ feet at the shaped stern.

Next, steel piles at the east end of the cofferdam were loosened with hydraulic jacks and pulled to provide the *Maine* with an exit. After noon on March 15, the hulk was towed out of the dam by the naval tug *Osceola* and two local tugs that assisted gingerly. The movement was not announced to the press. Few witnesses were present as the floating wreck was anchored alongside the dam with her stern pointing toward the harbor mouth. The *Maine* was ready for her last voyage, down in front as usual, even though it was the stern that was forward.

At sunrise on the morning of March 16, 1912, the *Maine*'s funeral began with a cannon shot from Fort Cabanas. From then on, a gun was fired at half-hour intervals, resembling the slow tolling of a bell.

The United States warships *Birmingham* and *North Carolina* arrived at eight o'clock. The *Birmingham* entered the harbor first and saluted the Cuban flag. Cabanas answered. The vessels were piloted to anchorages in front of the Machina wharf, near the cofferdam. Port and sanitary authorities quickly certified the two ships.

That was the moment when the Havana Corps of Port Pilots stepped in. The Corps contended that the battered and rudderless wreck was still a ship. Consequently, port regulations required the employment of a pilot even when the ship was being towed. In view of the historic occasion, however, the Corps accepted a compromise. Captain "Dynamite Johnny" O'Brien, the former filibusterer and now a Havana port pilot, was placed in charge, without compensation other than glory.

The glory was plenty for O'Brien. *Harper's Weekly* wrote that he "had helped more than any other to prolong the resistance of the Cuban patriots until freedom was assured by the sacrifice of the *Maine.*" In O'Brien's freebooting days, the *Maine* had vainly hunted for him on her Florida patrols and now he was the majordomo of her demise.

HOMAGE TO THE DEAD

Memorial services for the dead sailors whose remains had been removed from the dewatered *Maine* were also taking place in Havana to allow the Cuban Republic to display gratitude for the island's freedom. The bones of the 67 sailors, divided into 34 metal coffins, were symbols of the American sacrifice in the Spanish War.

Cuban architects had supervised the placement of special braces under the floor of Havana City Hall to prevent collapse from the weight of the coffins and the expected crowds. The entrance to the hall was draped with large U.S. and Cuban flags, and the three flights of marble stairs were hung with black and gold cloth softly illuminated. Heavy black cloth on the sides and galleries framed the central color.

The closed coffins were covered with scores of floral arrangements. Many had been sent by American politicians, but the largest was "From the People of Havana to the Victims of the *Maine.*" The honor guard for the caskets included General Bixby, members of the board of Army engineers, and Cuban notables.

At 2:15 P.M. on March 15, 1912, the City Hall doors were opened to the public. Hundreds of Cubans were waiting outside. From then on, a constant stream of silent visitors filed past the coffins. The number increased during the night. At least thirty thousand mourners attended.

Public viewing was terminated early the next morning. City Hall filled with officials who observed Father Chidwick while he presided over a requiem mass. At ten o'clock the coffins were carried down the three flights by Cuban artillerymen.

Twenty-five Havana policemen led the cortege. They were followed by the Havana Municipal Band, the *North Carolina*'s band, and three hundred American sailors and marines headed by Commander Charles "Handle Bars" Hughes of the *Baltimore*. He had been the recorder of the Vreeland board.

Next came the coffins. The first was borne on the shoulders of American sailors, the remainder by the Cuban artillerymen. Forty thousand Cubans lined the sidewalks between City Hall and the wharf. Rooftops and balconies were packed.

When the cortege arrived at the wharf, Havana's Mayor Cardenas formally delivered "the sacred relics of the brave mariners" to the United States. General Bixby replied as the United States's representative to receive the remains. At the conclusion of the orations, the coffins were taken to the *North Carolina* in launches.

Mayor Cardenas had prohibited the showing of a motion picture simulating the blowing up of the *Maine*. He declared the film to be in bad taste for exhibition on the sober occasion.

The only blot on the day was an article in the Spanish-bloc newspaper *El Diario de la Marina*, reprinting the old canard that Captain Sigsbee was off the *Maine* at a dance when the explosions occurred. The intimation was that he knew to take himself out of danger because the impending catastrophe was of American origination. After fourteen years, Spanish fanatics remained hostile to Sigsbee. Although absent from the ceremony, he was a lasting symbol of the 1898 U.S. intervention.

THE SEA BECKONED HER

Captain O'Brien was dressed in funereal black when he climbed aboard the *Maine* shortly after 1 P.M. on March 16. The wrecking crew was making final adjustments to the trim of the hulk while the *Osceola* stood by. On the tug were General Bixby and members of the board of Army engineers. Apart from Hughes, the Vreeland board was not represented.

According to O'Brien, "the first thing was to get the ship straightened out" so she could be towed stern foremost. "To keep control, the cable to the *Os-*

ceola was drawn short and a local tug was hooked to each side of the ship. At last she swung properly. The working crew went aboard one of the tugs, leaving me alone aboard the *Maine*. I took my stand at the foot of the makeshift mast near where the Captain's cabin had been.

"From the masthead floated the biggest navy ensign I ever saw. The flag had been run up by the halyards, then nailed to the mast so that by no possibility could the ship sink without carrying her flag with her." The deck was strewn with thousands of cut roses.

At 2 P.M. two guns at Cabanas boomed the signal for the start of the last voyage. Thereafter a cannon from the fort fired a salute every minute until the *Maine* passed. Along the waterfront, eighty thousand Cubans gathered. Roofs were filled with spectators. The ramparts of Morro and Cabanas were crowded. Thousands more, including American residents of Havana, were on boats in the harbor. The men took off their hats as the wreck was guided toward the channel.

The sailors and marines on the *North Carolina* and the *Birmingham* stood at attention while the hulk was towed past them. Then the two warships joined the nautical procession. Four gunboats of the Cuban navy were next, followed by steamers and tugs carrying officials of Havana's civic organizations. Private vessels were in the rear.

O'Brien recalled that "it was an anxious time going slowly down the harbor, for no man could tell how the hulk was liable to act. I was in plain view of both steering tugs and could signal them when to go ahead or astern. You took a long turn to port going out of the harbor, and when this was passed the flanking tugs cast off, the *Osceola* paid out her cable for sea towing, and we headed out. I was surprised to see what good weather the old hulk made of it. Only a little pitching from side to side as gently as a baby."

A heavy swell rocked the sea. Dark clouds spread appropriate gloom while the *North Carolina* fired a signal gun for each mile. To the right, the Ward liner *Saratoga* bound for New York City and the *Olivette* bound for Tampa kept pace.

"It was slow towing out," O'Brien added, "but at last came three whistles from the *North Carolina*, signaling that the voyage was over. Last rites were delayed to permit the escorting fleet to group themselves around." The U.S. warships halted to the right and the Cubans to the left about four miles from shore. The rest of the vessels formed the other two sides of the square.

"A tug put the working crew aboard again, and at a signal from the *Osceola* they opened the sea cocks in the ship's bottom and raised sluiceways in the bulkhead and returned to their boat, leaving me alone. The *Osceola* cast off her towline. I took one last look around, then dropped into the pilot boat, and stood by to wait for the end." Sailors and marines on the warships were at attention once more. Civilians bared their heads.

At first it appeared that the *Maine* would not go down. Romantics claimed she was fighting her fate. Then she began to sink very slowly while the Marine band on the *North Carolina* played the national anthem. Gradually she dropped lower and lower. The afterpart with the wooden bulkhead submerged until only the stern with the huge flag was above water.

At last she tilted to 45 degrees and sank out of sight at 5:30 P.M. There was a flash of colors as the ensign struck the waves and disappeared. Simultaneously, the decks were blown upward by air pressure, hurling jets of spray and masses of the roses into the air. Soon there was no trace of the ship except for the flowers on the sea's smooth surface. The death throes had taken only twenty-three minutes.

Just then, the clouds parted and the red rays of a lurid tropical sunset gave a parting touch of color. Taps were sounded and the warships' sirens wailed a dirge. When the lamentations died down, the *North Carolina* and the *Birmingham* fired final salutes and left for Virginia with the caskets containing the remains of the drowned sailors. The *Maine* sank in six hundred fathoms of water but was borne many miles north and east by the Gulf Stream before touching bottom.

Motion-picture cameramen on the *Osceola* took thousands of feet of film of the burial. Newspapermen wrote that no craft ever left port as oddly as this first battleship of the new U.S. Navy did when she was towed to her finish. O'Brien was pleased that "in no way could she have met a sweeter or more peaceful end. The sea beckoned to her and she went swiftly and gladly to its bosom."

SETS IN EVERY COFFIN

The burial of the *Maine* had been scheduled for 3 P.M. on March 16 to mark the last act of the naval ceremonies in Cuban waters. Not knowing that the ritual sinking would be delayed for two and a half hours, Americans across the country paid their final tribute to the ship at the original time.

Bells in New York City churches led by Old Trinity began tolling at three. Riverboats and ferries joined in by blowing their whistles. Flags that had hung at half-mast during the day were lowered. Work in the city ceased for a few moments to permit remembering the *Maine*.

In Washington, "a memorial service for the dead of the (old) U.S.S. *Maine*" had been set by President Taft for March 23 at 2:30 P.M. The morning of the twenty-third began with bright sunshine in the capital, although the air was chilly and rain was expected. Long before the funeral procession came through the city from the Navy Yard, the streets along the route were crowded with more people than had been seen on any day other than a presidential inauguration. Business had been suspended.

There were thirty-four horse-drawn caissons bearing the metal coffins in the cortege. Two skeletal sets were in every coffin but one, with the contents wrapped generously to prevent bare bones from rattling against the metal. Following the caissons was the Third Battalion of the Third Field Artillery with horses and gear. Two military bands played Grieg's "Dead March" and "The Dead March" from Handel's *Saul*.

The procession stepped slowly and solemnly along the avenue, taking an hour to reach the State, War, and Navy Building's rear entrance that was euphemistically called the south front. By then the rain had started. Few mourners were present to hear the eulogy by the President, the invocation, and the overlong oration by the ubiquitous Father Chidwick. Taft asserted that "every American can feel proud of that war because it was fought without a single selfish interest and was prompted by the most altruistic motives."

When the speeches ended, the cortege started off again in the continuing rain. At Arlington Cemetery, the coffins were lifted from the caissons and carried to open graves that surrounded an anchor from the *Maine*.

At that point, Admiral Sigsbee entered the enclosure reserved for survivors of the disaster. Twelve enlisted men were there, all past middle age and all still in the Navy, although one wore seven service stripes representing twenty-eight years. As Sigsbee reached the twelve, they stood at attention and prepared to salute. The moment the admiral saw them, however, he leaped forward, waved aside the salutes, and shook their hands with great warmth. Tears ran down the sailors' faces.

To begin the brief graveside ceremony, a marine rifle squad fired three volleys that broke the stillness. When the riflemen fell back, a Navy bugler sounded taps. Then the big guns at the fort boomed twenty-two times and the services were over.

The costly dewatering and the elaborate farewells to the *Maine* and her dead in Havana and Washington were intended to allay suspicions concerning the honesty and accuracy of the findings of the two American investigative commissions, the Sampson court and the Vreeland board. The attempt failed.

TRACES OF TRAGEDY WIPED AWAY

After Sigsbee saw the films of the *Maine*'s burial, he wrote that "the *Maine* floats desolate, but flying her national ensign above the rusted hull. Again and again the waves incline her gently. Then she bows to fate. She pauses for a moment on her deepest incline, and then glides down to her eternal grave. A sheet of ruffled water rolls its white mantle over the spot. She lies in water clear and cold. The waves resume their rhythm, and the material *Maine* merges into the memory of her dead." That was one of the few noncontroversial comments about her.

The hulk had sunk so deep and in such an indefinite location that promoters were precluded from sending divers to recover parts to sell as souvenirs. The burial place was in international waters, beyond the reach of any government. The only pieces given away by the board of Army engineers were for memorials. Two of the 10-inch guns and a gun turret were donated for the *Maine* memorial in Havana. The mainmast had been set up at Arlington Cemetery, along with the anchor. The foremast was at Annapolis flying weather signals.

The structure of the cofferdam and bits of wreckage were all that remained in Havana harbor. Rubble that protruded above the mud was broken up with small charges of dynamite. The pilings of the cofferdam were pulled and returned to the fabricator for scrap value. On December 3, 1912, the harbor bottom where the Maine had rested was graded to 37 1/2 feet, a little deeper than before the explosions. At that point, all traces of the tragedy were gone.

A monument to the *Maine* was dedicated at the Columbus Circle entrance to Central Park in New York City on Decoration Day in 1913. This was a prime location. George Hearst, the son of the publisher of the yellow press *Journal*, performed the unveiling as part of a lengthy naval and military pageant.

The architect was H. Van Buren Magonigle. Also, forty-seven sculptors had submitted models for the plum art job to be paid for by popular subscription. Attilio Piccirilli was chosen. He was an Italian-born associate of the National Academy of Art and one of six sculpting brothers who were themselves sons of a sculptor. The committee in charge called Piccirilli's model "the most appropriate and beautiful." An advisory group of prominent artists agreed with the selection which was also approved by the Municipal Art Commission.

The monument's base was a massive forty-foot shaft of Tennessee marble. Around the base were clusters of "symbolical statuary." On top was the gilded bronze figure of Columbia Triumphant cast from 6-inch gun barrels recovered from the *Maine*. She was poised on a chariot drawn by three seahorses.

As soon as the covering was removed, however, a dispute of national proportions arose. Letters to New York newspapers composed "a chorus of unfavorable criticism from artists and art-loving laymen."

In addition, correspondents from the state of Maine complained that New England marble would have been more appropriate. George Hearst was called ill suited for the unveiling because his father profited from the catastrophe. Some Americans regarded Triumphant Columbia as a poor choice because Spain had received a raw deal. Others were hostile to the glorification of war when a world conflict threatened. The feeling was of disillusionment, but the dispute soon died away and the monument stands as an overblown relic of former times.

Many regarded the *Maine*'s burial as one more act of deception by the naval establishment. "In 1911 [and 1912] when the *Maine* was raised, towed to sea and sunk in deep water," they claimed, "the mystery went down with her." The radical Industrial Workers of the World was more direct, maintaining that the submersion was intended so "there will be no chance of the true facts being revealed."

In *The Martial Spirit* published in 1931, Walter Millis repeated Bucknill's old saw by writing, "But if the first court had been so badly mistaken in holding that a charge exterior to the ship had been detonated 50 feet forward, the second one may have been mistaken also." Then he added, "At all events, the hull was towed out to sea and sunk, rendering any further study impossible." Millis was widely copied.

No one pointed out that the buried hulk was the undamaged part of the ship. Any study of the aft section would be meaningless. The debris forward was where the explosions had occurred. For that crucial area the board of Army engineers and the Vreeland board had accumulated a mountain of verbal description, photographs, drawings, charts, tables, and models.

The voluminous evidence compiled by the two boards was almost as good as having been there.

Rickover and the *Maine*

★ ★ ★ ★ ★ ★ ★ ★

PROLOGUE

In 1900 the English naval authority H. W. Wilson supported the Sampson court's finding of a mine explosion. He reversed his opinion in 1925 and joined other European experts by writing that "no scrap of evidence from Cubans or Spaniards in nearly 30 years has been forthcoming to show a mine was there. No trace of a mine could afterward be found. There was no upheaval of water. No dead fish were found." Hence, there was no mine.

He added that "supposing there was a mine, it must have been laid by the [Cuban] Republicans to secure the intervention of the United States. Spanish authorities would have been the last people to invite attack."

The difference between Wilson's positions in 1900 and in 1925 was caused partly by the intervention of World War I. The brutal struggle made it hard to believe that a sophisticated colonial power such as Spain would have committed a deadly assault leading inevitably to hostilities, even though the fighting was the comparatively picayune bloodletting of the Spanish-American War.

By the 1920s, war had also lost its glamor in America where public opinion followed a similar pacifist path. Noble Spain, it was said, could not have initiated the Cuban conflict. Moreover, the Weylerites who were the other possible malefactors were not guilty either. They were just young gentlemen employed by the gallant Spanish government as junior officers. Looking back from the 1920s, the *Maine* explosions were accidents precipitating a war that should never have been fought.

Author Millis concurred in opposing the mine theory: "In 30 years, no evidence has come to light to indicate a mine existed. The explanation seems to be that the *Maine* did destroy herself, through an act of God." Hearst's biographer Ferdinand Lundberg noted the continuing absence of a culprit's confession: "Nobody has come forward to acknowledge the deed. That makes the theory of accident stronger. Some parties to the conspiracy would surely have spoken out."

In 1935 Spain's innocence was recognized as official United States policy. At the request of Claude Bowers, the U.S. ambassador to Spain, President Franklin Delano Roosevelt acknowledged that Spain was not to blame for the *Maine* disaster. An indifferent Spanish government expressed polite appreciation.

By the 1960s, some writers had backed themselves into a neutral position: "Today, no more can be proved with regard to how the explosion took place or who may have planned it than could be demonstrated on February 16th. Nor is it likely to be." In 1970 the determination was the same: "We are no wiser seven decades after the event. At the time, people believed what they wanted to believe. Today, official Spanish culpability seems unlikely. The American rush to condemn Spain appears to have been a lapse into irrationality."

In 1974, the Washington *Star-News* printed J. M. Taylor's feature story "Returning to the Riddle of the Explosion that Sunk the Maine." The article cast doubt on both the mine theory and the integrity of the naval establishment.

The gist was that "the Sampson Court carried out a professional inquiry, but neither its procedures nor its conclusions were above reproach. Was there a mine at all? A popular theory was that Sigsbee's buoy was booby-trapped from the outset. But Sigsbee could have opted to anchor elsewhere and the Spanish authorities had only 18 hours' notice. Once in the harbor, Sigsbee maintained a 24-hour watch. It would have been theoretically possible for divers to attach a mine some dark night, but not a mine of sufficient size. Conclusive evidence is as elusive today as in 1898. And there is little prospect of any new inquiry."

Although the Taylor article was a rehash of disabused notions, the Navy Department retreated from the findings of the Sampson court and the Vreeland board. In 1975, a history of the Navy was approved by a committee of naval officers and copyrighted by the United States Naval Institute. The text maintained that "the cause of the explosion has never been determined. More than 75 years later, statements by a survivor indicated that the Spanish may have been correct; sailors smoking below decks in unauthorized places probably did cause the explosion."

This unlikely explanation was followed by the 1977 *History of the War at Sea* published by the Naval Institute Press: "In February 1898, the *Maine* explodes in Havana harbor, probably due to the spontaneous detonation of unstable explosives." The conflicting texts indicated how muddled the naval historians were on the cause of the destruction of the *Maine*. Both these theories had previously been refuted.

In the end, the Taylor article had greater impact than could have been expected. The piece happened to be read by Admiral Hyman Rickover. The combination of supposedly inconclusive evidence to support establishment findings and the unlikelihood of a new inquiry by Navy brass intrigued the admiral. He determined to solve the mystery, in a manner that suited his bent.

ENTER THE ADMIRAL

Hyman George Rickover was born in 1900 in Makowa, Poland. A Chicago congressman nominated him to the Naval Academy where his socialite classmates referred to him as "that little Jew" and claimed that "when he was circumcised they threw away the wrong end." Throughout his long Navy career, he displayed "an abrupt, uningratiating, and even obnoxious manner" that friends excused in terms of "the vicious anti-Semitism" he faced.

After graduating an undistinguished 107th in his 1922 class, he served as line officer on a surface ship, as a student of electrical engineering at Columbia University, and as executive officer of a submarine where the crew lacked confidence in his leadership. During World War II he was in charge of the Electrical Section of the Bureau of Ships. Associates were annoyed because he did the job well while ignoring the prescribed red tape.

In 1948 he was appointed head of the new Nuclear Power Division where he supervised design and construction of the first nuclear submarine, the *Nautilus*. The next year *Time* and *Life* magazines featured his achievements in harnessing atomic energy.

Despite the nation's need for nuclear submarines, Rickover's fellow officers disapproved of his penchant for personal publicity. They conspired to oust him from the service because he flouted conservative Navy traditions. Their vehicle was the Navy selection board which chose the officers to be promoted each year from the ranks of those eligible. Officers passed over for promotion twice were automatically retired. The board behaved like a private club in blackballing the unwanted.

Rickover changed his religion after marrying an Episcopalian, yet the 1951 selection board still passed over him. Because a second refusal would mean his compulsory retirement, the Chairman of the Joint Congressional Committee on Atomic Energy voiced concern. Secretary of the Navy Dan Kimball assured the chairman that failure to select Rickover was an oversight.

Rickover professed not to be surprised by the rejection but he became more antagonistic in his determination to continue his role in the Navy. He transferred his assistant to eliminate a possible successor. Meanwhile, Secretary Kimball awarded Rickover a second Legion of Merit for being "responsible for the most important work in the history of the Navy." The Secretary wanted to be sure the 1952 selection board got the message.

The next day, July 8, Kimball's plea was ignored as the board passed over Rickover again. The Navy brass said he would easily be replaced. Immediately, however, *Time* and *Life* expressed outrage against the naval establishment. In response, the Navy became more hostile toward Rickover, feeling that he was using the press to undermine the selection board instead of leaving quietly.

Federal agencies and Congress also supported Rickover. The Atomic Energy Commission released a statement that morale in the atomic program would suffer if Rickover was retired, but words had no impact on the Navy. Then Congress acted. The 1952 selection board had chosen thirty-nine other captains for promotion. Secretary Kimball and President Truman approved the list, but the Senate Armed Services Committee halted all promotions while the Rickover rejection was being investigated. The Navy saw itself as hostage to Rickover's advancement.

Truman gave in first. He had new Navy Secretary Robert Anderson convene an unprecedented special selection board to retain Rickover as captain for one year and also require that one captain be chosen for promotion in 1953 who was experienced in atomic propulsion. Rickover was the only captain who fit the description. Congress did not relent until he was retained and set for promotion.

The 1953 selection board still took five hours to approve Rickover's promotion. The vote was not unanimous. In 1958, political intervention was again required to force Rickover's promotion to vice admiral. In 1973, Rickover was made a four-star admiral by resolution of Congress.

To humiliate Rickover, he was barred from ceremonies for the *Nautilus* he had built. His wife was denied permission to launch a submarine. The admiral depicted himself as untouched by the snubs but he hated the naval establishment. He paid the brass back whenever he could. Attachment to his nuclear service was eagerly sought by young naval engineers. He interviewed applicants himself.

He enjoyed the prospect of getting even with the traditional Navy. Proving that the distinguished officers on the Sampson court and Vreeland board were inept or venal promised to provide a measure of satisfaction. He looked forward to the investigation.

CONTROLLING THOSE IN HIGH PLACES

Admiral Rickover recorded his findings in *How the Battleship* Maine *Was Destroyed*, a book published in 1976. The publisher was the Naval History Division of the Department of the Navy. Participants in the preparation of the manuscript were mainly government employees.

Vice Admiral Edwin Hooper (Ret.), the Director of Naval History, stated in the Foreword that his Advisory Committee approved the manuscript because "significant new insights" were provided. The book became the Navy's informal position on the *Maine* disaster.

In his Preface, Rickover acknowledged that the 1974 Taylor article had aroused his curiosity. "Mr. Taylor observed that no one had yet determined whether the *Maine* had been destroyed by a mine or an accidental explosion. That I knew." Rickover was starting on the premise that neither of the Navy's inquiries had produced sustainable conclusions.

"Taylor also remarked that Charles Sigsbee, commanding officer of the *Maine* and therefore an interested party, was allowed to attend sessions of the Navy's court of inquiry and even to question witnesses." Rickover was dissembling. He was aware that the court's precept entitled Sigsbee to these rights.

"Furthermore, Taylor pointed out that Rear Admiral George W. Melville, Chief of the Bureau of Steam Engineering, had said that the cause of the disaster was a magazine explosion. However, he was not asked to testify. These points raised in my mind questions as to how the Navy had investigated the event." Rickover charged the Sampson court with irregular proceedings, exclusion of vital testimony, and false conclusions.

Rickover then listed his key points: First, the *Maine*'s visit to Havana was a deliberate provocation contributing to increased tension between the United States and Spain.

Second, McKinley was poorly served by the *Maine*'s commanding officer. Sigsbee was isolated from day to day routine. He took only ordinary measures to guard against an accident, although he knew that other similar warships had bunker fires and that his bunker alarms were inaccurate. The *Kearsarge* and the *Texas* were found to be dirty while under his command.

Third, the Sampson court suffered from Secretary Long's failure to provide technical advice. After disposing of the possibility of an internal cause to its satisfaction, the court found that an external force raised the keel. However, "strained relations between the two nations, the warlike atmosphere in Congress and the press, and the natural tendency to look for reasons for the loss that did not reflect on the Navy" made the verdict one that could have been anticipated.

Fourth, the Spanish inquiry concentrated on spontaneous combustion. The Spaniards were astonished that magazines were adjacent to coal bunkers in the *Maine*.

Fifth, Rickover credited Colonel Bucknill with the most searching contemporary criticism. There had been two detonations. Self-ignition in the coal bunker caused an explosion in the reserve magazine. The second burst was in the 10-inch magazine.

Sixth, the 1911 Vreeland board was technically superior to the Sampson court. The board examined the dewatered wreck under the best circumstances and discovered that one section of bottom plating was bent inward and folded back. The board stated that a mine caused this damage, but the report is difficult to comprehend because the exhibits were not printed and the reasoning was not given. The board was without the advice of an outside expert.

Why the board took this stand is not understood, according to Rickover. Perhaps, he speculated, the board was unwilling to reopen the question of whether there had been a mine. Only thirteen years had elapsed since the war. It would have been difficult for the board to face the issue of whether the nation had made a grave error in 1898.

Subsequent to 1911, Rickover added, much experience has been gained in analyzing ship damage. In 1975, Ib Hansen, an expert on simulated weapons explosions, and Robert Price, a specialist in underwater photography of explosions, volunteered to look at the *Maine* evidence.

According to Rickover, Hansen-Price showed that the characteristics of the damage were consistent with a large internal explosion and the dynamic effects of the ship sinking. The analysis contradicted the 1911 board's findings. There was no evidence of a rupture or deformation which would have resulted from a contact or near contact mine. In one relatively small area the bottom plating was folded inward but there were several plausible explanations other than an external explosion.

What did happen, Rickover asked. Probably a fire in bunker A-16. There was no evidence that a mine destroyed the *Maine*.

"The *Maine* should impress us," Rickover concluded, "that technical problems must be examined by competent and qualified people; and that the results of their investigation must be fairly presented. With the vastness of our government and the difficulty of controlling it, we must make sure that those in 'high places' do not, without most careful consideration of the consequences, exert our prestige and might."

The moral he found at the end of his story was the same one he began with: (1) Engineers make the best analysts in a technological society. (2) The traditional Navy cannot always be trusted to act ethically or for the common good.

A TREMENDOUS IMPACT

Ten years after Admiral Rickover's book was published, there were still copies in stock from the short printing. Nevertheless, the impact of the book on public opinion was tremendous. There was no longer any doubt about the cause of the *Maine* disaster. Coal in the bunker adjacent to the reserve magazine had ignited by itself.

Rickover's decision that an accidental fire sparked the explosions was taken as fact. There was no analysis of his reasoning. He was incontrovertible within the Navy.

Yet Rickover's first point that the *Maine's* presence in Havana contributed to increased tension favored the mine theory, not the accidental fire. Anxiety would have ignited emotions, not things. When feelings ran hot, mines could well have been planted and detonated by fanatics. On the other hand, Spanish hatred could not have raised the temperature of bunker coal.

Next, Rickover attempted to set the stage for fire by portraying Sigsbee as negligent with respect to bunker alarms. In fact, the fault with the Maine's bunker alarms was that they were too sensitive. They rang twice when there was no fire. If there had been a fire, the alarms might well have rung. If not, there were the practical tests of touch, smell, and sight that had always worked before to find self-ignition on ships susceptible to fire.

Rickover's charge that Sigsbee knew of bunker fires on other warships was true. His executive officer Wainwright was a leading authority on spontaneous combustion. However, none of the causes was present on the *Maine* where there had never been spontaneous combustion. If there had been a reason for concern, Wainwright would have recognized and handled the symptoms.

It was also true as Rickover noted that two of Sigsbee's other ships had failed inspections. However, the infractions were explained satisfactorily to the authorities. Neither occurred on the *Maine*, which was spotless after three weeks in Havana harbor. Wainwright ran a clean ship. He was there to maintain routine while Sigsbee had been picked by McKinley and Long for his courage, quick thinking, and diplomacy.

In short, Sigsbee was the traditional Navy officer, a popular cog in the establishment. He had even been a member of a personnel examining and retiring board similar to the later one that passed over Rickover twice. The depiction of a careless captain who ran a slovenly *Maine* was a fabrication.

Most of Rickover's text was an attack against the Sampson court whose error had been corrected in 1898 by Colonel Bucknill and others. Yet, Rickover performed the refutations again seventy-eight years later so he could say that "the verdict of an external explosion could be expected. The finding of the court of 1898 appears to have been guided less by technical considerations and more by awareness that war was now inevitable." According to Rickover, the court's fault was inappropriate predetermination, not bad judgment.

The admiral was even testier with the 1911 board. First, he said, the Vreeland report was difficult to understand because the exhibits were not printed with the finding. That was true. Congress had not thought enough of the Vreeland board to spend the extra money to publish the photographs and charts. On the other hand, the original exhibits were retained in an envelope in the National Archives. When Rickover asked for the exhibits, the entire envelope was delivered to him. He was furnished with everything he needed.

Second, Rickover complained that the board's reasoning was not given. Actually, the board's finding was simply that 100 square feet of the *Maine's* bottom plating was bent inward and folded back. That was reason enough. Displacement inward presumed that a blow from outside had occurred. In response, Rickover cited Hansen-Price as only suggesting that this displacement "could have been accounted for by an internal explosion and the dynamic effects of the ship sinking." "Could have been" is not by itself a sufficient rebuttal.

Third, Rickover said the 1911 board was without the advice of an outside expert. In fact, the members were the most knowledgeable men in their fields. Rickover did not ask his own experts to call in outsiders, yet they were not as prominent in their fields as the board members were.

Beyond inducing his modern experts to perform their analysis, Rickover contributed little to substantiate his thesis that the traditional Navy had been unqualified and unfair in twice finding a mine as the cause of the *Maine* disaster and that in the process the Navy had dishonored itself. His text was not a historian's study but a sea lawyer's brief.

Yet, his analysis has endured. In 1991, a book published by the Naval Historical Center of the Department of the Navy claimed that "it was not until 1976 [in Rickover's book] that scientists and engineers established conclusively that the *Maine* was not destroyed by a mine but by internal implosion."

The Rickover rationale has since been revisited by its proponents, just as the faulty Sampson finding was modified over the years in order to correct what had become obvious errors. The current modification by some Rickover theorists is that a very slow, very localized burning had spontaneously combusted at high temperature, starting with the coal dust in the cracks at the bottom of the bunker. This location would have prevented the fire from being noticed by routine inspections, it is now said, and also the burning would have failed to set off the highly sensitive alarms installed on the bunker's overhead.

The only thing new about this, however, is the hot coal dust in the cracks. Actually, the coal and its dust are always on the floor, and the alarms are always on the ceiling. That is what "routine inspections" check.

In the end, how valid Rickover's position was would depend entirely on the Hansen-Price report. If Hansen-Price was correct, Rickover was also correct, and vice versa.

Survivors of his first-rate team state that they were given all the technical data they needed and they were told simply to find the truth. They believe that Rickover would have been just as happy if the study had concluded that a mine had sunk the *Maine*.

Hansen-Price and the *Maine*

★ ★ ★ ★ ★ ★ ★ ★

ENTER MR. H AND MR. P

Near the end of his book Admiral Rickover restated a version of the Hansen-Price analysis he simplified into seven steps:

1. Spontaneous combustion occurred in the bituminous coal in the *Maine*'s bunker A-16 due to inadequate ventilation. Similar fires had occurred in other warships.
2. Heat from the bunker fire ignited gunpowder in the adjacent reserve magazine.
3. Explosion of the reserve magazine resulted in detonation of nearby magazines.
4. Most of the bottom plating was blown outward.
5. The forward section of the ship capsized to starboard. The forward end of the undamaged after section began to sink. The keel between the forward and after sections was elevated into an inverted V by the motion of the ship.
6. The outer bottom plating was low-strength steel, half an inch thick. One section of this plating was bent upward into the reserve magazine. That was the key evidence for the 1911 board. Hansen-Price found, however, that the plating bent upward showed no evidence of the mangling or rupturing expected from an external explosion strong enough to initiate a magazine burst. Instead, the contour and position of this plating can be explained by dynamic effects of the magazine explosion or by the sudden inrush of water following the explosion.
7. Hansen-Price found no evidence of an external explosion.

Rickover's restatement was constructed on the assumption in step 1 that spontaneous combustion occurred due to inadequate ventilation. In fact, however, self-ignition of coal feeds on oxygen. When air is prevented from reaching the coal, there is no ignition. "Inadequate ventilation" halts spontaneous combustion rather than helps the process. Fortunately, the admiral's experts were more scientifically grounded than his simplifications made it appear.

The Hansen-Price analysis was called "The U.S.S. *Maine*: An Examination of Technical Evidence Bearing on Its Destruction." It was published as an appendix to the Rickover text. The Introduction provided that "the object was to determine if present-day knowledge of explosion phenomena and their effects on ship structures could provide new insight into the question of whether the explosion was initiated externally or internally. Although not exhaustive, the investigation covered the principal technical points on which the boards appear to have based their decisions."

Immediately, the Hansen-Price acknowledgment that their examination was "not exhaustive" contrasted with Rickover's complaint that the inquiries by the 1898 Sampson court and the 1911 Vreeland board were insufficient. The court took twenty-three days and the board twelve days while Hansen-Price appear to have worked part time on data and exhibits selected by Rickover's assistants. As a result, many of the Hansen-Price conclusions were based on incomplete and misleading information furnished to them. To fully "provide new insight," the investigation should perhaps have been all inclusive and undertaken as a full-time job.

The next part of the examination dealt with "present-day knowledge of explosion phenomena" related to the *Maine* wreckage: "In a recent study of warhead effectiveness, high explosive charges were fired inside destroyer hulks. Allowing for the differences in explosive type, size, and placement, the damage produced was remarkably similar to that found on the *Maine*." The differences were so basic, though, that claiming any sort of similarity was going beyond the facts. Besides, no detail or citation was given. No testing was done that was specific to the *Maine*. The comparison was weakened because it was unsupported.

After these preliminaries set the stage, the Hansen-Price examination probed the Vreeland findings concerning the *Maine*'s bottom plating. Their conclusion was, "The inward folded section 1 plating was bent smoothly, not severely mangled, and shows no evidence of the rupture or deformation typical of an external contact or near-contact explosion. The Spanish contact mines of the day contained a charge of 100 to 200 pounds of guncotton. Such a charge would have ruptured and mangled the outer bottom over an area of 15 to 25 feet in diameter and would most likely have ruptured the keel. It also appears that the inner bottom plating was more mangled than the outer bottom plating in the region, which again is contrary to expectations if an external burst had taken place."

This reasoning is not persuasive. How the Vreeland photographs are read is a matter of interpretation, but the devastation near section 1 was substantial. The relevant illustration was not reproduced in the Rickover book. It is here (see plates p. XIV).

Actually, engineers on the magazine *Scientific American* found at the time that the photographic exhibits confirmed the Vreeland report: "Had the mine contained a high explosive, a clean hole would have been cut through the bottom immediately over the mine. But being filled with a low explosive, probably black powder, the blow was distributed over a rather wide area which was dished upwardly, while the bottom plate [section 1] immediately above was torn loose from the adjoining plating and blown inwardly and to the rear until it was folded back in the tell-tale position shown in the photograph."

Inexplicably, Hansen-Price responded to the Vreeland report by assuming for no apparent reason that a mine would necessarily have come from the Spanish navy and therefore be charged with guncotton. In contrast, the Vreeland findings expressly specified a low form of explosive. This was interpreted as the 70 to 100 pounds of black musket powder needed to penetrate the bottom plate and detonate the reserve magazine.

Hansen-Price, however, followed their unfounded assumption by calling for twice that quantity, not of gunpowder at all but of the high-explosive guncotton. Then they described the massive destruction such an amount of high explosive would have effected. Their analysis is simply unresponsive to the Vreeland findings. They are at apples and oranges.

Although underwater bursts of guncotton and musket powder both produce two types of pressure waves, the heavier shock wave and the following pulse wave, there is a big disparity in kind as well as degree. Guncotton detonates with a rapid development of terrific energy. Maximum intensity is attained almost at once. There is a very steep front to the shock wave. In contrast, gunpowder burns more slowly. The front is more gradual. Peak intensity is not as high.

Again, a guncotton explosion is sharp and violent with an abrupt front while a gunpowder explosion produces a slower development of lesser potency. Against the low-strength bottom plates of the *Maine*, a guncotton explosion would cut and mangle, as Hansen-Price maintained. A gunpowder explosion would tear along the weaker seams and then bend, just as section 1 was torn and folded.

A 1952 inquiry concerning underwater explosions in California is relevant to the contrast between guncotton and gunpowder bursts. The inquiry also bears on the Spaniards' "fish story," as Sigsbee called it. The violent explosions that blew up the *Maine* killed no fish. Yet when a Havana engineer set off small amounts of dynamite to clear harbor obstructions, fish died. Why?

In a submarine canyon off San Diego, dynamite explosions employed in offshore oil explorations killed fish. Local anglers objected. In a series of tests, scientists discovered that charges as small as one pound of a high explosive decimated fish while 90 pounds of black powder did not cause significant injury. Fish survive black powder bursts because energy from low explosives is not concentrated into an abrupt cutting and mangling front.

As an indication of the significant difference there would have been between charges of guncotton and of black powder bursting against the *Maine*'s bottom, fish are now safe from explosions off San Diego. Oil explorers have switched to the milder gunpowder.

Finally, Hansen-Price cite as fact that damage to the *Maine*'s inner bottom was greater than to the outer bottom. This is evidence to them that there was no outside explosion.

It is not clear, however, that there was more damage to the inner bottom of section 1. In the illustration of the photograph Hansen-Price examined, the section's inner bottom was folded back and was not readily visible. Second, if there really was greater internal damage, it may be that such a variation is common. In the Danish report on *Foersigtigheten* test no. 12, an external blast caused internal damage of 71 square feet compared to 64.6 square feet of external damage. Third, the *Maine*'s internal magazine blast that followed the detonation of the external mine was much heavier and did do more internal injury than the mine caused externally.

Further, Hansen-Price may not have been provided with all relevant data. The outer bottom steel was half an inch thick, as given, but they were not told that the inner bottom was only five-sixteenths of an inch thick. The inner bottom was thinner, weaker, and more readily displaced.

Besides, the Vreeland board was on the scene. The members examined the bottom plating in three dimensions. They actually touched section 1, which was in living color, 100 square feet in area, as big as a wall. In contrast, Hansen-Price looked at an eight by ten inch black-and-white photograph. The green paint of the outer bottom was not distinguishable because green photographed black. There is no doubt about which would be better evidence, the thing itself or a small colorless picture of it.

Moreover, there is little "present-day knowledge of explosion phenomena" that could aid Hansen-Price. This mine was an antique, probably homemade so primitively that engineers in the age of modern missiles could not believe it functioned. The charge was a black musket powder seen today only in Civil War pageants. The mine's target was bottom plating made of a soft, bendable steel outmoded since the turn of the century.

More reliance should have been placed on naval historians. "Present-day knowledge" does not help when elements of the explosions are outside the experience of present-day engineers.

Hansen-Price brought nuclear technology as excess baggage to the examination of the workings of antique musket powder.

THE MORE THE MANGLING

Because Hansen-Price found no mine in their scenario of the *Maine* disaster, they had to account for the inboard folding of section 1 by other means.

At the outset they confessed that "a simple explanation is not to be found," although there were "some possible ways" the inboard folding could have occurred. Presumably their most likely explanation was, "The 6-inch reserve magazine was bounded by transverse bulkheads. There was also a longitudinal web at the B strake. When the magazine exploded, both bottom platings and the bulkheads were ruptured. It appears plausible that the inner bottom around section 1 could have ruptured prior to the bulkheads. Then, when the bulkheads were displaced violently an instant later, the attached pieces of the bottom structure were whipped upward. In the process, the inner bottom plating became folded up and the longitudinal web was torn loose and also whipped up."

After presenting this implausibly convoluted sequential phenomenon that ignored section 2, Hansen-Price offered three alternate explanations. Each contradicted the others. The last one hypothesized that the inward bending of section 1 was from "the force of hitting the harbor bottom when the ship sank." What the ship sank into was slime, however, and not a solid bottom. There was no resistance when the wreck came to rest in the deep mud that cushioned a descent continuing for days.

As Hansen-Price admitted, "these explanations of the condition of the plate [at section 1] are conjectural." Despite the crucial lack of proof, however, Rickover accounted for the inward bending of section 1 by generalizing about "the dynamic effects or the sudden inrush." The admiral did, though, tiptoe around the force-of-hitting-the-slime theory.

Most of the Hansen-Price examination was either surplusage or foreign to the "technical points" that were their field of expertise. "Damage to Keel and Bow" was another attack on the Sampson court. "Evaluation of Eyewitness Reports" concluded that witnesses "cannot provide positive proof that an external explosion did or did not occur." One of the prepublication reviewers of this text commented that Rickover's technical experts attacked witnesses' testimony that there were two explosions by pointing out that sound travels faster in water than in air, so that witnesses would *feel* the same explosion twice, whereas there were in fact testimonies from witnesses who *saw* two explosions.

In "Evaluation of Miscellaneous Evidence," there was a discussion of "Feasibility of Placing a Mine Near the *Maine*" in terms of Viet-Cong training of underwater sappers who were able to handle 200-pound explosive devices.

In reviewing the "Capability of an External Burst to Ignite the Magazine," Hansen-Price determined that "a burst in contact with the ship bottom directly below the magazine will immediately transmit shock and hot gases into the magazine, provided the charge is big enough. A charge of at least 50 to 100 pounds is believed to have been required," although "it is most unlikely that the *Maine* explosion was indeed initiated by a mine." The reason for the improbability was the same absence of the "mangling" that would have resulted from a Spanish navy mine containing guncotton.

Finally, Hansen-Price considered "Possible Internal Sources of Explosion." A bunker fire was judged most probable because (1) bunker fires did occur frequently in 1898; (2) New River coal [Pocahontas] was known to have ignited itself in other ships; (3) the coal had been in bunker A-16 for three months; (4) the bulkhead between the bunker and the reserve magazine was a single plate; (5) brown and black powder were stored in the reserve magazine near the bulkhead; and (6) the forward stack that vented the bunker was not in use, making ventilation insufficient.

Actually, the coal would have been more stable after three months in the closed bunker, not more volatile. Further, the primary function of the forward stack was to vent the forward boilers when they were in use. The forward boilers had not been lit. No air had been drawn from bunker A-16 for weeks.

There was no proof at all that a bunker fire had caused the *Maine* explosions or that section 1 was bent inward by an internal force. The idea of a burst from inside thrusting the bottom plating back inside against the force of the same inner burst is confusing.

A GOLD SEAL ON A BLUE COVER

Rickover's book received a limited number of reviews. Despite the physical and philosophical thinness of the volume, however, substantially every comment was at least favorable. Some were raves.

The *Saturday Evening Post* observed editorially that the Navy's gold seal was embossed on the book's blue cover. "We cannot think of another instance," the *Post* remarked, "where a nation went to war on false pretenses and later came out with a government document admitting its error. Admiral Rickover points out that this [catastrophe] was a turning point in history, based on a gigantic error which many at the time recognized as such. All of the press, politicians, bureaucrats, and professional naval officers, however, told the story as they wished it might have been. That one such as Rickover, while serving in the government, can speak the unvarnished truth is a hopeful sign."

Rickover had successfully lambasted the judgment and honesty of the Navy's "professional officers." In addition, he enhanced his own image with the public he had needed in years past to rescue him from attacks by the same class of officers.

In a review titled, "Explosive Evidence" the *Post* also printed: "Admiral Rickover has written a book employing the best modern-day naval-laboratory techniques about explosions inside and outside steel ships. In spite of two naval investigations which concluded that the *Maine* had been blown up by an external explosion, Rickover decided that the explosion occurred within the ship in one of the ammunition magazines. Except for exacting thoroughness, there is nothing really new here."

The Marine historian Graham Cosmas wrote an approving article in the *Naval War College Review*, a periodical that was read by Rickover's peers: "Rickover demolishes the theory that the ship was mined and proclaims that the explosion was an accident resulting from a cause within the *Maine*. His civilian experts concluded the cause was a fire started by spontaneous combustion in an adjacent coal bunker.

"Rickover sharply criticizes the conduct of the two Navy investigations. The Sampson court did not call for the advice of available technical experts, many of whom doubted the mine hypothesis. Rickover strongly implies that influential individuals in the Navy Department had made up their minds about the cause before the investigation started. Rickover insists the 1911 board also reached the wrong conclusion, possibly for political reasons."

Similarly, a 1981 history of the Spanish-American War stated that "it is now almost universally believed that the Spanish view was correct, but the situation in 1898 did not permit a comprehensive and objective inquiry. Recently Admiral Rickover arranged for a modern engineering analysis. The two experts argue convincingly that a fire in bunker A-16 caused by spontaneous combustion led to the explosion."

Rickover's biographer Norman Polmar was caustic about the admiral, but he too gave credit to the book. Polmar had barbs only for the preparation at government expense: "At Rickover's request, Spanish, British, and French naval attachés supplied documents, translated by the Office of Naval Intelligence. The Director of Naval Telecommunications, Director of the National Security Agency, Archivist of the United States, and National Archives specialists did research. The Director of Naval History suggested the book be published by a commercial publisher. Rickover refused, and the Naval History Advisory Board accepted Admiral Hooper's suggestion of publication by the Navy."

Even the one doubter of Rickover's theory was polite. A 1984 history of the war noted that "in 1976 Rickover published his study, concluding there is no evidence that an external explosion initiated the destruction of the *Maine*. It is reasonable to ask, though, why the coal ignited in Havana harbor, the only case of an explosion out of 20 coal bunker fires."

The one comment that irritated Rickover was Cosmas' summing up. After the favorable observations that Rickover "sharply criticizes," "strongly implies," and "furnishes expert confirmation," the reviewer classified the book as a scientific treatise rather than literature.

In addition, Cosmas maintained that "the *Maine* disaster offers the historian the chance to examine late 19th century military and governmental institutions under stress. Rickover merely touches upon the political and bureaucratic interplay and his book is less than a complete historical study. Another study remains to be done on the human elements. The definitive account of the fate of the *Maine* remains to be written."

In Rickover's opinion he had already published the definitive account. He reacted by contacting Vice Admiral James Stockdale, the President of the Naval War College whose *Review* had printed the Cosmas article. First, Rickover asserted, Cosmas did not have the technical background necessary to evaluate the book and should not have been selected. Second, the *Naval War College Review* itself could be eliminated by having its funds cut off because bad judgment had been displayed.

As biographer Polmar observed, Rickover used government resources to do research. He controlled the project and induced the Navy to print the manuscript. Then he took steps to retaliate against criticism, although Admiral Stockdale would not have been fazed by the querulous complaints.

COAL THAT LIT ITSELF, OR DID IT?

At the end of a 1924 article on "Coal Piles That Light Themselves," the editor of *Scientific American* inserted a postscript: "The phrase spontaneous combustion is a familiar friend of long standing but the average person might be pardoned for feeling that it represented merely a convenient alibi to cover fires that cannot be explained in any easier fashion. The fact is, conditions under which coal will ignite itself, to burn more or less vigorously, are fairly well determined, and the means of prevention are fairly well indicated."

According to the editor, spontaneous combustion is only a scapegoat. When Rickover wanted to find a way to hang the *Maine* explosions on the Navy, he asserted that (1) bituminous coal can combust spontaneously; (2) there was bituminous coal on the *Maine* that was adjacent to a magazine; (3) therefore, the bituminous coal self-ignited and detonated the gunpowder in the magazine. Because he had no alternative, he fell back on spontaneous combustion, the "familiar friend."

As *Scientific American* pointed out, however, spontaneous ignition is a scientific fact of defined origin. Bituminous coal absorbs available oxygen. Absorption is accompanied by the development of heat. The temperature of the coal rises slowly and steadily. The process is accelerated on shipboard if there is a high temperature near the coal bunker.

Ignition requires a continuous replacement of air to maintain oxidation. If there is no supply of new air, the available oxygen will be exhausted. Heating will not proceed to ignition.

Coal is most apt to self-ignite when newly mined. The likelihood of spontaneous heating decreases during the first three months of undisturbed coal storage. Thereafter, the coal is stable if not handled and self-ignition would be unlikely.

The simplest inspection of coal stored on shipboard is by sight, smell, and touch rather than with instruments. The sight of coal smoke is the most frequent warning on a warship. The distinctive odor of heating coal is another indication. The smell is similar to burning sulphur and is overwhelming in close confinement such as the hold of a warship.

The critical temperature for commencement of ignition is between 140 and 180 degrees F. To test by touch, an inspector presses his bare hand around the pile for signs of warmth. The maximum temperature the average palm can bear is the crucial level of 150 degrees F., so the hand is a practical indicator.

The 1898 voyage of the USS *Oregon* furnished a telling example of spontaneous combustion on shipboard. On March 19 the battleship was ordered to leave San Francisco for Key West because of the approaching Spanish war. With the *Maine*'s experience in mind, the *Oregon*'s captain had his steam launch circle the vessel when in port at night to detect fanatics with mines. No incident occurred.

Due to the *Oregon's* tight construction, the interior became hot after only a few days at sea. The fireroom temperature around the bunkers rose to 150 degrees F. One afternoon in the Pacific near Peru, smoke came from a bunker containing 70 tons of Cardiff coal that was equivalent to the *Maine's* Pocahontas fuel. The coal had ignited itself. Sailors working ten-minute shifts dug down to the flame in four hours. The burning coal was extinguished with water. No further trouble was experienced.

The *Oregon* passed through the Straits of Magellan on April 17, just before the declaration of war. The ship's chief engineer found that Cardiff coal was superior to coal supplied by American colliers in the South Atlantic. He had the Cardiff coal shoveled into "the fighting bunkers" adjacent to the firerooms and he locked the doors although regulations called for daily inspections. Because new air was excluded from the bunkers, the coal did not ignite itself in spite of extreme heat nearby.

The *Oregon* reached Key West April 26 and was assigned to the Santiago blockade. On the day of the naval battle, July 3, the chief engineer opened the doors to the bunkers containing the Cardiff coal he had saved for an emergency. The fuel's superior steaming quality generated the *Oregon's* sustained high speed in the chase after the Spanish fleet.

The facts about self-ignition and the *Oregon* example are relevant to conditions on the *Maine*. The door to the *Maine's* bunker A-16 was closed. The ventilating stack was inoperative. There was no new air to sustain oxidation. The coal had been stored on the *Maine* for three months and was stable. The air in the bunker, in the magazine, and in the area was cool.

Moreover, the *Maine's* assistant engineer had been near bunker A-16 an hour and forty-five minutes before the explosions. There was no coal smoke or stink. The officers and crew customarily put their hands on the bunker's bulkheads and there was no heat.

All that was left, as Sigsbee said, was the fairy tale about what resulted from the mere proximity of the coal to the powder. Spontaneous combustion was Rickover's "convenient alibi."

Who Was the Perpetrator

★ ★ ★ ★ ★ ★ ★ ★

McKINLEY'S FACE

To counter the current conclusions that the *Maine* disaster was caused by a small homemade mine rather than by spontaneous combustion a la Admiral Rickover, a few modern critics are harping on two questions that have remained unanswered: If there was a mine under the *Maine*, why can't we say who planted it there? And, in the decades since the catastrophe, why has the guilty party not come forward to confess?

This demand for the identification of the specific culprits who blew up the *Maine* was started long ago by the Englishman, Bucknill. Some of the later experts such as Rickover have emphasized the lack of an acknowledgment of guilt by the miscreant: "There is an absence of any claim by a Cuban, American, or Spaniard of knowledge about sabotage of the *Maine*. It seems contrary to human nature that on his death bed if not before, some participant would not have confessed."

To take the first question first, there is information at hand concerning the identity of the perpetrators that came from a reliable source known to and suppressed by Consul General Lee, Secretary of State Day, and President McKinley.

Alexander Brice was an Iowa businessman and bridge builder born in 1844. A Democrat, he was appointed by President Cleveland to the consular service in Cuba. By February 1898 he had been on the island for eight years. He was stationed in Matanzas where he had an extensive network of informants.

At midnight on February 13, a former Spanish officer Brice knew made a secret call at the official residence. The officer who had resigned from the Spanish army because he sympathized with the movement for Cuban autonomy demanded assurance that the two were alone. He then told Brice that he had a warning of great importance to communicate, but according to Brice, "it meant death to him if he was ever found out. Upon receiving my promise never to reveal his name, he said the *Maine* was to be blown up."

"He said he did not know just how it was to be done," Brice continued, "whether the boat was located so that the wind would bring it around to the point of destruction or whether mines were to be placed at a desired point. But he advised that there was no time for delay." It was implied that the malefactors were the officer's former associates, the Weylerites.

Brice believed the officer. He knew the man, and the details about the mine and the wind were convincing. Although the hour was late, he sent for his secretary Fred Delgado who arrived at 2 A.M. "Meantime," Brice added, "I prepared a despatch to Fitzhugh Lee, consul general at Havana. Being unable myself to leave until afternoon, I sent my secretary. He returned as I was leaving [for Havana] and reported that no credence was given to the warning. The message was difficult to believe, but something, perhaps the manner it was impressed upon me by my informant, made me feel that it was true. My visit to Havana did not change the situation."

Lee had been receiving daily barrages of alarms about the violent intentions of the Weylerites. After three weeks he became indifferent to the warnings. His options were few. He could have asked Sigsbee to sweep the harbor bottom for mines or he could have ordered the *Maine* back to Key West. The first would have angered the Spanish authorities, contrary to his instructions, and the second would have required permission from Washington that he would not get without firmer data. Consequently, he kept the warning to himself.

The *Maine* blew up the next evening.

"When I came to the United States," Brice went on, "my first official visit was to President McKinley and to him and to his Secretary of State I told the incident. I shall never forget the grief upon McKinley's face. He asked me not to make public my information at this time. Knowing the effort McKinley was making to avoid war, I obeyed his request." Accordingly, when Brice was interviewed after his meeting with the President, he divulged only the bare fact that "I was in Havana the next day after the *Maine*'s destruction. The *Maine* was destroyed by Spaniards and the Spanish government knows it."

Brice disclosed the whole story in 1911, after McKinley and Lee were dead and the Vreeland report confirmed his view of how the *Maine* was destroyed. The *New York Times* reported Brice's experiences. He was an unimpeachable witness.

The miscreants were thus the Spanish junior officers who supported General Weyler. "The butcher" had asked that there "be a Spanish hand to punish" the *Maine* for her insulting presence in Havana harbor. The chastisement Weyler called for was meted out by his disciples.

WHO WOULD KNOW

Fixing the onus on the Weylerites still left open the question of why there had been no deathbed confession. Critics claimed that a dying man would not have feared retribution.

To this there are three possible answers. First, the swimmer who set the mine under cover of the *City of Washington*'s arrival on the night of the explosions might have been killed by the blast before he could get away. His body parts would not have been distinguishable from the remains of mangled American sailors. He may have been buried with honors in Arlington Cemetery.

Second, claiming credit for a terrorist act is a modern phenomenon. Terrorists use publicity to induce mass fear of further random violence. That was not applicable to the attack on the *Maine*. The guilty Weylerite officer probably employed only one small homemade gunpowder mine. No one knew for sure in 1898 that such an exterior explosive device could detonate a magazine. He could not have expected to blow up the ship. He probably wanted only to damage the *Maine* enough to compel her to return to the United States for repairs, and thus start the war with an advantage. The unintended consequences of his action were too horrible to be acknowledged.

Finally, the guilty Spaniard would probably have been a Roman Catholic. Any deathbed confession would have been made to a priest who is obliged to treat everything revealed by a penitent as confidential. The priest would not have betrayed the officer. If the perpetrator did make a deathbed confession, who would know?

REPRISE

In January 1898, President McKinley gambled when he ordered the *Maine* into Havana harbor to intimidate the Spanish officials. Instead, he cost the nation its first modern battleship and most of the crew. He had unintentionally imposed the ultimate insult on Spanish fanatics who responded by blowing up the *Maine* as an act of defiance.

The cause of the explosions was not resolved at the time. Some authorities called the catastrophe an accident, while the majority blamed a mine. Following its regulations, the Navy Department initiated a prompt inquiry headed by Captain Sampson of the *Iowa*. The court heard evidence disclosing all the meaningful facts, but unaccountably based its conclusions on an obviously wrong understanding of the locus of the mine.

Despite the Sampson court's flagrantly erroneous analysis, its published record is the only reliable source for the official testimony of eyewitnesses. The testimony is divided into two theories, the accident theory involving spontaneous combustion and the mine theory. In support of the mine theory, reputable witnesses on a nearby liner testified that there had been two explosions, the first like a shot from a gun and the second a sustained burst that was taken as the firing of the magazines. The first explosion was the mine.

Negating the possibility of spontaneous combustion, the *Maine*'s assistant engineer testified that he had been near the coal bunker in question less than two hours before the explosions and there had been no smoke, no odor, and no heat. These were the practical tests for ignition. Also, there was no supply of fresh air to support burning in the coal bunker, and the adjacent boilers which might have heated the bunker had not been lit. There had never been an incident of spontaneous combustion on the *Maine*.

More than a decade after the Spanish-American War that had been sparked by the explosion on the *Maine*, the ship was dewatered to recover the bones of the victims, to give the vessel a proper burial, and to make a final judgment concerning the cause of the disaster. A board headed by Admiral Vreeland was composed of leading experts in all the relevant specialties. The Vreeland board took no testimony but instead had the dewatered ship itself to examine. The board found a 100-square-foot segment of bottom plating that was blown in, immediately under the reserve magazine, while the neighboring segments were blown out. The board took this indisputable fact to mean that an external burst from a mine with a low form of explosive had set off the gunpowder in the forward magazines.

For some remote romantic reason, the demise of the *Maine* has continued to live in the public mind. The explanation of the ship's death, however, gradually changed to favor the accident theory. There were even some calls for a new inquiry, but the hulk of the *Maine* and the rubble at the point of the explosions had long since been dumped in the open ocean. The Navy Department was not officially interested in a third investigation.

In 1974, though, Admiral Rickover said that neither the Sampson court nor the Vreeland board had settled the issue to his satifaction. He determined to hold his own investigation and he engaged the assistance of two technical analysts who were honored to volunteer their services for the renowned officer.

The report of the two scientists contradicted the Sampson and Vreeland conclusions. First, the explosion of a Spanish contact mine containing 100 to 200 pounds of guncotton would have produced more mangling of the bottom plating than the Vreeland board found. Consequently, there was no mine. Second, the magazines were ignited by spontaneous combustion in the adjacent coal bunker. Thus the cause was accidental and internal. Third, the bending upward of a section of the bottom plating was probably caused by an inrush of water following the explosion. This explains away the prima facie case for a mine explosion that was established by finding the section bent upward and inward.

The Rickover report was extensively researched, but each of these conclusions was specious. First, the mine used was not the heavy Spanish guncotton type that did not fit the indicia of the explosion, but probably was homemade in the form of a keg filled with musket powder. Second, there was no evidence at all of spontaneous combustion on the *Maine*. Third, the inwardly bent segment of bottom plating could not be satisfactorily explained other than by the explosion of a small external gunpowder mine. It certainly convinced the members of the Vreeland board, the only experts to have seen the wreck itself.

Ergo, the culprits were Spanish fanatics who obeyed their charismatic leader, General Weyler. They had the opportunity, the means, and the motivation, and they blew up the *Maine* with a small low-strength mine they made themselves.

A GREAT AMERICAN NAVAL MYSTERY

The *Maine* disaster and its Cuban consequences should have taught the United States a lasting lesson. Yet subsequent U.S. presidents have ordered equally unnecessary aggressive acts in foreign lands, with varying results. There are Third World countries that continue to see Uncle Sam as just a warship diplomat.

The U.S. imperialism that led to the Spanish-American War and the *Maine*'s destruction that triggered the war were seminal factors in setting a course of foreign policy for the United States. Current international relationships are still affected by the events and the aftermath of 1898.

The cause of the *Maine* disaster was a great American mystery for many decades. In *Remembering the Maine*, officers with long and brilliant naval careers reached radically different conclusions about what caused the ship to explode. In addition, personal bias, professional blunders, and political pressure played their part.

The moral is that the findings of honest judges are sometimes attacked by men such as Bucknill and Rickover who begin with points to prove. The Bucknills and the Rickovers may succeed on the assumption that judgments in favor of the establishment are wrong simply because the court that makes them is presumably predisposed toward the establishment.

Notes

★ ★ ★ ★ ★ ★ ★ ★

RESOLVING A NAVAL MYSTERY
pg. 4   additional background material: Melia, *"Damn the Torpedoes"*; Offner, *An Unwanted War: The Diplomacy of the United States and Spain over Cuba, 1885–1898*; Blow, *A Ship to Remember*.

REBELLION IN CUBA
5   late nineteenth-century view of Spain: Green, *Our Naval Heritage* (p. 271); *Harper's Pictorial History of the War with Spain* (p. 74).
5   revolt in Cuba had become chronic: West, *The American People* (p. 532).
5   recall of Campos: Ferrara, *The Last Spanish War* (p. 14).
6   Weyler's welcome: Morris, *The War with Spain* (p. 731).
6   description of Weyler: Halstead, *The Story of Cuba* (n.p.).
6   ratio of Spanish soldiers to Cuban populace: West, *Admirals of American Empire* (p. 133).
7   Cuban peasants forced into concentration camps: Green, *Our Naval Heritage* (p. 271).
7   insurgents inspired to greater resistance: Ferrara, *The Last Spanish War* (p. 14).
7   disastrous consequences: Morris, *The War with Spain* (pp. 73, 92).
7   official investigation of Weyler by President McKinley: *Harper's pictorial History* (p. 75).
7   In United States, popular opinion outraged by Cuban carnage: Hume, *Modern Spain 1788–1898* (p. 558).
7   general incensed at failure of United States to prevent sympathizers; and O'Brien's story: Horace Smith, *A Captain Unafraid* (pp. 2, 192).
8   Castillo murder: Hume, *Modern Spain 1788–1898* (p. 558).
8   Sagasta came back to power: Carr, *Spain 1808–1975* (p. 386).
8   coalition of European powers: Ferrara, *Last Spanish War* (p. 82).
8   insurrection stalemated: Morris, *The War with Spain* (p. 79).

8   Blanco's mission: Hume, *Modern Spain* (p. 558).

8   Blanco offered home rule: *Harper's Weekly*, Jan. 8, 1898.

9   on the Continent there was animosity: Ferrara, *Last Spanish War* (p. 82).

9   withdrawal of concentration order: Morris, *The War with Spain* (p. 109).

9   Blanco granted autonomy: Holman, "The Destruction of the *Maine* February 15, 1898" (p. 148).

9   reform never had a chance: LeFeber, *The New Empire* (p. 342).

9   amnesty offer: Morris, *The War with Spain* (p. 79).

9   Conservatives opposed autonomy: Carr, *Spain 1808–1975* (p. 386).

9   Cubans considered to be radicals: Wisan, *The Cuban Crisis as Reflected in the New York Press* (p. 372).

9   Weyler back in Spain: *Encyclopedia Britannica* (vol. 23, p. 552).

10 dishonorable acquiescence: O'Toole, *The Spanish War* (p. 19).

10 heralded autonomy less than anticipated: *Harper's Weekly*, Jan. 8, 1898.

10 Dupuy on the "political situation": *Spanish Diplomatic Correspondence and Documents 1896–1900* (p. 43).

10 Woodford note to Gullon: Santovenia, *Memorial Book of the Inauguration of the Maine Plaza at Havana* (p. 90).

11 Lee named consul general by Cleveland: Eggert, "Our Man in Havana" (p. 464).

11 Washington feared Spain might cede Cuba: Engle and Lott, *America's Maritime Heritage* (p. 214).

12 present appraisal of McKinley: Gould, *The Presidency of William McKinley* (n.p.).

12 McKinley referred back to Weyler's "cruel policy": *Harper's Pictorial History* (p. 75).

13 Cuban issue fading from headlines: Millis, *The Martial Spirit* (p. 93).

THE NEW U.S. NAVY

15 when the war was over: Engle and Lott, *America's Maritime History* (p. 212).

15 U.S. fleet offered pleasant outdoor jobs: Young, *History of Our War with Spain* (p. 84).

15 ships almost useless for warfare: Grupp, "Rear Admiral Wallace Melville" (p. 614).

15 "the darned thing is hollow": Chidwick, *Remember the Maine!* (n.p.).

15 some secretaries of Navy ignorant of battleships: ibid.

16 Chilean navy: Engle and Lott, *America's Maritime History* (p. 213).

16 fewer opportunities for advancement: Karsten, "No Room for Young Turks?" (p. 39).

16 benefits of the Navy for "the governing class": Bennett, *Roosevelt and the Republic* (p. 61).

16 reversal of naval policy in 1881: Weems, *Fate of the Maine* (p. 5).

16 survey of naval needs: Young, *History of Our War with Spain* (p. 84).

16 replacement of wooden ships recommended: *Harper's Pictorial History* (p. 94).

16 construction of three cruisers authorized: ibid.

17 only 25 seaworthy ships: Engle and Lott, *America's Maritime History* (p. 212).

17 Congress appropriated money: *Harper's Pictorial History* (p. 94).

17 Congress halted progress toward a new Navy: West, *Admirals of American Empire* (p. 187).

17 never tested under demanding conditions: Trask, *War with Spain in 1898* (p. 30).

17 Chadwick sent to Europe in 1877: Dorwart, *The Office of Naval Intelligence* (p. 8).

18 competition for promotion: Karsten, "No Room for Young Turks?" (p. 39).

18 old organizational structure of Navy Department: Luce, *The Text-Book of Seamanship* (pp. 158–61).

18 chiefs of bureaus of Equipment and Ordnance were line officers: Rickover, *How the Battleship* Maine *Was Destroyed* (p. 19).

18 funding legislation for the *Maine*: Pulsifer, ed., *Navy Yearbook* (p. 49).

18 armor, engines, boilers of domestic manufacture: O'Neil, "The Development of Modern Ordnance and Armor in the United States," (p. 259).

18 warships repaired in country's navy yards but no battleships built in one: Spears, *Our Navy in the War with Spain* (p. 47).

19 Chief Constructor Wilson directed planning of hull: Wright, *Official and Pictorial Record of the War with Spain* (p. 65).

19 Constructor Wilson had no technical experience: Cummings, *Admiral Richard Wainwright* (p. 85).

19 eccentricity of ship design in 1880s: Cummings, ibid.

19 combination canvas and coal: O'Toole, *Spanish War* (p. 22).

19 Wilson of old school: *New York Journal*, Feb. 17, 1898.

19 more than 7,000 square feet of canvas; rig to be either bark or barkentine: *Harper's Pictorial History* (p. 94).

19 end of era of wind power: O'Toole, *Spanish War* (p. 22).

20 classified as armored cruiser: *Harper's Pictorial History* (p. 94).

20 no enemy ship her size: *New York Herald*, Feb. 17, 1898.

20 design completed and bids taken: *Scientific American*, Nov. 29, 1890.

20 quotation of Bethlehem Iron: O'Neil, *Development of Modern Ordnance and Armor* (p. 259).

20 engines designed by Melville: *Scientific American*, Nov. 29, 1890.

20 keel laid after thunderstorm: Weems, *Fate of the Maine* (p. 6).

20   hull of mild steel: Morley, "Contract Trial of the United States Armored-Cruiser Maine" (p. 196).

21   total coal capacity: ibid. (p. 197).

21   armament: *New York Times*, Jan. 25, 1898.

21   beak for ramming: *New York Herald*, Feb. 17, 1898.

21   a homemade ship: *New York Times*, Nov. 19, 1898.

CONSTRUCTING THE *MAINE*

23   new science of steel shipbuilding: *Scientific American*, Oct. 5, 1889.

25   Secretary Tracy set high noon: *New York Times*, Oct. 20, 1890.

25   Monday night stormy: Weems, *Fate of the Maine* (p. 6).

25   special guests received formal invitations: *Scientific American*, Nov. 29, 1890 (p. 340).

26   story of the launch: *Scientific American*, Nov. 29, 1890 (p. 340).

28   nation becoming an international power: Herrick, *American Naval Revolution* (p. 83).

29   materials available for armor overtaken by advanced methods of treating steel: O'Neil, "Development of Modern Ordnance and Armor" (p. 259).

29   plans redrawn: O'Toole, *Spanish War* (p. 22).

29   *Maine* easily distinguishable from other warships: *Harper's Pictorial History* (p. 94).

29   three separate superstructures: Wilson, *Downfall of Spain* (p. 8).

29   placement of "winged" turrets: Sigsbee, *The "Maine"* (p. 7).

29   doubt about turret design: *New York Times*, Nov. 19, 1890.

30   the armor belt: Morley, "Contract Trial" (p. 196).

30   V-shaped bulkheads to protect against projectiles: *New York Times*, Feb. 16, 1898.

30   thin steel bottom: Morley, "Contract Trial" (p. 197).

30   specifications: *Dictionary of American Naval Fighting Ships*, vol. 3 (p. 189).

30   draft when stowed with stores: Harris, *Age of the Battleship* (p. 14).

30   peacetime paint colors: Rickover, *How the Battleship* Maine *Was Destroyed* (p. 3).

30   ship's commissioning: *New York Times*, Sept. 18, 1895.

31   crew took bags aboard: Weems, *Fate of the Maine* (p. 10).

31   shakedown cruise: Herrick, *American Naval Revolution* (p. 191).

31   George B. Dewey, President of Board of Inspection: West, *Admirals of American Empire* (p. 140).

32   stars foretold destruction: *New York Herald*, Feb. 27, 1898.

32   oil-soaked waste had ignited: *New York Herald*, Feb. 16, 1898.

32   details of shakedown cruise, November 1895: Chidwick, *Remember the Maine!* (n.p.); and Weems, *Fate of the Maine* (p. 17).

32   Newport trials postponed: Chidwick, *Remember the Maine!* (n.p.).

33 silver service for the *San Francisco*: West, *Admirals of American Empire* (p. 174).

34 mishaps on other ships: *New York Times*, Jan. 29, 1898.

THE CAPTAIN OF THE *MAINE*

35 *Maine* left New London on July 28: Johnson, "Battleship *Maine* and Pier 46" (p. 1295).

35 next day at 11A.M.: *Army and Navy Journal*, July 28, 1923 (p. 1157).

36 coming upstream along Brooklyn shore: *New York Times*, July 30, 1897.

36 Aboard the steamer *Chancellor*: Johnson, "Battleship *Maine* and Pier 46" (p. 1295).

37 last warning blast: *New York Herald*, Mar. 6, 1898.

38 *Concord* incident at Hell Gate: *New York Times*, Nov. 19, 1890.

38 naval board of inquiry found: Johnson, "Battleship *Maine* and Pier 46" (p. 1295).

38 place and date of Sigsbee's birth: *Army and Navy Journal*, July 28, 1923 (p. 1157).

38 appointment by Erastus Corning: *New York Herald*, Mar. 6, 1898.

39 Sigsbee "bilged": Clark, *My Fifty Years in the Navy* (p. 6).

39 Sigsbee's rapid progress: *New York Herald*, Mar. 6, 1898.

39 Professor Alexander Agassiz gives reasons for team's success: *Army and Navy Journal*, Mar. 5, 1898.

40 *Blake* caught in hurricane: *New York Times*, July 29, 1923.

40 Sigsbee given command of *Maine*: Weems, *Fate of the Maine* (p. 33).

40 affable manners: Chidwick, *Remember the Maine!* (n.p.).

SENDING THE *MAINE*

43 Sigsbee took command and *Maria Teresa* incident: Weems, *Fate of the Maine* (p. 34).

44 *Maine* detached from North Atlantic Squadron: Brown, *Correspondents' War* (p. 110).

44 *Maine* to take on coal and be put in shape: Rickover, *How the Battleship Maine Was Destroyed* (p. 22).

44 *Maine* ordered to Key West: Brown, *Correspondents' War* (p. 110).

44 orders confidential: Sigsbee, *The "Maine"* (p. 9).

45 General Lee and Captain Sigsbee test Havana cable service: ibid. (p. 10).

45 "very nice" luncheons: Sigsbee, letter to his wife, Jan. 18, 1898.

46 "I have doubts": Sigsbee, letter to his wife, Jan. 21, 1898.

46 Sigsbee refuses flagship: Sigsbee, *The "Maine"* (p. 18).

46 revised warning signal "pay nothing": Weems, *Fate of the Maine* (p. 41).

47 Sigsbee and Key West pilots: Sigsbee, *The "Maine"* (p. 18).

47 transfer of apprentices: Jones, *Chaplain's Experience*, (p. 146).

47 Captain Chadwick relay of confidential directions: Meriwether, "Unremembered Maine" (p. 10).

48 Cuba not in headlines: Millis, *The Martial Spirit* (p. 93).

48 *Voluntarios:* Trask, *War with Spain in 1898* (p. 24).

48 rioting began Wednesday morning: Pepper, *To-Morrow in Cuba* (p. 90).

48 pro-Blanco newspapers: *The World*, Jan. 13, 1898.

48 shouts of "Long live Spain!": Foner, *Spanish-Cuban-American War* (p. 227).

49 cable to put *Maine* on alert: O'Toole, *The Spanish War* (p. 21).

49 second cable never sent: Millis, *The Martial Spirit* (p. 95).

49 Blanco achieves control: Pepper, *To-Morrow in Cuba* (p. 91).

50 Lee cable re "presence of ships": Eggert, "Our Man in Havana" (p. 479).

50 Lee credited with averting war: Brown, *Correspondents' War* (p. 111).

50 sending *Maine* to Havana desirable: O'Toole, *The Spanish War* (p. 19).

50 goals of Spain and United States same: *New York Herald*, Jan. 4, 1898.

51 "Although I have been present": *New York Herald*, Jan. 16, 1898.

51 McKinley's excuse for sending warship: Foner, *The Spanish-Cuban-American War* (p. 227).

51 rebels growing more confident: *New York Times*, Jan. 15, 1898.

52 decision to send *Maine* not made in haste: *Evening Star*, Jan. 24, 1898.

52 aim was to place battleship in Havana: Long, ed., *Journal of John D. Long*, Jan. 24, 1898 entry.

52 the faulty rationale for keeping warships away: *Leslie's Official History of the Spanish-American War* (p. 55).

52 two Spanish cruisers: *New York Times*, Oct. 23, 1897.

52 Spanish antipathy had always given way to good manners: Melville, "Destruction of the Battleship 'Maine'" (p. 833).

52 gaining entrance to Havana harbor by stages: *Evening Star*, Jan. 24, 1898.

53 policy called for overseas bases: Engle and Lott, *American Maritime Heritage* (p. 213).

53 Germany's imperialist stratagems: O'Toole, *The Spanish War* (p. 115).

53 warship in Havana natural: *Harper's Weekly*, Feb. 5, 1898.

53 potency of United States: Dobson, *America's Ascent* (p. 104).

53 legislative moves quieted: *Evening Star*, Jan. 24, 1898.

53 be held responsible: Harris, *Age of the Battleship* (p. 41).

53 no emergency in Havana: Eggert, "Our Man in Havana" (p. 481).

54 Long, Day, and President confer: *Evening Star*, Jan. 24, 1898.

54 Madrid newspapers react: *New York Herald*, Jan. 24, 1898.

54 rumor Lee assassinated: *New York Times*, Jan. 24, 1898.

54 dispatching *Maine* an error: Hofstadter, *Paranoid Style in American Politics* (p. 155).

54 Long has misgivings: Grenville and Young, *Politics, Strategy, and American Diplomacy* (p. 255).

54 *Maine* picked for medium size: *Harper's Pictorial History* (p. 94).

55 considered modest vessel: Long, *New American Navy* (p. 136).

55 more expendable than a newer, bigger ship: *Evening Star*, Jan. 25, 1898.

55 *Maine* would make a strong defense and reasons for choice of Sigsbee: Long, *New American Navy* (p. 136).

55 Sigsbee able to cope: *Leslie's Offical History of the Spanish American War* (p. 58).

55 Sigsbee's coolness: *New York Herald*, Jan. 15, 1898.

55 among most popular officers: *Army and Navy Journal*, Mar. 5, 1898.

THE *MAINE* ARRIVES

57 "Lee has reported autonomy has failed": *Spanish Diplomatic Correspondence and Documents* (p. 66).

57 Spain "miffed": *Evening Star*, Jan. 24, 1898.

57 Dupuy enraged: Lodge, *Spanish-American War* (p. 28).

58 Day told Dupuy "he went to see President": *Spanish Diplomatic Correspondence* (p. 68).

58 Dupuy recognized wisdom: Long, *New American Navy* (p. 24).

58 "Spanish Minister fully informed": *New York Times*, Jan. 25, 1898.

58 "it is the purpose of this Government": *Papers Relating to the Foreign Relations of United States, 1898* (p. 1025).

58 *Maine's* visit meant intervention: Herrick, *American Naval Revolution* (p. 210).

59 move applauded in Congress: Rickover, *How the Battleship* Maine *Was Destroyed* (p. 31).

59 "the danger of resentment": *Evening Star*, Jan. 25, 1898.

59 Day's reply to Lee: *Papers Relating to the Foreign Relations of United States, 1898* (p. 1026).

59 Long issued *Maine's* actual sailing orders: *Evening Star*, Jan. 24, 1898.

59 "Notice given by the Spanish Minister": Long, ed., *Journal of John D. Long* (n.p.).

59 "portended nothing serious": *Evening Star*, Jan. 24, 1898.

60 John Caldwell: Smith, *A Captain Unafraid* (p. 259).

61 *Herald* shipped a revolver: Meriwether, "Remembering the *Maine*" (p. 550).

61 lookout on the *Maine*: Sigsbee, letter to his wife, Jan. 25, 1898.

62 the impatient Sigsbee: Sigsbee, *The "Maine"* (p. 20).

62 instructions: Rickover, *How the Battleship* Maine *Was Destroyed* (p. 34).

62 "left to act according to own judgment": Sigsbee, *The "Maine"* (p. 23).

62 formidable fleet assembled: *New York Times*, Jan. 25, 1898.

63 decks cleared for action: Chidwick, *Remember the Maine!* (n.p.).

63 a last shaping up: Sigsbee, letter to his wife, Jan. 25, 1898.

63 "in a state of readiness": Sigsbee, "My Story of the *Maine*" (p. 157).

63 port regulations: *Evening Star,* Jan. 25, 1898.

63 habitual aversion to commercial pilots: Weems, *Fate of the Maine* (p. 48).

64 Senator Teller: *New York Times,* Jan. 25, 1898.

64 device to keep Congress quiet: *The World,* Jan. 26, 1898.

64 Cuban junta's warning: *New York Times,* Jan. 25, 1898.

64 Caldwell tells Lee *Maine* is coming: Meriwether, "Remembering the *Maine."*

64 *Maine* waited under guns of Spanish forts: Sigsbee, *The "Maine"* (p. 26).

65 without clean bill of health: Rickover, *How the Battleship* Maine *Was Destroyed* (p. 34).

65 pilot Garcia: ibid.

65 port peculiarly shaped: *New York Journal,* Feb. 17, 1898.

66 *Maine* proceeded leisurely: Sigsbee, letter to his wife, Jan. 25, 1898.

66 no overt demonstration: Crabtree, *The Passing of Spain* (p. 420).

66 Sigsbee shown location on chart: *Report of the Spanish Naval Board of Inquiry* (p. 610).

66 Sigsbee complimented Garcia: Sigsbee, *The "Maine"* (p. 25).

66 two Spanish naval officers: *New York Times,* Jan. 26, 1898.

67 reality of formal visits: Sigsbee, letter to his wife, Jan. 25, 1898.

67 "*Maine* came gliding": Eggert, "Our Man in Havana" (p. 481).

THE *MAINE* IN HAVANA HARBOR

69 a friendly call: Smith, *A Captain Unafraid* (p. 268).

70 Lee sent frequent cables: Chadwick, *Relations of the United States to Spain* (p. 6).

70 McKinley greatly relieved: Leech, *In the Days of McKinley* (p. 164).

70 Weylerite ringleaders under house arrest: *Leslie's Official History* (p. 58).

70 agitated night talk: *New York Herald,* Jan. 27, 1898.

70 Spanish newspapers not restrained: *New York Journal,* Jan. 26, 1898.

71 Blanco government had betrayed Spanish cause: *New York Herald,* Jan. 27, 1898.

71 "cooped up like chickens": Sigsbee, letter to his wife, Jan. 25, 1898.

71 mooring 500 yards from Spanish magazine: March, *The History and Conquest of the Philippines* (p. 318).

71 poorly ventilated steel ship: Rickover, *How the Battleship* Maine *Was Destroyed* (p. 38).

72 Chilean and Brazilian insurrections: Dorwart, *The Office of Naval Intelligence* (pp. 40, 50).

72 health hazard: Sigsbee, letter to his wife, Jan. 25, 1898.

72 belief that filth from harbor bottom would breed yellow fever: *New York Journal,* Jan. 26, 1898.

72 letters sent home by crew: *New York Times,* Feb. 18, 1898.

73 Lt. Jenkins of Office of Naval Intelligence: *New York Herald*, Feb. 18, 1898.

74 Sigsbee's conclusion reassured officers: *New York Herald*, Feb. 18, 1898.

74 *Maine* responded by playing her searchlights: *New York Times*, Jan. 26, 1898.

74 spick-and-span warship: Meriwether, "Remembering the *Maine*" (p. 551).

75 extraordinary vigilance: Sigsbee, *The "Maine"* (p. 42).

75 Seaman Ericksen: Weems, *Fate of the Maine* (p. 48).

76 "every rifle belt filled for firing": *New York Journal*, Feb. 19, 1898.

76 "don't want these people to burn our clothes": Sigsbee, letter to his wife, Jan. 25, 1898.

76 banned use of harbor water: Weems, *Fate of the Maine* (p. 61).

76 fiction of friendly visit: Green, *Our Naval Heritage* (p. 276).

76 police boat run discontinued: *New York Journal*, Feb. 19, 1898.

77 serving as "red rag": Sigsbee, letter to his wife, Jan. 29, 1898.

77 Sigsbee as eyes and ears: Long, *New American Navy* (p. 136).

QUIET WEEKS ON THE *MAINE*

79 Spanish officials punctilious: (Woodford) *The American-Spanish War* (p. 95).

79 Parrado and his sister: Sigsbee, letter to his wife, Jan. 29, 1898.

79 *Maine* appeared enormous: Sigsbee, *The "Maine"* (p. 54).

80 composition of crew: *Army and Navy Journal*, Mar. 5, 1898.

80 ready to leave for next assignment: Sigsbee, letter to his wife, Jan. 29, 1898.

80 Spaniards happier than Sigsbee: Foner, *The Spanish-Cuban-American War* (p. 231).

81 presence might lead "to a conflict": Millis, *The Martial Spirit* (p. 96).

81 problem of switching ships: Long, *New American Navy* (p. 137).

81 social engagements and bullfights: Sigsbee, *The "Maine"* (p. 34).

82 in great danger at bullfight: Sigsbee, "My Story of the 'Maine'" (p. 375).

83 small printed circular: Sigsbee, letter to his wife, Jan. 30, 1898.

83 anti-American handbill commonplace: Sigsbee, *The "Maine"* (p. 34).

84 no one thought admonition serious: *New York Herald*, Feb. 18, 1898.

84 ferryboat incident: Sigsbee, letter to his wife, Jan. 30, 1898.

85 asking for regular torpedo-boat service: Eggert, "Our Man in Havana" (p. 481).

85 the *Cushing* cast off early: Rickover, *How the Battleship* Maine *Was Destroyed* (p. 40).

85 *Cushing* most vulnerable in heavy weather: Sigsbee, letter to his wife, Feb. 11, 1898.

85 formal call on Blanco: Sigsbee, *The "Maine"* (p. 49).

85 "difficult to grasp the Spanish character": Sigsbee, letter to his wife, Feb. 11, 1898.

85 incident that changed Sigsbee's opinion: Sigsbee, "Personal Narrative of the 'Maine'" (p. 94).

86 failure to call on Autonomous Council: Rickover, *How the Battleship* Maine *Was Destroyed* (p. 36).

86 Sigsbee call on council: Holman, "Destruction of the *Maine*" (p. 150).

86 at an afternoon tea: Cummings, *Admiral Richard Wainwright* (p. 83).

86 Spanish people bitterly opposed to U.S. policy: *New York Herald*, Feb. 16, 1898.

87 Office of Naval Intelligence overstated Spanish preparedness: Dorwart, *The Office of Naval Intelligence* (p. 61).

87 sending *Maine* to Havana would not be regarded as aggressive act: *Evening Star*, Jan. 24, 1898.

87 *Vizcaya* would soon be sailing to New York City: *New York Times*, Jan. 27, 1898.

87 stroke of diplomacy: *New York Herald*, Jan. 30, 1898.

87 *Montgomery* dispatched: *New York Herald*, Feb. 3, 1898.

88 Day cable to Lee and Lee's response: Chadwick, *Relations of the United States and Spain* (p. 1027).

88 reports of untroubled scene: Leech, *In the Days of McKinley* (p. 166).

88 Gullon's tough stance: Gould, *Presidency of William McKinley* (p. 72).

88 Gullon's misgivings: Santovenia, *Memorial Book of the Inauguration of the Maine Plaza* (p. 91).

89 Spain's forces ready by April: Foner, *Spanish-Cuban-American War* (p. 231).

89 Dupuy's letter: Wisan, *Cuban Crisis as Reflected in the New York Press* (p. 380).

89 Dupuy resigns and U.S. demands apology: *The World*, Feb. 12, 1898.

89 supplies reaching Cuban rebels increased: *New York Herald*, Feb. 15, 1898.

89 Pinkerton's detectives: *New York Times*, Feb. 14, 1898.

90 the constellation Orion: Brown, *Correspondents' War* (p. 114).

90 winter sun had set: *New York Times*, Feb. 15, 1898.

90 atmosphere oppressively hot; *Maine* heading northwest: Sigsbee, *The "Maine"* (p. 57).

91 sounds of pre-Lenten carnival: *Harper's Weekly*, Mar. 5, 1898.

91 El Prado illuminated for week of fiestas: Musgrave, *Under Three Flags in Cuba* (p. 225).

91 ships' anchorages: Beehler, "Experiences of a Naval Attaché," (p. 949).

91 separate admiral's and captain's staterooms: Sigsbee, *The "Maine"* (p. 62).

92 the 328 members of the crew: ibid. (p. 61).

92 captain responded to letter from Roosevelt: Sigsbee, letter to his wife, Feb. 17, 1898.

92 crew turned in at nine: Sigsbee, *The "Maine"* (p. 63).

93 only visible movement: *Harper's Weekly*, Mar. 5, 1898.

93   afternoon had begun no differently: Basoco, "What Really Happened to the *Maine?*" (p. 12).

93   Wainwright directed setting up for rifle practice: Cummings, *Admiral Richard Wainwright* (p. 86).

94   Jenkins sailing around the harbor: *New York Herald*, Feb. 18, 1898.

94   great event going to happen: Chidwick, *Remember the Maine!* (n.p.).

94   Chidwick climbed into his bunk: O'Toole, *The Spanish War* (p. 27).

94   Cluverius read petty officers' reports: Weems, *Fate of the Maine* (p. 61).

94   Blandin on watch: *New York Times*, Feb. 18, 1898.

95   Marine Lt. Catlin recollection: *New York Times*, Feb. 21, 1898.

95   Corporal Thompson and Apprentice Ham saw small boat(s): Weems, *Fate of the Maine* (p. 65).

95   Passengers Rothschild and Wertheimer were chatting: *Report of the Naval Court of Inquiry* (p. 58).

95   Weinheimer on waterfront: *New York Times*, Feb. 22, 1898.

96   Martin Bunting story: *New York Journal*, Feb. 22, 1898.

96   Meriwether's standing order: Meriwether, "Remembering the *Maine*" (p. 552).

96   Clara Barton at her writing table: Epler, *The Life of Clara Barton* (p. 286).

THE BIG BANG ON THE *MAINE*

98   Catlin's recollection: *New York Times*, Feb. 21, 1898.

98   description of crew's reaction: Sigsbee, letter to his wife, Feb. 17, 1898.

98   "suddenly the lights went out": Cummings, *Admiral Richard Wainwright* (p. 86).

98   initial burst as more violent: *New York Herald*, Feb. 17, 1898.

98   Lt. Blandin told the press: *New York Times*, Feb. 17, 1898.

99   "When disaster came": Sigsbee, letter to his wife, Feb. 17, 1898.

99   "I was enclosing": Sigsbee, *The "Maine"* (p. 63).

99   "heard two different reports": ibid. (p. 98).

100 Essence of what men said: *New York Times*, Feb. 17, 1898.

101 Thompson firm in stating: ibid., Feb. 21, 1898.

101 In contrast, the observers on *City of Washington*: *Report of the Naval Court of Inquiry* (pp. 57–65).

101 Passenger Rothschild "heard a shot": ibid. (pp. 57–62).

102 Passenger Mann in the saloon: *New York Times*, Feb. 17, 1898.

102 Capt. Stevens a most experienced witness: ibid., March 10, 1898.

102 Officer Sullivan affirmed: ibid.

102 Assistant Purser Reynolds: ibid.

102 Francis Weinheimer heard: *New York Times*, Feb. 21, 1898.

102 Martin Bunting also on wharf: *New York Journal*, Feb. 22, 1898.

102 windows broken, doors shaken: *Harper's Weekly*, Mar. 5, 1898.

103 thought the *Maine* being attacked: Sigsbee, *The "Maine"* (p. 67).

103 Lee could see flames: Foner, *The Spanish-Cuban-American War* (p. 236).

103 Clara Barton was still at work: Epler, *The Life of Clara Barton* (p. 286).

103 Meriwether entering a café: Meriwether, "Remembering the *Maine.*"

103 hurried up the slanted floor: Sigsbee, *The "Maine"* (p. 64).

104 two sailors heard the captain: *New York Journal*, Feb. 24, 1898.

104 Chidwick reading Rea: Chidwick, *Remember the Maine!*

104 asked Anthony for the time: Sigsbee, *The "Maine"* (p. 65).

104 Lt. Catlin located the ladder: *New York Times*, Feb. 21, 1898.

104 sailors' death-defying tales: ibid., Feb. 20, 1898.

105 The captain's first hint of the immensity: Sigsbee, *The "Maine"* (p. 68).

105 "The forward part of the ship": Chidwick, *Remember the Maine!*

106 Once he saw the bodies: Sigsbee, *The "Maine"* (p. 69).

106 lifeboats from the *Alfonso XII*: *New York Times*, Feb. 17, 1898.

107 Lt. Blow overcome: Chidwick, *Remember the Maine!* (n.p.).

107 "If there is anyone living": *Scientific American*, Feb. 26, 1898.

107 captain's dog Peggy: Weems, *Fate of the Maine* (p. 88).

107 two boats headed for *City of Washington*: Sigsbee, *The "Maine"* (p. 73).

108 "Ah Americanos": *New York Times*, Feb. 23, 1898.

108 shouts of exultation: Sigsbee, "My Story of the 'Maine'" (p. 378).

108 statistics: Holman, "The Destruction of the *Maine*" (p. 153).

THE *MAINE* DESTROYED

109 "cool but changed": Weems, *Fate of the Maine* (p. 91).

109 "No one can ever know": Sigsbee, *The "Maine"* (p. 81).

110 report on letterhead of the New York and Cuba Mail Steamship Company: Brown, *Correspondents' War* (p. 116).

110 model of clarity: Taylor, "Returning to the Riddle of the Explosion that Sunk the Maine" (n.p.).

111 General Solano came aboard: Sigsbee, letter to his wife, Feb. 17, 1898.

111 Congosto ungracious: Meriwether, "Remembering the *Maine*" (p. 552).

111 Sigsbee handed Rea two messages: Brown, *Correspondents' War* (p. 116).

112 General Solano gave his word: Sigsbee, *The "Maine"* (p. 80).

112 police launches sped up the bay: *New York Journal*, Feb. 17, 1898.

113 Sigsbee could not sleep: Sigsbee, letter to his wife Feb. 17, 1898.

113 cable office reopened: Meriwether, "Remembering the *Maine*" (p. 553).

113 Spaniards jeered at Weinheimer: *New York Herald*, Feb. 22, 1898.

113 Sigsbee awakened: Sigsbee, *The "Maine"* (p. 100).

114 Meriwether visiting the injured: Brown, *Correspondents' War* (p. 119).

114 Clara Barton: Epler, *Life of Clara Barton* (p. 287).

114 Sigsbee's second report: Sigsbee, "My Story of the 'Maine'" (p. 151).

115 Lee's reaction: Foner, *The Spanish-Cuban-American War* (p. 236); Eggert, "Our Man in Havana" (p. 481).

115 Lee's cables: *New York Times*, Feb. 17, 1898.

116 "a light struck me!": Meriwether, "Remembering the *Maine*" (p. 553).

116 retaining only nine officers and enlisted men: Sigsbee, "My Story of the 'Maine'" (p. 379).

116 engage telegraph wire that ran to Punta Rassa: *Key West Citizen*, Feb. 1, 1968.

116 arrival of *Mangrove* and *Fern*: Sigsbee, *The "Maine"* (p. 101).

117 placard to remove hats: Millis, *The Martial Spirit* (p. 106).

117 feelings for wounded: Sigsbee, "My Story of the 'Maine'" (p. 379).

117 "A better and more docile crew": Sigsbee, letter to his wife, Feb. 17, 1898.

117 no *gran* aspect: *The American Navy* (p. 9).

117 Blanco request to hold public burial ceremony: Sigsbee, letter to his wife, Feb. 17, 1898.

118 Martin Hellings in Key West: Goode, *With Sampson Through the War* (p. 2).

118 Hellings goes to *Cushing*: O'Toole, *The Spanish War* (p. 32).

118 rumors circulated in Key West every day: Chadwick, *Relations of the United States and Spain* (p. 9).

119 Sicard had *Mangrove* and *Fern* made ready to depart: Goode, *With Sampson Through the War* (p. 2).

119 Helen Long found messenger: Leech, *In the Days of McKinley* (p. 166).

119 she awakened her father: (Woodford), *The American-Spanish War* (p. 341).

119 "it was almost impossible to believe": O'Toole, *The Spanish War* (p. 34).

119 Dickins reported to Long: Long, ed., *Journal of John D. Long* (p. 214).

120 telephones in White House twenty-one years: Loomis, "The White House Telephone and Crisis Management," (p. 64).

120 report that Long telephoned the White House: Millis, *The Martial Spirit* (p. 102).

120 "The President came out": Gould, *The Presidency of William McKinley* (p. 74).

120 *Mangrove*, with doctors aboard, had sailed: *The Times*, Feb. 17, 1898.

120 Hearst worked until midnight: Swanberg, *Citizen Hearst* (p. 136).

120 conscientious doorman was waiting: Coblentz, ed. *William Randolph Hearst* (p. 58).

121 "colors be half-masted": Weems, *Fate of the Maine* (p. 91).

121 expressions of grief widespread: Leech, *In the Days of McKinley* (p. 166).

REPORTING THE MAINE DISASTER

123 slant of articles determined by bias: Mayo, ed., *America of Yesterday* (p. 163).

123 speculation about spontaneous combustion in the coal bunkers: *Evening Star*, Feb. 16, 1898; *New York Herald*, Feb. 17, 1898.

124 location of magazines and bunkers: Wright, *Official and Pictorial Record of the War with Spain* (p. 80).

125 Hearst's promotional proclivities took over: Lundberg, *Imperial Hearst* (p. 72).

125 fanciful illustration: Wilkerson, *Public Opinion and the Spanish-American War* (p. 101).

125 difference between black and brown gunpowder: O'Neil, "Development of Modern Ordnance and Armor" (p. 245).

126 Smokeless gunpowder invented: *Historical Transactions 1893–1943* (p. 270).

126 buoyant contact mine simplest explosive device: *The Literary Digest*, Mar. 26, 1898.

126 If mine homemade: Beehler, "Experiences of a Naval Attaché" (p. 949).

126 disadvantages of contact mines, deep water applications, and bottom mines in Havana harbor: *New York Herald*, Feb. 27, 1898.

127 sphere of gas began to rise: Beehler, "Scandinavian Experiments with Submarine Mines" (p. 122).

127 officers and enlisted men had feared the harbor was planted: *Harper's Weekly*, Mar. 12, 1898.

127 captain had a launch drag a grappling iron: *Army and Navy Journal*, Mar. 5, 1898.

128 Spanish government stated officially: ibid.

128 "It seems absurd": *New York Times*, Apr. 19, 1898.

128 Charles Crandall story: New York *World*, Apr. 15, 1898.

128 explosion in Havana harbor in 1897: *Evening Star*, Feb. 28, 1898.

129 deathbed confession: Grieg, *The Immediate Cause of the War with Spain* (pp. 28–43).

SPONTANEOUS COMBUSTION ON THE *MAINE*

133 *Maine* a bad luck ship: *New York Herald*, Feb. 17, 1898.

134 Wainwright determined that the danger of self-ignition: *New York Times*, Feb. 18, 1898.

135 the board reported to Secretary: *Report of Efficiency of Various Coals* (pp. 81–85).

136 comparable disasters began with the *Demologos*: Melville, "The Destruction of the Battleship 'Maine'" (p. 839).

136 *Missouri* was wrecked: *New York Times*, Feb. 17, 1898.

137 *Philadelphia* in dry dock: *New York Journal*, Feb. 17, 1898.

137 Captain Henry Glass remembered: *Army and Navy Journal*, Feb. 19, 1898.

138 cruiser *New York* experience with self-ignition: ibid.

138 seven recent fires on *Indiana*: *New York Herald*, Feb. 18, 1898.

139 no warship destroyed by explosion from coal fire: Melville, "The Destruction of the Battleship 'Maine'" (p. 846).

139 spontaneous ignition not common: *Report of Efficiency of Various Coals* (p. 82).

139 HMS *Captain* had capsized: *The World*, Feb. 17, 1898.

139 HMS *Doterel's* and *Triumph's* paint lockers: *New York Times*, Feb. 17, 1898.

WHY DID THE *MAINE* EXPLODE?

142 background of Professor Alger: Knight, "Professor Philip Rounseville Alger, U.S. Navy" (p. 2).

142 "We know of no instance": *New York Times*, Feb. 19, 1898.

143 Marix opted for guncotton explanation: *New York Journal*, Feb. 18, 1898.

143 O'Neil asked whether *Maine* had gone into harbor with warheads on torpedoes: Rickover, *How the Battleship* Maine *Was Destroyed* (p. 46).

143 possibility of methane gas: Naisawald, "Destruction of the USS *Maine*— Accident or Sabotage?" (p. 98).

143 "fire damp effected destruction": Basoco, "What Really Happened to the *Maine*?" (p. 15).

143 Stanford professor: ibid.

144 circulation of *Journal* rose: Wisan, *The Cuban Crisis as Reflected in the New York Press* (p. 388).

144 Many newspapers across the country copied: Foner, *Spanish-Cuban-American War* (p. 238).

144 Boyton's fame had spread to Congress: *New York Times*, Feb. 17, 1898.

145 *Herald* printed a diagram: *New York Herald*, Feb. 18, 1898.

145 Boyton outlines his method: *The World*, Feb. 17, 1898.

145 Secretary Long encouraging accident theory: Young, *History of Our War with Spain* (p. 55).

145 finding of accident would demoralize the Navy: *New York Times* Feb. 18, 1898.

146 "It may be impossible": Allen, *Papers of John D. Long* (p. 53).

146 "The *Maine* was sunk": Roosevelt, letter to B. Diblee, Feb. 16, 1898 (Letters on the Battleship *Maine*).

146 "Long and Roosevelt at Loggerheads": *New York Journal*, Feb. 17, 1898.

146 Professor Alger free to make statements: *Harper's Weekly*, Mar. 5, 1898.

146 "don't you think it inadvisable": Roosevelt, letter to Captain Charles O'Neil, Feb. 28, 1898 (Letters on the Battleship *Maine*).

146 Alger denied taking "the Spanish side": *New York Times*, Feb. 17, 1898.

146 Bradford asserted Alger was wrong: *Evening Star*, Feb. 17, 1898.

147 Navy records showed 87 degrees F. maximum temperature: ibid., Feb. 16, 1898.

147 disclosure of untold history of self-ignition: *New York Times*, Mar. 26, 1898.

147 "There is little doubt in the minds of any of us": McKinley Presidential Papers, letter from H. D. Geddings to Mrs. E. R. Moses.

147 Spaniards had sworn to blow up the *Maine*: *The World*, Feb. 17, 1898.

148 Cuban junta trying to make Spaniards appear guilty: *New York Herald*, Feb. 17, 1898.

148 Cuban junta counting on sinking of *Maine*: *The Times*, Feb. 17, 1898.
148 "character of the hole would show": *New York Times*, Feb. 17, 1898.
149 "I am glad": Roosevelt, letter to William S. Cowles, Feb. 23, 1898 (Letters on the Battleship *Maine*).
149 complete American war plan: Nuñez, *The Spanish-American War* (p. 15).
150 "Spain must bust!": Samuels, *Henry Adams the Major Phase* (p. 185).
150 Frederic Remington complained: Greene, *American Imperialism in 1898* (p. 53).
150 "orgasmic acme": Swanberg, *Citizen Hearst* (p. 177).
150 Sigsbee convinced Hearst had known in advance: Lundberg, *Imperial Hearst* (p. 72).
150 Sigsbee's effectiveness confirmed by Captain Puri: *New York Herald*, Feb. 24, 1898.
150 Spanish warships employed picket boats: Sigsbee, *The "Maine"* (p. 136).
150 Cuban rebels claimed they did not want intervention: Foner, *Spanish-American-Cuban War* (p. 245).
151 *Maine* could have been moored over mine: Harris, *Age of the Battleship* (p. 43).
151 could have accidentally tripped the key: Jane, "The *Maine* Disaster and After" (p. 640).
151 Spaniards were capable of choosing hour for explosion: Spears, *History of Our Navy* (p. 80).
151 Emperor of Germany was sure: White, *Autobiography* (p. 164).
151 "General Lee is of the opinion": Mayo, ed., *America of Yesterday* (p. 171).
151 "It was my official duty": Sigsbee, "My Story of the 'Maine'" (p. 150).
152 Even after "irrefutable proof": Schroeder, *A Half Century of Naval Service* (p. 212).
152 General Blanco with General Marinas: *The World*, Feb. 24, 1898.
152 detailed indictment: *Evening Star*, Feb. 28, 1898.
153 "Send the *Maine* Away!": *The World*, Mar. 3, 1898.
153 Weylerites wanted war with the United States: *New York Journal*, Feb. 26, 1898.
153 Weylerites had the knowledge to build a mine: Mayo, *America of Yesterday* (p. 171).
154 higher Spanish officials made protestations of grief: Pepper, *To-morrow in Cuba* (p. 99).
154 "*Maine* soup" on the menu: Musgrave, *Under Three Flags in Cuba* (p. 225).
154 "colors no longer be at half-mast": *New York Times*, Feb. 20, 1898.

THE INQUIRY ON THE *MAINE*

155 views in the House and Senate: *New York Times*, Feb. 17, 1898.
155 Navy regulations provided for a court of inquiry: Rickover, *How the Battleship* Maine *Was Destroyed* (p. 48).

156 "the people are coming to the conclusion": *Congressional Record* (Senate), Feb. 18, 1898.

157 composition of the court of inquiry: *New York Times*, Feb. 18, 1898.

157 Marix selected as judge advocate: *Evening Star*, Feb. 17, 1898.

157 Sampson and Chadwick beyond reproach: *Leslie's Official History* (p. 77).

158 no specialist in combustion or construction on court: *New York Journal*, Feb. 18, 1898.

158 Secretary Long gave lip service to jingoes and Spaniards: *New York Times*, Feb. 18, 1898.

158 preliminaries began with board of investigation: *The World*, Feb. 21, 1898.

158 court to convene in Havana: *Report of the Naval Court of Inquiry* (p. 4).

159 Sampson "a son of the plain people": Crabtree, *The Passing of Spain* (p. 356).

159 elected student leader: Chadwick, *Relations of the United States and Spain* (p. 20).

159 Younger men like Chadwick and Sigsbee: West, *Admirals of American Empire* (p. 55).

159 Sampson on the *Patapsco*: Reynolds, *Famous American Admirals* (p. 293).

159 "reputation as most brilliant officer": West, *Admirals of American Empire* (p. 115).

159 Sampson advanced over seventeen senior captains: Chadwick, *Relations of the United States and Spain* (p. 20).

159 a martinet: Coblentz, ed., *William Randolph Hearst* (p. 63).

160 explosives were his specialty: Long, *New American Navy* (p. 142).

160 Chadwick background: Coletta, *French Ensor Chadwick: Scholarly Warrior* (pp. 4, 11, 57, 58, 69).

160 Potter's background: Hamersly, *Records of the Living Officers of the United States Navy and Marine Corps* (p. 168).

160 Marix's background: *Who's Who in America 1918–1919.*

160 Long cabled Admiral Dewey: Bishop, *Theodore Roosevelt and His Time* (p. 94).

161 *Vizcaya* arrived off New York City: *The Times*, Feb. 19, 1898.

161 funeral for *Maine* dead: *New York Times*, Feb. 19, 1898.

161 permission to have Protestant prayers: Millis, *The Martial Spirit* (p. 106).

161 read Book of Common Prayer to himself: Sigsbee, letter to his wife, Feb. 22, 1898.

161 Blanco did not participate: Wright, *The Official and Pictorial Record of the War with Spain* (p. 74).

161 Cowles mistaken for Sigsbee: Sigsbee, letter to his wife, Feb. 22, 1898.

162 "dead Americans were carried": McKinley Presidential Papers, letter from H. D. Geddings to Mrs. E. R. Moses, Feb. 18, 1898.

162 "it would be foolish": Mahan, *Lessons of the War with Spain* (p. 30).

162 Roosevelt concerned: Rickover, *How the Battleship* Maine *Was Destroyed* (p. 47).

162   "there are risks in battleships": *New York Times*, Feb. 23, 1898.

162   naval budget had been cut: Wisan, *The Cuban Crisis as Reflected in the New York Press* (p. 408).

163   *Texas* had sunk at her dock: *New York Herald*, Feb. 18, 1898.

163   Secretly McKinley had acknowledged war was coming: Foner, *Spanish-Cuban-American War* (p. 243).

163   "it was manifest that the loss of the *Maine*": Long, *The New American Navy* (p. 140).

163   "Chaplain, if it had not been for Providence": Jones, *A Chaplain's Experience Ashore and Afloat* (p. 150).

163   tabby cat found: *New York Times*, Feb. 19, 1898.

164   "Assuming the cause was a mine": *Literary Digest*, Mar. 5, 1898 (p. 271).

164   Professor Hermann Von Holst: ibid.

164   if *Maine* had exploded due to internal accident, Spain had no liability: "Response of Spain," *Army and Navy Journal*, Feb. 26, 1898 (p. 473).

164   Captain Peral ordered to investigate disaster: Foner, *Spanish-Cuban-American War* (p. 237).

165   Manterola confronted Sigsbee: Sigsbee, *The "Maine"* (p. 129).

167   Mason offered a resolution: *The Times*, Feb. 21, 1898.

167   "he would not sit at the table with a Spaniard": *New York Times*, Feb. 19, 1898.

168   "we never could convince the people-at-large": Allen, *Papers of John D. Long* (p. 57).

168   "I put in my oar": Roosevelt, letter to William S. Cowles, Feb. 23, 1898.

168   McKinley told Spanish chargé d'affaires: *Spanish Diplomatic Correspondence and Documents* (p. 89).

168   "Spanish divers to examine the wreck": *The Times*, Feb. 21, 1898.

GETTING THE INQUIRY STARTED

169   Peral at a standstill: Rickover, *How the Battleship* Maine *Was Destroyed* (p. 52).

169   sharp protest to Blanco: Long, *The New American Navy* (p. 143).

170   keel had settled deeper: *New York Journal*, Feb. 18, 1898.

170   three heaps of crumpled metal visible: Wilson, *The Downfall of Spain* (p. 14).

170   A tour around the wreck: *Scientific American*, Mar. 12, 1898.

170   Sigsbee had been visiting the hospitals: Sigsbee, letter to his wife, Feb. 22, 1898.

171   court's hearings would be open to press: *The World*, Feb. 19, 1898.

171   "Will the Inquiry be behind closed doors?": ibid.

171   proceedings "strictly secret": *New York Times*, Feb. 23, 1898.

172   first assignment to secure Navy code book: Sigsbee, letter to his wife, Feb. 25, 1898.

172 Washington feared loss of ciphers to Spaniards: Roosevelt memo to Long, Feb. 17, 1898.
172 divers told to retrieve bodies: *New York Times*, Feb. 23, 1898.
172 Spanish patrol boat towed bodies: *New York Herald*, Feb. 23, 1898.
173 yellow press went further: Wilkerson, *Public Opinion and the Spanish-American War* (p. 101).
174 *La Lucha* printed the canard: *New York Journal*, Feb. 19, 1898.
174 Marix brought joyous tidings: Sigsbee, letter to his wife, Feb. 22, 1898.
175 "Evidence beginning to prove": *Message of the President on the Relations of the United States to Spain*, Feb. 21, 1898.
175 the English had proved: *New York Herald*, Feb. 24, 1898.
175 Charles Cramp declared American people would repudiate: *New York Journal*, Feb. 19, 1898.
176 Sigsbee expected to direct wrecking crew: Sigsbee, letter to his wife, Feb. 22, 1898.

IDENTIFYING THE *MAINE*'S KEEL
177 view that issue could be settled through observation of hull: *New York Times*, Feb. 17, 1898.
178 Powelson transferred to the *Fern* too recently: *New York Herald*, Feb. 25, 1898.
178 Powelson's background: ibid.
179 Powelson expected to be assigned to *Maine*: Cummings, *Admiral Richard Wainwright* (p. 89).
179 Morgan and Meriwether story: Meriwether, "Remembering the *Maine*" (p. 554).
181 Cowles quoted the two officers: Cowles letter to Roosevelt, in Cowles, *Letters from Theodore Roosevelt to Anna Roosevelt* (p. 208).
182 "The *Maine* was clean on her bottom": *The World*, Feb. 25, 1898.
183 "in Ensign Powelson's evidence": *Evening Star*, Feb. 28, 1898.
183 "A rumor based on an alleged statement": *The Times*, Feb. 26, 1898.
184 Madrid newspapers printed tirades: *New York Journal*, Mar. 3, 1898.
184 Eulate had admired New York City; sighting of unidentified wooden barrel: *New York Times*, Feb. 24, 1898.
184 the *Vizcaya* entered Havana harbor: Sigsbee, letter to his wife, Mar. 1, 1898.
184 impediment to peace: *The Nation*, Mar. 3, 1898.
184 how easy a take-over of Cuba would be: *New York Times*, Feb. 24, 1898.
185 the Kaiser's oath: *The Times*, Mar. 28, 1898.
185 Sigsbee made divers a present: *Army and Navy Journal*, Feb. 26, 1898.
185 the correspondents' most gruesome job: *New York Times*, Feb. 25, 1898.
186 Commander West visited Havana: Sigsbee, letter to his wife, Feb. 25, 1898.
186 bill to appropriate $50,000,000 "for national defense": Spears, *Our Navy in the War with Spain* (p. 85).

186 the Spaniards had just bought two cruisers: *New York Times*, Mar. 5, 1898.

186 deathblow to peace: Chadwick, *Relations of the United States and Spain—Diplomacy* (p. 544).

THE PRESIDENT'S MESSAGE

187 Lloyd's odds: *New York Times*, Feb. 27, 1898.

187 Sigsbee pleased by newspaper articles: Sigsbee, *The "Maine"* (p. 123).

187 enlisted men were fitted into rubber suits: Weems, *Fate of the Maine* (p. 101).

188 men were let down into the wreck by winches: *New York Times*, Feb. 23, 1898.

188 "It was suggested": Sigsbee, *The "Maine"* (p. 164).

189 permission for detonation of small dynamite charges: *New York Herald*, Mar. 24, 1898.

189 "showing the cloven hoof": Sigsbee, letter to his wife, Mar. 21, 1898.

189 "I did not fancy the berth": Sigsbee, *The "Maine"* (p. 135).

190 Sigsbee "fears a collapse": *New York Herald*, Mar. 9, 1898.

191 Sigsbee watched the Spaniards derisively: Sigsbee, *The "Maine"* (p. 161).

191 diver Olsen surpassed naval record: *New York Times*, Mar. 7, 1898.

191 Spanish divers explored the harbor bottom: ibid.

191 Peral preliminary finding: *New York Herald*, Mar. 12, 1898.

192 young daughter of *Mangrove*'s commanding officer: *New York Herald*, Feb. 26, 1898.

192 "never in the history": Brown, *Correspondents' War* (p. 127).

193 Chadwick's original view that magazine had exploded: *New York Journal*, Mar. 20, 1898.

193 hasty judgment might be contradicted: *Evening Star*, Feb. 28, 1898.

194 "How Long Stirred a Storm": *The World*, Mar. 4, 1898.

194 Spanish newspapers erroneously reporting: *The World*, Feb. 25, 1898.

194 "reports from Cuba": *Spanish Diplomatic Correspondence and Documents* (p. 88).

195 Sicard had alerted Long: Rickover, *How the Battleship* Maine *Was Destroyed* (p. 69).

196 "had no knowledge as what findings of the court will be": Sigsbee, letter to his wife, Mar. 8, 1898.

196 "Don't forget that": ibid., Mar. 15, 1898.

197 Marix and three armed officers: *New York Journal*, Mar. 23, 1898.

197 officers stood continuous watches: *New York Times*, Mar. 25, 1898.

197 enormous crowd gathered in Union Station: Leech, *In the Days of McKinley* (p. 174).

197 unrestrained throng jostled Holman: *New York Journal*, Mar. 25, 1898.

197 Marix gave a short interview: *The World*, Mar. 25, 1898.

198 "to place before an assembly": Chadwick, *The Relations of United States and Spain—Diplomacy* (p. 555).

198 Lemly and Marix went to Long's office: *New York Times*, Mar. 26, 1898.

198 Long and Marix drove to White House: Leech, *In the Days of McKinley* (p. 174).

199 Police estimated at least 6,000 visitors: *New York Herald*, Mar. 29, 1898.

199 There had been two distinct explosions: *Papers Relating to the Foreign Relations of the United States* (p. 1041).

199 The court found: *Report of the Naval Court of Inquiry* (p. 279).

199 President's message anticlimatic, Leech, *In the Days of McKinley* (p. 178).

200 Senator Davis asked for a reading: O'Toole, *The Spanish War* (p. 160).

TESTIMONY CONCERNING THE *MAINE*

201 Sigsbee's testimony: *Report of the Naval Court of Inquiry* (pp. 10–19; 41–42).

201 Sigsbee had showed himself to be remote: Rickover, *How the Battleship Maine Was Destroyed* (p. 55).

202 Holman's testimony: *Report of the Naval Court of Inquiry* (pp. 20–24; 36–37).

202 Wainwright's testimony: ibid. (pp. 25–29).

202 Cluverius' testimony: ibid. (pp. 29–30).

202 Holden's testimony: ibid. (pp. 30–31).

203 Howell's testimony: ibid. (pp. 32–36; 51–52).

204 Powelson's testimony: ibid. (pp. 43–48; 57).

205 Teasdale's testimony: ibid. (pp. 52–55).

205 Rothschild's testimony: ibid. (pp. 57–65).

206 divers' testimony: ibid. (pp. 66–93).

THE TELLTALE PLATES

209ff. all testimony: *Report of the Naval Court of Inquiry* (pp. 43–48; 57).

THE SAMPSON FINDINGS

219 findings of the court: *Report of the Naval Court of Inquiry* (p. 281).

220 "we may never know": Weems, *Fate of the Maine* (p. 116).

221 "every decent citizen": *Harper's Weekly*, Apr. 9, 1898.

221 "sensational testimony . . . withheld from public": *New York Journal*, Apr. 2, 1898.

221 one witness' name withheld: Basoco, "What Really Happened to the *Maine*?" (p. 19).

222 "we know the *Maine* was blown up": *New York Journal*, Mar. 31, 1898.

222 Marix spoke freely: *New York Herald*, Mar. 30, 1898.

222 "the presence of the *Maine*": Chadwick, *Relations of the United States and Spain—Diplomacy* (p. 561).

222 Chadwick "intimately acquainted" with *Maine's* construction: Meriwether, "The Unremembered *Maine.*"

223 "a perfectly safe ship": Chadwick, *Relations of the United States and Spain—Diplomacy* (p. 561).

224 nine of the eleven: *The Times*, Apr. 11, 1898.

224 Sigsbee had asked Powelson to prepare a private report: Sigsbee, *The "Maine"* (p. 169).

224 Sigsbee before Senate committee: *Report of the Committee on Foreign Relations* (pp. 481–92).

225 "They admitted the plan was feasible": Sigsbee, *The "Maine"* (p. 183).

225 "Spanish officials blew up the *Maine*": *The World*, Apr. 10, 1898.

225 Lee's and Laine's testimony before Senate: *Report of the Committee on Foreign Relations* (Lee, pp. 534–48; Laine, pp. 503–11).

226 Weyler had bought dynamite in London: March, *The History and Conquest of the Philippines* (p. 328).

226 hearings in House of Representatives where "Men fought," *The Times*, Apr. 14, 1898.

227 no physical indication of a mine explosion: *Report of the Spanish Naval Board of Inquiry* (p. 634).

228 "We regarded that excuse": *Report of the Committee on Foreign Relations* (p. 485).

228 "the keel did not appear to have suffered": Chadwick, *Relations of the United States and Spain—Diplomacy* (p. 561).

228 "no American appeared before Spanish Court": Sigsbee, *The "Maine"* (p. 171).

DECLARATION OF WAR

229 Congressman Smith told Sigsbee: Sigsbee, letter to his wife, Mar. 12, 1898.

229 choice of receptions: Sigsbee, *The "Maine"* (p. 177).

229 Sampson named commander: West, *Admirals of American Empire* (p. 193).

229 final disposition of the *Maine*: Sigsbee, *The "Maine"* (p. 176).

230 "Tell the officer in charge": Cummings, *Admiral Richard Wainwright* (p. 91).

230 McKinley insisted that Spain withdraw: Gould, *The Presidency of William McKinley* (p. 78).

230 prospects for peace looked favorable: *The Times*, Apr. 11 and 12, 1898.

230 McKinley was rebuffing the European powers' overtures: Gould, *The Presidency of William McKinley* (p. 81).

231 "You will win the fight": Wisan, *The Cuban Crisis as Reflected in the New York Press* (p. 422).

231 Beranger admitted Havana harbor mined: *The Times*, Apr. 12, 1898.

231 Powelson ordered off: *New York Herald*, Apr. 7, 1898.

231   thousands of Spaniards lined the shore: Sigsbee, *The "Maine"* (p. 176).

231   Lee challenged to duel: *New York Times*, Apr. 19, 1898.

232   McKinley sent war message to Congress: Wisan, *The Cuban Crisis as Reflected in the New York Press* (p. 439).

232   Militancy was widespread: Leech, *In the Days of McKinley* (p. 178).

233   destruction of *Maine* credited with having stampeded: Smith, "The Moral of the Cuban War" (p. 283).

233   bonds to be redeemed at full value: Smith, *A Captain Unafraid* (p. 284).

233   "a matter of small import": Green, *Our Naval Heritage* (p. 271).

234   war natural outgrowth of expansionist U.S. foreign policy: Grenville, "American Naval Preparations for War with Spain."

234   drive for overseas markets: Hofstadter, *The Paranoid Style in American Politics* (pp. 146, 147).

THE VIEW FROM THE OTHER SIDE

235   European newspapers sympathized with the Spaniards: *The Times*, Apr. 22, 1898.

235   Austrian and Italian naval officers: *New York Herald*, Apr. 12, 1898.

237   "it might appear": Jane, "The 'Maine' Disaster and After" (p. 640).

237   background of Bucknill: *The Times*, Aug. 26, 1935, obit.; *Supplement to the Royal Engineers Journal*, Oct. 1935 (obit.); letter from E. D. Norris, Librarian, Royal Engineering Corps Library.

238   Bucknill's articles, pts. 2–5: *Engineering*, June 3, June 10, June 17, June 24, 1898.

239   "a sharp jar on the ankle bones": *Supplement to the Royal Engineers Journal*, Oct. 1935 (obit.).

242   a thoughtful reply: *Engineering*, July 1, 1898, letter from F. M. Barber.

243   Sampson court was prejudiced: Beggs, *The Mystery of the Maine*.

243   the most formidable of the American dissenters: Grupp, *Rear Admiral Wallace Melville* (pp. 613, 614); and Hamersly, *Records of Living Officers of the U.S. Navy and Marine Corps* (p. 93).

AMERICAN REBUTTAL

245   Sampson appointed board of survey to examine wrecked Spanish warships: Young, *Reminiscences and Thrilling Stories of the War* (pp. 140, 141); and *Annual Reports of the Navy Department for the Year 1898* (pp. 574, 578, 581, 583).

245   Sampson asked board to report on damage from magazine explosions: (Woodford), *The American-Spanish War* (p. 8).

245   *Almirante Oquendo* had been armor-belted cruiser: Wilson, *The Downfall of Spain* (p. 358).

245   description of structural damage to the *Oquendo*: Goode, *With Sampson through the War* (p. 222).

246   The *Vizcaya* in identical battle class as *Maine*: Young, *Reminiscences and Thrilling Stories of the War* (p. 141).

246   "Any doubt that the *Maine* was blown up": ibid. (p. 140).

247   destruction of Admiral Makaroff's flagship: Meriwether, "The Unremembered *Maine*."

247   Danish naval report from 1873: Beehler, "Scandinavian Experiments with Submarine Mines" (pp. 121–54); idem, "Experiences of a Naval Attaché" (pp. 949–51).

248   employment of phrase "Remember the *Maine!*" prohibited: Sigsbee, *The "Maine"* (p. 190).

249   "swearing like pirates": Long, ed., *Journal of John D. Long* (p. 228).

249   sailors scratched "Remember the *Maine!*": *New York Times*, July 14, 1898.

249   Wainwright in time for battle of Santiago: *Dictionary of American Biography* (vol. 19, p. 319).

249   "The *Maine* is avenged!": *New York Times*, July 6, 1898.

250   Sigsbee denied making oral report: West, *Admirals of American Empire* (p. 240).

250   ten U.S. sailors killed: Rickover, *How the Battleship* Maine *Was Destroyed* (p. 75).

250   commissioners proposed a joint Spanish-American board: Foner, *The Spanish-Cuban-American War* (p. 244).

250   United States refused to participate in new inquiry: Trask, *The War with Spain in 1898* (p. 466).

250   "this illustrated anew": *Life*, Dec. 22, 1898.

RAISING THE *MAINE*

251   *Texas* inspection found dirt and rust: Rickover, *How the Battleship* Maine *Was Destroyed* (p. 75).

251   unrepentant Sigsbee told Secretary Long: Allen, *Papers of John D. Long 1897–1904* (p. 361).

251   bodies of *Maine* sailors disinterred: Sigsbee, "My Story of the 'Maine'" (p. 380).

252   reburial of the *Maine* dead: *New York Times*, Dec. 29, 1899; Long, ed., *Journal of John D. Long* (p. 240).

253   explanations for the explosions on the *Maine*: Holman, "The Destruction of the *Maine*" (p. 159).

254   sunken vessel had created a shoal: Weems, *Fate of the Maine* (p. 156).

255   "Why has the American government not raised the wreck?": Meriwether, "The Unremembered Maine."

255 Meyer would never have reopened Sampson inquiry voluntarily: Coletta, *The Presidency of William Howard Taft* (p. 213).

255 New York's Congressman Sulzer spoke: *Congressional Record*, 60th Cong., 1st sess. (pp. 6154–57).

256 "There is still a mystery of the *Maine*": *New York Times*, Apr. 14, 1908.

257 "I call up the bill": *Congressional Record*, 61st Cong., 2d sess. (p. 3223).

257 the bill Congress enacted provided: *Congressional Record, Final Report on Removing Wreck of Battleship "Maine"* (pp. 5, 6).

258 board whose members were better qualified: Rickover, *How the Battleship Maine Was Destroyed* (p. 96).

258 General Bixby reported: *Congressional Record, Raising Wreck of Battleship "Maine,"* document no. 96.

259 Constructor William Ferguson to act as liaison: Rickover, *How the Battleship Maine Was Destroyed* (p. 79).

261 Army Corps of Engineers congratulated: *Scientific American*, Dec. 23, 1911.

THE SECOND AMERICAN INQUIRY

263 precept for the Board to Inspect: *Congressional Record, Raising Wreck of Battleship "Maine,"* Exhibit A (p. 5).

263 Admiral Charles Vreeland's background: Hamersly, *Records of the Living Officers of the U.S. Navy* (p. 213).

264 background on Chief Constructor Richard Watt: *Who's Who in America, 1920–21.*

264 background on Commander Joseph Strauss: *Who's Who in America, 1914–15.*

264 Colonel William Black's background: *Who's Who in America, 1920–21.*

264 background on Commander Charles Hughes: Reynolds, *Famous American Admirals* (pp. 156, 157).

264 first meeting of the board: *Congressional Record, Raising Wreck of Battleship "Maine,"* Exhibit B (p. 5).

264 heavy rain: *New York Times*, Nov. 23, 1911.

266 the board provided a detailed description of the wreck: *Raising Wreck of Battleship "Maine"* (pp. 7–10).

270 "a second Court of Inquiry upheld": Basoco, "What Really Happened to the *Maine*?" (p. 22).

270 Samuel Eliot Morison observed: Morison, *The Oxford History of the American People* (p. 800).

271 "Its findings were no more conclusive": Harris, *The Age of the Battleship* (p. 48).

271 "found that what the initial Court had taken as evidence": Brown, *Correspondents' War* (p. 143).

271 "In 1911, a thorough investigation showed": Werstein, *Turning Point for America* (p. 61).

271 "A joint board reported in 1911": Sigsbee, "My Story of the 'Maine'" (p. 381).

271 "I have never had a doubt": *New York Times*, July 30, 1923.

271 Bucknill in touch with Bixby: Bucknill, "The U.S. Battleship 'Maine,'" (pp. 827–29).

THE END OF THE *MAINE*

273 amendment to permit hull to be sold: *New York Times*, Dec. 17, 1911.

273 debate on proposed sale: *Congressional Record*, 61st Cong., 3d sess.

273 penny pinchers had suggested: *Scientific American*, Mar. 30, 1912.

274 Army engineers had resumed control: *Congressional Record, Final Report on Removing Wreck* (p. 28).

274 hulk towed out of dam: *New York Times*, Mar. 15, 1912.

274 At sunrise, the *Maine*'s funeral began: *Scientific American*, Mar. 30, 1912.

275 port regulations required employment of a pilot: Caldwell, "The Most Mournful of Sea Pageants" (p. 20).

275 memorial services for the dead sailors: *Outlook*, Mar. 30, 1912 (p. 715).

276 Captain O'Brien climbed aboard the *Maine*: Caldwell, "The Most Mournful of Sea Pageants" (p. 20).

278 at first it appeared the *Maine* would not go down: *New York Times*, Mar. 24, 1912.

278 Romantics claimed she was fighting: Weems, *Fate of the Maine* (p. 162).

280 hulk sunk in such an indefinite location: *New York Times*, Mar. 17, 1912.

280 disposal of cofferdam, etc.: *Congressional Record, Final Report on Removing Wreck*.

281 monument to the *Maine*: *The Literary Digest*, June 7, 1913.

281 George Hearst called ill suited for the unveiling: Weems, *Fate of the Maine* (p. 176).

281 "In 1911 when the *Maine* was raised": Dierks, *A Leap to Arms* (p. 21).

281 "there will be no chance of the true facts being revealed": Foner, *Spanish-Cuban-American War* (p. 245).

RICKOVER AND THE *MAINE*

283 "no scrap of evidence": Wilson, *Battleships in Action* (p. 118).

283 "In 30 years, no evidence has come to light": Millis, *The Martial Spirit* (p. 128).

284 "Nobody has come forward to acknowledge the deed": Lundberg, *Imperial Hearst* (p. 73).

284 "no more can be proved": Basoco, "What Really Happened to the *Maine*?" (p. 22).

284 "no wiser seven decades after": Dierks, *A Leap to Arms* (p. 21).

284 Taylor's feature story: Washington *Star-News*, Sept. 1, 1974.

285 "sailors smoking probably did cause": Engle and Lott, *America's Maritime Heritage* (p. 214).

285 "spontaneous detonation of unstable explosives": Pemsel, *History of War at Sea* (n.p.).

285 Rickover background and "vicious anti-Semitism": Reynolds, *Famous American Admirals* (pp. 277–79).

285 "that little Jew": Polmar and Allen, *Rickover* (p. 191).

285 pre–World War II naval career: Reynolds, *Famous American Admirals* (p. 278).

286 1951 board's passing over Rickover: Blair, *The Atomic Submarine and Admiral Rickover* (p. 180).

286 1952 selection board's actions: Blair (p. 193).

286 Navy became more hostile; and 1953 board still took five hours: Polmar and Allen, *Rickover* (pp. 189, 191, 203).

287 Rickover findings: Rickover, *How the Battleship* Maine *Was Destroyed*.

HANSEN-PRICE AND THE *MAINE*

294 self-ignition of coal feeds on oxygen: Hoskins, *A Study of Spontaneous Combustion in Storage Coal* (pp. 22–24); and Springer, "Coal Piles that Light Themselves," *Scientific American*, Aug. 1924 (p. 104).

294 Hansen-Price investigation "not exhaustive": Hansen and Price in Rickover, *How the Battleship* Maine *Was Destroyed* (p. 108).

295 engineers found photographic exhibits confirmed: *Scientific American*, Dec. 23, 1911 (pp. 578–79).

296 A 1952 inquiry concerning underwater explosions: Hubbs and Rechnitzer, "Report on Experiments Designed to Determine Effects of Underwater Explosions on Fish Life" (p. 334).

296 series of tests of underwater bursts of both high and low explosives: ibid. (p. 345).

296 Danish report: Beehler, "Scandinavian Experiments with Submarine Mines" (p. 124).

297 The outer bottom steel: Morley, "Contract Trial of the U.S. Armored-Cruiser *Maine*" (p. 196).

299 "We cannot think of another instance": *Saturday Evening Post*, Nov. 1976, editorial.

300 "Rickover demolishes the theory": Cosmas, *Naval War College Review*, Fall 1977 (p. 139).

300 a 1981 history of the Spanish-American War: Trask, *The War with Spain in 1898* (p. 35).

300 "At Rickover's request": Polmar and Allen, *Rickover* (p. 524).

301   A 1984 history of the war: O'Toole, *The Spanish War* (p. 400).

301   "The phrase spontaneous combustion": Springer, "Coal Piles that Light Themselves," *Scientific American*, Aug. 1924 (p. 104).

302   ignition requires a continuous replacement of air: Hoskins, *Study of Spontaneous Combustion in Storage Coal* (p. 24).

302   coal stable if not handled: Stoek, *Fires in Steamship Bunkers and Cargo Coal* (p. 21).

302   spontaneous combustion on shipboard: *Engineering*, Sept. 9, 1898 (p. 327).

302   the captain had steam launch circle the vessel: Sternlicht, *McKinley's Bulldog: The Battleship Oregon* (p. 58).

303   temperature around bunkers rose to 150 degrees F.: (Woodford) *American-Spanish War* (p. 165).

303   smoke came from a bunker: O'Toole, *The Spanish War* (p. 160).

303   the fuel's superior steaming quality: *North American Review*, Mar. 1902 (p. 338).

WHO WAS THE PERPETRATOR

305   "There is an absence of any claim": Naisawald, "Destruction of the USS Maine" (p. 98).

305   background of Alexander C. Brice: *History of Taylor County* (pp. 339–41).

305   at midnight on Feb. 13: *New York Times*, Dec. 12, 1911.

306   "He said he did not know": *Times-Republican* (Bedford, Iowa), Dec. 14, 1911.

307   no deathbed confession: *New Catholic Encyclopedia* (pp. 133–36).

Bibliography

★ ★ ★ ★ ★ ★ ★ ★

Academic American Encyclopedia. Danbury, Conn.: Grolier, Inc., 1983.

Alden, John D. *The American Steel Navy.* Annapolis: Naval Institute Press/American Heritage Press, 1989.

Alger, R. A. *The Spanish-American War.* New York: Harper and Brothers, 1901.

Allen, Gardner Weld. *Papers of John D. Long 1897–1904.* Boston: The Massachusetts Historical Society, 1939.

The American Navy. Chicago: George M. Hill & Co., 1898.

Annual Reports of the Navy Department for the Year 1898. Washington, D.C.: Government Printing Office, 1898.

———. *Appendix to the Report of the Chief of the Bureau of Navigation.* Washington, D.C.: Government Printing Office, 1898.

Armstrong, Leroy. *Pictorial Atlas Illustrating the Spanish-American War.* N.p.: Souvenir Publishing, 1898.

Army and Navy Journal. "The Loss of the U.S.S. Maine." Feb. 19, 1898.

———. "Various Opinions Concerning the Disaster." Feb. 19, 1898.

———. "The Loss of the Maine." Feb. 26, 1898.

———. "Responsibility of Spain." Feb. 26, 1898.

———. "To Relieve the Maine Sufferers." Feb. 26, 1898.

———. "Loss of the Maine." Mar. 5, 1898.

———. "English Sympathy on the Loss of the Maine." Mar. 5, 1898.

———. "The Captain of the Maine." Mar. 5, 1898.

———. "Is Our Discipline Lax?" Mar. 12, 1898.

———. "Sigsbee's Obit." July 28, 1923.

Atkins, Edwin F. *Sixty Years in Cuba.* New York: Arno Press, 1980.

Atkins, John B. *The War in Cuba.* London: Smith, Elder & Co., 1899.

Barry, David S. *Forty Years in Washington.* Boston: Little, Brown, and Co., 1924.

Basoco, Richard M. "What Really Happened to the *Maine?*" *American History Illustrated.* June 1966.

Bassler, R. E. "The Origin of Engineering Duty Only." *Journal of the American Society of Naval Engineers.* Nov. 1953.

Beach, Edward L. *The United States Navy: A 200-Year History*. Boston: Houghton Mifflin, 1987.

Beale, Howard K. *Theodore Roosevelt and the Rise of America to World Power*. Baltimore: The Johns Hopkins Press, 1956.

Beehler, Commodore W. H. "Experiences of a Naval Attaché." *Century*. Oct. 1908.

———. "Scandinavian Experiments with Submarine Mines." United States Naval Institute *Proceedings*, vol. 7:16 (1881).

Beer, Thomas. *Stephen Crane*. New York: Alfred A. Knopf, 1923.

Beers, Henry P. "The Development of the Office of the Chief of Naval Operations." *Military Affairs*. Spring 1946.

Beggs, Robert H. *The Mystery of the Maine*. Washington, D.C.: The Carnahan Press, 1912.

Bennett, John W. *Roosevelt and the Republic*. New York: Broadway Publishing Co., 1908.

Benton, Elbert J. *International Law and Diplomacy of the Spanish-American War*. Baltimore: The Johns Hopkins Press, 1908.

Bishop, Joseph Bucklin. *Theodore Roosevelt and His Time*. Vol. 2. New York: Charles Scribner's Sons, 1920.

Blair, Jr., Clay. *The Atomic Submarine and Admiral Rickover*. New York: Henry Holt and Co., 1954.

Blasters' Handbook. Wilmington, Del.: E. I. du Pont de Nemours & Co., 1966.

Blow, Michael. *A Ship To Remember*. New York: William Morrow and Company, Inc., 1992.

Bonsal, Stephen. *The Fight for Santiago*. New York: Doubleday & McClure Co., 1899.

Booklist. Review of *How the Battleship Maine Was Destroyed*. Oct. 15, 1976.

Bourne, Henry E., and Elbert Jay Benton. *American History*. Boston: D. C. Heath and Co., 1925.

Bowers, Claude G. *Beveridge and the Progressive Era*. Cambridge: Houghton Mifflin Co., 1932.

Bradford, Gershom. *A Glossary of Sea Terms*. New York: Dodd, Mead & Co, 1942.

Brooks, Elbridge S. *The Story of Our War with Spain*. Boston: Lothrop Publishing Co., 1899.

Brown, Charles H. *The Correspondents' War*. New York: Charles Scribner's Sons, 1967.

Brownlee, James Henry. *War-Time Echoes*. New York: The Werner Co., 1898.

(Bucknill) Letter from E. D. Norris, RE Corps Library, Institute of Royal Engineers, Brompton Barracks, Chatham, Kent, England.

———. Obit., *The Times*, Aug. 26, 1935.

———. Obit., Supplement to the *RE Journal*, Oct. 1935.

Bucknill, Lt. Col. John Townshend. *Back Along*. N.p.: 1935.

————. "The Destruction of the United States Battleship 'Maine.'" Parts 1–5. *Engineering*, May 27, June 3, June 10, June 17, June 24, 1898.

————. Letters to Editor on Bucknill articles. *Engineering*, July 1, July 8, July 15, July 22, July 29, Aug. 12, and Aug. 19, 1898.

————. "The Raising of the Wreck of the U.S. Battleship 'Maine.'" *Engineering*, Mar. 15, 1912.

————. "The U.S. Battleship 'Maine.'" *Engineering*, June 21, 1912.

Bullard, F. Lauriston. *Famous War Correspondents*. Boston: Little, Brown and Co., 1914.

Caldwell, John Randolph. "The Most Mournful of Sea Pageants." *Harper's Weekly*, May 11, 1912.

Carlson, Oliver. *Brisbane*. New York: Stackpole Sons, 1937.

Carr, Raymond. *Spain 1808–1975*. Oxford: Clarendon Press, 1982.

Carter, Lt. Col. W. H. *From Yorktown to Santiago with the Sixth U.S. Cavalry*. Baltimore: The Lord Baltimore Press, 1900.

Carter, William Harding. *The Life of Lieutenant General Chaffee*. Chicago: The University of Chicago Press, 1917.

Catchpool, Edmund, and John Satterly. *Textbook of Sound*. London: University Tutorial Press Ltd., 1947.

Catlin, Dorothy Warren. "Remember the Maine." *Shipmate*, Feb. 1968.

(Chadwick) *Dictionary of American Biography*. Vol. 3. New York: Charles Scribner's Sons, 1929.

Chadwick, French Ensor. *The Relations of the United States and Spain*. New York: Charles Scribner's Sons, 1911.

————. *The Relations of the United States and Spain—Diplomacy*. New York: Charles Scribner's Sons, 1909.

Chidwick, John P., as told to Harry T. Cook. *Remember the Maine!* Winchester, Va.: Winchester Printers and Stationers, 1935.

Christian, Ermine A. *The Effects of Underwater Explosions on Swimbladder Fish*. Technical Report 73–103. Naval Ordnance Station, July 1973.

Clark, Charles E. *My Fifty Years in the Navy*. Annapolis: Naval Institute Press, 1984.

Cluverius, Commander W. T. "A Midshipman on the *Maine*." United States Naval Institute *Proceedings*, Feb. 1918.

Coblentz, Edmond D., ed. *William Randolph Hearst*. New York: Simon and Schuster, 1952.

Coletta, Paolo E. *A Bibliography of American Naval History*. Annapolis: Naval Institute Press, 1981.

————. *French Ensor Chadwick: Scholarly Warrior*. Boston: University Press of America, 1980.

————. *The Presidency of William Howard Taft*. Lawrence, Kans.: The University Press of Kansas, 1973.

Columb, F. H. "First Impressions of the War." *National Review* (London). June 1898.

Congressional Record. The Proceedings and Debates of the 55th Cong., 2d sess. Washington, D.C.: Government Printing Office, 1898.

———. Proceedings and Debates of the 60th Cong., 1st sess. Washington, D.C.: Government Printing Office, 1908.

———. Proceedings and Debates of the 60th Cong., 2d sess. Washington, D.C.: Government Printing Office, 1909.

———. Proceedings and Debates of the 61st Cong., 2d sess. Washington, D.C.: Government Printing Office, 1910.

———. *Raising Wreck of Battleship "Maine."* 62nd Cong., 1st sess., document no. 96. Washington, D.C.: Government Printing Office, 1911.

———. *Final Report on Removing Wreck of Battleship "Maine" from Habana, Cuba.* 63rd Cong., 2d sess., document no. 480. Washington, D.C.: Government Printing Office, 1914.

Cosmas, Graham A. *An Army for the Empire.* Columbia, Mo.: University of Missouri, 1971.

———. Review of *How the Battleship Maine Was Destroyed*, by H. G. Rickover. *Naval War College Review.* Fall 1977.

Coward, H. F., G. W. Jones, C. G. Dunkle, and B. E. Hess. *The Explosibility of Methane and Natural Gas.* U.S. Publication Bulletin 30. Pittsburgh: Carnegie Institute of Technology, 1926.

Cowles, Anna Roosevelt. *Letters from Theodore Roosevelt to Anna Roosevelt 1870–1918.* New York: Charles Scribner's Sons, 1924.

Crabtree, J. B. *The Passing of Spain.* Springfield: The King-Richardson Publishing Co., 1898.

Croly, Herbert. *Marcus Alonzo Hanna.* New York: The Macmillan Co., 1923.

Cummings, Captain Damon E. *Admiral Richard Wainwright and the United States Fleet.* Washington, D.C.: Office of Naval Operations, 1962.

Dennis, Alfred L. P. *Adventures in American Diplomacy 1896–1906.* New York: E. P. Dutton & Co., 1928.

Dictionary of American Biography. Dumas Malone, ed. New York: Charles Scribner's Sons, 1936.

Dictionary of American Naval Fighting Ships. Vols. 1 and 3. Washington, D.C.: Navy Department, Navy History Division, 1959.

Dierks, Jack Cameron. *A Leap to Arms.* Philadelphia: J. B. Lippincott Co., 1970.

Diller, Ludwig. "The Mystery of the Maine." *Scientific American*, Sept. 2, 1911.

Dinger, Capt. H. C. "More About the U.S. Maine." *Shipmate*, May 1948.

Dobson, John M. *America's Ascent.* De Kalb, Ill.: Northern Illinois University Press, 1978.

Donahue, William J. "The United States Newspaper Press Reaction to the Maine Incident." Ph.D. thesis, University of Colorado, 1970.

Dorwart, Jeffery M. *The Office of Naval Intelligence.* Annapolis: Naval Institute Press, 1979.

Dulles, Foster Rhea. *Prelude to World Power.* New York: The Macmillan Co., 1965.

Dunn, Arthur Wallace. *From Harrison to Harding.* New York: G. P. Putnam's Sons, 1922.

Dyson, C. W. "A Fifty Year Retrospect of Naval Engineering." *Journal of the American Society of Naval Engineers,* May 1918.

Earle, Lt. Com. Ralph. "The Destruction of the Liberté." United States Naval Institute *Proceedings,* Dec. 1911.

Eggert, Gerald G. "Our Man in Havana: Fitzhugh Lee." *The Hispanic American Historical Review,* Nov. 1967.

The Encyclopedia Britannica. 14th ed., 1930.

Engineering. Note on "Woodwork in Ships of War," Sept. 2, 1898.

———. Note on fire in bunkers of battleship "Oregon," Sept. 9, 1898.

Engle, Eloise, and Arnold S. Lott. *America's Maritime Heritage.* Annapolis: Naval Institute Press, 1975.

Epler, Percy H. *The Life of Clara Barton.* New York: Macmillan Co., 1937.

Evans, Robley D. *A Sailor's Log.* New York: D. Appleton and Co., 1901.

The Evening Star (Washington, D.C.). Jan. 24, 1898–Mar. 19, 1899.

Ferrara, Orestes. *The Last Spanish War.* New York: The Paisley Press, 1937.

Flack, Horace Edgar. "Spanish-American Diplomatic Relations Preceding the War of 1898." *Johns Hopkins University Studies in Historical and Political Science,* ser. 24, nos. 1–2. Jan.–Feb. 1906.

Foner, Philip S. *The Spanish-Cuban-American War.* New York: Monthly Review Press, 1972.

Garraty, John A. *The American Nation.* New York: Harper and Row, 1966.

Gauvreau, Charles F. *Reminiscences of the Spanish-American War.* Rouses Point, N.Y.: The Authors Publishing Co., 1915.

Goode, W. A. M. *With Sampson Through the War.* New York: Doubleday & McClure Co., 1899.

Gould, Lewis L. *The Presidency of William McKinley.* Lawrence, Kans.: The Regents Press of Kansas, 1980.

Green, Fitzhugh. *Our Naval Heritage.* New York: The Century Co., 1925.

Greene, Theodore P. *American Imperialism in 1898.* Boston: D. C. Heath & Co., 1955.

Grenville, John A. S. "American Naval Preparations for War with Spain, 1896–1898." *Journal of American Studies,* April 1968.

———, and George Berkeley Young. *Politics, Strategy, and American Diplomacy.* New Haven: Yale University Press, 1966.

Grieg, Julius, as told to Charles H. McLellan. *The Immediate Cause of the War with Spain.* N.p., n.d.

Grupp, George W. "Rear Admiral Wallace Melville as a Man and Engineer-in-Chief of the Navy." United States Naval Institute *Proceedings*, May 1948.

Gulliver, Commander Louis J. "Our First Pearl Harbor." *Shipmate*, Mar. 1948.

Hagan, Kenneth J. *The People's Navy: The Making of American Sea Power*. New York: The Free Press, 1991.

Halstead, Murat. *The Story of Cuba*. Chicago: The Werner Co., 1896.

Hamersly, Lewis Randolph. *Records of the Living Officers of the U.S. Navy and Marine Corps*. Philadelphia: L. R. Hamersly & Co., 1894 and 1902.

Hansen, Ib S. Letter to authors, Aug. 10, 1985.

Hansen, Ib S., and Robert S. Price. "The U.S.S. Maine: An Examination of the Technical Evidence Bearing on Its Destruction," in H. G. Rickover, *How the Battleship* Maine *Was Destroyed*. Washington, D.C.: Department of the Navy, 1976.

Harper's Pictorial History of the War with Spain. New York: Harper and Brothers, 1899.

Harper's Weekly. Jan. 1898–May 1898.

Harris, Brayton. *The Age of the Battleship: 1890–1922*. New York: Franklin Watts, Inc., 1965.

Hartmann, Gregory K. *Weapons That Wait: Mine Warfare in the United States*. Annapolis: Naval Institute Press, 1979.

Hero Tales of the American Soldier and Sailor. N.p.: A. Holloway, 1899.

Herrick, Jr., Walter R. *The American Naval Revolution*. Baton Rouge: Louisiana State University Press, 1966.

Historical Transactions 1893–1943. "Types of Naval Ships," Pt. 3. New York: The Society of Naval Architects and Marine Engineers, 1945.

History of Taylor County. 1910. "Alexander C. Brice."

Hofstadter, Richard. *The Paranoid Style in American Politics*. New York: Alfred A. Knopf, 1965.

Holman, Donald A. "The Destruction of the *Maine* February 15, 1898." *Michigan Alumnus Quarterly*, Feb. 27, 1954.

Hoskins, A. J. *A Study of Spontaneous Combustion in Storage Coal*. Bulletin no. 30. Lafayette, Ind.: Purdue University, April 1928.

Hovgaard, William. *Modern History of Warships*. London: Spon & Chamberlain, 1920.

Howarth, Stephen. *To Shining Sea: A History of the United States Navy 1775–1991*. New York: Random House, 1991.

Hubbs, Carl L., and Andreas B. Rechnitzer. "Report on Experiments Designed to Determine Effects of Underwater Explosions on Fish Life." *California Fish and Game*, July 1952.

Hume, Martin A. S. *Modern Spain 1788–1898*. New York: G. P. Putnam's Sons, 1899.

J, Commander. "Sketches from the Spanish-American War." United States Naval Institute *Proceedings*, March 1899.

Jane, Fred T. *All the World's Fighting Ships*. London: St. Dunstan's House, 1898.
————. "The 'Maine' Disaster and After. The Naval Positions of Spain and the United States." *Fortnightly Review*, April 1898.
Johnson, Arthur M. "The Battleship Maine and Pier 46, East River." United States Naval Institute *Proceedings*, Nov. 1955.
Jones, Rev. Harry W. *A Chaplain's Experience Ashore and Afloat*. New York: A. G. Sherwood & Co., 1901.
Josephson, Matthew. *The President Makers*. New York: Harcourt, Brace and Co., 1940.
Journal-Miner Weekly (Prescott, Ariz.). Apr.–Dec. 1898.
Journal of the American Society of Naval Engineers. "Ships, the French Naval Disaster." Vol. 19, 1907.
Kane, Joseph Nathan. *Famous First Facts*. New York: The H. W. Wilson Co., 1950.
Kansas City *Star*. Dispatch about A. C. Brice, Dec. 17, 1911.
Karsten, Peter. "No Room for Young Turks?" United States Naval Institute *Proceedings*, March 1973.
Keil, A. B. "The Response of Ships to Underwater Explosions." *Society of Naval Architects and Marine Engineers*, Report no. 1576, 1961.
Key West *Citizen*. "First Man to Hear About the Maine Disaster." Feb. 15, 1974.
————. "That Gallant Lady Was Laid to Rest." Feb. 1, 1968.
King, W. Nephew. *The Story of the Spanish-American War*. New York: Peter Fenelon Collier & Son, 1900.
Knight, Rear-Admiral Austin. "Professor Philip Rounseville Alger, U.S. Navy. An Appreciation." United States Naval Institute *Proceedings*, Mar. 1912.
Langley, Lester D. *The United States and the Caribbean in the Twentieth Century*. Athens, Ga.: University of Georgia Press, 1985.
Leavitt, Professor Chris. University of New Mexico professor who discussed theory of sound with the authors. Feb. 20, 1986.
Leech, Margaret. *In the Days of McKinley*. New York: Harper and Brothers, 1959.
LeFeber, Walter. *The New Empire*. Ithaca, N.Y.: Cornell University Press, 1963.
Leslie's Official History of the Spanish-American War. 1899.
Leslie's Weekly Supplement. "Uncle Sam's Latest Greatest Shortest War." 1898.
Life magazine. Jan.–Dec. 1898.
Linderman, Gerald F. *The Mirror of War*. Ann Arbor: University of Michigan Press, 1974.
The Literary Digest. "The Disaster to the 'Maine,'" Feb. 26, 1898.
————. "International Law and the 'Maine' Disaster," Mar. 5, 1898.
————. "Relations between the United States and Spain and Cuba," Mar. 12, 1898.
————. "Measures of National Defense," Mar. 19, 1898.
————. "Views of the 'Maine' Catastrophe," Mar. 19, 1898.
————. "Topics in Brief," Mar. 19, 1898.

———. "Submarine Mines and Electricity," Mar. 26, 1898.

———. "How the Report of a Cannon Travels," Apr. 2, 1898.

———. "How the 'Maine' Will Be Raised," Nov. 12, 1910.

———. "Flaws in the 'Maine' Memorial," June 7, 1913.

Livezey, William E. *Mahan on Sea Power*. Norman, Okla.: University of Oklahoma Press, 1981.

Lodge, Henry Cabot. *The Spanish-American War*. New York: Harper and Brothers, 1899.

Long, John D. *The New American Navy*. New York: The Outlook Co., 1903.

Long, Margaret, ed. *The Journal of John D. Long*. Rindge, N.H.: Richard R. Smith Publishers, 1956.

Loomis, Richard T. "The White House Telephone and Crisis Management." United States Naval Institute *Proceedings*, Dec. 1969.

Lorant, Stephen. *The Life and Times of Theodore Roosevelt*. New York: Doubleday & Co., 1959.

Luce, Rear Admiral S. B. *Text-Book of Seamanship*. New York: D. Van Nostrand Co., 1898.

Lundberg, Ferdinand. *Imperial Hearst*. New York: Equinox Cooperative Press, 1936.

Madden, Robert B. "The Bureau of Ships and Its E.O.D. Officers." *Journal of the American Society of Naval Engineers*, Feb. 1954.

Mahan, Captain Alfred T. *Lessons of the War with Spain*. Boston: Little, Brown & Co., 1899.

———. *Retrospect and Prospect*. Port Washington, N.Y.: Kennikat Press (reprint 1968).

March, Alden. *The History and Conquest of the Philippines*. Philadelphia: International Publishing, 1899.

(Marix) *Who's Who in America 1918–19*. Chicago: A. N. Marquis & Co., 1918.

Mason, Gregory. *Remember the Maine*. New York: Henry Holt and Co., 1939.

May, Ernest R. *American Imperialism*. New York: Atheneum, 1968.

———. *Imperial Democracy*. New York: Harcourt, Brace & World, 1961.

Mayo, Lawrence Shaw, ed. *America of Yesterday*. Boston: The Atlantic Monthly Press, 1923.

McCalmont, Scott D. *Absorption of Water and Methane on Western Subbituminous Coals*. Abstract of thesis, University of New Mexico.

McKinley Presidential Papers. One letter of H. D. Giddings, Treasury Department, Havana Club, to Mrs. E. R. Moses, Treasury Department, Washington, D.C., Feb. 18, 1898.

Melia, Tamara Moser. *'Damn the Torpedoes.'* Washington, D.C.: Naval Historical Center, 1991.

Melville, G. W. "The Destruction of the Battleship 'Maine.'" *North American Review*, June 1911.

Memorial Services for the Dead of the U.S.S. Maine. Message from the President of the United States. House of Representatives, 62d Cong., 2d sess., document no. 630.

Meriwether, Walter Scott. "Remembering the *Maine.*" United States Naval Institute *Proceedings*, May 1948.

———. "The Unremembered Maine." *Harper's Weekly*, July 11, 1908.

Message of the President of the United States on the Relations of the United States to Spain by Reason of Warfare in the Island of Cuba. House of Representatives, 55th Cong., 2d sess., document no. 405.

Millis, Walter. *The Martial Spirit.* Cambridge: The Riverside Press, 1911.

Miscoski, Vincent T. "United States Naval Oceanography. . . . A Look Back." United States Naval Institute *Proceedings*, Feb. 1968.

Morgan, H. Wayne. *America's Road to Empire.* New York: John Wiley and Sons, 1965.

———. *William McKinley and His America.* Syracuse, N.Y.: Syracuse University Press, 1963.

Morison, Samuel Eliot. *The Oxford History of the American People.* New York: Oxford University Press, 1965.

Morley, A. W. "Contract Trial of the United States Armored-Cruiser Maine." *Journal of the Society of American Engineers*, Feb. 1895.

Morris, Charles. *The War with Spain.* Philadelphia: J. B. Lippincott Co., 1899.

Musicant, Ivan. *The Banana Wars: A History of the United States Intervention in Latin America from the Spanish-American War to the Invasion of Panama.* New York: Macmillan, 1990.

Musgrave, George Clarke. *Under Three Flags in Cuba.* Boston: Little, Brown and Co., 1899.

Naisawald, Lt. Col. L. VanLoan. "Destruction of the USS Maine—Accident or Sabotage?" United States Naval Institute *Proceedings*, Feb. 1972.

The Nation. Feb. 24–May 5, 1898.

National Archives. Charles D. Sisgsbee's military records.

Navy Department. *Destruction of the Maine.* Washington, D.C.: Government Printing Office, 1898.

Neuhaus, Herbert M. "Fifty Years of Naval Engineering." *Journal of the American Society of Naval Engineers*, Feb. 1938.

New Catholic Encyclopedia. New York: McGraw-Hill Book Co., 1967.

New York Herald, "Naval Institute Papers, May 11, 1895.

———. "N.Y. Navy Yard News," May 11, 1895.

———. Jan. 10–April 18, 1898.

New York Journal. Jan. 13–Apr. 20, 1898.

New York Times. "Laying of the Keel," Oct. 20, 1888.

———. "The Concord's Trial Trip"; "The Launch of the Maine." Nov. 19, 1890.

———. "The Maine in Service," Sept. 18, 1895.

————. "Collision on East River," July 30, 1897.

————. "Spanish Cruisers Arrive," Oct. 23, 1897.

————. Jan. 24–July 18, 1898.

————. "The Maine Dead Interred," Dec. 29, 1899.

————. Nov. 23–Dec. 18, 1911.

————. "Hulk of the Maine to be Buried at Sea," Mar. 16, 1912.

————. "The Maine Sinks to Ocean Grave," Mar. 17, 1912.

————. "Maine Dead Receive the Nation's Homage," Mar. 24, 1912.

————. "Admiral Sigsbee of the Maine Dies"; "Sigsbee of the Maine," July 20, 1923.

————. May 24–June 11, 1985.

North American Review. "Some Neglected Naval Lessons of the Spanish War," Mar. 1902.

Nuñez, Servero Gomez. *The Spanish-American War*. Washington, D.C.: Government Printing Office, 1899.

Office of Naval Intelligence. *Comments of Rear Admiral Pluddemann*. Washington, D.C.: Government Printing Office, 1899.

————. *The Spanish-American War*. Washington, D.C.: Government Printing Office, 1899.

————. *The Squadron of Admiral Cervera*. Washington, D.C.: Government Printing Office, 1900.

Offner, John L. *An Unwanted War: The Diplomacy of the United States and Spain Over Cuba 1895–98*. Chapel Hill: University of North Carolina Press, 1992.

O'Neil, Rear Admiral Charles. "The Development of Modern Ordnance and Armor in the United States." *Transactions of the Society of Naval Architects and Marine Engineers*, vol. 10, 1902.

O'Toole, G. J .A. *The Spanish War*. New York: W. W. Norton & Co., 1984.

Outlook. "The Burial of the Maine," Mar. 30, 1912.

Paine, Ralph D. *Roads of Adventure*. Boston: Houghton Mifflin Co., 1922.

Palmer, Joseph, comp. *Jane's Dictionary of Naval Terms*. London: Macdonald and Jane's, 1975.

Papers Relating to the Foreign Relations of the United States, 1898. Washington, D.C.: Government Printing Office, 1901. House of Representatives, 55th Cong., 3d sess., document no. 1.

Pemsel, Helmut. *A History of War at Sea*. Annapolis: Naval Institute Press, 1977.

Pepper, Charles M. *To-Morrow in Cuba*. New York: Harper & Bros., 1899.

Plesur, Milton. *Creating an American Empire 1865–1914*. New York: Pitman Publishing Co., 1971.

Polmar, Norman, and Thomas B. Allen. *Rickover*. New York: Simon and Schuster, 1982.

(Potter) *Who's Who in America 1910–11*. Chicago: A. N. Marquis & Co., 1910.

(Powelson) *Who's Who in America 1912–13*. Chicago: A. N. Marquis & Co.,
1912.

Powelson, Wilfred V. N. "Ensign Powelson's Personal Report to Captain Sigsbee
on the Cause of the Explosion of the Maine," in Charles D. Sigsbee, *The
"Maine."* New York: The Century Co., 1899.

Pulsifer, Woodbury, ed. *Navy Yearbook*. Washington, D.C.: Government Printing
Office, 1911.

Raising the Wreck of the Battleship Maine. U.S. Senate, 61st Cong., 3d sess., document no. 765. Washington, D.C.: Government Printing Office, 1911.

———. House of Representatives, 62d Cong., 1st sess., document no. 96. Washington, D.C.: Government Printing Office, 1911.

*Record of Proceedings of a Court of Inquiry in the Case of Rear-Admiral Winfield S.
Schley, U.S. Navy*. House of Representatives, 57th Cong., 1st sess., document
no. 485. Washington, D.C.: Government Printing Office, 1902.

*Record of the Proceedings of the Naval Examining Board convened at the Navy De-
partment, Washington D.C. in the case of Lt. Commander Charles D. Sigsbee,
May 6, 1882*. National Archives, Military Field Branch, Military Archives Division, Sigsbee File RG-125 Entry 58.

Regulations for the Government of the Navy of the United States. Washington,
D.C.: Government Printing Office, 1896.

Reich, Robert B. "Political Parables for Today." *The New York Times Magazine*,
Nov. 17, 1895.

Report of Efficiency of Various Coals 1896–1898. U.S. Senate Report, 59th Cong.,
1st sess., document no. 313. Washington, D.C.: Government Printing Office,
1906.

*Report of the Committee on Foreign Relations, United States Senate, Relative to
Affairs in Cuba*. Apr. 13, 1898. Report no. 885, 55th Cong., 2d sess. Washington, D.C.: Government Printing office, 1898.

*Report of the Naval Court of Inquiry Upon the Destruction of the United States
Battleship Maine in Havana Harbor, Feb. 15, 1898, Together with the Testimony
Taken Before the Court*. U.S. Senate document 207, 55th Cong., 2d sess.

*Report of the Spanish Naval Board of Inquiry as the Cause of the Destruction of the
U.S.S. Maine*. Transmitted Apr. 2, 1898 to the Secretary of State. Found in *Re-
port of the Committee on Foreign Relations, United States Senate, Relative to
Affairs in Cuba* (see above).

Report on the Wreck of the Maine. Message from the President of the United States
Transmitting Report of Board Convened at Habana, Cuba, by Order of the Secretary of the Navy, to Inspect and Report on the Wreck of the Maine (Old). Document no. 310, 62nd Cong., 2d sess., House of Representatives. Washington,
D.C.: Government Printing Office, 1912.

Reynolds, Clark G. *Famous American Admirals*. New York: Van Nostrand Rein-
hold Co., 1978.

Rhodes, James Ford. *The McKinley and Roosevelt Administrations*. New York: Macmillan Co., 1922.

Rickover, H. G. *Eminent Americans*. Washington, D.C.: United States Printing Office, 1972.

———. *How the Battleship* Maine *Was Destroyed*. Washington, D.C.: Department of the Navy, 1976.

———. *Swiss Schools and Ours*. Boston: Little, Brown and Co., 1962.

Roosevelt, Theodore. *An Autobiography*. New York: The Macmillan Co., 1913.

———. (Letters on the Battleship *Maine*.) Theodore Roosevelt Collection, Library of Congress.

———. (Letters on Naval Matters.) Theodore Roosevelt Collection, Library of Congress.

Royal Engineers Journal. Supplement. Oct. 1935.

Samuels, Ernest. *Henry Adams the Major Phase*. Cambridge: Harvard University Press, 1964.

Santovenia, Emeterio S. *Memorial Book of the Inauguration of the Maine Plaza at Havana*. La Habana, 1928.

Sargent, Herbert H. *The Campaign of Santiago de Cuba*. Chicago: A. C. McClurg & Co., 1907.

Saturday Evening Post. "Explosive Evidence." Nov. 1976.

Schroeder, Seaton. *A Half Century of Naval Service*. New York: D. Appleton and Co., 1922.

Scientific American. "Building the Armored Cruiser 'Maine.'" Oct. 5, 1889.

———. "The Launch of the Armored Cruiser 'Maine' at the Brooklyn Navy Yard." Nov. 29, 1890.

———. "The Loss of the Battleship 'Maine.'" Feb. 26, 1898.

———. "The 'Maine' Disaster." Mar. 12, 1898.

———. "Foreign Expert Opinion of the 'Maine' Disaster." May 21, 1898.

———. "The Mystery of the 'Maine.'" Sept. 2, 1911.

———. "The 'Liberté' and the 'Maine.'" Oct. 7, 1911.

———. "The Pumps Used in Uncovering the 'Maine.'" Nov. 4, 1911.

———. "Destruction of the 'Maine' by a Low-Explosive Mine and Her Own Magazine." Dec. 23, 1911.

———. "'Maine' Explosion No Longer a Mystery." Jan. 27, 1912.

———. "Exploitation of the 'Maine' Wreck." Feb. 3, 1912.

———. "The Last of the 'Maine,' A Fitting Burial at Sea." Mar. 30, 1912.

Seitz, Don C. *Joseph Pulitzer: His Life and Letters*. New York: Simon & Schuster, 1924.

Sigsbee, Charles D. *The Log of the Howard Watch*. N.p.: E. Howard Watch Works, 1911.

———. *The "Maine."* New York: The Century Co., 1899.

———. "My Story of the 'Maine.'" *Cosmopolitan*. July–Aug. 1912.

———. "Personal Narrative of the 'Maine.'" *Century Magazine*. Nov. 1898.

————. Letters to his wife, Jan. 15–Mar. 31, 1898. The New York State Library, Manuscripts and Special Collections, Box 1, Folder 23.

————. Reports of the Maine's Crew, Feb. 16, 1898. The New York State Library, Manuscripts and Special Collections, Box IV, Folder 94.

————. "Papers from the Commission of Pensions." National Archives, Washington, D.C.

Sleeman, C. *Torpedoes and Torpedo Warfare*. Portsmouth: Griffin & Co., 1889.

Smith, Goldwin. "The Moral of the Cuban War. *Forum*, Nov. 1898.

Smith, Horace. *A Captain Unafraid*. New York: Harper & Bros. Publishers, 1912.

Spanish Diplomatic Correspondence and Documents 1896–1900. Washington, D.C.: Government Printing Office, 1905.

Spears, John R. *The History of Our Navy*. Vol. 5, *The War with Spain*. New York: Charles Scribner's Sons, 1899.

————. *A History of the United States Navy*. New York: Charles Scribner's Sons, 1919.

————. *Our Navy in the War with Spain*. New York: Charles Scribner's Sons, 1898.

Springer, J. F. "Coal Piles that Light Themselves." *Scientific American*, Aug. 1924.

Sternlicht, Sanford. *McKinley's Bulldog: The Battleship Oregon*. Chicago: Nelson Hall, 1977.

Stoek, H. H. *Fires in Steamship Bunkers and Cargo Coal*. Technical Paper 126, Department of Interior, Bureau of Mines. Washington, D.C.: Government Printing Office, 1923.

(Strauss, Joseph) *Who's Who in America 1914–15*. Chicago: Marquis & Co., 1914.

Sumner, William Graham. *War and Other Essays*. New Haven: Yale University tPress, 1911.

Swanberg, W. A. *Citizen Hearst*. New York: Charles Scribner's Sons, 1961.

Taylor, John M. "Returning to the Riddle of the Explosion that Sunk the Maine." *Star News* (Washington D.C.), Sept. 1974.

Thrush, Paul, and Staff of Bureau of Mines. *A Dictionary of Mining, Mineral, and Related Terms*. United States Department of the Interior, 1968.

The Times (London). Feb.–Apr. 1898.

The Times-Republican (Bedford, Iowa). "A. C. Brice Says He Was Warned Maine Would Be Blown Up in Harbor," Dec. 14, 1911.

Trask, David F. *The War With Spain in 1898*. New York: Macmillan, 1981.

A Treaty of Peace Between the United States and Spain. 55th Cong., 3d sess., document no. 62, pt. 1. Washington, D.C.: Government Printing Office, 1899.

United States Naval Institute *Proceedings*. "Professional Notes: Ship's Magazines." Mar. 1912.

USS *Kearsarge*. Letter Admiral D. D. Porter to Secretary of Navy, Nov. 22, 1886. National Archives, RG 125, Records of the Office of the Judge Advocate General (Navy), Case No. 72, Vol. 1369, Charles D. Sigsbee.

————. Letter Rear Admiral J. E. Jouett to Secretary of Navy, July 1, 1895.

————. Letter Commodore P. C. Johnson to Secretary of Navy, Dec. 2, 1886.

———. Letter and enclosures Commander C. D. Sigsbee to President of Examining Board, Nov. 30, 1896.

USS Portsmouth. Report of the Portsmouth under command of Charles D. Sigsbee by Captain F. M. Bunce, Oct. 12, 1892. National Archives, RG 125, Records of the Judge Advocate General (Navy), Case No. 72, Vol. 1369.

USS Texas. Letter Charles A. Allen, Acting Secretary of Navy to Charles D. Sigsbee, Mar. 29, 1899. National Archives, RG 125, Records of the Judge Advocate General (Navy), Case No. 72, Vol. 1369.

———. Letter Charles D. Sigsbee to Secretary of Navy, Apr. 25, 1899.

———. Letter John D. Long, Secretary of Navy, to Charles D. Sigsbee, Jan. 31, 1900.

(Wainright, Richard) *Dictionary of American Biography.* New York: Charles Scribner's Sons, 1937.

(Watt, Richard Morgan) *Who's Who in America 1920–21.* Chicago: A. N. Marquis & Co., 1920.

Weems, John Edward. *The Fate of the Maine.* New York: Henry Holt and Co., 1958.

Werstein, Irving. *Turning Point for America.* New York: Julian Messner, 1964.

West, Richard S., Jr. *Admirals of American Empire.* New York: The Bobbs-Merrill Co., 1948.

West, Willis Mason. *The American People.* New York: Allyn and Bacon, 1928.

White, Andrew Dickson. *Autobiography.* New York: The Century Co., 1906.

Wilkerson, Marcus M. *Public Opinion and the Spanish-American War.* Baton Rouge: Louisiana State University Press, 1932.

Wilson, Herbert W. *Battleships in Action.* Boston: Little, Brown, reprint 1969.

———. *The Downfall of Spain.* Middletown: Wesleyan University Library, 1900.

———. *Ironclads in Action.* Vol. 2. Boston: Little, Brown and Co., 1896.

———. "The Truth about the Maine." *National Review* (London), July 1898.

Wisan, Joseph E. *The Cuban Crisis as Reflected in the New York Press.* Boston: D. C. Heath and Co., 1955.

(Woodford) *The American-Spanish War.* A History by the War Leaders. Norwich: Charles C. Haskell & Son, 1899.

The World (New York). Jan.–Apr. 1898.

Wreck of the Battleship Maine. Letter from Secretary of War to Congress. House of Representatives, 62d Cong., 1st sess., document no. 60.

———. Message from the President of the United States. House of Representatives, 62d Cong., 1st sess., document no. 113.

———. Message from the President of the United States. U.S. Senate, 62d Cong., 1st sess., document no. 107.

Wright, Marcus F. *The Official and Pictorial Record of the War With Spain.* N.p.: 1902.

Young, James Rankin. *History of Our War with Spain.* N.p.: J. R. Jones, 1898.

———. *Reminiscences and Thrilling Stories of the War by Returning Heroes.* Chicago: Providence Publishing Co., 1899.

Index

★ ★ ★ ★ ★ ★ ★ ★